Grounds for Comparison

Harvard Studies in Comparative Literature
Founded by William Henry Schofield

32

Grounds for Comparison *Harry Levin*

Harvard University Press   Cambridge, Massachusetts   1972

To My Teachers, Colleagues, and Students at Harvard University (*1929–1972*)

This volume of Harvard Studies in Comparative Literature has been sponsored by his friends and colleagues as a special tribute to the author on the occasion of his sixtieth birthday. Though it was our idea to assemble his uncollected writing and to include his bibliography, in every other respect he is the only begetter of this book; and we recognize that in seeking to honor him with the publication of his own work we have largely honored ourselves. Nonetheless, our sponsorship—*parvum non parvae amicitiae pignus*—is meant to express our abiding affection and esteem for Harry Levin, who, through three decades, has inspired, guided, and, indeed, personified Comparative Literature at Harvard.

W. K.

18 July 1972

CONTENTS

x   Contents

Grounds for Comparison

A PERSONAL RETROSPECT

Headnotes to the regathered pieces that follow will record their original circumstances of publication and acknowledge the author's gratitude to their various publishers and sponsors for permission to reprint them here. Since this introductory sketch was written to be published directly in the present volume, it has no prehistory; rather, such as it is, it is a prehistory. Hence the opening headnote provides me with the best opportunity for expressing my warmest thanks to Elizabeth Ann Farmer, Marina Levin Frederiksen, and Anna-Maria Kovacs for the unfailing helpfulness and reassuring patience with which they have shared the tasks of collection under pressures of time. And, as always, Elena Zarudnaya Levin has not only screened every word, checked elusive details, and helped in an indescribable number of ways; she has also found an apt quotation from the Russian poets for almost every happening of our lives.

I

This is an irredeemably miscellaneous volume, which rambles on desultorily from the Homeric Question to questions of censorship now *sub judice,* unified by little more than the fact that the thirty-six papers it contains were written by the same author—and when I reread some of the earliest, I do not even feel quite sure of that. All of them were written to meet an occasion—which means that the conjunction of author and subject generally originated in the minds of others, though I had much leeway of incidental choice, and would not presumably have been called upon in the first place if I had not manifested some sort of predisposition for the task at hand. Many of the occasions were academic: *Festschrift-en,* symposia, congresses, controversies, surveys, and necrologies, frankly conducing to a professional or pedagogical tone. Those communications which dwell at length on problems of scholarly method may be some-what alleviated by those evoking personal recollections of individual scholars. Those which bear on critical theory are, in large part, general-izations supported in some detail by my full-length studies in thematics and in modes of narration. Practical criticism is represented by several revaluations of classic novels and, in one case, a classic novelist. The reviews included were first encounters with four books of significance. A number of articles, having been commissioned as introductions, do their best to epitomize; others may be regarded as marginalia, such as the notations on marginal aspects of four American poets. Fully a dozen were conceived as lectures or addresses and first presented orally, one of which is here appearing for the first time in print. I have passed over some of my uncollected essays on Shakespeare and the drama, in the hope that this book might not be my last.

The heterogeneous form that its contents have taken—including at one point an exchange of letters, which affords me the opportunity to call in an eminent collaborator—is variegated further by the time-span they bridge. Half of them indeed have appeared within the last five or six years, and naturally it is with these that I am most willing to be identified today. But the other half are dated sporadically across the antecedent thirty years, and the only confidence I have in reprinting some of them is that they will not testify to a record of consistent decline. Afterthoughts and corrections have been held to a minimum. As the bibliography will show, my publications have been widely scattered; perhaps the lack of unity could be explained by what seems to have been, in retrospect, a restless movement from one publishing organ to another. But if I have drifted, the current has changed. No more than six of these pieces made their appearance in what might be described as a general periodical; sponsorship was more specialized, for most of the others, and circulation was more limited. That, of course, would be no excuse for republishing them in this compendious and presentable format, if it turned out that they might better have been left in the files. However, the responsibility for risking such a judgment is, under the present circumstances, shared with me by trusting colleagues, especially Walter Kaiser. Deeply grateful to them as I am for their friendly endeavors to ease the rites of passage into gafferhood, I have faced with mixed feelings the exercise in retrospection that has thus been set for me. Happily, although it has compelled a hesitant indulgence in the first person singular, any emergent pattern will owe its real meaning to the encounters along the road.

Self-repetition, though more or less unavoidable for a teacher, is not a tactic that I have ever set much store by. Since the article that follows this was my answer to a questionnaire probing explicitly into the nature of one's critical outlook, I shall try not to overanticipate its points. My immediate cue was supplied by a "veteran of letters"—Edmund Wilson's apt phrase for himself—when, for his fiftieth birthday, he was presented with a bibliography of his writings in the *Princeton University Library Chronicle* (February, 1944). Let me say at once, as a lifelong admirer of his art and scope, that I would hardly venture to press an analogy; if I mention him now, it is because his "Thoughts on Being Bibliographed" mentioned me, in a context which might help me to locate my own position. Mr. Wilson located himself in a line of free-lance journalists serving the cause of cultural enlightenment, such as H. L. Mencken, J. G. Huneker, and G. B. Shaw—truly an unassuming self-appraisal since, purely as a literary critic, he has far outranked those predecessors. As for his potential successors, he expressed regret that younger men, possibly in recoil from the confusions and constrictions of the thirties, were turning from the present to the past and from Bohemia to Academe. He was struck by "the curious phenomenon—which would have been quite inconceivable in my college days—of young men teaching English or French in the most venerable schools and universities at the same time that they hold radical political opinions and contribute to 'advanced' magazines." Probably he chose his specific example because of my recent little book on Joyce: "In the twenties, Mr. Harry Levin . . . would undoubtedly have been editing the *Dial* and going to bat for *Ulysses* in its pages."

Well, I am immensely flattered by the thought; nothing like it would have occurred to me; but, after having been so authoritatively suggested, it has haunted my fantasies. I was an avid reader of the *Dial* for the three years preceding its termination in 1929—that historic year in which my class happened to enter college. The previous decade had been climactic for the brilliant constellation of writers that figured in those pages, both European and American. In the author of *Axel's Castle* they encountered, while their best books were still coming out, what Joyce would characterize as "that ideal reader suffering from that ideal insomnia." Largely thanks to such responsive interpretation, they were approaching classical status by the time I started reviewing in the late thirties; and no one has lamented more poignantly than Mr. Wilson himself the comparatively anticlimactic trends of the subsequent decades. I was fortunate enough to review some of the later works of contemporary masters, and to meet with gracious acknowledgements from James Joyce and Thomas Mann. It was Joyce's response to my temerarious review-article on *Finnegans Wake* that prompted James Laughlin to commission my critical introduction to Joyce, as the first volume in the Makers of Modern Literature series sponsored by the incipient New Directions. When I had my first chance to teach a course in comparative literature, I persuaded my rather skeptical senior colleagues, mainly by a stiff reading-list and a language requirement, to let it be Proust, Joyce, and Mann—even though the last two were then alive, and consequently suspect as material for college study. The change, in this regard, has been so complete that it dizzies me to think about it, and it was already giving Mr. Wilson some concern in 1944.

As a reviewer, I seem to have served a kind of apprenticeship for other gambits. Writing with some regularity in succession for the *Nation*, the *New Republic,* and the *New York Times Book Review*, I found myself specializing in new books from abroad and specifically concerned with the quality of the translations. I was so fiercely caustic as to be labeled a young Turk (along with Randall Jarrell) by Allen Tate, and guarded my independence so jealously that I withdrew from the *Partisan Review* because of its doctrinaire partisanship in those days and disappointed the editor of the *Kenyon Review* by taking a middle ground between New Criticism and old scholarship. Having friends in many different camps, and having had before me the monitory example of Irving Babbitt's New Humanism, I have gone out of my way to avoid identification with any particular school or coterie or set of dogmas. It has always seemed to me that, if it is truth we seek, then every conceivable path to it should be considered viable, and that the seeker should try as many of them as he can, or at least do his best to keep them open. For the fact that my reviews have so decreased with the years, I suppose I could point to a number of reasons: that my criticism has been taking other forms, that reviewing may be primarily a young man's game, that it has so largely been pre-empted by the English in our most widely circulating journals, that the special challenge of Joyce and Mann has had few later counterparts. Such as they have been, my later reviews have tended to deal with critical commentaries and reeditions of classics. My only regular associations in this field now are with the editorial boards of two scholarly journals: *Comparative Literature* and the *Journal of the History of Ideas*.

But though I still find hospitality in the quarterlies and receive enough invitations to keep me busy, I occasionally regret the loss of contact with a wider public and the lack of opportunity to greet some of the literary productions of this latter day—which I continue to read with the unique interest that attaches to the contemporaneous, for better or for worse. The problem would not be worth raising if it did not have a broader application, if it had not limited the audiences of other critics who are probably more deserving of them. Long ago the editor of the *Atlantic Monthly* very kindly offered me a contract to contribute four articles a year. On a trial basis, he published such a sequence, each of which had been written with some other purpose in mind. When, after discussing further possibilities with him, I sat down to write a piece expressly for his magazine, I was blocked by my inability to envision the reader I would be addressing. That may well have provided a negative insight into the question of why we have no adequate literary reviews in this country, or what impedes a meeting of minds between readers and critics. Having often had better luck in England and on the Continent, I sometimes feel that I have been crumpling my manuscripts into bottles and casting them into the sea. Yet any sense of isolation suggested by that metaphor has been compensated many times over by the continual rewards of verbal communication with students and colleagues—a procedure so personally rewarding, when literature is its object, that I would not have traded it for the editorship of the *Dial*. This, at any rate, is my subjective response to the historical point that Edmund Wilson was making, when he used me as an illustration.

Mr. Wilson has reminded us that, when he was at college (seventeen years before me), scholarship and criticism were looked upon as mutually exclusive, and most professors relegated the latter to the dilettantes and journalists. That was not an inevitable disjunction, nor was it necessarily so in the past or elsewhere; but literary studies at American universities had been constrained within a Germanized philological system, which was only beginning to loosen its hold at the time I graduated. Methodological and curricular changes have come thick and fast during the four decades that have been passing since then. The analysis of texts has shifted from a linguistic to an esthetic focus. The chronological emphasis, no longer concentrated on the Middle Ages, has been rushing toward the modern period. There have been losses as well as gains in all that, particularly in the sense of history and the acquisition of languages. Psychological and mythic approaches have both illuminated and obscured. These reservations may serve to indicate that, insofar as I have been a participant in a movement, at this stage it has been carried well beyond any intentions or expectations of mine. I seem to have started out as a young critic who had a certain amount of scholarly background. Nowadays I am likely to be viewed—if at all—as an elder scholar who has, or else had, certain critical interests. Since I do not believe that my interests or viewpoints have changed all that much, the difference may be a measure of the extent to which my world has changed. What I had hoped to see was a *rapprochement* between, as I once put it, learning and discerning. But the academy has been going journalistic, while even Mr.

Wilson has deigned to teach at times, and paradoxically few of my professorial colleagues would be able to match his erudition today.

2

Scholar or critic, teacher or student—I would gladly give up any claim to such titles for that which Stephen Dedalus settled on: learner. It so happens that I am one of those to whom the smell of chalk-dust has always acted as the most powerful of stimulants. Scratch a teacher, and you will sense the influence of his teachers; ask him what his reward has been, and he will boast of his pupils. I have kept warm memories of high school, and especially of two English teachers: E. Dudley Parsons, radical and local historian, and Hannah M. Griffith, a Radcliffe-trained Quakeress who headed me in the direction of Harvard. Neither of my parents had gone to college; though interested in music and the theater, neither had the slightest interest in literature; but, being Jewish and having arrived at comfortable circumstances, they wanted their children to have the good education they had missed. Roughly speaking, the teens of my career coincided with the twenties of the century. To grow up then in the middle west was to feel that life was secure and solid, pleasant enough but utterly uneventful. History was something that had already taken place, mostly on the other side of the ocean. As I became absorbed in reading about more colorful epochs and localities, I became less satisfied with the flatness of the contemporary landscape. In this I was abetted by the novels of two fellow Minnesotans then in their heyday, Sinclair Lewis and F. Scott Fitzgerald. H. L. Mencken's *American Mercury* taught me the invidious comparison between the cult of the Almighty Dollar and the cultural values symbolized far away by the Old World. My adolescent reaction from the middle class was reinforced by sympathies with the populist Farmer-Labor Party, and also by the institutional sociology of Thorstein Veblen, which has had a lasting impact on my work.

To leave Minneapolis for Cambridge—where, of course, I had no notion that I would be spending the rest of my life—was to immerse oneself in a live tradition, a central concern for intellectual matters which might elsewhere have been regarded as on the fringe. Had I remained at home and studied at the University of Minnesota, as I came to realize upon later acquaintance, I would have learned more about Shakespeare from E. E. Stoll than I did at the feet of the arch-philologist G. L. Kittredge. But I attended his courses more or less faithfully, along with those of other great philologists then in their last teaching days: F. N. Robinson, J. L. Lowes, C. H. Grandgent, E. K. Rand. I was also lucky enough to make friends with three beginning instructors, each of them ten years older than myself, each of them destined to die prematurely, each of them in vital touch with a different aspect of literary experience: Milman Parry, F. O. Matthiessen, Theodore Spencer. The master I most revered was the philosopher A. N. Whitehead, and I gained much from the counsel and hospitality of the esthetician D. W. Prall, at whose rooms one met such developing talents as Leonard Bernstein and Robert Motherwell. As for my ambivalent debt to Irving Babbitt, I have sought to acknowledge it by my inaugural lecture on assuming the chair named for him in 1960. His ever-apt citation of ready texts, his continued redefinition of critical terms, and his use of the past as a critique of the present left an ineradicable impression. An essay on the classicism of the English Romantics, which I wrote for his course in my sophomore year, *The Broken Column,* won a prize and was published by the university press, to my future embarrassment. This unripe garland lessened the reverence with which I looked at anything in print, and possibly retarded books more fully meditated.

The pedagogical event of my senior year at Harvard was the presence of T. S. Eliot as Charles Eliot Norton Professor of Poetry. For my generation, which had read him early enough to experience the tensions of novelty, he was still the poetic revolutionary as well as the critical arbiter. And here was a legend become a reality before our very eyes—the legendary reality of a middlewestern boy who, by way of New England, had somehow managed to enter the mainstream of English literature. It was quite improbable and, obviously, inimitable. Yet his example gave heart to youthful admirers, like myself, by demonstrating that there could be lines of connection between Middle America and European culture. I had written a paper on a minor Metaphysical poet, which was shown to Eliot by Ted Spencer, exercising a characteristic talent for bringing people together. Though the paper took issue with some of Eliot's views, his generous response was to accept it for publication in his *Criterion.* Another article, accepted the following year, was returned and printed elsewhere when that periodical folded; indeed it was through Eliot, not long afterward, that his firm became my British publisher. His deep sense of *pietas* came out strongly with regard to his university, particularly in his later years; and I suppose that, after Spencer's death, I became a personal link with it. During the closing cycle of his pilgrimage, he seemed to take pleasure in revisiting American haunts and introducing his sympathetic new wife to American friends. With the momentum of his expatriation, he had out-Englished the English in certain respects. But he did not expect us to go along with this traditionalism, and he much preferred a relationship based on mutual irony to the kind of adulation that all but overwhelmed him.

Graduation led to a European *Wanderjahr* on a traveling fellowship, with encouragement from Eliot and Babbitt (who died before my return). I had previously been abroad on a grand tour with my family, guided by couriers, stopping at *de luxe* hotels, and staying no more than three days in any single place. As a student, my year was divided mainly between the British Museum and the Sorbonne, though I began by joining my classmate Henry Hatfield on a bicycle trip through England and concluded with a brief journey to Greece and Palestine. This was a quest for history with a vengeance. I had come to the Old World, like many a passionate pilgrim before me, intending to lose myself in the storied past; that was being rapidly overtaken by the ominous present in the Europe of 1933. I was fascinated by debates between Fascists and Communists at the Speakers' Corner in Hyde Park, and attended a performance at the Comédie Française which broke out into a political riot. Within the Neo-Humanist ivory tower, I had resisted Marxism; now I saw that any realistic view of modern culture must come to terms with it; but, since it taught me that ideologies could be utilized as instruments of repression, I never joined the Communist Party as some of my friends did. I did help to organize a teachers' union at Harvard a few years later, and reported in one or two articles on the left-wing politics of my native state. Meanwhile, my sojourn in Europe had enlarged my conception of America, as well as my sense of their interdependence. I had commenced to read American history along with American literature. On the homeward voyage I shared a cabin with a young German émigré, and shared his feelings when the Ile de France passed the Statue of Liberty.

A friend who shared my bookish interests in college, and who went out into the wider world to practise law in Washington, now and then comes back to Cambridge and asks me: "What are you going to do when you grow up?" As a matter of fact, I have never faced that decision. My father hoped I would enter the family business; I had seen enough, in the apprentice jobs he assigned me during vacations, to know that I would never be a businessman; nonetheless I am glad to have had those assignments, since they gave me a clearer impression of how most Americans pass their lives. Though I had done the usual dabbling in verse and fiction, I knew I lacked that special concentration of the ego which enables the truly imaginative writer to discover the powers within himself. I was already enough of a critic to be aware that analysis brings a wholly different set of gears into play. In the life of letters, I suspected, there would be room for a commitment founded upon a detachment from the mixed motives of creative ambition. But where? In the university—and this would mean undergoing the conventional propaedeutics of graduate school. I was sure I did not want to go back to Harvard in order to take the doctorate in English; and I was not sure, after my continental term, that English would remain the focal point of my literary studies. My preliminary exposures to the classical literatures and to French had been at least sufficient to frame an enlarging perspective; and I looked forward to sporadic excursions with German, Russian, Spanish, and Italian authors, if not to systematic training in those additional fields. Moreover, if Harvard was limiting, the genteel insularity of most other English departments in the United States was even less inviting.

More and more, at Paris during the spring of 1934, I found myself hoping to stay and round out my education in Europe—an uncertain hope, since it was dependent upon my parents. I had some thought of studying with either Fernand Baldensperger at the Sorbonne or with I. A. Richards at Cambridge University. By a fortunate irony, I was to find myself their junior colleague at Harvard within five years. Those intervening years were heralded by a sudden and unexpected call from the sky, as it were, a cablegram from the Dean of the Harvard Faculty, Kenneth Murdock, inviting me to join the newly established Society of Fellows. As a Junior Fellow, I was to enjoy the exhilarating freedom of the university with only one restriction: I could not be a doctoral candidate. Free to indulge my curiosities by reading widely in areas far from the purview of any degree, as well as to sharpen tools and practise techniques by occasional writing and varied research, I was enabled to acquire a backlog which would serve for projects and commissions in years to come. The Society's only regular observances were its Monday evening dinners with its founder, the former President Lowell, and the other Senior Fellows. The tone, both culinary and dialectical, was set by the chairman, Lawrence J. Henderson, a tough-minded and many-sided biochemist, noted for the methodological rigor with which he challenged the respective disciplines represented by his junior colleagues. A student of the humanities, which were decidedly in the minority, would be pressed to justify assumptions taken for granted in graduate school and to phrase his formulations precisely, lest he demonstrate the softheadedness of his subject. More positively, he could learn the value of an interdisciplinary approach from his contemporaries in the physical and social sciences.

Hence, without acquiring professional accreditation in any field, I was encouraged to trespass in more than one. Though my original teaching appointment was to the Department of English, where I have continued to offer instruction chiefly in Shakespearean drama, and fond as I am of my colleagues at Warren House, their patience may well have been tried at times by my tendency to go whoring after the strange gods of *Grenz-wissenschaft*. My principal involvement in this area has been with the Department of Comparative Literature, which I was called upon to reorganize after its dormant period during the Second World War. But I have done some interdepartmental roving in other directions, having been administratively involved with the first Committee on General Education, the Division of Modern Languages, the Loeb Drama Center, and the Society of Fellows again for twenty years as a senior member. Stimulus has often come through congenial interaction with such personalities as my versatile neighbor, the clinical psychologist Henry A. Murray, with whom I jointly conducted three seminars, much to my own enlightenment. Though such associations and undertakings had their venturesome side, they all had the limitation of being confined to Harvard. Therefore I have been especially gratified by those opportunities to break through my Harvardian confinement and fill in my educational gaps, which have presented themselves by way of visiting lectures and temporary appointments at other institutions. Thus I returned to the Sorbonne as exchange professor twenty years after my student days. I have likewise profited from terms at Salzburg, Tokyo, Berkeley, Princeton, Indiana, and Cambridge. More than anything else I have ever met with, these visits have sustained the old notion of a republic of letters, where men speak a common language in spite of distances and relate to one another through ideas and books.

3

To look back on one's preoccupations over a long interim is to contemplate a pattern interwoven by chance and choice. Yet there are such things as elective affinities, with regard to a critic's subject matter. Insofar as his intentions are serious, they may well be focused on problems rather than authors in themselves—or even better, on authors who constitute problems, as Homer did for Parry or Shakespeare for Stoll. Joyce, though he has since become a mine for notes and queries or else an echo-chamber for overreadings and tautologies, was a problem when *Finnegans Wake* came out and when I wrote my little handbook in the year of his death (1941). Not that the problem is solved; we are still living with the crisis of the novel that he precipitated, and to which later novelists have reacted in their several ways, regressive more often than experimental. Viewing such work as a culmination of the symbolist movement, in *Axel's Castle* ten years before, Edmund Wilson had predicted a *détente*, a reversion to some more pedestrian plane of naturalism. That prediction came true in part, but only at a lower level, where the novel had always been predominantly naturalistic. At the end of the thirties, after proletarian novels had shown their limitations and the emergence of Kafka had signalized a renewal of fantasy, it could be seen more clearly that the symbolic strain was deep and lasting and anything but a recent development. *Ulysses* was so paradigmatic because, as Eliot had noted in relating it to his own work and that of Yeats, it so magisterially handled the parallelism between the mythical and the realistic. But the observation could be generalized and applied to the whole of literature—or rather, to the imaginative process that brings it into being—inasmuch as all fiction must combine, though in widely varying proportions, symbolism with realism.

Joyce the modernist pointed back to the *Odyssey,* which had outlined the situation in parable. Yet those two metaphorical gates—the ivory of romance, the horn of reality—coexisted not merely as alternatives but as poles at the ends of a sliding scale. In recounting men's actions and projecting their values by means of fabulation—here I adapted the term that Henri Bergson employed for the imagination, *la fonction fabulatrice* —narrative has fluctuated between the poles, depending at every stage on social conditions and modes of communication. The novel from Cervantes onward has been increasingly rigorous in its observation of life, habitually tending toward the realistic pole; and there my early theorizing found rich confirmation in the stylistic studies of Erich Auerbach. Style was the immediate vehicle for a changing world-view, not least in that explicit repudiation of literary artifice which I have come to call the Quixotic principle; but, along with the texture, one also had to consider the structure of the critique that the realists were engaged in, to compare their versions of actuality with the historical ways in which it might be documented. France was the exemplary terrain for such a demonstration, as Babbitt had affirmed, even though he had not cared for this part of its literary history. Nowadays Paris is no longer the center for artistic movements that it was through the earlier years of our century; indeed the empiricism and the lucidity that long made French thought a cultural model have been giving way to obfuscation and subjectivity; one cannot view that horizon without regretfully noting, as Wordsworth did after having derived so much of his earlier inspiration from it, "a want of books and men." However, it had furnished the books and men, from Stendhal to Proust, for the central movement in the history of realistic fiction.

My resulting study, *The Gates of Horn*, was put together and partially published at intervals over a twenty-five-year period, during which I was mainly occupied with other commitments. Since I had taken so long to digest its substance, I could not be surprised or disappointed if its readers did likewise. If the forest had been somewhat obscured by the trees, if the theory of realism itself was overshadowed by the five novelists I had selected for monographic illustration, it may have been my fault; yet I think it may have been inherent in a thesis which could only be demonstrated by a detailed sequence of case histories. "It is the method, one feels, that Mr. Levin most urgently wanted to formulate," wrote Germaine Brée in an exceptionally sensitive review. Many of the book's other reviewers were also professors of French, who were indulgent in welcoming a nonspecialist into their field. I had aimed at contributing to a more general type of criticism, which was well grounded in the Anglo-American novel and its Jamesian canons of formal analysis, but heretofore rather deficient in theoretical groundwork and sociohistorical correlation. From my own reviewing I had learned something about the vicissitudes one might expect as a reviewee, and cared less about approval than understanding. As matters ordinarily work out, the appreciations greatly outnumber the denigrations; judgments err more frequently on the side of lenience than of severity. One gets used, of course, to seeing a transitional phrase quoted as a brilliant *aperçu* while one's most original formulation may be passed over as conventional stuff. I have no complaints about the reception of *The Gates of Horn* so far, nor the fact that it has been read for its critical revaluations, and I still hope that someone will some day pick up the message within its *bouteille à la mer*.

Meanwhile the other pole had attracted me, the one toward which American fiction inclined through its classic preference for the romance above the novel. The title I echoed from Melville, *The Power of Black-*

ness, stood for the pessimistic side of our literature—not quite for what has since been called "black power," though I felt honored when my book was banned from a public library in the south. Here the method was thematic, tracing a set of recurrent symbols as they had functioned in highly idiosyncratic contexts. My more recent venture into what I had described as literary iconology, *The Myth of the Golden Age in the Renaissance,* searched for the history of ideas in a cluster of images relating to utopia and paradise, innocence and experience, past and future, property and communism, love and war. Insofar as an academic must specialize in a period, I have been happy to bask in the Renaissance, though the concerns of my writing have often been updated by the pressures of modernity. Shakespeare, in his age and theater and language, has been the major subject of my teaching throughout my career. Since he is so infinitely various, it has never palled. Otherwise, I have seldom repeated a course more than five times; the classroom or the seminar has presented a kind of humanistic equivalent to the scientist's laboratory; and every such experiment in interpretation has led to an article or two, if not a book. Conversely, I would not ever want to give a course where everything that got said was already in print. Out of those classes and public lectures have come editions, more or less technical articles, and my books on *Hamlet* and on Marlowe. Latterly my interest has been turning from the tragic to the comic viewpoint, and what I go on to write may lie within that sphere.

My collections of essays are *parerga,* by-products of more sustained researches, applications of their methods to further material, exercises in stylistics, structure, and critical definition, efforts to keep criticism in touch with other disciplines and with social responsibilities. If they embody any range or depth of scholarship, this should be attributed to the sheer advantage of having a room of one's own in Widener and immediate access to the treasures of the Houghton Library. Merely browsing there holds a serendipity which will be forever lost when stacks and shelves are replaced by catalogued microfilms and data-banks. Theodore Spencer, in his sympathetic yet searching way, once told me that I was striving toward two incompatible ideals: an ideal of fact and an ideal of form. On the one hand, I acknowledge an urge to exhaust the bibliographies of my subjects, which complicates the process of assimilation. On the other, though I tend by nature to be skeptical and rationalistic, I have an almost intuitive faith in "the figure in the carpet": not only the emergent profile of the author or object studied but the structural and verbal configuration of the study itself. Yet all who try to be both scholars and critics must face such dilemmas, making their own approximations and compromises. The tensions may be registered in my discrepant use of footnotes. Recoiling from the institutionalized pedantry that had its monument in *PMLA,* I intermittently tried to do without them or else to put them in the least conspicuous place; and when I used them, I generally held myself down to the simplest bibliographical references, in order not to be tempted into digression. This meant that the texts were sometimes heavily loaded with parenthetical details, while at other times the train of allusion may not have made its intended connection.

My own consciousness of the deficiencies in my writings was acute enough, I trust, to have improved them while they were still in the course of being written; my judgment or misjudgment, in having finally published them without still further revision, is for others to judge. To be bibliographed—if I may borrow Edmund Wilson's expression—is to be dated in more ways than one, to be fitted more definitively into the past dimension than could be envisaged through the continuities of personal reminiscence. Seeking to take my chronological bearings, I cite another witness; and if I transcribe half a page from Norman Mailer's novel, *The Naked and the Dead* (1948), it is because his first paragraph was transcribed from one of my lectures:

The number seven has a deep significance to Mann. Hans Castorp spends seven years on the mountain, and if you will remember the first seven days are given great emphasis. Most of the major characters have seven letters in their name, Castorp, Clavdia, Joachim, even Settembrini fulfills it in that the Latin root of his name stands for seven.

The scribbling of notes, the pious acceptance. Sir, Hearn asks, what's the importance of that? I mean frankly I found the novel a pompous bore, and I think this seven business is a perfect example of German didacticness, expanding a whim into all kinds of critical claptrap, virtuosity perhaps but it leaves me unmoved.

His speech causes a minor stir in the class, a polite discussion which the lecturer sums up gently before continuing, but it is a significant impatience for Hearn. He would not have said that the preceding year.

So far as the lecturer remembers—and Mr. Mailer treats him very gently —the episode is apocryphal. He would share some of Hearn's impatience over Mann's numerology, and indeed gave up on *Finnegans Wake* because of its numbers games. Yet such virtuosity is the defect of Mann's or Joyce's artistic virtue, a sense of design, a sense which is conspicuously absent from Mr. Mailer's shaggy ego-trips. Hearn's boredom would be justified if that design were no more than mandarin filigree; but the visions of those seven sleepers on their magic mountain offer keys to the significance of life and death in the years between the wars. For those of us who formed our reading habits during those years it is hard not to feel that, despite the urgency and openness of Mailer's generation, something has become attenuated, oversimplified, twisted, diffused, or forced. I have considered some of the reasons for this flow and ebb of talent in my essay, "What Was Modernism?," and have taken note that Lionel Trilling reached a parallel view by a different route. Not long ago he asked me what three contemporaries I would choose, if I were attempting a latter-day counterpart of my course in Proust, Joyce, and Mann. By tentatively suggesting Nabokov, Borges, and Robbe-Grillet, I earned his irrefutable comment that the course would be less interesting than its predecessor. Currently we are living in what Arnold Toynbee has termed the Post-Modern period. The cultural epoch that began with the Renaissance, and proceeded through the Enlightenment into the nineteenth century, may have ended with the Second World War. If we now are facing an apocalypse, then perhaps we may need critics with apocalyptic sensibilities, like George Steiner, rather than stodgy old humanistic liberals like Professor Trilling and myself.

At all events, to have lived through a length of time that would be commonly reckoned as two generations, almost inevitably, is to have become somewhat detached from the contingencies of the passing moment. It should likewise have broadened one's perspective, deepened one's humility, and tested one's attachment to the less ephemeral values. Though the word *culture* is probably enunciated today more than it ever was in Matthew Arnold's prime, he would never have recognized some of its newer connotations. One word that induces louder reverberations, particularly in educational circles, is *relevance*. Having as a student criticized the antiquarianism of the curriculum on just that ground, I cannot but sympathize with the present attitude of the young—that is to say, their concern for the pressing problems of our society and our world. Yet human life has dimensions that are historic as well as social, and relevance can be vertical as well as horizontal. Besides our moral obligation to the claims of our day, in other words, we should also be concerned with our role in the chain of lives extending backward into the past and forward into the future. To preserve this vital relationship thus becomes a special responsibility for students and teachers, writers and critics, if whatever wisdom men have learned is to go down to their posterity, if intercommunication is to be sustained beyond the narrow limits of the single life-span. The more we are socially menaced by forces of destruction, the more important it seems to shore up our fragments and to hand on the intellectual heritage. To play any part, however small, linked with that far-ranging continuum of minds, is a privileged dispensation. I feel gratitude—if not guilt—for the privileges I have enjoyed, the friends and circumstances that have made it possible for me to spend most of my own life doing the very things I most wanted to do.

LEECH-GATHERING

This was one reply to a question posed by the London *Times Literary Supplement*, when it asked a number of critics to explain what they thought they had been doing all along. I had never reviewed for the *TLS*, never having quite assented to their policy of anonymity. However, I had anonymously contributed one article to their first issue on American literature, with the understanding that it could be reclaimed and legitimatized; it was, as an appendix to *The Power of Blackness*. Of course there would have been no point to the symposium in which the present statement appeared, had not all the articles been signed—an indication that the policy may, to some extent, be changing. As chance would have it (and it could not have been anything other than chance), the issue that contained my critical statement also contained a patronizing and deprecatory review of *The Gates of Horn* (July 26, 1963). The impression left on other readers besides myself was one of editorial inconsistency: that the *TLS* would do a critic the honor of inviting him to discuss his viewpoint, while at that very moment disparaging his most substantial work, much of which had been previously in print. Shortly afterward I was enlightened by re-reading the same review, somewhat expanded and modulated, in *Ramparts* (Autumn, 1963), over the signature of Martin Turnell. *Tout comprendre, c'est tout pardonner*. Given Mr. Turnell's dogmatic commitments, plus his expressed antipathies toward some of the authors involved and toward all literary theories, he was merely exercising his critical franchise. But it made some difference, in common fairness, for him to do so over his own name rather than under the mantle of Jupiter Tonans. The fact that he has reprinted his critique elsewhere suggests that he too might not have been satisfied by its conjunction with my piece in the *TLS*. Herewith I am following his example and completing the disengagement. I should add that the symposium later came out as a book, *The Critical Moment* (London, 1964), and was published in German translation under the editorship of Hans Mayer, *Kritiker unserer Zeit* (Stuttgart, 1964). Needless to say, my title—or rather, Wordsworth's—proved untranslatable, and yielded to the sobriety of *Das Metier des Kritikers*.

It is probably a healthy thing to be questioned about one's professional reasons for existence; and when one's questioner coexists in a comparable sphere of endeavor, one can only hope that the question itself will not turn out to be mutually rhetorical. Academic it is bound to be in the present instance, since the respondent happens to be a professor by calling and a critic mainly by courtesy. This means that he has managed to gain his living through certain activities which he is not ordinarily called upon to justify: by reading as much as he could, by mulling it over, by discussing it orally with students and now and then with other readers through print. It has been so purely pleasurable an assignment that I sometimes feel guilty at being paid for doing so little else. Hence I find myself extremely vulnerable to the sort of query that Wordsworth repeatedly put to his old Leech-Gatherer on that lonely moor. Just exactly what is it that one does? And how is it that one lives? "What occupation do you there pursue?" I would that I could answer by patient example, and show no less resolution or independence than did Wordsworth's dogged interlocutor. But criticism is never in its nature a solitary pursuit, and whether or not its gleanings are salutary must be considered a moot point. Happily, the invitation calls for a credo rather than a confession, and one is not necessarily expected to live up to everything that one professes to believe.

Professes? To believe? There is where the trouble begins. The classical periods were field days for criticism precisely because they could afford to take such professions of faith for granted; though opinions might individually differ, everyone could appeal to a single accepted code. If Samuel Johnson could lay down the law so authoritatively, it was because his literary authority rested upon authoritarian attitudes toward religion and politics. The subsequent growth of science and democracy, by fostering the development of alternative attitudes, challenged the traditional notion of culture and thereby created the dilemma that so perplexed Matthew Arnold. Latter-day critics have had to face it in one way or another. Those who continue to play a judicial role have maintained their jurisdiction by narrowing their view: by embracing a dogma and addressing the faithful. Neo-orthodoxy has proved itself capable of moving in diametrically opposite directions: of excommunicating D. H. Lawrence, with T. S. Eliot, or proscribing Boris Pasternak, with the editors of the *Literaturnaya Gazeta*. In fairness to Mr. Eliot it should be remarked that his dogmatizing, unlike the Soviet kind, presupposes the prevalence of heresy. Yet heresy—which I can merely equate with a liberal outlook—thrives upon the stalemate of such conflicting attempts to conceive the world as a smaller and simpler place than the course of experience has actually shown it to be. Its very largeness may indeed have instigated partial viewpoints, party lines, and *Partisan Reviews*. In any case, the application of dogmatic principles, theological or ideological, is more objective than the unprincipled dogmatism of coteries.

Objectivity, in matters involving human responses, may at best be an approximation; nonetheless it lies within the critic's power to aim at Arnold's goal of "disinterestedness"—to do his best, in other words, to detach himself from preconceptions and prejudices. Hence a credo may be somewhat less germane to his efforts than, in Holofernes' phrase, a *haud credo,* an emphatic disclaimer of all beliefs except an infrangible belief in literature itself. It is not for nothing that the commonest meaning of "criticize" is to censure, to dispense blame more readily than praise. The uncomfortable privilege of expressing discontent with the status quo, the skeptical habit of seeing through and beyond the trivial immediacies of man's condition, may well be man's clearest way of distinguishing himself from the animals. It is to be noted that Jean-Paul Sartre and his fellow proponents of *la littérature engagée* have been more effectual in their critique of things-as-they-are than in their commitment to a succession of causes. Literature itself, to be sure, would quickly cease to exist, if it were not constantly taking sides and projecting values; and every value judgment has its significance in reckoning the total impact of any given work. All the more reason why literary criticism should stand by in sympathetic detachment, and set its sights by an ultimate prospect of understanding, rather than engage in the fluctuating traffic of revaluation. Too many Olympian verdicts have been reversed; too many hot tips have grown cold; too many absolutes have, with the passage of time, revealed limitations.

These cautionary reflections leave me open to the charge of being a relativist. I am quite willing to accept the term, if I am allowed the right to choose my definition. Relativism, for the absolutist, is a wholly negative conception, implying the absence of standards. I should prefer to regard it as a concern for ever-changing standards, both in their variety and in their continuity, as well as, much more positively, a sense of universal interrelatedness—a sense which, insofar as I possess it at all, I owe to Alfred North Whitehead. Now every intellectual discipline is devoted to the study of certain unique relationships, large and small. Literary criticism, understandably, has found it more attractive to dwell upon the smaller particularities. But insofar as it constitutes a mode of knowledge, it must likewise deal with broad and basic points of connection. My own critical focus has centered on two or three of these points: first and primordially, on the relation between literature and life. Perhaps no complex variable has been subject to more drastic oversimplifications. On the one hand, Marxists, publicists, and censors have confounded the two categories. On the other hand, the adherents of art-for-art's-sake have refused to recognize any linkage between them. Each of those extreme positions has its characteristic source of strength. The social critics have well understood how art could be a weapon, and how its emotional charge could affect and reflect men's lives. In their turn, the formalists have insisted that it is first and last art, and have quickened appreciation of it with their intensive scrutinies.

This is not so much a contradiction as it is a complementarity. Of course the critic's starting point is literature, though in a larger sense he has already started with life. The works that he examines are verbal artifacts which give sensuous pleasure, and may incidentally communicate ideas, through the writer's mastery of their esthetic medium. Consequently there can be no adequate substitute for informed stylistic explication or detailed structural analysis; yet all such interpretation would be barren if it did not lead toward a meeting of minds between writer and reader. My own realizations of the interplay between form and function, as demonstrated *a fortiori* through the elaborate conventions of the Homeric epic, was one of the lessons I learned from Milman Parry. I have tried to generalize the problem under the concept of "Literature as an Institution," a highly tentative formulation which seeks to reconcile the autonomy of artistic usages with the responsive counterclaims of society. More concretely, I have been studying that conscious tendency on the part of writers to imitate life—moreover, to criticize it —which is so very loosely known as realism, and possibly to pin it down with a little more precision by relating it to the rise and decline of middle-class culture. Its special paradox is the unremitting competition between fact and fiction, which has *Don Quixote* as its paradigm and which accelerates into the modern novel. Although the latter stresses novelty and lets the analytic viewpoint prevail, a longer view would also emphasize the persistence of archetypes, the adaptation of recurrent themes, and the ascendancy of poetry over prose—in short, the continuous unfoldment of the storytelling faculty from primitive myth to *le nouveau roman*.

Thus I am brought to the second of my coordinates: the relation of the past to the present. That literature is the testament of tradition, which orients us to the perspectives of time, furnishes us with ever-living patterns of behavior, and links us directly with our remote progenitors and ultimate progeny—I shall not labor this Arnoldian *topos*, which has done its duty in many an argument on behalf of the humanities. Those who take a strictly formal stance may still reject it, on the grounds that it subordinates pure artistry to the stuff of human experience. Yet even to extract such testimony requires some awareness of the techniques through which it has been transmitted. Conversely, the very closest reading of a text is likely to go astray when it is pursued without reference to the historical context. Furthermore, I am concerned at this point, not simply with the usefulness of literature as an illustrated supplement to history, but with the convergence of the two, and the reshaping of literature by history through the evolution of genres. Every genre would seem to run its organic cycle. After the long and rich harvest of the novel, latterly we are beginning to ask ourselves whether its season has not been declining. The drama, because of technical requirements, and especially because of its audiences, has flourished at particular times and places. The remarkable train of circumstance that made it possible for Shakespeare to write his plays is, for me, the central epoch of literary history, and to it I return with perennial enthusiasm in my teaching and in occasional writing.

As we draw near to Shakespeare's four-hundredth anniversary, I am convinced that he stands nearer to us then he did to his readers and spectators during most of the intervening years. That proximity is partly due to a renewed concentration on him in his natural habitat, the theater, and partly to the accumulation of studies casting light on his original texts, his rhetorical means, his antiquarian background, and his intellectual climate. Scholars of E. K. Chambers' generation spent industrious and productive careers in gaining public access to the facts, the documents, and the other relevant materials, so that the next generation —not without gratitude—could undertake to synthesize and interpret with more freedom and more security. One could set out to be a Renaissance scholar, as I once did, be deflected by the urgency of more recent manifestations, and yet not altogether lose touch—I trust—with one's field of predilection. The gap between scholarship and criticism, which in the earlier years of our century sometimes took on the aspect of a quarrel between pedants and dilettantes, has been gradually closing. The fabric of learning will always need to be filled in and kept up to date, but today it is relatively well organized. What with the available editions, works of reference, research libraries, technological aids, and facilities for travel, the interpreter of literature has no excuse for not solidly grounding his observations or widely testing his speculations. Nor can he expect to take his bearings, in this increasingly polyglot era, unless he is at home in more than one language and a venturesome tourist in several others.

Just as the belatedness of our age has its compensation in historical consciousness, which can emancipate us from provinciality in time, so a heightened geographical consciousness can free us from parochialism in space. My mentor in this respect was Iriving Babbitt, who taught his students to trace their cultural inheritance back to its cisatlantic origins. My third and last coordinate is therefore, as it must be for any American who is interested in the arts and in ideas, the span between the United States and Europe. The tides have ebbed and flowed appreciably since the days of passionate pilgrims, innocents abroad, and condescending visitors from England to America; the approach, from either side, is no longer dialectic but dialogue, as the presence of this very deposition attests. The immeasurable blessing of having been born to the English language is perhaps one which a native of another country may acknowledge without incurring the imputation of Podsnappery. While remaining aware that his ear may not be fully attuned to some of the subtle cadences and local associations of English literature, he would like to think that his visitor's eye could catch a few nuances or discern some analogies which might not have occurred to observers more familiar with the terrain. Again, having had a German-born father, having a Russian-born wife, and having studied and taught on occasion in France, he would almost habitually frame his Anglo-American interests within a broadly European perspective. This orientation has been strengthened by friends and colleagues expatriated westward by the political pressures of our century—I must name, from among them, the late Renato Poggioli.

Looking back, I suppose I should not be surprised at having found a university niche in the hospitably conceived, if awkwardly titled, subject of Comparative Literature; for it is really not so much a subject as an object: an attempt to pool the resources of the variously related literatures, to cross the linguistic barriers that confine them within the framework of national histories, and to provide an area for the consideration of their common features and underlying forces. As attention has tended to shift, in recent years, from reciprocal influences and parallel movements to the permutation of forms and the diffusion of motifs, criticism has been accorded more of the scope it needs for rising to a theoretical plane. Bacon spoke of "a science pertaining to the imagination," and though no one has developed that conception, it might well emerge from the middle ground between criticism and psychology. Psychoanalysis has thus far been using literature to document its own fascinating inquiries, rather than to illuminate it per se. Something more to the purpose might be hoped for from a newer line of investigation which is coming to be known as thematics, whereby the effects of fantasy can be studied through the progressive transformation of images or myths. All this foreshadows a greater emphasis on literature as a process, the component parts of which—even the works of Shakespeare—are subsumed and surpassed by the workings of the whole, as we come to understand it. Needless to say, no one individual or self-limiting group could carry out such a program; it would demand international cooperation on a high level and in a hopeful future.

However, it does not envisage itself as a school of thought, or urge the adoption of any prescriptive method. Poets, playwrights, and novelists may justifiably venture to found schools, take stands, or issue manifestos; for they are involved and licensed, committed to experiment and one-sided by design. Critics can scarcely be other than open-minded, unblushingly eclectic rather than doctrinaire, ready to entertain any possibility—to exclude no insight or procedure—that promises to illuminate or enrich the matter at hand. But I am speaking in the optative mood; in practice the exceptions outnumber such rules; and there are too many critics who glory in their one-sidedness. Half-truths are usually more arresting than whole truths, and ignorance can inspire more striking generalizations than a thoughtful canvass of the facts. Since one can never be sure of being absolutely right, why not be wrong in an interesting fashion? Without trading Shakespeare's plays for the laws of thermodynamics, criticism would benefit from more rigorous criteria. Possibly the most confusing hazard is the frustrated author who turns critic: either he overingeniously rewrites the books he reviews or else, Stanislavsky-like, he identifies himself subjectively with the writers he revaluates. In spite of all the poets who have written effective propaganda for their poetry, there is a good deal to be said for a separation of powers. Wordsworth, after all, was so absorbed in thinking of Burns and Chatterton and himself that he failed to understand the Leech-Gatherer's first reply, albeit the second stayed so memorably with him after he departed—leaving the feeble old man to putter on somehow with his humble, old-fashioned, increasingly difficult, thoroughly repellent, and conceivably therapeutic task.

THE MODERN HUMANITIES IN
HISTORICAL PERSPECTIVE

In sweeping contrast to the self-limited outlook of the previous paper, the next one has attempted to take a long view—a view so long, perhaps, as to bedim its horizon. I should scarcely have dared to make the attempt, if I had not so cordially been invited, and been confronted with so challenging a title, by the officers of the Modern Humanities Research Association. This response to their challenge was read and discussed, as the first of a sequence of ten papers, during the fiftieth annual meeting of the MHRA at Cambridge University on August 26, 1968, and these proceedings were published in a volume entitled *The Future of the Humanities* (Cambridge, 1969). The gardens by the Cam seemed far away from the current disruptions at Columbia and the Sorbonne, to which I felt uneasy enough to refer, not without expectation of the storm that would hit my local Cambridge within the next year. For such academic discourses as this, the conventional premise has been what the nineteenth century liked to call "the march of intellect." That triumphal progression can no longer be taken for granted, to say the least, and we face the alternatives of lag, retrogression, or change of direction in the continuity of ideas. Clearly the humanities, as traditionally defined, can no longer claim the cultural predominance that they once enjoyed. Yet they "persist and endure," in Faulkner's phrase, so long as culture is molded by its consciousness of human persistence and endurance. I am sorry that I was unable to avail myself of the searching historical sketch, "Shifting Definitions and Evaluations of the Humanities from the Renaissance to the Present," first published in the collected essays of the late R. S. Crane, *The Idea of the Humanities* (Chicago, 1967). However, I venture to think that my briefer essay, ranging over a longer period, complements some of Professor Crane's observations.

Fifty years of scholarly interchange and advancement are all the worthier of commemoration when the jubilee falls at a moment of uncertainty, a crisis in the universities which reverberates to a greater turbulence in the extramural world. Here, in this most serenely beautiful of university towns, it is tempting to look the other way; but our congratulations would not ring true, if they were not mingled with some degree of concern. After the student barricades on the Boulevard Saint-Michel, after the occupation and evacuation of Morningside Heights, none of us can take refuge in cloistered immunity. Recently a French colleague sent me a copy of a manifesto, wherewith not only the students but also the *concierges* demanded the right to participate in the appointment of faculty and the supervision of examinations. It would be vain to reply, in the heat of the argument, that the structure of knowledge is hierarchical rather than democratic, and that the best a democracy can do is to open careers to talents which it has recruited and trained for them. All of us have taken certain steps up the academic *gradus ad Parnassum,* or else we would not be here, and there are some among us whose example points on toward the upper reaches. We cannot help our pupils without explaining to them that valid rights are those which have been earned.

Any responsible body of scholars meeting today cannot altogether detach its thoughts from such pressures, even though the problems they raise may seem to be out of order, being less directly related to research than to pedagogy. Yet at a time when the multiplication of students must be met by a rapid increase of teachers, and so long as the license to teach at the highest level is more or less equivalent to the doctoral thesis, it follows that the quality of research stands in some danger of being diluted. It will not be my part in these discussions either to prescribe or to predict, happily for you as well as me. Nor am I sure that historical perspectives, insofar as I can make it out, can do much to clarify a situation which may strike you as all but unprecedented. Notwithstanding, if we have any professional obligation, it is to history: to the interpretation of recorded experience in its continuities, from whenever they started until now—or rather, from the present to the past, as Diderot saw when he pointed out that we reverse the order of history in becoming conscious of it. No form of provinciality is more confining than ignorance of other times than one's own. No intellectual exercise can be more liberating than the attempt to look before and after the limits of contemporaneity.

To glance back, after all, is to be reminded that institutions of higher learning have lived upon an accumulation of precedent which, because they have always dealt with youth, has seldom gone unchallenged. For whatever the reassurance might be worth, the record of student protest is coextensive with the annals of the faculties. Rioting against the papal authorities took place at the University of Paris as early as 1229, a generation before Robert de Sorbon set up his house of studies on the Rue Coup-Gorge for impoverished students of theology. The rioters were young men known as Goliards, who—when not professionally angry— liked to sing about their potations and fornications, and preferred that vagabond existence to the quiddities of the subtle doctors; in short, they were not unlike those latter-day *vagantes* who have fringed our campuses with ear-piercing music and a slightly narcotic haze. The Sorbonne, in spite or perhaps because of its international centrality, has in each of its many centuries been a target of vocal criticism and an object of administrative reform. Because it persisted into the Renaissance as a bulwark of medieval scholasticism, Francis I was compelled to found a rival and superior institution for the pursuit of the new learning, the Collège de France. The restored Sorbonne is already falling down, jeered the wits when Richelieu rebuilt it a century afterward.

> Instaurata ruet jamjam Sorbona. Caduca
> dum fuit, inconcussa stetit; renovata peribit.

Frequent renewal has not yet killed it off, though its effectual survival is once more at stake. As of 1968 we can no longer say that, while it was in decline, it stood unshaken. Organs for the preservation and transmission of culture are peculiarly subject to the cultural lag, so that intermittent progress makes itself manifest through shake-ups and showdowns, demonstrations and confrontations. Faust's revulsion from an encrusted and etiolated curriculum marks the beginning of his quest for realities. He is a more auspicious mentor for Goethe than for Marlowe. Even while our wandering scholars were rioting on the Left Bank, a curricular battle was being fought, which has been narrated by the *trouvère* Henri d'Andeli in his allegorical mock-epic, *La Bataille des set ars*. Those were the seven liberal arts, of course, and we tend to imagine them standing in undisrupted alignment. Seneca had distinguished the *artes liberales* from the *artes mechanicae* on the grounds that the former offered no mercenary rewards; therefore they were worthy of free men, and indeed were agents of liberation. Richard of Bury was to condense this relationship between liberty and liberality into a double pun on his much-loved books: "O libri soli liberales et liberi!" But impracticality is not in itself a criterion for a liberal education, and usefulness has unexpected ways of breaking in.

Art and science were roughly interchangeable concepts during the Middle Ages; the subjects of the Quadrivium—arithmetic, geometry, and astronomy, if not music—were predominantly scientific, from our point of view. The Trivium came first, and the first of all the arts—Dante's *prima arte*—was grammar, not merely the principles of the Latin language but the study of selected classical authors. Rhetoric. which came second, and Logic or Dialectic, in the third place, were increasingly to be regarded as practical instruments rather than modes of inquiry. "Is to dispute well Logic's chiefest end?" asks Dr. Faustus wearily, answering himself, "Then read no more, thou hast attained that end." As for Rhetoric, during the thirteenth century it took the expedient and popular form of the *ars dictaminis,* the technique of letter-writing. Clerics became clerks in the secretarial sense, utilizing their literacy to enter worldly service, where they contributed public documents as notaries, diplomats, and administrators. Under the influence of *dictamen* the University of Paris had virtually become a business school, according to Henri d'Andeli, while the classics had retreated to the University of Orleans. His rueful poem depicts the grammarians sallying forth to a military fray with the rhetoricians on the Hill of Saint Genevieve. But alas, the old *auctores* are routed by the contemporary utilitarians. Logic attracts the students, while Grammar is outnumbered.

> Logique a les clers en ses mains
> Et Grammaire rest mis au mains.

The pattern looks so familiar that we are almost shocked to realize for how long it has been applicable, in one way or another. It was not simply the nineteenth-century *Zeitgeist* which James Russell Lowell was opposing, when he asserted that the university was a place where nothing useful should be taught. Nor was Herbert Spencer introducing a novel proposition, when he maintained at the other extreme: "Just as the Orinoco Indian paints and tattoos himself, so the child in this country learns Latin because it forms a part of the education of a gentleman." Battles of the books have been waged again and again, moving into fresh territory at every engagement, since their issue is the adaptation of literary traditions and conventions to the demands and concerns of a newer day. So Greek was propagated in the West against the initial opposition of belated Latin-speaking schoolmen, who were styled Trojans. The *Querelle des anciens et des modernes* registered the coming-of-age of vernacular literature and ended with a relativistic acceptance of both parties on their own terms. Swift's *Battle of the Books,* some five hundred years after Henri d'Andeli's satire, brought Homeric reinforcements to the ranks of the classicists. Since it is fragmentary by design, the outcome is inconclusive; but there can be no question regarding the author's sympathies, as elucidated in his insect-fable of the spider and the bee.

The moral is brought home by his spokesman, Aesop: ". . . was ever anything so modern as the spider in his air, his turns, and his paradoxes," in his squalid webs spun out of his entrails, his pride in his mechanical ingenuity, and little else save "a large vein of wrangling and satire?"

Instead of such "dirt and poison" the Ancients, like the bee, offer "honey and wax, thus furnishing mankind with the two noblest of things, sweetness and light." And Swift thus furnished Matthew Arnold with a noble catch-phrase, which subsequent apologists for the classics have somewhat cloyed and bedimmed. Swift could scarcely have been unaware of his own paradoxical stance in the controversy, as a satirist and as a Modern. He balanced it with a further paradox when he singled out the redoubtable Hellenist, Richard Bentley, as the leader of the attack on the Ancients. The latter had precipitated debate by attacking Charles Boyle, whose Latin phrasing is echoed in Swift's description of Bentley, "chiefly renowned for his humanity." The epithet, well deserved insofar as it refers to classical scholarship, waxes ironic as a characterization of Bentley's overbearing pedantry. The ambiguity becomes explicit when he is rebuked by Scaliger ". . . thy learning makes thee more barbarous, thy study of humanity more inhuman." Swift's lampoon on Bentley signalized the turning point from humanism to classical philology.

The larger irony is that, despite such tactical triumphs, the Moderns were bound to win out in the long run—as inevitably they must, inasmuch as time is on their side. Then, if they survive, it is their turn to assume what Dr. Johnson would claim for Shakespeare, "the dignity of an ancient," and to redistribute sweetness and light. Stendhal would turn this sequence upside down in his maxim that every classic had been romantic in its heyday. The consequence, for Stendhal, was the obsolescence of the classics. As modernity found its own expression, they were destined to recede more obscurely into the background. Henceforth their domain, once the common possession of educated men, would be chiefly accessible through the experts, the antiquaries and the archeologists for whom Bentley had prepared the way. Duty, in the guise of school assignments, would keep up a superficial conversance; but a diminishing few, primarily dons, would be reading dead languages for the pleasure of seeing them come alive. Meanwhile Swift and Voltaire would move to a foreground in the pantheon of taste, even as Juvenal and Lucian were transferred to its subsidiary niches. As satirists, more closely involved than most other writers with ephemeral circumstances, all of them were especially vulnerable to the erosions of change. The cycle of tradition and innovation brings us to the sphere of the modern humanities.

The Modern Humanities. May I venture, as an American, to suggest that the very phrase is a Briticism? It had to be coined, I should suppose, because of the dominating position occupied by the Greco-Roman classics in the leading British universities until the present century, and I should not be surprised if you told me that there were still classicists who considered the term a self-contradiction. The standard rubric, *litterae humaniores* (which has been ambiguously translated as "the so-called humanities" in *Tom Brown at Oxford*), is comparative and therefore invidious, implying as it does that some letters are more humane than others. But that reflects the inherited distinction between the liberal and the mechanical arts, just as the French do when they speak of *beaux-arts* and *belles-lettres*. If, in Oxonian parlance, the *litterae humaniores* are "Greats," it might seem to the outsider that the modern humanities ought to constitute the "Modern Greats"; but I am told that this is not the case, that Philosophy, Politics, and Economics have an ascendancy comparable to the *sciences humaines* in France and the social sciences in the United States. In my country we now have an official definition, thanks to Public Law 89-209 establishing the National Endowment for the Humanities. Though the legislative language may seem arbitrary and somewhat circular, it cannot be faulted for lack of breadth:

The term "humanities" includes, but is not limited to, the study of the following: languages, both modern and classic; linguistics; literature; history; jurisprudence; philosophy; archeology; the history, criticism, theory and practice of the arts; and those aspects of the social sciences which have humanistic content and employ humanistic methods.

I am sorry to report to my British colleagues that this open-ended definition has not yet been matched by open-handed generosity on the part of the Congress in appropriating funds. When your organization was established in 1918, as I understand, it was first called the Modern Language Research Association—a title interlinking its purposes with those of the Modern Language Association of America, which had been established thirty-five years before. The broadening of modern philology in relation to neighboring disciplines was acknowledged when you changed to your present title in 1920. It is a little awkward when the English language, lacking adjectives for certain nouns, must line up substantives in Germanic fashion, so that the compound "Research Association" must be doubly compounded with "Humanities Research." But it is a testimonial to your corporate accomplishment that your trademark has been recognized by at least one lexicon. In the latest edition of

Cassell's English-German Dictionary, where "humanities" is defined as "klassische Philologie," "modern humanities" is defined as "neuere Sprachen und Literatur." Evidently, so far as the Germans are concerned, you need not have bothered to change your name. The pluralization of the key word ("humanity"/"humanities") is an eighteenth-century refinement, a tardy recognition that the house of learning has more than one mansion. The singular is so all-encompassing in its purview that, to transpose Terence, no one can feel alien to it.

To be sure, Herman Melville uses the plural when Captain Peleg tells Ishmael in *Moby-Dick:* "No, no, my lad; stricken, blasted if he be, Ahab has his humanities." This is the kind of exception that proves a rule, since the sequel will corroborate our suspicion that Captain Ahab most lamentably wants the human touch. It is curious how the word "science," which comprehended all knowledge originally, and still does in other languages, has been technically specialized in English, where too frequently it denotes the opposite of the humanities. The word "anthropology" takes on a scientific tone from its suffix, though its root is the Greek counterpart of the Latin-based "humanity;" it betokens the science or study of *homo sapiens* as distinguished from the proper study of mankind. The basic formulation, *studia humanitatis,* appears to be one of the many reverberant phrases that we owe to Cicero. Typically, he announced that he had come to the defense of Archias because that poet, immersed in the study of humanity, was unversed in legal technicalities. A revealing comment by Aulus Gellius later objects, in the name of pure Ciceronian usage, to the loose employment of *humanitas* as a synonym for philanthropy—a failure to discriminate between the humane and what we term the humanitarian. Whereas the true equivalence is with what the Greeks termed παιδεία, that discipline of the mind which sets man apart from the animals.

"Humanism," like "humanitarianism," is a coinage of the nineteenth century, though we retrospectively apply it to the first important movement of modern intellectual history. The Italian humanists, when they descended from Ciceronian Latin to the vernacular, spoke of *umanità,* which comprised their interests in grammar, rhetoric, poetry, history, and moral philosophy. The designation of *umanista,* for a scholar or teacher of these studies, goes back to the student slang of the Quattrocento, as Professor Kristeller has shown. Such cognates, in the Renaissance, conveyed an inflection which was missing in ancient Rome—where education was secular—and which replied to the religious constraints of the

Middle Ages. There was an implicit and diametrical contrast between scholastic dogma and the humanistic outlook, with the added implication that the latter was a deliverance from the former. Few of the humanists were antireligious, and most of them were in orders; many of their efforts were directed toward ecclesiastical reform, theological *aggiornamento,* and the editing, the translation, and the higher criticism of canonical texts. But a clear line seems to have differentiated the two kinds of knowledge, divinity and humanity, and the second was clearly the promising innovation, the prospect of discovery for open and fertile minds. This dichotomy, which was generally accepted, became a triad in Bacon's *Advancement of Learning,* where natural philosophy or physical science sets forth upon its independent career:

In philosophy, the contemplations of man do either penetrate unto God, or are circumferred to nature, or are reflected or reverted upon himself. Out of which several inquiries there do arise three knowledges, divine philosophy, natural philosophy, and human philosophy or humanity.

Since it is man who is making these inquiries, the third of them—the reflection or reversion upon himself—has a unique immediacy. More rarely than the others is it an end in itself; more commonly it is a means of self-cultivation, a program for the formation of character. The effect on the student becomes the object of the study, while investigative curiosity gives way to pedagogical responsibility. The article in Diderot's *Encyclopédie* (written by the Abbé Mallet) argues that *les humanités* have been so named because, by polishing the intellect and mollifying the manners, they humanize those who cultivate them. Man's innate superiority to the beasts, who want discourse of reason, should be reinforced by this process of humanization. Yet the schoolboy idiom, *faire ses humanités,* came to stand for little more than taking the regular course at *lycée,* particularly the second-year class devoted to rhetoric. The *Dictionnaire de l'Académie* of 1778 is as categorical on the subject as only French schooling could be. *Les humanités,* it explains, are "Ce qu'on apprend ordinairment dans les collèges jusqu'à la Philosophie exclusivement." This may throw some light on the special charm that philosophy has held for Frenchmen; they equate it with their last year of school. Who can wonder why some of them moved so far in the other direction that the journalistic organ of their communist party is denominated *L'Humanité?*

Obviously—and who would know it better than the members of this association?—there are humanities and humanities. The humanistic ideal, the *cortegiano* or the *honnête homme,* was the scholar-gentleman, equally adept at arms and letters, whom Don Quixote strove to emulate. More clerk than knight himself, he survives as an object lesson in the hazards of disequilibrium; and yet less hazardous withal than if he were overbalanced on the other side, if he were more of a rider than a reader. If an immersion in humane letters was humanizing, some of the deepest immersions tended to bring out all too human failings. Witness the brutal exchanges between the learned Poggio and the erudite Filelfo, where matters of state and of syntax are debated on the same plane of personal scurrility and in the most pretentious Latin verse. Milton himself was not above trading such invectives with Salmasius. The mastery of polite learning, as Swift would prove on Bentley, was not necessarily the mother of *politesse.* Montaigne recalls an encounter with two scholars walking fifty paces apart, followed at a distance by a gentleman after whose identity he inquired. The first scholar, mistakenly thinking that the second was meant, responded: "He is not a gentleman; he is a grammarian, and I am a logician." Even more naïve than the confusion between the scholar and the gentleman was the expectation that two scholarly specialists might have something in common.

Such obtuse professionalism could be a foible of the learned at any given period. If Montaigne's anecdote looks ahead toward an era of narrowing specialization, then it also looks back to the warring factions within the Trivium. His habitual quotations from Greek and Latin, some of them inscribed upon the actual roof-beams of his study, illustrate how a literary revival could stimulate a rediscovery of life. Life could thereupon collaborate in a rebirth of literature, which in turn would be handed over to criticism, finally subsiding into the ministrations of philology. Our semantic soundings confirm the dictum, "Tout finit en Sorbonne." Dr. Johnson defines a humanist as "a philologer; a grammarian; a term used in the schools of Scotland." Would he have included himself in this reductive category? The Scottish term may well have been synonymous with *Latinist,* for the chair of Humanity was occupied by the Professor of Latin at the University of Edinburgh. That identification had been justified throughout the long interval when Latinity was the universal medium of literate discourse and high culture in Western Europe. The conception of an international republic of letters was, to a large extent, grounded upon it. Though it was in gradual retreat before the advancing babel of the various vernaculars, it managed to maintain its institutional and educational hold through those densely woven ties which—to Herbert Spencer—seemed the outmoded marks of caste.

Insofar as that caste could be viewed as a clerisy, the sociological point has a certain substance. The social function of the European clerk was not so definitely fixed as that of the Chinese Mandarin; but, in both cases, the shibboleth of the educated class was a language esoteric to the population at large. This elite tongue had been Greek among the Romans, whose own language doubled the patrimony of the Renaissance humanists. The Latin had a substantial preponderance over the Greek, because of its linguistic proximity as well as its residual bases in the church, the law, and the sciences. But, as it relinquished its active and functional role for a purely educational one, the two literatures came to occupy their coequal places at the center of the curriculum, with Greek reclaiming its inherent advantages in the esthetic and philosophical spheres. Milton's tractate *On Education* is based on the simple notion of subdividing the Greco-Latin corpus according to subject matter and expecting his dauntless pupils to read through all the authors systematically. Thus they will learn about agriculture from Cato, Varro, and Columella (Hesiod is probably too old-fashioned), and this pragmatic lesson will teach them how "to improve the tillage of their country." In addition to the classical tongues, they will naturally have acquired the Hebrew, not to mention "the Chaldee and the Syriac dialect."

Somehow Milton contrives to make his "complete and generous education," like his way to establish a free commonwealth, sound both ready and easy. His sole provision for the modern languages is laid down in a single and casual sentence: "And either now or before this, they may have easily learnt at any odd hour the Italian language." A similar assumption, that foreign tongues were souvenirs picked up by their pupils on continental vacations, seems to have prevailed among English educators well into the nineteenth century. If Milton's odd hour from a heavy schedule left room for only one contemporary language, the obvious choice was Italian; and he has given rich evidence of his own proficiency in it and his acquaintance with its poetry; but the only Italian works he recommended were three commentaries on Aristotle's *Poetics*. Milton's poetic achievement looms large as a monument to both the Renaissance and the Reformation, a distinctive yet characteristic fusion of classicism and Christianity. Like Dante's in Italian or the Pléiade's in French, it demonstrated that the vulgar tongue could be rendered illustrious. Milton could even assume the battered dignity of an ancient, prematurely worn down by ruthless emendation, when Bentley published his edition of *Paradise Lost* in 1732. Yet it was not until 1917 that Milton, among the great masters of English literature, could have figured in a Tripos at his own university.

Cambridge and Oxford were preceded by London, in this field, and by several among the provincial and Scottish universities. Faculties in English were generally preceded by the establishment of teaching staffs in the modern languages. There the language barrier interposed a pedagogic rigor which was thought to be missing from mere literature. In both fields the chronological emphasis was less likely to be modern than medieval. The Modern Humanities Research Association could never have been founded without a strenuous generation or two of pioneering and campaigning. Great Britain has had the habit, appropriate to an empire, of taking its own culture for granted, in contradistinction to France, where the attitudes toward language and literature have been standardized by an Academy, promulgated by the schools, and disseminated abroad by the *services culturels*. The other Romance countries, though less central, have been no less self-regarding. The smaller nations have been the most outgoing in their polyglot intercultural contacts: Switzerland, the Netherlands, Scandinavia. Germany, the most nationalistic in some respects, has in others been the most appreciative of the other national identities. It is German scholarship that we have to thank not only for *Germanistik*, but for some of the earliest and most important researches in *Romanistik* and *Anglistik*. The pioneers of English studies in the United States had to go to Germany for their training.

Such obligations were repaid when Britain and America welcomed a brilliant succession of German scholars, forced into dispersion by an anti-intellectual regime. The migrations of the intellectuals, through artistic expatriation when not through political exile, have helped to frame a supranational attitude toward ideas and the arts, harking back to the old republic of letters and sharing in Goethe's vision of world literature. It is the special illumination of the modern humanities that, beyond our immediate culture, they foster an understanding of others, with which they keep in close touch. Since those other cultures are likewise endeavoring to understand ours, their endeavors hold mirrors up to us, as it were. And since each culture thus has outposts in other countries, and every faculty has representatives of a wide range of cultures, the possibilities for stimulus and collaboration are panoramic. We are in no danger of neutralizing the many shadings, the striking differences, and the immense variety among peoples. The ethnic, the linguistic, the ideological, and the geographical boundaries between them are sharply drawn. Cosmopolitan critics, like Madame de Staël, have emphasized the national characteristics of the different literatures. But there is a broader cosmopolitanism which is more interested in parallels, recurrences, and interconnections. The comparative method, drawing material from diversified sources in order to trace themes and delineate forms, contemplates all literature as one organic continuum.

This continuum is plainly visible in the network of tradition extending through the Occident from Greece, Rome, and Judea. Few of us have much occasion to stray beyond it; yet, at the stage of history we have reached, its cultural hegemony is no longer accepted; and, since increasing cognizance will be taken of Asia and Africa, we must try to discern the relation between their humanities and ours. But, although such an orientation can extend our perspectives, it can never take the place of our basic occidentation, if I may risk a neologism: our commitment to that train of European values whose prior stages are outlined by Jaeger's *Paedeia* and Curtius' *Lateinisches Mittelalter*. Truly the Renaissance was preoccupied with the ancient humanities. It is to the Enlightenment that we must look for the proclamation of modernism, of a modernist spirit conveyed in a neoclassical style. Significantly, its organon of knowledge was not a synthesis but an encyclopedia, a collection of critical surveys and up-to-date articles linked together by no less random an arrangement than the alphabet. Diversity and particularity were soon carried much farther by the Romantic Movement. And it is here, in the self-realization of concurrent nationalities, in the recovery of the vernacular literatures of the Middle Ages, and in the emergence of such mediatory disciplines as comparative philology and folklore, that we find the matrix of the modern humanities.

Here too we can watch the rise of historicism, the imaginative reconstruction of the past, the sympathetic rather than moralistic approach to each successive period in the light of its own presumptions and aspirations, with a consequent acknowledgment of their manifold variation and their relative validity. Literature, the most expressive source of documentation, was the final residue of the historical process. The history of literature, as soon as it went beyond the listing of names and the cataloguing of titles, had to proceed along evolutionary lines and to relate its developments to those of society as a whole. Moreover, in the selection and treatment of authors, it utilized a canon predetermined by criticism and responsive to changeable tastes. This was simplest when a literature began with a founding father, as it did with Dante in Italy. It was not before an interim of critical probation that Shakespeare was accorded the primacy in England. Unlike the English—whose Royal Society, despite an early mandate to deal with the language, concentrated more professionally upon scientific experiment—the French empowered their Academy to be the arbiter of literary standards. Poets who came before Malherbe were summarily dismissed, and the heroic drama of Corneille was condemned for overstepping the confines of neoclassicism. Such exercises of authority were incitements to revolt; but revolutions, when they occurred in France, set up their own canons and fomented counter-movements.

Germany and Russia followed a slower rhythm, possibly because of political retardation; for their respective father-figures, Goethe and Pushkin, though they transcended Romanticism, were its contemporaries. The designation of certain ages as golden is retrospective as well as subjective; it was not until the nostalgic nineteenth century that *floruit 1600* became the *siglo de oro* of Spain. How much is due to patriotic self-consciousness, to the state of the language, or to the contingent presence of individual genius will vary from one cultural apogee to another. Contagion from one country to another has proved a powerful agency for the introduction of movements and the renovation of genres, so that it can be as meaningful to consider several related literatures at a particular period as it is to study a single literature in its full chronological span. Unhappily specialization has narrowed so many horizons that, more often than not, the specialist is not simply an Anglicist, a Germanist, or a Hispanist; he is self-limited further by circumscription within a specific century. He may even hesitate, if he is professionally committed to the eighteenth century, whether to focus his expertise on the age of Swift or the age of Johnson. When we talk about a Renaissance man, in the Modern Language Association, we do not mean a polymath like Erasmus; we have in mind a man who knows his way through Pollard and Redgrave's *Short-Title Catalogue*.

If our adjective *modern* signifies anything more than distance from antiquity, it should indicate the relevance of our studies to the present, and vice versa. This association's first ten years coincided with a decade of peculiar brilliance for continental European and Anglo-American letters. A number of the modernists then emerging would now be granted the status of hallowed ancients, and they themselves would not have been unprepared to play their canonical parts. Thomas Mann admitted to rehearsing the *imitatio Goethe;* T. S. Eliot garlanded *The Waste Land* with his own footnotes; Paul Valéry sat in the lecture hall when Gustave Cohen lectured on *Le Cimetière marin.* The commentaries that James Joyce demanded and has been receiving bid fair to fill an Alexandrian library, albeit the comparison breaks down when we think of incineration as an irreparable loss. Universities have been traditionally laggard in coming to terms with the times; given the times, that procrastination could be a virtue, which would have merited the praise of Arnold. Some of the newer programs, keenly aware of past evasions, are striving frantically to be "with it"—with what? We cannot help, nor should we avoid, being with the third generation of the twentieth century. But it is also our vocation to be, if coexistence is possible, with minds of those who have already lived. As custodians of their memory, we must do whatever we can to keep their words alive.

This is not so grateful a task as it ought to be and has been, in view of the multiplying distractions: the *trahison des clercs* seduced by journalism, the trespasses of the mechanical upon the liberal arts. The mechanization of life has led, as Ortega y Gasset predicted, to the dehumanization of art. If man is the measure of the humanities, our progression may be reckoned by his changing image of himself. The scholar-gentleman yields to the underground man; and the antiheroes of Dostoevsky and Kafka, clambering to the surface with Beckett and Genet, do not cringe but domineer. Swift, who had his own deep vein of subterranean insight, was prophetic when he chose the spider as a prototype of the latest moderns, with their ingenious mechanisms, their cobwebs spun from entrails, and their renunciation of sweetness and light in favor of dirt and poison. We should be deceiving ourselves if we underestimated the antihumanistic thrust of so much recent writing. When the annual series of *entretiens* was conducted at the Abbaye de Pontigny in 1923, one of the questions propounded was: "LES HUMANITÉS, sont-elles irremplaçables pour former une Élite?" The participants in that discussion, who included André Gide, Charles Du Bos, Roger Martin du Gard, Heinrich Mann, and Lytton Strachey, exemplified their theme by both their formation and their standing, and thereby lent extra weight to the premise that the humanities were on the wane.

As to what has been replacing them, we now have Lord Snow's unsurprising answer. We also have the candid testimony of my biological colleague, James D. Watson, suggesting that even a scientific formation at the Cavendish Laboratory—while it may lead to major discoveries—produces something less than an intellectual elite. "The humanities need to be defended today," wrote Irving Babbitt just sixty years ago, "against the encroachments of physical science, as they once needed to be against the encroachments of theology." That defense, which Babbitt sought in vain to rally under the slogan of New Humanism, was essentially a rearguard action. We have long since passed the point where it seems pertinent to conduct metaphorical battles of books against test tubes. Parting from Divinity in the Renaissance, Humanity was on the side of nature. Naturalism is still a bond between Bacon's natural philosophy and what has been made of human philosophy by Bergson, Freud, William James, and Bertrand Russell. Currently, applied science has been lending us helpful instruments, such as the computerized concordance to Shakespeare edited in Germany by the American *Anglist,* Marvin Spevack; and certain branches of humanistic research, notably structural linguistics and analytic bibliography, have become so systematic as to be at home among the exact sciences. Meanwhile, among both the scientists and the humanists, the beleaguered spirit of disinterested inquiry needs all the defenders it can command.

The irresistible menace to both, to all, is the encroachment of technology. We have been living through a five-hundred-year cycle, during which the principal medium of communication and information and expression has been the book. The transposition to it, from the manuscript, inaugurated the recognizable world; a shift away from it, portended by the audiovisual media, beckons us toward a realm of science fiction. No one who has used a library or taught the young over the past thirty years can have failed to notice signs of crucial change, though our vested interests as scholars may have put blinkers on our eyes. Marshall McLuhan deserves much credit for having made an issue of what has been happening. But he does not analyze, he embraces it, with the paternal fondness of a Frankenstein for his monster. Culture is obsolete, for Professor McLuhan, in the humanistic sense; in the anthropological sense, he swings with the customs of the tribe, however barbaric. His prognosis may be right, the more the pity. What would be worse is the supposition that the humanities are replaceable, since their falling-off would be part of a general declination. It is heartening to recollect that they have not heretofore needed replacement, that they have disappeared and reappeared, that their prolonged confinement to the scriptorium did not abate their essential vitality, that they have shown a limitless capacity for renascence and metamorphosis.

WHY LITERARY CRITICISM IS NOT
AN EXACT SCIENCE

For a student in the humanities, I have had more than usual opportunity to associate with scientists—which is why they have never to me been the bugbears feared and deplored by some of my more immediate colleagues. The most exciting course I took in college was one offered by A. N. Whitehead in cosmology from Plato to Einstein. Since my graduate studies were not undertaken under a department of English or comparative literature, but in the new freedom of Harvard's Society of Fellows, I had the privilege of seeing Whitehead and other Senior Fellows in both the sciences and the arts on an informal basis every week, and later of joining them. Meanwhile, as one of the early Junior Fellows, I felt challenged and stimulated by the friendship of B. F. Skinner and W. V. Quine, as I have continued to be throughout my career. These circumstances may have moved me to take a special interest in the more recent foundation of Churchill College at Cambridge University, where a predominant emphasis upon science was to be infiltrated by a fair number of students and fellows from the humanistic disciplines. The Vergilian—or else Lucretian—motto of the College, *Felix qui potuit rerum cognoscere causas,* has always seemed to me to speak for the common strain of intellectual curiosity that the interpreter of art ought to share with interpreters of nature, even though he may work with less tractable or predictable material. When, as Overseas Fellow at Churchill during the spring of 1967, I was asked to give a public lecture (May 12), my subject was virtually suggested by the occasion. Hence my title was at least half-serious. I should own that I was also moved by the thought that Cambridge had been the late battleground of *The Two Cultures,* and that the assailant in that battle was not necessarily to be complied with as the ultimate spokesman for literary criticism. The lecture was published by Heffers in the College's pamphlet series the following year and republished in the United States by the Harvard University Press. I might add here that, having previously refused several invitations to review both *Anatomy of Criticism* and the first four volumes of *A History of Modern Criticism* because I did not want to qualify the greeting that I thought they both deserved, I welcomed a more detached occasion for seeking to understand what they had and had not contributed to the advance of criticism as a general enterprise. I am happy to say that my friendship with Professor Richards, Wellek, and Frye has continued intact. In afterthought I also must admit that, when I charged Sartre with critical malpractice vis-à-vis Flaubert, I did not dream that he would offer such monstrous corroboration as he now has done in *L'Idiot de la famille.*

It is with some diffidence that I have chosen my title, and with a considered awareness of how little it promises. It may well seem to underline the obvious, to undertake an explanation of what has been all too self-evident, by twisting a simple axiom into a rhetorical question. Scientists perhaps may raise their eyebrows, while literary critics—who are notoriously more touchy and more on the defensive today—may even take umbrage, over the merest possibility that their respective pursuits might have anything in common. The likeliest sign of mutual agreement would seem to be the scorn that both sides join in heaping upon the unwary man of good will who gets in their way by attempting to mediate between them. But there has not always been such a sense of disjunction; the sciences and the arts were on interchangeable terms within the medieval curriculum; and men of letters were prominent among the founders of the Royal Society. Inasmuch as science has comprised the sum of human endeavors to gather knowledge, knowledge about the existence of man as well as the conditions under which he exists, much of its history has been preoccupied with what we call the humanities. Since these belong to us all by definition, they have a certain priority upon culture; but this does not mean that they have any monopoly over it. On the contrary, the cultural achievements of the past three centuries have been most spectacular in the fields of scientific experiment, discovery, and speculation.

So much would go without saying, if the more bookish humanists had not been unduly reluctant to make the acknowledgment. On the other hand, there can be no future in the assumption that the experimental sciences constitute by themselves a rival culture. This has served its purpose by bringing us back to the realization that all culture is, or should be, a continuous and pluralistic whole. Here, if anywhere, that completeness should be exemplified: in the university of Spenser, Milton, and Wordsworth, which is also the university of Newton, Darwin, and Rutherford. This College, dedicated to scientific advance in the name of a great humanist, has extended its hospitality not merely to visitors from overseas but to exponents of the humanistic disciplines. Yet even Cambridge, one gathers, has not quite settled the escalating intracultural war. In approaching that situation from the other side, I can reduce it to the smallest dimensions by linking it with an episode in my own education. It is now thirty-three years since I first visited Cambridge, having then just graduated from its academic offshoot in Cambridge, Massachusetts. My favorite teacher at Harvard, Alfred North Whitehead, may have pointed the direction by having reversed it himself. I arrived with a letter to I. A. Richards, whose welcome was the best possible introduction and whose friendship has been a happy circumstance of my subsequent life. He was then in the limelight, and was most appealing to me, as the man who seemed destined to solve the problems of literary criticism by the application of scientific methods.

Richards had been recruited by the developing English Faculty after having taken his undergraduate degree in Moral Sciences—mainly, I believe, in logic and psychology. Hence he not only brought new and sharp instruments to the study of literature but, since he was untrammeled by the clutter of literary history and philology that passed for scholarly training in those days, he was freer to take a more strictly analytic approach. All this would have been of no avail, had he not possessed an intelligence which was subtle as well as ingenious, sympathetic as well as penetrating, and sensitively attuned to the novel effects that Anglo-American poetry was currently achieving. Indeed he has turned out, belatedly, to be a poet himself—but I must not anticipate the point of my object lesson. It is at once the glory and the limitation of literary criticism in England that it has been dominated by a line of poets, from Sir Philip Sidney to T. S. Eliot. As practitioners, they have given us a uniquely valuable sequence of insights into the nature of their art. They have also defended it against the perennial philistines, waged campaigns for more or less noble causes, and propagandized for the styles and tastes they were interested in promoting, not least their own. The defect of their virtue has been its lack of what Matthew Arnold considered prerequisite to criticism, namely disinterestedness. The main alternative to their professional involvement has been, in the words of a French scholar-critic, Henri Peyre, "the whimsical amateurishness dear to an English gentleman touching on literature."

The conception of the critic as an amateur, though it sounds more affirmative in the French sense of the term, has left him with an inferiority complex which he has not invariably deserved. It has subjected him to the condescension of writers who, however slight their original talent, look down on him as a failed writer, an envious parasite, or at best a publicist for his betters. "I am always amused," said Oscar Wilde, "by the silly vanity of those writers and artists of our day who seem to imagine that the primary function of the critic is to chatter about their second-rate work." That may be a secondary function, especially congenial to the amateurish, and it reaps due recognition in the quoted blurb. But if we think of the critic's subject matter as the body of man's verbal expression, together with the artistic forms it has taken and the modes of experience it has projected and preserved, then we have our business cut out for us on a more serious plane. If English literature was to become a university subject, it had to be professionalized in some measure. Many students of it set out to become authorities on special periods or particular authors.

Dr. Richards had the courage to deal with the underlying processes, particularly with communication and with imagination. The poems of his good friend Eliot, then regarded as the ultimate in modernism, plus the contemporaneous rediscovery of the Metaphysical poets, raised difficulties which in turn gave rigor to Richards' program of interpretation, and to that explication of texts for which he revealed so illuminating a flair.

It is worthy of note that his earlier books were published in the International Library of Psychology, Philosophy, and Scientific Method. Two of them were produced in collaboration with the editor of the series, that enterprising polymath, C. K. Ogden. Their path-breaking tract on semantics, *The Meaning of Meaning,* called into question much that had been taken for granted about the fundamental use of words to convey ideas and emotions. *The Foundations of Aesthetics,* written with James Wood as a third collaborator, undermined those ponderous substructures of esthetic theory whereupon so disappointingly little had been built that conduced to a practical grasp of the arts. Having thus been helped to clear the way, to dispel the dogmas that surrounded his subject, and—as he professed—"to write in a scientific spirit," Richards formulated his own position with *The Principles of Literary Criticism* in 1925. It would be unfair to view so problematic an undertaking as a literary sequel to the *Principia Mathematica* either of Newton or of Whitehead and Russell, though it comes close to the *Principia Ethica* of G. E. Moore and bears out *a fortiori* the Cantabrigian genius for getting down to first principles. What it really has to offer is a methodology of doubts—or, as the author puts it, "a machine to think" whose operations culminate in "the analysis of a poem." Insofar as values are involved in this process, they are naturalistically inferred; and, among the tabulations and redefinitions, there is even a diagram which illustrates the stabilizing effect of poetry upon the nervous system.

The monograph that appeared in the following year, *Science and Poetry,* was most explicit in its mediation between the two. We can now see that it belongs among the classic apologies of the poets, along with Sidney's defense against Puritanism and Shelley's against Utilitarianism. By the time he rewrote it, shortly less than a decade later, Richards' conciliatory position had shifted into a virtual counterattack. Meanwhile, in 1929, he had made his most striking contribution with a book whose originality was based, just as far as criticism can be, on first-hand experimentation. Since those experiments were conducted in his classes at Cambridge, and since they have affected and improved the teaching of literature and language all over the world, I scarcely need to emphasize his account of them in *Practical Criticism*. Teachers had long been familiar with their pupils' capacities for misunderstanding. But no one had previously tried to control the problem by selecting and assigning texts which embodied significant ambiguities, analyzing the patterns of variance among the responses to them, and diagnosing the blocks and biases that gave rise to misreadings. It is true that the experimentalist was no more than another reader himself, albeit an incomparably perceptive one. Moreover, unlike the other readers, he was not shielded from his own preconceptions by being kept in the dark about the identity of the testing passages. In reserving the rights to determine the central line from which the interpretations of his guinea-pig students were to be regarded as deviations, he reintroduced an element of that old-fashioned dogmatism which he had been striving to avoid.

Yet the venture held out, for my generation, concrete hopes of pursuing the writer's thought from the printed page to the reader's mind, of breaking down such opaque conceptions as universality into the particulars that make them meaningful, of investigating the precise effect of a given work rather than pronouncing a facile judgment upon it. In turning his attention next from the work's impact to its inception, and from the psychology of the reader toward that of the writer, Richards sought to open up an even more promising domain. However, it proved to be jealously haunted by an elusive ghost who delighted in leading clearer minds into the shadows and quagmires of his own excogitation, Samuel Taylor Coleridge. If ever a failure in creativity was rationalized by a resort to criticism, that was the case with Coleridge's celebrated theory of the imagination. No one celebrated it more fervently than its theorist, whose doctrine of organic wholeness may have consoled him for the self-confessed disintegration of his poetic career. The parallel career of Wordsworth reached its climax with *The Prelude, or the Growth of the Poet's Mind*. Coleridge's fragmentary counterpart in prose, the *Biographia Literaria,* was foredoomed to be an anticlimactic medley of philosophical autobiography and critical apologia. Yet it discloses an overarching pattern if we read it as a case history of disappointed radicalism turned reactionary, cultivating German metaphysics in atonement for the French Revolution and repudiating British empiricism to enwrap itself in transcendental idealism.

Bacon, in surveying the ground for the provinces of modern knowledge, had indicated the necessity for "a science pertaining to the imagination." Hobbes and Locke had carried the inquiry into the mental sphere, and Coleridge had begun his speculations under the influence of the pioneering psychologist, David Hartley. His breakdown as a poet seems to have been accompanied by a conversion from the psychological to the metaphysical viewpoint. In the categorical phraseology of his new mentor, Kant, it was a transposition from mere Understanding to the higher Reason. Such dichotomizing must have encouraged Coleridge to leave pragmatic considerations behind him, to take refuge in more intuitive concepts, and to elaborate his qualitative distinction between Fancy and Imagination. Whatever was analyzable now seemed to him mechanical, not to say neoclassical, and he relegated its productions to the patronizing category of Fancy. The truly creative power, Imagination, partaking as it did of the divine, was by that very token inexpressible, in spite of his gyrations to express it. He pretended to have worked out his argument in more than a hundred pages, so abstruse that the world was not ready for them: "holding the same relation in abstruseness to Plotinus, as Plotinus does to Plato." Consequently he was withholding them, on the advice of an invented friend—or should we say that the person from Porlock was interrupting the damsel with the dulcimer once more? Coleridge's definition of the imagination is promulgated on a single page, and is less of a reasoned statement than a theological edict *ex cathedra*.

Elsewhere he abounds in suggestive notations and pertinent comments, and he uses the categories of the imaginative and the fanciful as value judgments to signalize the beauties and faults of Shakespeare, Wordsworth, and others. But, to be quite candid with ourselves, we should admit that an important path of criticism either took a wrong turn or came to a dead end in the thirteenth chapter of the *Biographia Literaria*. The compulsive monologue of Coleridge still goes on, like that of his Ancient Mariner, and exerts a peculiar fascination over the most gracious wedding guests. It is not too hard to comprehend why he attracted so agile a mountain climber is Ivor Richards, with a latent strain of Welch mysticism in his own temperament, to the loftier and cloudier regions of critical discourse. Yet some of us, who feel immensely indebted to Richards for the stimulus of his bold and fresh researches, felt that we might be losing a leader when—instead of attacking the subject directly—he brought out his commentary on *Coleridge on the Imagination* in 1934. He had begun it in the empirical vein, as a self-professed Benthamite; but by the time he had retraced the course of his more visionary predecessor, he himself emerged as a full-fledged Platonist. As irony would have it, our first meeting was the only occasion on which I could count myself among his disciples. Although we became colleagues at Harvard soon afterward, most of his work there was centered at the School of Education, and its remarkable benefits have been chiefly registered in the fields of linguistics and pedagogy.

Richards' contributions to literary criticism and to the revival of rhetoric are all the more strategic because, professionally speaking, he seems to have functioned as an interdisciplinary messenger from the outer world of the behavioral sciences. The disciple best qualified to continue and advance his theoretical interests, William Empson, has preferred the role of a crotchety virtuoso to that of a systematic investigator. The habit of close reading, developed into an educational discipline by Richards and his successors, has left its mark on English departments everywhere. But, whereas it had served him as an instrument for open-ended curiosity which he was willing to follow wherever it led, others would frame it with canons of what to read and regulate it by sanctions on how to judge, just as dogmatic critics had done in the past. Their dogmas had been different, to be sure, and the fact that these have fallen into disuse is one of the reasons for distrusting such dogmas as happen to be current today. The critic, seeking a basis for his authority, finds it easier to model himself on the schoolmaster than on the scientist. Readers, hot for certainties, are more readily convinced by emphatic oversimplifications than by a patient and searching effort to grapple with things in their inherent complexity. Writers can be marked and ranked like schoolboys, though none but schoolboys need respect such ratings. When names are cited to be conjured with, when touchstones are held up for concerted approval, when penalties are exacted for disagreement, we are still in the schoolroom.

Coleridge was fond of saying that every man was either a Platonist or an Aristotelian. Though he may have overrated the average citizen, one way or another, there could be no question where he stood; and, if my impressions of Professor Richards are warranted, it could be said that he started on the ground as an Aristotelian and moved upward into the stratosphere of eternal ideas. Plato, of course, is a somewhat equivocal sponsor for criticism, given his views on the irrationality of poetic inspiration, on the falsity of artistic representation, and on the undesirability of poets within the ideal commonwealth. Aristotle, in this as in so many other respects, is the master of those that would know. He approached literature as an omniscient naturalist, whose studies of the natural order (physics, zoology) extended to human activities (ethics, politics) as well as to the basic ways of thinking (logic, metaphysics). Though his *Rhetoric* sets forth an impure science, the modern science of public relations, it is characteristically observant in discerning the springs of motivation and indicating how they could be manipulated. Though his *Poetics* was necessarily limited by the genres available for his scrutiny—principally tragedy and epic—and by the peculiarities of their Hellenic manifestations, he made some defining observations which apply to all drama and narrative. What were to be even more significant, and to be discussed and reinterpreted from his day through our own, were his formulas for the relationship between art and reality ($\mu\acute{\iota}\mu\eta\sigma\iota\varsigma$) and for the psychological or moral reaction to art ($\kappa\acute{\alpha}\theta\alpha\rho\sigma\iota\varsigma$).

It is evident that, after twenty-three centuries, Aristotle's critical works are far less out of date than his scientific writings. The inference might be that criticism has not progressed much since its origins. The counter-argument would then be that it is not a progressive discipline, that—being more of an art than a science—it does not depend so much on the collective deployment of accumulations and breakthroughs. If it does not build on what has gone before but must start all over again each time, that would explain why great critics have been so few and far between. But this supposition would be challenged by the paradox of Aristotle himself, who clearly wrote in a scientific spirit and thereby provided a point of departure for all too much of the ensuing discussion. For example, when Richards drew his diagram to illustrate how poetry soothes the nerves, he was simply updating the concept of catharsis, which Aristotle had derived from the Hippocratic writings and utilized to refute the Platonic charge that poetry had a demoralizing effect. Whether or not the metaphor provides a valid description of the emotional process is a question which ought to be referred, at long last, to the physiologists and the clinical psychologists. Nowadays it would seem more important than ever to understand, if we can, whether a vicarious participation in lust and murder at an esthetic distance purges the spectator's mind of its antisocial impulses, as Aristotle claimed, or whether these are incited and abetted by pornography and crime fiction, as some of our contemporary moralists have admonished.

In the context of ancient thought, or as an encouragement to the Arabs or later empiricists, the essence of Aristotelianism could have been summed up—with Pope's phrase—as "Nature methodized." Its teachings had been findings originally, rather than the doctrines they arbitrarily became; they had been "discovered, not devised." Aristotelian philosophy became so rigidly identified with medieval scholasticism that it had to be repudiated as an enemy to intellectual progress. Now the *Poetics,* curiously enough, was not known to the Middle Ages. Critical tradition was accordingly founded on the *Ars Poetica* of Horace, which—as a handbook for would-be poets—was prescriptive rather than descriptive in its emphasis. It is not Aristotle but Horace who was responsible for the imposition of schoolmasterly notions of correctness, such as the insistence that a proper tragedy must have neither more nor less than five acts. Since the manuscript of Aristotle's *Poetics* was a rediscovery of the Renaissance, there seemed to be no dead hand set upon it. It was hailed as a source for the liberations and the renovations of the new age; and for a while, to some extent, it was. But, after the intensive labors of its editors and commentators had canonized it as the supreme authority, it was calculated to be an agent of petrifaction. Observations stiffened into precepts, and precepts finally ossified into rules. Critics saw themselves as judges, interpreting the law; but, since their interpretations continued to differ, they could more appropriately be compared to litigants; and in order to enforce their decrees, they established legislative bodies in the form of academies.

Thanks to Bernard Weinberg, we can now consult a monumental *History of Criticism in the Italian Renaissance.* As we might expect, the name of Aristotle figures strategically on nearly every page. Yet far from being wholly static as it might appear, the chronicle is riven with controversies, literary quarrels in which each faction calls upon the Stagirite as its protector. We are reminded of Communist polemics, where the conflicting opinions are all put forward in the sacred name of Karl Marx. Surely it is one of the ironies of European history that its most trenchant social critic has become the patron saint of its authoritarian societies. Just as Marx once declared that he was no Marxist, so Aristotle might have dissociated himself from the rigidities of the Aristotelians. Their shibboleth, the doctrine of the Three Unities, is very tentatively adumbrated in the *Poetics.* No mention whatsoever is made of the so-called Unity of Place, which had not always been observed in Greek drama, but which was imposed on the Italian theater by its development of scenery. The codification of laws made it possible to hand down official judgments, as the French Academy did when it censured Corneille for having committed tragicomedy in *The Cid.* The disparity between these neoclassical criteria and the consummated actualities of literature itself, in the instance of Shakespeare, became so flagrant that it all but discredited the critical establishment. Dr. Johnson redeemed it by his famous appeal "from criticism to nature," pointing out that the unities were artificial restrictions, after all, and that life itself was considerably larger than either tragedy or comedy.

By proceeding "not dogmatically, but deliberately," Johnson rescued criticism from the oppressive letter of the Aristotelians and directed it back toward the inquiring spirit of Aristotle. Thus it rounded a cycle which paralleled the formation and the diffusion of classical culture in the West, and which conferred a unity and a continuity on the first two volumes of George Saintsbury's *History of Criticism*. Though his taste was mildly romantic and his manner rather impressionistic, Saintsbury tended to fall off in his third and last volume. His treatment of the nineteenth century was, to use his typical expression, a "topsyturvyfication." His background in the classics was a credit to his Tory prejudices; and he loved French wine, if not French rationalism; but disorganization tripped him up and he bogged down into insularity, when he attempted to cope with the variety and the individuality of what was then the modern period. It has remained for René Wellek to accomplish this task on a scale commensurate with its importance in his *History of Modern Criticism, 1750–1950*, the fifth and final volume of which should be appearing within the next year or so. As a Czech-born scholar of English literature, now the leading practitioner of comparative literature in the United States, Professor Wellek is magisterially fitted for his demanding assignment. It would be difficult to think of any other person who could bring it off single-handedly. Since I have one or two slight reservations to make, let me make it clear how much I admire his encyclopedic learning, his tireless industry, and his shrewd common sense.

Professor Wellek's period, roughly the two centuries between Johnson and ourselves, has been truly an age of criticism. It was heralded as such by Kant, who would be echoed by Renan and Arnold. To view that age in "international perspective" is to diminish the stature of Coleridge; Professor Wellek stresses "his importance for the transmission of German literary ideas to the English-speaking world." I have no quarrel with this devaluation, and I rejoice at seeing intellectual currents traced across political boundaries. But when the Russian ideologue Belinsky is accorded more space than Baudelaire, I wonder whether some principle of national representation is not being given precedence over a record of substantive achievement. These are open questions, on which Professor

Wellek's convictions should carry much weight. He is frank in announcing that "sides have to be taken," and—as a former member of the Cercle Linguistique de Prague who is now a colleague of the New Critics at Yale—he comes by his formalistic bias honestly. In short, he is a critic of critics as well as a historian of criticism. But since he is primarily a historian, and since generations of students will be depending upon his erudition, should not he have shown more concern for objectivity? When he tells us that he subscribes to "neither relativism nor absolutism," he seems to opt for an excluded middle: to promise us that he will not be swerved by partiality, on the one hand, or by impartiality on the other. The history of earlier criticism has taught us nothing, if it has not warned us against absolutes. The logical option is to accept the consequences of historical relativism.

Professor Wellek even speaks of transcending historicism, and discerns "no causality" in his material. Obviously, he has no ambition to be a scientist—*qui potuit rerum cognoscere causas*. Why then should he be writing history, which, if it be not a meaningless succession of unconnected events, is precisely an investigation into the causes of things? Actually, no one could be more expert than he is at conducting such investigations into the evolution of literary concepts, notably his genetic studies on the idea of romanticism or of the baroque. These are so illuminating as to suggest that his *History* might have been more rigorously, and more instructively, organized around the development of such key ideas. Apparently Professor Wellek had thought of employing a more synoptic method, which would have put a more impersonal stress on the growth of the field, but had decided the time was not yet ripe. As matters stand, he focuses on critical personalities, summarizing their individual contributions with a good deal of conceptual cross-reference. Analysis is blended with appraisal, and value judgments are rendered on value judgments. The protean character of the critic makes him a slippery unit to handle. Now he is an esthetician; again he is a book- or play-reviewer; often he plays the moralist, sometimes the philologist; at other times he can be a biographer or a pamphleteer. He engages in such varied kinds of activity—or rather, critics vary so much in their numerous concerns—that the late Erich Auerbach, in his review of Wellek, doubted whether criticism should be construed as a self-sufficient or unified subject.

We could meet this objection by defining criticism, in the broadest and most democratic terms, as the totality of discourse about literature. Everyone is a potential critic, inasmuch as he reads and responds to his reading.

To the extent that his response is informed and sharpened and refined, he fulfills his potentiality. This is the area that Richards called practical criticism, in contradistinction to the sphere of critical principles. Wellek's unifying concern has been with the latter, as he demonstrated twenty years ago, when he collaborated with Austin Warren in the methodological survey, *Theory of Literature,* which has so widely influenced graduate studies and research. One would not want to draw so sharp a distinction as to imply that the practice of criticism was unprincipled, though one might gain that impression from book-reviewing today. If the reviewer, who began as a judge, but lost his jurisdiction when the classical rules were abrogated—if the reviewer has become a tipster, so have many other figures in public life. As a taste-maker or an opinion-monger, he bears the same relation to the scholar-critic that the journalist does to the historian; and there too, as I realize, the line is hard to draw. The word *opinion* presupposes differences; the word *taste* presupposes, not disputes we trust, but changes of fashion; and the rate of change for literary fashions, like *la haute couture,* is so ephemeral and so contrived that it has become smart to cultivate bad taste, or "camp." The test of the journalistic critic, like that of the politician, is whether he leads or follows the public-opinion polls.

In a book entitled *Writers and Their Critics,* Henri Peyre has drawn up an impressive list of masterpieces—so we have come to regard them—which went unappreciated by the reviewers or were misunderstood by their earliest critics. We know that Meredith, as a publisher's reader, turned down a novel by Hardy, just as Gide in the same position turned down a novel by Proust. Meredith and Gide had been fashionable; Hardy and Proust would be unique. Proust has a passage which throws light on such misunderstandings; he argues that all genuine innovation is bound to go unrecognized upon its first appearance; it must gradually pave its own way and create its own audience. Critics do not discover it by the frenetic desire to be "with it," which cannot but unearth more dross than gold. The meeting of minds between writer and critic, the aim of Pater "to see the object as it really is," demands not only alertness but a certain measure of selflessness, which is not quite the same thing as the tactical anonymity of the *Times Literary Supplement.* At least, the anonymous critic is prevented from practising that cult of personality which can end by turning criticism into an irresponsible medium of self-expression. A case in point is that of Jean-Paul Sartre, who, despite his high pretensions to intellectual honesty, cannot write about some other writer without grinding some ulterior axe of his own, whether in his vendetta against Flaubert or in his canonization of Genet. There are no safeguards against this kind of critical malpractice, except the old liberal hope that truth may ultimately prevail against the winds of doctrine.

Happily, the truth is by no means inaccessible. The objects of our study coincide with its documentation, which is much richer and more immediate than that of any other discipline. The specific concreteness of words gets diffused in transit, to be sure. Documents must be deciphered, and the possibilities for divergent readings are unlimited. Yet, in the long run, meanings are subject to the corroboration and verification of a consensus among the decipherers. Furthermore, the record is not less expressive when the document turns out to be a palimpsest. The very accretion of comment around a major text, while testifying to its powers of suggestion, becomes a part of its ultimate significance. Richards' students responded to the poems he set before them with varying degrees of aptness and irrelevance, but they all were undergoing a simultaneous and interrelated series of experiences. "What's aught, save as 'tis valued?," Hector asks in *Troilus and Cressida*. The answer is that value cannot be an innate property; it is a rating placed upon a work by observers. Hence it must express their scheme of values, while it reflects some feature of the work which has elicited their interest. Works of art exist, not in the timeless vacuum of a House Beautiful or a Temple of Fame, but in a continual flux of evaluation and revaluation. Critics have very properly taken the lead in these appraisals and testimonials; yet far too frequently, they have confused their own value judgments with the eternal verities. Perhaps they should remind themselves that the verb *to criticize* was derived from the Greek κρίνειν, which meant to distinguish before it meant to judge.

There have been some palpable signs of late that criticism is ready to abandon its besetting legalism and to resume that analytic attitude which has characterized its more effective procedures. Northrop Frye's *Anatomy of Criticism,* which has been increasingly influential during the decade since its publication, begins with a "Polemical Introduction" maintaining that value judgments should be excluded from the systematic study of literature. They may be indulged in afterward, but that is a private matter. Professor Frye, one of those brilliant Canadian theorists who have undertaken to rearrange our outlook, disarms himself in a "Tentative Conclusion," and his treatise bears the tentative subtitle, *Four Essays.* His title is ambiguous, since *anatomy* can signify either the technique of dissection or the body to be dissected. Which of the two definitions applies to criticism? Initially, it seems, Professor Frye had planned to entitle his book *Structural Poetics*. The noun would have set it in the appropriate literary tradition, and the adjective would have allied it with recent developments in other areas, for example structural linguistics and structural anthropology. Similarly, the term *anatomy* sounds both scientific and old-fashioned. What Professor Frye has envisioned, somewhat along the lines of Arnold Toynbee's morphology of history, is nothing less than a morphology of literature. But it is less concerned with the actual forms than with a formal pattern embracing them. Viewed more closely, it might be termed a typology, and might find a closer analogue in Biblical exegesis.

Professor Frye describes his large objective as "a conceptual framework derived from an inductive survey of the literary field." In practice, he is inevitably forced—by the very expanse of the territory he covers—to rely on deduction most of the time, to synthesize and to extrapolate on the basis of his framing propositions. His four essays deal respectively with modes, which are historical; symbols, which are ethical; myths, which are archetypal; and genres, which are rhetorical. This fourfold symmetry, which entails a certain amount of lopping and stretching, finds its sanction not in Saint Thomas Aquinas but in nature itself. Each of the modes—which I find hard to distinguish taxonomically from the genres—is associated with a season of the year: romance with summer, tragedy with autumn, irony with winter, and comedy with spring. All four, since they are "all episodes in a total quest-myth," coalesce into one quintessential fiction. Cambridge scholars were severely criticized, two generations ago, for exaggerating the connections between ancient drama and vegetation rites. What a vindication it would be for them to behold Professor Frye reducing the entire corpus of literature to a seasonal myth! But the efficacy of magic numbers is never beyond dispute. There were seven liberal arts in the Middle Ages because there were seven days in the week—and seven planets in the sky, or so the Schoolmen believed. After the pseudo-science of astrology had yielded to the science of astronomy, the correspondences seemed less direct between the academic curriculum and the structure of the universe.

The schematic overingenuity of Professor Frye's grand design should not keep us from appreciating the well-informed acumen with which he incidentally handles a multitude of challenging topics. As an accomplished musician, he is able to illuminate the delicate relations between music and metrics. On irony and the theory of comedy, he has much of his own to contribute; but he depends at second hand for his classical generalizations, rather more heavily than he acknowledges, on the work of F. M. Cornford and J. A. K. Thomson. It is not surprising that Professor Frye should have given us one of the best books on William Blake, for his critical apparatus seems best adapted to the hieratic English poets: Blake and Yeats, Spenser and Milton, and the Shakespeare of the late romances. The *Anatomy of Criticism* enjoys and deserves popularity as a key to the esoteric. We may set it on our shelves beside Yeats's *Vision*. But it is not that anatomy of literature for which Bacon left a place in his *Novum Organum*. We might almost have guessed that, when Professor Frye turned to modern prose, he would discover that there were four types of novels. He manages to pigeonhole so capacious and multiform a genre by defining his fourth type as the anatomy—a species so miscellaneous that it makes a novelist out of Robert Burton, not to mention Mr. Frye himself. He does not throw much light on realism by labeling it—in rhetorical terminology—"a low mimetic mode," after all we have been learning from Auerbach's *Mimesis* about the persistent and ever-changing effort to convey realities through words.

There is nothing like philology for positivistic exactitude, when the empirical scrutiny of literary texts is alerted to the relevance of historical contexts. Its painstaking and detailed inductions, at the opposite extreme from Professor Frye, have been inclined to shy away from theories. But scholarship, like science, fits its results together into a corporate enterprise, which neutralizes the subjectivity of the various personal approaches, and practises a discriminating eclecticism to guard against the doctrinaire limitations of any one school of thought. In our understanding of our greatest writer, it can therefore be maintained that we have positively progressed. We have ampler means of acquainting ourselves with Shakespeare's text, his language, his theater, and his cultural environment than have been available to readers or spectators in the years between his lifetime and today, plus the perspectives of the intervening period. Computers are now being programmed to solve the stylistic problems that dismayed and disintegrated the Shakespeare Society in the nineteenth century. With the exacting techniques of descriptive bibliography, including a collating machine of his own invention, Charlton Hinman has minutely examined the eighty-odd copies in the Folger Library and has meticulously reconstructed the printing and proofreading of the First Folio, page by page and line for line. Unfortunately, all his efforts could not have turned up any new evidence which would help us to decide whether Hamlet meant to speak of "too too solid flesh" or of "too too sullied flesh."

However, we now possess more exact data about the professional habits of the five compositors who set up the type for the Folio than we have about the life of Shakespeare. A. L. Rowse's biography, claiming that the popular historian has an insight denied to the literary scholar, recently revived an old conjecture identifying the young man of the Sonnets with the Earl of Southampton. Within a year two Shakespearean experts, Dover Wilson and Leslie Hotson, had brought out books proposing two other identifications for the same personage. We need scarcely complicate discussion at this point by recalling the lunatic fringes that question the identity of Shakespeare himself, since the relevance of the biographical aspect is marginal at most. What matters is what we have learned about the writing and the staging of his plays. The commentaries of Granville-Barker—who was an actor-playwright, like Shakespeare, as well as a scholar-critic—set standards based on the cumulative experience of both stage and study. But theatrical performance is even more prone to vagaries and vicissitudes than critical interpretation has been. The very fact that the repertory has been performed so many times before, that it is so thoroughly familiar to its audiences, has accelerated the striving for novelty with each new production. The successful director is he who plays tricks with the script, who contrives things unattempted yet in the way of gags and gimmicks, who resets his scene in some unlikely country or dresses his actors up in anachronistic costumes—the farther-fetched the better, no matter how irrelevant.

The actor who interpolates a line or deviates from the score of a Gilbert and Sullivan operetta brings the wrath of the loyal Savoyards down on his head. But the Royal Shakespeare Company is licensed, in more ways than one, to victimize their Bard by every conceivable sort of distortion. Witness Peter Brook's version of *King Lear,* which stripped the king of every shred of dignity and invited us to sympathize with Goneril and Regan. Mr. Brook was inspired by the essay of the Polish critic, Jan Kott, "*King Lear* or *Endgame.*" Mr. Kott, who has suffered gallantly under both the Nazis and the Communists, has earned the right to dissent from the humane ethos of Shakespeare; but he has no authority for recasting the tragedy in the mold of Samuel Beckett's farcical nihilism. This determination to strike an original note at all costs, to be arresting at the expense of being merely cogent, is not confined to the playhouse. An American critic has lately declared that the quality he rates most highly in a work of literature is the will to outrage. We have come a long way since the dull old days when propriety was the criterion. Criticism, at the forensic level, has acted as a voice of dissidence breaking with a more traditional past. Critiques of philosophy, religion, and social institutions were characteristic organs of the Enlightenment and accompanied the rise of science. The image of the critic as a dissenter and an enlightener has faded, under the somewhat apocalyptic conditions of the later twentieth century. Youthful seekers after guidance seem to favor the guru and the shaman. The most devout coteries spring up at the feet of the angriest oracles.

If I have dwelt too long on the peccant humors of my theme, I hope that Baconian phrase may be accepted as my excuse, since it suggests a preliminary need for clearing the air. In the underwoods of criticism, we are still at the stage of botanizing or indulging in the hobbies of natural history. Some of the more impatient and inventive critics have striven to square the circle or to arrive at the Philosopher's Stone. They will be finding out—what you know—that the shortcuts are few, and that the answers are not always elegant, assuming that one is lucky enough to find them. You—if I may address this word to my scientific colleagues—are well aware that knowledge is an endless approximation, that it exacts much waste for every gain, and that those very gains are constantly being rendered obsolete by further discoveries. The humanities may not search so far, but they do not obsolesce so fast. Meanwhile, and at all events, we have the pleasure of immersing ourselves in the richest of human materials. I suspect that the very pleasures of that immersion may have hindered us from viewing our subject matter in clearer detachment. But, in spite of having made no attempt to suppress my misgivings or to soften my strictures, I share the hopes of those critics whom I have criticized, and I am grateful to them for holding before us a larger vision of what criticism might some day become. It is a prospect which completes and redeems the broken-down speculations of Coleridge, which enables Richards to round out his own researches into the imagination, which allows Wellek to record a history of advancing ideas rather than of idiosyncratic personalities, and which verifies the hypotheses of Frye by an unflagging exploration of the material facts.

ENGLISH, AMERICAN, AND
COMPARATIVE LITERATURE

These remarks were prompted by the curiosity—and, in some cases, the anxiety—of colleagues, both in Canada and England, as to the relationship of traditional English studies to the two newer disciplines more lately being developed in the United States. The original version was presented on November 25, 1966, as the Sedgewick Lecture at the University of British Columbia. Under the same auspices, and under the original title, *Countercurrents in the Study of English,* it was published as a pamphlet in 1967. Meanwhile, as revised for another audience, it was delivered under the present title at Cambridge and at several other English universities. The text below has been modified somewhat further, with the American reader in mind.

The poet's problem of gaining a livelihood was so acute for William Butler Yeats in 1911 that he even thought of applying for the professorship of English literature at Trinity College, Dublin. In response to his letter of inquiry, he was flatly told by the eminent professor of Ancient History, John Pentland Mahaffy: "Literature is not a subject for tuition." How much trouble many of us might have saved ourselves if, like Yeats, we had listened to Mahaffy's advice—which, of course, was the most respectable opinion in university circles two generations ago! If Yeats had taken that post at Trinity, if (as seemed probable the following year) James Joyce had been appointed a lecturer on Italian at University College, Dublin, if Ezra Pound had not been dismissed from Wabash College a few years before, if T. S. Eliot had returned to take his Ph.D. orals and to teach metaphysics at Harvard—well, it gives us pause to imagine the course that Anglo-American letters might have followed.

It needs no gift for retrospective prophecy to surmise that the academy's gain might have entailed some loss to the world at large. Those writers have enshrined themselves among the English classics of our century. We shuffle over them and cough in ink, as Yeats once said. Yet in his day he was a revolutionist; Joyce saw his books banned everywhere; Pound was committed to an insane asylum; and even Eliot, whom we regard as the very pillar of tradition, was considered dangerously subversive, especially by professors of literature. The gulf was all but absolute between the groves of Academe and those purlieus of Bohemia where creative genius was permitted to struggle through its wayward career, whether in Bloomsbury, on the Rive Gauche, or at Greenwich Village. The rift was almost as sharp within the university between the consecrated routines of scholarship, on the one hand, and, on the other, a quasi-heretical interest in criticism.

Critics like J. E. Spingarn or Stuart P. Sherman had given up their professorships for publishing or journalism. Spingarn, the American apostle of Benedetto Croce and one of the pioneers of comparative literature, was calling for a thoughtful reconsideration in 1911 with a little book entitled *The New Criticism*. All too little heed was paid to it; but just a generation later, in 1941, John Crowe Ransom issued another call, with a book also entitled *The New Criticism;* and this time spirits came from the vasty deep. This is where some of our most respected teacher-critics came in, and I need not dwell on the benefits we have enjoyed under their dispensation over the last generation. Another pair of books, emanating from Oxford and Cambridge, *The Muse in Chains* by Stephen Potter and *The Muse Unchained* by E. M. W. Tillyard, would testify to comparable developments at the English universities.

Meanwhile Eliot, remaining in England, had virtually revised its poetic canon, while making a substantial place within it for his own poetry. I. A. Richards, who had devised a critical method subtle enough for the subtleties of such poets, redressed the transatlantic equilibrium by settling in the United States. Not only did our critics return to the campus, but they brought a new generation of poets and novelists with them, and together they brought up a still newer generation on the works of such Bohemian masters—erudite artists, if not professors *manqués*—as Yeats and Joyce and Pound and Eliot. It follows that the nineteen-sixties teem not so much with geniuses as with epigones. It is the nature of the Academy to exert an academic influence, just as conservatories turn out conservatives; and conservatives are notoriously staunch at upholding yesterday's innovations. When the novelist is a professor, it is not surprising if his novel turns out to be what the Germans call a *Professorenroman,* or else what I am sometimes tempted to call an English Department Novel. So much current fiction tends to be written by and for and even about members of English departments that we may wonder what interest it retains for the general public.

Recently Saul Bellow has complained about the resulting trend toward self-conscious pastiche, and the trend has been confirmed by Professor Bellow's complaints. It is hard to think of a serious writer, among his contemporaries, who has not been at least a part-time teacher, ordinarily a teacher of writing. Since most of these would rather write than teach, their *modus vivendi* involves a compromise which is better calculated to enrich their teaching than their own writing. Obviously, we have come a long way since Yeats made his timid and tentative application to old Mahaffy. The latter doubted whether appreciation was teachable; blithely we assume that creation is. Whether or not we have refuted his dictum that literature is no subject for tuition—that is another question, to be sure, which we beg by considering it here. Let us try to keep it at the back of our minds for the light it may cast on further questions: whence we have come, and whither we may be going?

Now Mahaffy, although he was German-trained, was neither a pedant nor a philistine; his historical works were literary as well as social in their purview; he was, for better or worse, an early mentor of Oscar Wilde; and his remarks about the chair of English were not made to disparage its retiring occupant, Edward Dowden, or to discourage the applicant Yeats, whom he would have welcomed as a purely ornamental poet in residence. But, as a classical scholar, Mahaffy firmly believed that there could be only one true basis for pedagogy, namely *paideia.* Trinity, as a sort of Anglican outpost in Ireland, was possibly more Oxonian than Oxford in its emphasis on *litterae humaniores,* the great books of Greece and Rome, the texts interpreted by philology and set into the contexts of history. Such an education was undeniably based upon works of literature, yet these were hedged in by such strict prerequisites that they could hardly be dallied with as *belles-lettres.*

Literature is in itself an enjoyment; consequently educators are always trying to make the sweet pill morally acceptable by coating it with the bitter taste of didacticism. There could be no imputation of esthetic softness in a subject whose access presented so many obstacles, textual and linguistic, or whose substance afforded so many object lessons, moral and social. We stand in some awe before the fact that generations of statesmen and civil servants were successfully trained through this mode of discipline—and "discipline" is the word, here if anywhere. At its best, it was nothing less than culture itself, as envisaged by its most devoted celebrant, Matthew Arnold. At its worst, as recollected in *Tom Brown's School Days* (which, after all, were spent at Arnold's father's school), it became a sequence of exercises in parsing and scanning, and was reduced to the intellectual plane of fagging and flogging and other public-school sports.

Dr. Johnson's epigram about Greek—that it resembled lace, that every man got as much of it as he could—was all too soon outmoded by alterations of fashion. Greek and even Latin are much greater rarities today than lace was in the eighteenth century, and are not so much coveted by men. But the cultural lag worked in their favor at British schools and universities. Rather less happily, it worked against the recognition of English culture within the curriculum. While the dons reedited and commented upon the Greco-Roman classics, the care and maintenance of the older English authors was left in the hands of bookstall browsers like Charles Lamb or antiquarian parsons like the Reverend Alexander Dyce. Among the exclusive minority that got formally educated, a casual conversance was taken for granted. "It was generally thought that one knew English, and could read Milton when one liked," recounts G. S. Gordon, implying that one very seldom did and probably couldn't. English studies were the poor man's classics, as D. J. Palmer has shown in an interesting monograph, and they got their start in dissenting academies and mechanics' institutes.

Systematic research and graduate training in the literary history of England were first conducted in Germany. They developed in this hemisphere shortly afterward on a scale commensurate with American industry, exfoliating into the Chaucer laboratory at the University of Chicago or the Walpole factory associated with Yale. After a chair of English had been set up at Oxford, belatedly toward the end of the nineteenth century, the first Merton Professor—the philologist A. S. Napier—is quoted as saying: "Since you could not make a discipline out of a modern literature, you must stiffen the course with linguistics." It is not the positive burden of this remark, it is the negative undertone that reverberates so harshly. There is justification for insisting that the student of English cannot fully appreciate its unmatched expressibility unless he understands the development of its structure and the sources of its vocabulary, until he has a modicum of grounding in Latin, French, and German as well as Old and Middle English.

But Napier's attitude betrayed the same suspicion of the belletristic as Mahaffy's, along with a puritanical belief in discipline more for its own sake than for some cogent purpose. A similar point of view was sternly held by George Lyman Kittredge, whose principles—or rather, whose hobbies—dominated English scholarship in America from the last decade of the nineteenth through the first third of the twentieth century. His conception of literary history did not extend beyond the Middle Ages; and they were intensively studied, not for the value of their literature nor for the significance of their culture, but for the philological debris they had left behind them. As a result, his students were better versed in Ulfilas than in Keats. Ends had superseded means to such an extent that, when one graduate student sought his permission to write a doctoral dissertation on Ruskin, after some objection Professor Kittredge reluctantly agreed; but he stipulated that it should be unusually well written, since the subject matter was too recent to be susceptible of scholarly treatment.

This tacit and grudging acknowledgment that style could be a saving grace is the kind of touch that still endears him to those who studied under him, regardless of our exasperations with him or his with us. If he insisted on Gothic, he assumed that every man had Greek; and that assumption must have been roughly warranted when his principles were first laid down. Nowadays, when Ruskin himself seems medieval and we are deluged with badly written theses on the symbolism of Lawrence Durrell or the neuroses of J. D. Salinger, I sometimes find myself preferring those dull and stodgy disquisitions fostered by Kittredge on the comparative grammar of the Scottish dialects or the weaknesses of the Middle English verb. At all events, they embodied honest labor; they did no harm by misleading anyone; and they might conceivably have been useful under certain limited circumstances. That, I fear, is more than one can say for an embarrassing amount of what currently appears in the critical quarterlies.

The fundamental and inescapable premise for the study of English is that it is a language, and that it is our language: our language with a difference, admittedly. The differences between the mother tongue and that demotic dialect of it which we speak, to our minds, must constitute one of its most interesting features. Ever since the breakdown of philology a generation ago, students of language and of literature have tended to go their several ways, to the disadvantage of both. Structural linguistics has found its closest allies in cultural anthropology and analytic philosophy. Criticism, though it has concentrated more and more on stylistic scrutiny and the close reading of texts, has missed many a nuance by not being linguistically oriented. Rhetoric, the twofold art of putting words together and taking them apart, of composition at every level from the barest freshman literacy to the English Department Novel or Poem, and of analysis, of examining models and showing what techniques are used to gain what effects—rhetoric is a good two thousand years older than English as a subject for tuition.

At the moment or all too soon, we may find ourselves referring to it as Communication Arts, having forgotten most of the older and more elaborate terminology. Yet, insofar as its point of departure has been the spoken word, the uses and the abuses of oratory, it has lately undergone a revival prompted by a concern for the audiovisual media. (The hazard is that this revival, insofar as its prophet is Marshall McLuhan, may prove to be a dissolution of literature itself under the dizzying impact of electronics.) What we could term the rhetorical aspect of English —the verbal, the formal, the technical, then—must claim a shared priority for all speakers and readers who are to the language born or bred. The major books, both English and American, must be accorded a central position in our libraries as models of styles, even before we consider them as paradigms of experience or patterns of behavior.

For there, confronting the historical context of English, is where we encounter a bifurcation and where we have some degree of choice, in the sense that we Americans elect what the British inherit. Their literature is their racial memory, linked to them personally by a common past and a topographic continuity. If Sherwood Forest was dug up to make way for the Nottinghamshire collieries, that was an elegiac presupposition for D. H. Lawrence. Canada, in this respect as in others, stands closer to her sister country than to the mother culture. I would hope that students in the British Commonwealth have a more concrete and precise acquaintance with the factual background than some of our American majors in English, whose knowledge of kings and reigns seldom rises above the schoolboy howlers of *1066 and All That*. Even our doctoral candidates are not likely to know that a Jacobite could have been anything other than an admirer of Henry James, whom they are much likelier to have read than Walter Scott.

English for the English holds an immediacy to which we can never quite attain. For us, approaching it from a cultural distance, albeit with a linguistic identification more or less, it has the countervailing qualities of a perspective. The exemplary role that Greek literature played in Roman civilization, or that Greco-Roman literature has played in British education, such is the function that English literature can best perform for us. This is no occasion for reflections on the vicissitudes of empire, and in a changing world we adjust as best we can to changes in the curriculum. Suffice it to recognize that the fortunes of the language, its polyglot origin and its worldwide spread, are paralleled by the strains of the literature, its scope, its variety, its individuality. Viewed as a corpus from *Beowulf* to Virginia Woolf, it is panoramic in its commentary on life and strategic in its critique of recurrent issues. It could not lend itself more helpfully than it has done to our pedagogical purposes.

The special and fruitful tension that can exist between the model kingdom of one's reading and the mental climate in which one happens to grow up is particularly stressed by Lionel Trilling, who has scarcely been less concerned than Arnold himself with the relation of literature to the formation of character. Since Mr. Trilling's lecture, "The Two Environments: Reflections on the Study of English," was addressed to an English university audience, his American colleagues might feel as if they were eavesdropping on it. But they are bound to be pleasantly surprised by the statement: "In America at least, the study of English has come to be thought of as the most usual and the most natural preparation for taking one's place in the intellectual life of the nation." Certainly, if we equate the intellectual life of the nation with the literary reviews and the publishing houses of New York City, there could be no better preparation for taking one's place in it than studying English at Columbia with Professor Trilling.

But when we stop to contemplate the broad diversity of artistic, scientific, and other activities that have contributed to the march of intellect across the country, and when we note that Professor Trilling is exceptionally humane in his approach to his calling, we may well feel less confident than he about making so large a claim for our specialty. His notion of English as the most liberal of the arts is both welcome and reassuring, after the chilly sufferance of the classicists and the inferiority complex of the apologists. It puts the primary responsibilities where— from an educational standpoint—they have generally belonged: on instruction rather than investigation, on moral influence rather than scientific curiosity, on the cultivation of sensibility rather than the promotion of knowledge. In short, it becomes a question of college teaching rather than university research.

However, at a time when half of our undergraduates are heading for graduate schools, it may seem unduly old-fashioned to draw too sharp a line between the propaedeutic task of forming the taste and informing the mind, of rounding out the intelligent reader, and the more advanced initiation of the speaker, the writer, the person who is destined to become —through his capacities and his qualifications—the expert. It is precisely the adjustment between the second stage and the first, between accomplished *expertise* and budding connoisseurship, that can make literature a subject for tuition. An unduly categorical distinction between the two in the past has led to the gushing dilettantism of classroom appreciators, reacting against the myopic professionalism of library scholars. It has encouraged the simple-minded legend that the great teacher is he who can staunchly resist the distraction of keeping up with his field and the drain of publishing contributions to it.

At a time when unprecedented numbers of students are going to college, when the base of the academic pyramid has overwhelmingly broadened, we must not overlook the point—that is to say, the apex, which should be higher but can be no broader than before. Its attainment should therefore continue to depend on quality rather than quantity; excellence, by definition, is never overabundant, since it means doing better than most of the others; yet the demands of higher education are so much more pressing than the available supply of abilities that publication, though it be rigorously exacted from candidates for teaching positions, is judged by the most perfunctory standards. Monographs make an impression, even when they demonstrate nothing but the incompetence of the monographers. Professorial reputations thrive upon that discreet application of scissors and paste which produces paperback anthologies. Learned journals multiply for the advancement, not of learning, but of assistant professors.

The intellectual interplay that Mr. Trilling underlines has the advantage of adding another landscape to our horizon; but distance raises some unavoidable problems of relevance. What is commonplace to the native may look exotic to the foreigner; conversely, what is pertinent to our interests can be overlooked in favor of what is more tangential. For example, remember the thousands of copies of *Silas Marner* that have been worn out in our schools by pupils who had never heard about the indigenous Silas Lapham. Although T. S. Eliot passed his boyhood on the banks of the Mississippi River, so to speak, he did not read *Tom Sawyer* or *Hucklebery Finn* until late in his life. If colonial attitudes persisted well into the present century, many of them could be traced to our English departments, which have been garrisons of Anglophilia as well as sanctuaries for the Genteel Tradition. Indeed our metropolitan book-reviewing has yet to free itself from a posture of subservience to the British, against which Poe and James Russell Lowell protested in their time.

The process of self-discovery started slowly, and naturally emphasized the more traditional elements. Barrett Wendell's *Literary History of America,* appearing in 1900, was so narrowly regional that it has been rechristened *A Literary History of Harvard College.* When F. O. Matthiessen was designated as assistant professor at Harvard in 1930, he was permitted to move beyond the New England orbit of Wendell with a course which figured in the catalogue as "American Writers of the South and West." South and west, in this context, meant southward and westward of Boston, Cambridge, and Concord. Mainly a vehicle for introducing Whitman and Melville into the curriculum, it got as far south as Camden, New Jersey, and as far west as Pittsfield, Massachusetts. V. L. Parrington's *Main Currents* had just thrown into bold relief the contrast between Yankee provinciality and the wider regions of American thought. Pioneering scholars had been preceded by such freelance critics as Van Wyck Brooks—above all, by the prophetic insight of one Englishman, Lawrence.

The extension of the frontier to the Pacific, and to the Mexican and northwestern borders, has been paralleled by the expansion and settlement of our literary history—so neglected until the middle years of the twentieth century. Paths through the backwoods have been transformed into freeways, and our national monuments and local landmarks have been surrounded by the motels of scholarship and the service stations of criticism, not to mention the obfuscations of smog. The earlier neglect of American literature has been compensated for many times over. Thanks to the well-organized endeavors of an ever-enlarging body of specialists, it has found its curricular identity. The least that can now be said is that it occupies an imposing mansion in the great house of English literature, and there are even pressures in some quarters to set up a separate establishment.

This is not simply the expression of eagle-screaming chauvinism or know-nothing obscurantism, although these have not been without their academic exponents. Since the Second World War, Anglicists have often been succeeded by Americanists in the chairs of English at some of the continental universities. They have been abetted by Fulbright lecturers, who have reversed the missionary errand into the wilderness by converting European palefaces to redskin styles of thought, while the missionaries in their turn have been acquiring an air of cosmopolitanism, each being modified by the other's example. Over the past decade the movement has very appreciably outdistanced the two-volume historical survey, *American Studies in Europe,* published in 1958 by the Norwegian poet, Sigmund Skard, who had been appointed after the last war to a newly established professorship of Literature, Especially American, at the University of Oslo.

There is a slight but significant disparity between the title of Professor Skard's post and that of his book, which points the two directions that have latterly been taken. American literature can be the center of a widening gyre which spirals outward into English and other literatures. "Literature, Especially American," would seem to be the normal starting point for Americans with literary interests—so long as we do not stop there. The alternative, which even in England has been becoming a subject for tuition, though rather at the urban universities than at Oxford or Cambridge, invites a combination with history and the social sciences. In 1866 Henry Yates Thompson of Liverpool offered to endow Cambridge University with a lectureship in the "History, Literature, and Institutions of the United States." The offer was rejected by the Senate with a vote of 110 to 82. Nor were the authorities willing to allow the use of a room for a single experimental course.

There were several grounds for this rejection: that such a course might have an unduly democratizing influence; that it might encourage American self-conceit, which needed no further encouragement even at that time; and that Mr. Thompson had unfortunately suggested the appointment of the incumbent through Harvard, which was fairly suspected of then inclining toward Unitarianism. During the intervening century, I understand that a few American names have crept into the English Tripos, and that America has made some entry into the historical syllabus. But there is no need to evangelize. If I have any lesson to preach, it would be that American literature has its place in English and English has its place in European literature. American studies, since they are not necessarily stiffened by language requirements, are at once less opaque and less demanding than those programs of Area Studies which the foundations have been focusing upon the troubled areas of our times.

We cannot view the Americans with quite such anthropological detachment, or with such dedicated hostility; but when we read their books —when we reread our books for such a purpose—we are merely using them as historical documents. It must be admitted that rather too many of them play a part in the syllabus chiefly because of their documentary values. Candor might also compel us to admit that, with a few exceptions, our literary scholars lag far behind our historians in the solidity and the distinction of their collective achievement. The explanation might be inherent in their material. American literature may be treated either as an illustrated supplement to American history or as a distinctive but continuous sequel to English literature. It has neither the esthetic richness nor the historic range to comprise a discipline by itself.

It has its major figures, whose vitality and originality we can unite in admiring; yet those we could agree upon, whose works belong among the world's undoubted masterpieces, could be counted on the fingers of both hands, if not of one. The accumulation of theses reinforces a natural tendency to promote and magnify writers of slighter stature; but we should try, by keeping our sense of proportion, to avoid the temptation of confusing our geese with swans. When Lydia Huntley Sigourney was characterized as "the Felicia Dorothea Hemans of America," she was put in a properly modest niche of the pantheon, and Mrs. Julia A. Moore was relegated to her provincial place when she was saluted as "the Sweet Singer of Michigan." We are sufficiently fortunate in possessing so pure a voice as that of Emily Dickinson, whose lyrics have deservedly been ranked among the greatest of any era or culture, though they were muted during her lifetime and all but lost to posterity.

Yet surely this constant search for whilom talent has overprized such incorrigibly minor poets as Jones Very and F. G. Tuckerman. It has made culture heroes of Hart Crane and James Agee in order to dramatize our sentimental image of the man of letters as a gifted failure, an inheritor of unfulfilled reknown whose fragments must be shored against his ruins. A figure like Henry Adams, at the uttermost an important but highly prejudiced witness, is not only accepted at his own excessive self-valuation but is praised for his art—doubtless because the truly original artists are few and far between in any reckoning. To signalize Eugene O'Neill as our greatest dramatist, alas, when we consider how his theatrical skill is overweighed by self-indulgence and tedium or how his emotional power is diluted by the crudity of his diction and the naïveté of his ideas, is to concede that ours is one of those nations which providence has not favored with authentic greatness in the dramatic sphere.

In pleading for a more objective balance, I do not want to overemphasize what Henry James described as "the negative side of the spectacle," or to echo his discredited litany on the absence of notable institutions or picturesque scenery. The peculiar conditions of American literary development made possible that strongly ethical and uniquely imaginative form of fiction practised by our nineteenth-century masters, the romance. Moreover, we must make due allowance for the limits of chronology, the relatively short span of our literature, if we would brave comparison with other nationalities. Yet terms like "American Gothic" or "American Renaissance" are no more than nostalgic metaphors, ghosts that never lived or memories of hopes. Our so-called Renaissance, historically speaking, was a part of the Romantic Movement. Nonetheless, its leading writers held their own with the leading European Romanticists, just as our contemporaries can do with their peers abroad.

On the other hand, these very linkages ought to teach us Americans that, instead of vaunting our uniqueness, we should be looking for universals. We might as well confess that, when all is said and done, we are not more closely related to Adam than the rest of his living progeny. We should be wary of becoming entrammeled in a self-centered mystique, like that of the Russians. Having exhausted the theme of lost innocence, we should be old enough to sound the theme of ripe experience. Neither dependence on the Old World nor independence from it but interdependence with it has become the keynote of this once-new world. Its citizens have been—and are more and more—what Melville and Whitman greeted as "a race of races," an ethnic intermixture inheriting many traditions. That they were expected to simmer down into a bland uniformity seems unlikely when we recall how the concept of the melting-pot was first enunciated by a French émigré, Hector St. John Crèvecoeur, who must have had in mind some variegated and pungent *ragoût*.

If the ingredients are far from exclusively British, this is no departure from Anglo-Saxon tradition; for, as the hyphenated term implies, the Anglo-Saxons themselves were a mixed breed, a race of races from the beginning. It may be a little more than a curious coincidence that their worst enemies, the Danes, supplied the setting for their earliest epic as well as for the most famous of English tragedies. It was not an internationalist, it was Rudyard Kipling, who asked:

> What shall they know of England
> That only England know?

The rhetorical question could be transposed and applied to America with even more devastating implications. Kipling's works remind us, like the novels of Conrad and the best-known novel of E. M. Forster, how far the reach of England has extended beyond the British Isles. Kipling, himself a scion of colonial India, overprotested when he professed his imperial allegiance. But if, to Conrad the Pole, we add the Americans James and Eliot, along with Shaw and other noteworthy Anglo-Irishmen, we are forced to conclude—as does the *Oxford History of English Literature*—that most of twentieth-century England's major writers were not native Englishmen.

Shaw's campaigns for Ibsen and Wagner brought about artistic revolutions; and if we assume that his imitation of Chekhov in *Heartbreak House* could only have been effected by a cosmopolitan modernist, we should remember likewise that Fielding began his career as a novelist with *Joseph Andrews* by frankly proclaiming himself an imitator of Cervantes. The language and the literature of England have been so intertwined with those of France, from the Norman Conquest to the conquest of that Anglicized *patois* known as *franglais,* that an understanding of either presupposes their complementary relationship. Both cultures presuppose the classics, each after its fashion, even as Hellenism had been presupposed by Latinity. Both have a common substratum in the Middle Ages, when all occidental culture was looked upon as a comprehensive unity. Given so late and eclectic a subculture as that of the United States, we have no reason to approach it in isolation.

Here you may suspect me of riding a hobbyhorse toward a foregone conclusion, if I suggest that comparative literature has opened a way out of these dilemmas. Yet the suggestion would be no more than a recapitulation, in general terms, of the motives and concerns that have drawn me in that direction, as an American student of English literature. A more impressive witness would have been my late colleague, Perry Miller, whose researches in New England thought carried him farther and farther back into the realm of European ideas. Had he lived to complete that splendid torso, *The Life of the Mind in America,* it would have been—as he himself has declared—a work of comparative literature. Hence I am not proposing a field to rival those I have already been discussing. Elsewhere I have ventured to define comparative literature as an object rather than a subject—an objective which Anglicists and Americanists will share with classicists or specialists in Romance, Germanic, Slavic, and Asiatic literatures, when they view their respective fields in the fullest orientation.

Under ideal conditions we should be able to talk about literature *tout court* as the object of our common pursuit, implying that we could pursue it wherever it happened to lead us. We could take the awkward adjective for granted, since all criticism—all intellectual judgment— implies some degree of comparison. Not that any responsible scholar or critic would presume to take the whole of literature for his domain. What should be important is the habit of thinking about it as a whole— or, at all events, as something infinitely larger than the ten books that, say, Dr. F. R. Leavis might take with him to a desert island. The well-attested appeal of particular works, which we run no risk of overlooking, should not deter us from exploring beyond them and discerning the structural modes that they exemplify. Our commitment to individual authors is transcended by the art in which they find their place. Yet dogmatic critics habitually endeavor to limit our curiosity, making a canon of their prejudices and a virtue of their ignorance.

For sake of our own convenience, in dealing with literature, we divide it vertically by languages and often horizontally by periods, so that we frequently end by trimming and watering a neat little plot of ground in which we feel thoroughly at home and into which we don't like to see strangers intruding. To accept a scheme of organization along such lines is to mistake the Modern Language Association of America for the cosmos or the mind of God. Scientists would never have found out much about the universe if they ignored what they could not see with the naked eye. Students of literature, all too frequently, have allowed themselves to superimpose their own limitations upon their subject matter. They should frankly recognize the nature of such limitations, while seeking to transcend them collectively if not individually.

Most of us, as individuals, find it most practical to start from what is closest at hand, although a clearer vista may be attained at a further remove. We cannot ignore the language barriers. Our attempts to hurdle them may interpose a relevant stiffening, a disciplinary rigor which should meet the objections of our elders at last and lend its moral sanction to literature as an admissible subject for tuition. But few of us are linguists by endowment, and few linguists seem to have much literary flair. We try to get as far as we can by our own efforts; and we lift ourselves by our bootstraps, as it were, in paying careful attention to the technique of translation, which can be a helpful servant if we retain control over it, though it is an unreliable master, if we are at its mercy. Classicists who deal with both Greek and Latin, students of a foreign language whose native speech is English are already potential comparatists. The growing body of literary theory offers a conceptual frame-work to build upon, without which criticism would soon bog down into sheer dogmatism or—what is much the same—subjectivity.

But concepts cannot be derived from accidentals. A viable methodol-ogy must be free to cross and recross linguistic and national boundaries. Otherwise, the genres are so imperfectly represented in English that we cannot mention them without borrowing a French word. The epic, in particular, has been sporadic and idiosyncratic in its manifestations. Students depending on translations for their awareness of it, in any case, would be better off with Homer than with *Beowulf*. It is too bad that Keats knew no Greek, but it seems unlikely that he would have got more from *Beowulf* than he did from Homer in Chapman's translation. Not until we have looked beyond the literary epic, beyond Milton and Vergil and Homer himself to the use of oral composition, will we comprehend it as more than a mere form: as an outlook, an institution, a way of life. Then again if we try to deal with the *-isms,* those currents of ideas which flow through literature, we realize that so many of them were labeled if not invented in France: Symbolism, through Baudelaire, hails Poe as its precursor, and the French cycle culminates with the Anglo-American Eliot.

More profoundly, the basic concept reaches into the dim backward of history and the abyss of psychology to illuminate the dynamic processes of the imagination. Neither the evolution of forms nor the history of ideas could be satisfactorily traced within the confines of a single liter-ature. It is true that he who ranges widely faces certain dangers, that his escape from the parochial may lead to the superficial. Yet narrowness has never served as a guarantee of depth. The reader of *Paradise Lost* has but skimmed the surface, if he remains unaware of the *Aeneid* or of the Italian heroic romance, let alone the Bible and the Fathers. For the immediate act of communion between him and his text, there can be no ultimate substitute. But that act cannot be meaningful unless he has been culturally alerted. Furthermore, to counterbalance the dangers of specialization and the provincialism of coteries, the urgent need is for breadth: a loyalty to literature in the aggregate, not a partisanship in favor of who's in and against who's out.

There can still be a dash of adventure in the enterprise of comparative literature. It came to the surface in the Soviet Union not very long ago, when a concern for the literature of the West was attacked by official spokesmen for the prevailing nationalism, and so-called "comparativism" became a charge of treason—or perhaps, through Western eyes, a gesture of liberation. Fortunately, it has not been regarded as an un-American activity. On the contrary, it has been sponsored by our government through the support of teaching programs in foreign languages. But the decisive influence for us has been the intellectual diaspora, the migration of European scholars to American universities during the nineteen-thirties. It would have been impossible to conceive the flowering of departments, journals, and other professional activities without the presence in the United States of Leo Spitzer, Erich Auerbach, Renato Poggioli, Américo Castro, René Wellek, Henri Peyre, and other inspiriting *savants,* from whose expatriation we have benefited immeasurably; and who in turn have been sustained by our cultural pluralism.

France, although its literature has been so internally centralized, though it has exhibited a model of literary history, was the principal home of comparative literature during the early years of this century; and its critics have been particularly sensitive in responding to the distinctive qualities of writers from other countries. Taine has thus responded to the English, Madame de Staël to the Germans, the Vicomte de Vogüé to the Russians; and, since the last war, Claude-Edmonde Magny has proposed that the new epoch be titled *L'Age du roman américain.* Though our leading novelists—notably Hemingway and Faulkner—may have deserved that homage, it is doubtful whether any nation should have the hegemony at this stage. It is too late for nationalistic rivalries in the literary sphere. Better a return to the borderless old Republic of Letters, which had no checkpoints and required no visas, or—better still—a projection into the future such as Goethe once envisioned.

"Poetry is the universal possession of mankind," he declared to his confidant Eckermann in 1829. "National literature is now rather an unmeaning term; the epoch of World Literature is at hand, and everyone must strive to hasten its approach." Though the meaning of Goethe's declaration has still to be clarified, it succeeded in launching the watchword *Weltliteratur;* and, significantly enough, it had been stimulated by a German translation of a Chinese novel. We have yet to adopt the procedure advocated by Professor Etiemble of the Sorbonne, whereby comparatists would address one another by transliterating their own languages into Chinese characters. Goethe, as usual, was far ahead of his time, and he remains far ahead of ours. Nevertheless we gain a glimpse of what the state of World Literature might be like when contemporary letters owe so much of their luster to cosmopolites like Vladimir Nabokov, Jorge Luis Borges, Nathalie Sarraute, and W. H. Auden.

It is the general effect of such countercurrents to broaden the mainstream. The artistic heritage of all countries and ages, available for contemplation at once, has been metaphorically conceived by André Malraux as an imaginary museum. We need not tax our imaginations to line up the world's great books in a similar continuum, or to rearrange them critically in what Eliot would have termed "an ideal order." For they await us at the nearest bookshop or library, all too tangible in their serried neutrality, dusty and dog-eared more often than not. No wonder they repel the semiliterate with their apparent lifelessness, so long as they stand inert! Yet, for the sentient observer, sparks are struck by their very collocation. They are marshaled to do battle, as Swift observed in a pamphlet which was nothing if not comparative. They can be reactivated by the energies and the sympathies that we can bring to them. They are ready to crown our personal experience, whatever and whenever it may have been or may be, with a sense of spatial interconnection and temporal relevance.

COMPARING THE LITERATURE

Whereas the foregoing paper sought to present the idea of comparative literature to a general audience, this one was addressed to a body of specialists in the field. Therefore it is set at a more narrowly professional level, though I trust it indicates that the profession involved is by no means a narrow one—or, at any rate, ought not to be. This was the presidential address at the third triennial meeting of the American Comparative Literature Association on the campus of Indiana University, April 19, 1968. It was printed in the *Comparative Literature Yearbook* (Bloomington, 1969).

Called upon to hold forth in a general way on matters of professional concern, to extend shop-talk into ritual, one seeks to muster the support of a text. My lack of assurance may be gauged from the fact that, for the present occasion, I have armed myself with two texts. Unfortunately, neither of them carries any real authority. Both of them have been passed on to me, out of the air, through hearsay. One was the most casual and cavalier of passing remarks; the other violates the privacy of a total stranger's dreams. What they illustrate, if anything, is the extent to which the repute of our discipline has, or has not, sunk into the collective subconsciousness. My first text has been transmitted through the good offices of a colleague, whom I shall not embarrass by naming here. He enjoyed the precarious privilege of being introduced to Dylan Thomas, during one of that gifted poet's tours of American campuses. As soon as Thomas learned that my informant was—like most of us— a professor of comparative literature, he asked: "What do you compare it with?" And in his inimitable, uninhibited, and explosive manner, he went on to offer a monosyllabic suggestion, which we could not permit ourselves to entertain.

What, then, do we compare it with? With no other mode of human expression, inasmuch as we start from the awareness that literature is quite incomparable. The repeated attempt to compare it with religion has not thrown much light upon either subject. Invidious comparisons between literature and science bog down into sterile academic controversies, such as the British argument over two cultures. Analogies with the visual arts make for pleasant conversation, but so far they have scarcely risen above the verbal plane. This is not to deny the important relations that literature has with art, with science, with religion, with all of man's institutions and artifacts, nor to rule out their frequent relevance in our studies. It is merely to affirm that our subject matter, in its basic autonomy, is beyond compare. As Hamlet might say, its semblable is its mirror; in other words, it can only be compared with itself. Every work of literature tends, if I may risk the qualification, to be more or less unique. Since it must share certain characteristics with other works, we must approach it in the relative—that is to say, the comparative—degree. To believe in absolute uniqueness is, like Benedetto Croce, to forbid comparison and hence to inhibit criticism.

"La littérature comparée n'est pas la comparaison littéraire," wrote Jean-Marie Carré. Those of us who remember his charm, his courage, and his courtesy may regret that he felt constrained to fight a rear-guard action for a national conception of literary history which relegated comparative literature to a kind of extraterritorial supplement. Since the act of comparison is central to the critical process, why should we—of all people—tie our own hands? A noncomparing comparatist might be compared with a violinist who disdains to use a bow and thereby limits his performances to a sequence of *pizzicati*. Our traditional exemplar is the anatomist, who understands the forms and functions of a given body by implicitly comparing it with innumerable other organisms. Similar comparisons have taught us all we know about the evolution of genres and the norms of literary technique. Without them we could reach no value judgments; we could spot no trends nor trace developments; we could not tell a masterpiece from journeywork. Nor should we forget that the ultimate comparison, as Dylan Thomas may have been obscenely hinting, measures literature against life itself, authenticating the one while enhancing the other.

But I see that I am preaching to the converted. This, of course, is part of our organizational liturgy. We attend these meetings in order to be confirmed in our faith and strengthened in our zeal, so that we may withstand the suspicion—if not the opposition—of departments less enlightened than ours, when we return on the morrow to our respective universities. I hope that I make no breach in our common cause if, along with loyalties, I voice a few misgivings. My second text is based on one of those mythical anecdotes which the protagonist is the last person to hear. Several years ago, I have been told, the wife of a graduate student dreamed that they were awakened late at night by the sound of a truck and a knocking at the door. Her husband arose and went downstairs to find out what was happening. Standing there were two men in over-alls, who turned out on further inspection to be Renato Poggioli and myself. The student reacted with that *savoir-faire* which is always so happy a feature of dreams. He simply remounted the stairs and reported to his wife: "The men are here to compare the literature." How she responded, or what she thought it meant, she could not recall. Her waking dream has yet to meet its Joseph, and I do not presume to venture any interpretation.

It is an axiom, and it should be a law, that no one is responsible for the role he may happen to play in someone else's dream-work. Nonetheless I feel highly honored that, even in so tenuous a figment of local mythology, I should be so closely and vigorously identified with my field and with my friend. There cannot be many native Americans of my generation who can claim, as our students now happily can, to have taken a doctorate or to have had much graduate training in comparative literature as such. I cannot, and by this time I have chaired so many examinations which I might have had difficulty in passing that I hardly blush in making the admission. How did one ever get into this association? Somewhat autodidactically. If you started amid the classics and found yourself straying after the strange gods of modernity, if the circumstances of education gave you some exposure to life abroad, if you had a naturalized parent—or, better still, a spouse—with a constant recollection of other worlds, if more of your apprenticeship was served in freelancing for critical journals than in fulfilling the doctoral requirements of an English department, then pure luck had set you on the path and pointed out the destination.

In contrast to this desultory formation, my collaborator had the fullest and deepest vocation for comparative literature that I have been privileged to witness at first hand. Poggioli was a poet and critic as well as a scholar, and to the very end of his tragically shortened career he continued to publish Italian translations from a dozen other languages. Trained as a Slavist in Italy and Czechoslovakia, he lectured on Romance languages in Poland and the United States before coming to Harvard in 1946. A Florentine, with cultural tradition as his birthright, he was an enthusiastic modernist in his esthetic, intellectual, and social sympathies; consequently his response to his adopted country was wholehearted and well rounded. From his polyglot experience he had gained a special insight into the dynamics of literary movements and the principles of artistic innovation, which he formulated in his last completed book, *The*

Theory of the Avant-Garde. An English translation by his former pupil Gerald Fitzgerald, which has recently been published, will increase his humane and vitalizing influence among American comparatists. Significantly, the volume is dedicated to four fellow-scholars from Europe who hold their professorships in America: Herbert Dieckmann, Erich Heller, Henri Peyre, and René Wellek.

In my private dream-vision the figure who stands at the side of Renato Poggioli, comparing the literature, is not myself but Professor Wellek. Their strategic contributions have been as complementary as their differing temperaments: the Italian so intuitive and evocative, the Czech so thoroughgoing and systematic. Though I am no mystic, I am inclined to discern something providential in the coincidence that called Wellek to Yale in the year of Poggioli's arrival at Harvard, both to chairs combining Slavic with comparative literature. It seems clear enough, some twenty years afterward, that their synonymous Christian names portended a renascence. Others, arriving from other countries and settling at other universities, have contributed vitally to that rebirth. My point is that so large a proportion of those who brought it about were expatriates, propelled hitherward—to our eternal benefit—by the great political dispersion of the nineteen-thirties. Consider the editorial board of the journal *Comparative Literature,* currently in its twentieth year. Our editor, Chandler Beall, has been a pioneer among Americans; so has the Swiss-born associate editor, Werner Friederich. Three of the five advisory editors, active from the beginning, are émigrés: Helmut Hatzfeld, Victor Lange, and again René Wellek.

Such an undertaking as this—or, more recently, Indiana's *Yearbook* or Illinois' *Comparative Literature Studies*—could not have been sustained at a previous period. *The Journal of Comparative Literature* sponsored by Columbia University, which deserved a friendlier welcome than Croce vouchsafed it, did not last beyond its year of inception, 1903. Columbia had established the first American department of comparative literature in 1899. Harvard, which had already been offering courses for several years, did not offer degrees until 1906. It salves its institutional vanity by recalling that Columbia's first professor, G. E. Woodberry, was a Harvard alumnus. His pupil and colleague, J. E. Spingarn, had emerged as America's most promising comparatist when, for personal reasons, he resigned and retired from academic life. Comparative literature at Columbia, to its disadvantage and our loss, was subsequently annexed by the English department. In recognizing those quantitative and qualitative changes which have given new impetus to our subject during the postwar period, while signalizing that transatlantic reversal which has Americanized so brilliant a group of European intellectuals, we do not want to overlook the full half-century of earlier development or to underrate the effort and foresight of our indigenous predecessors.

Looking farther backward, we could note precedents for the practice of comparative literature *avant la lettre.* Before there were professors of English or the separate modern tongues, a cultivated man of letters like James Russell Lowell could lecture on *belles-lettres,* moving with ease from Dante and Cervantes to Chaucer and the Elizabethans. The ancient pedagogical tradition of rhetoric would develop, with Lane Cooper at Cornell, into what he persisted in calling "the comparative study of literature." Within the philological departments—Germanic, Romanic—the related clusters of required languages furnished a basis for comparative studies, howbeit pedestrian. One could never be a medievalist without first becoming a comparatist. As for the classicists, they were at home in the double realm of Greco-Roman cross-reference, and some of them were curious about the continuing impact of the ancients. From his stylistic analyses of Homer's formulas, Milman Parry was led to investigate the parallels afforded by oral poetry, and to clinch his demonstration by collecting the repertory of the Serbian bards. His theory of epic composition, together with the supporting field work, must stand among the few humanistic researches of our day that have gained the sort of recognition accorded to a scientific discovery.

It was my good fortune to encounter Milman Parry as a freshman instructor, and to be in fairly close touch with him through his all too brief remaining lustrum. The incisive impression that he left—the measured speech, the adventurous thought, the Parisianized tastes, the Californian energies—has proved ineradicable. I think of him whenever I really try to grasp the fundamentals of literature: what it is made of, how it works, the part it plays in men's lives. Though I also studied with Irving Babbitt, and have tried to express my admiration for him elsewhere, I never counted myself among his numerous disciples. If he succeeded more fully than any American before him in animating and projecting our discipline, it was because he utilized comparative literature as a backdrop for moral drama. One might resist his doctrines, but one could not keep from being swept along by his panoramic sense of continuity, his encyclopedic skill at interrelating current ideas or issues with classical traditions and even the wisdom of the East. Those to whom the names of certain writers were no more than names saw no more than name-dropping in his majestic roll calls. It took a textual knowledge approaching his own to verify his juxtapositions and linkages.

Men like Babbitt and Spingarn functioned both as critics and as comparatists at a time when scholars in the more restricted literary fields cultivated history at the expense of criticism. As late as 1935 R. S. Crane, while crossing from the one domain to the other, declared that the two were mutually exclusive. To look upon them so often as coextensive has been a distinctively American attitude toward comparative literature. European comparatists, at least until lately, have been more strictly historical in their purview. I hesitate to draw these hemispheric distinctions because I firmly believe in the ecumenical principle defended by Cornelis de Deugd in his Dutch brochure, *De Eenheid van het Comparatisme:* the unity of comparative literature. One of our underlying assumptions, surely, has been the transcendence of nationalism. To speak of an American school seems especially shortsighted, when so many of our leading lights are of European origin. But we may observe that this continent has provided them with a much wider prospect than they might ever have attained in their fatherlands. The ethnic precondition of our culture, the very fact that here they mix with colleagues of different provenance, makes for a cross-fertilization of minds. Our objective is not a national school but an international perspective.

Smaller nations, whose languages are not widely spoken, enjoy the compensating advantage of multilingualism. Georg Brandes lamented that most of his readers could not read him in the original Danish; on the other hand, his command of foreign literatures made him the most cosmopolitan of critics. It is no accident that Switzerland and Alsace-Lorraine have produced comparatists, who in turn concentrated their pioneering endeavors on Franco-German relations, largely within the romantic epoch. As these areas have been staked and charted, the emphasis has been shifting culturally toward the Slavic regions and historically to other periods. An imperial culture like that of Great Britain, having imposed its language on tributary lands, has been less receptive to rival cultures. At any rate, the British have been slow to display an interest in comparative literature—though some of them, like H. M. Chadwick, W. P. Ker, and Sir Maurice Bowra, have discreetly practised it under more conventional rubrics. The United States, although predominantly English-speaking, has been in a rather different position. Its colonial past, its continental isolation, its continuous series of emigrations, not to mention the restlessness of its writers contemplating the American scene, have conditioned it to look outward, eastward toward Europe.

If our tendency has been centrifugal, France has unwaveringly tended in a centripetal direction. So many foreign roads have led to Paris, whence they have carried back the thriving exports of language and culture. It is not altogether surprising that the *comparatiste* has sometimes confused his task with that of the *douanier*. The French, on their side, have taken considerable interest in other lands, the kind of interest Athenians took in barbarians, and have augmented their lore with exotic tales which their travelers, like Herodotus, bring home. Their consciousness of living at the center of western civilization, by and large, has been justified by the course of events. More than any other people, they have set the pace, coined the terms, and framed the patterns for literary history. It seems logical that France should have been the birthplace, and for long intervals the chief sustainer, of comparative literature. That is one of the many intellectual debts to her which the rest of the world should gratefully acknowledge. It seems natural, too, that her scholars and critics should be centrally preoccupied with her own literature, and that her concern for other literatures should be regulated by their degree of relationship to the matter of France.

During the era of *l'entre-deux-guerres,* when the intellectuals of all nations gravitated toward their second fatherland and Paris was the capital of the arts and of ideas, foreign students of the humanities were finding a congenial haven in the Institut de Littérature Comparée at the Sorbonne, founded and directed by Fernand Baldensperger. Understandably, their studies were likely to focus upon some point of contact between French literature and their own. Now, when Leon Edel wanted to work on whom but Henry James, he got no encouragement from American graduate schools—how long ago it all seems! Ultimately he was to write his two path-breaking theses under the first French professor of American literature, Charles Cestre. But, when Edel arrived at the University of Paris, he had naturally begun by consulting Baldensperger. The latter, though by no means unsympathetic, explained that it was too late; the topic had just been covered. Whereupon he exhibited the thesis of Marie-Reine Garnier, *Henry James et la France.* That conjunction has indeed proved a fruitful one, to which Professor Edel has added further nuances. It is a pity that so small a number of writers lend themselves as generously as James to the automatic application of Baldensperger's formula.

Much later, when I was teaching for a term at the Sorbonne, I was given a glimpse of the medallion's other side. A student of comparative literature came to consult me in some bewilderment over the thesis topic assigned to him: André Gide and America. Since Gide had never visited the United States and had touched but marginally upon its literature, it would seem that this was expected to be a study in reception and influence. Unluckily for the candidate, the American reaction had been relatively slight and sporadic, so that it could barely have furnished the literary material for a short critical essay. The presumption behind such assignments, unchecked against the facts at the receiving end, is that somehow every distinguished French author must have had a substantial *fortune* in every country, worth investigating in detail. The value of the investigation is likewise thrown in doubt when the merits of the *récepteur* are appreciably inferior to those of the *émetteur:* for example, the influence of Flaubert on Lafcadio Hearn. The Francocentric approach was reduced to absurdity in the little manual of M. F. Guyard, where an appended table indicates what claims have been staked out and what unclaimed spheres of influence await the enterprising prospector.

The method is easily transferred to other bases of operation. As Jan Brandt Corstius puts it, in the latest *Introduction to the Comparative Study of Literature,* "the number of books dealing with author X in country Y is legion." In their concurrent handbook, *La Littérature comparée,* Claude Pichois and A. M. Rousseau use exactly the same formulation: "la formule X et Y." This seems well suited to that algebraic spirit which presided over us for too long. We trust that it is being supplanted by an *esprit de finesse.* However, we must be grateful to Baldensperger for pulling things together at the right time and place, for imposing concreteness on a subject which had theretofore been too diffuse. I have stressed his positive contribution in a memoir for the Harvard faculty, to which he belonged for six years; I owe him personal gratitude for having first encouraged me to teach a course in comparative literature. Perhaps he is best understood as a scholarly contemporary of Romain Rolland and Jean Giraudoux, who shared their good intentions with regard to frontiers, notably the Rhine. Academically, it could be argued that the chauvinism and provincialism of the other literary departments warranted the emergence of comparative literature as a border discipline, *Grenzwissenschaft*.

The trouble was that it spent too much of its energy patrolling those borders rather than crossing them; it paid the most attention to such writers as happened to travel most, intermediaries rather than innovators; and, by that reckoning, its greatest genius appeared to be Madame de Staël. Paul Hazard, primarily a literary historian of France, or Marcel Bataillon, mainly a Hispanist, could highlight a French or Spanish foreground against a comparative background. Baldensperger, committed to the professionalism of the arch-comparatist, was less interested in literature itself than in its "orientations étrangères." He could enliven matters with topical innuendos—as when, during the scandal of Edward VIII's abdication, Baldensperger addressed the Alliance Française on "Une Amie du Roi d'Angleterre," a French mistress of Charles II. When his collaborator, Paul Van Tieghem, relinquished these particularities to compile a historical conspectus of European and American literatures, it had no standing in *littérature comparée;* it was presented under the more synthetic category of *littérature générale.* Alas for such well-meaning internationalism! The first edition of the book, which came out during the German occupation of Paris, was not permitted to recognize the existence of either Heinrich Heine or Thomas Mann.

Van Tieghem's publishers have replaced his introductory guide of 1931 with that of Messrs. Pichois and Rousseau. To compare the comparative, across a span of thirty-six years, is to mark increases in both flexibility and breadth. Francocentricity seems to have been chastened and modified. Not unnaturally, the authors dwell on the early "conquêtes" of the French movement; but they also handsomely concede that American comparatism, "sur bien des points désormais, a plus de leçons à donner qu'à recevoir." If the viewpoint seems eclectic, so much the better; there has been too much single-mindedness in what should be a many-minded enterprise; all procedures genuinely illuminating the object should be relevant to it, and consequently to us. Messrs. Pichois and Rousseau begin conventionally enough, with sources and influences and the old-fashioned mechanics of exchange. Quickly they pass on to the history of ideas, the significance of themes, and a catchall dignified by the catchword of structuralism. I confess I feel somewhat like Monsieur Jourdain at his lessons when I see my own name listed in flattering company under the heading: "*Phénoménologie de la transposition littéraire.*" Yet, apart from such unaccountable aberrations, the volume has an open-ended quality which invites a resurgence for French comparative literature.

That would be an exhilarating change; for, if we scan the whole field candidly, we find ourselves looking in vain for a major work from France since 1937, the year that witnessed the publication of Albert Béguin's *L'Ame romantique et le rêve* as well as Marcel Bataillon's *Erasme en Espagne*. René Etiemble has evidently been rearing a monument of some kind in his *Le Mythe de Rimbaud*. But this is *Überlieferungsgeschichte,* anti-clerical hagiography, an exhaustive and exhausting study in misconception. The author himself calls it "sociologie religieuse," documents it to the point of obsession or parody, and admits that it rarely touches upon comparative literature. Little of what is written in France today, "sous le titre officiel de littérature comparée," satisfies the canons set forth in the pamphlet he issued upon his accession to a chair at Paris, *Comparaison n'est pas raison*. He is a cantankerous, if ardent, internationalist, who is not above resorting to *franglais* when he refers to *les yanquis*. But he has taken shrewd cognizance of professional discussions both east and west of France. American readers have no reason to be surprised at his recommendations, insofar as these involve thematology, imagery, translation, and poetics. What may surprise us is that such approaches have found a rostrum at the Sorbonne.

The most striking aspect of M. Etiemble's platform is its far-flung cosmopolitanism. There are so many nations in the world whose literature is still to be compared. Our discipline will not have completely realized its potentialities or objectives until its network has embraced them all. Meanwhile we do everything we can to establish programs of cooperation with the small and highly qualified band of available experts on nonoccidental literatures, such as the conferences held at Indiana University. The usual links, the intercultural borrowings, the reciprocal images and mirages, though interesting, are often disappointingly sparse and superficial. The exciting challenge of this gambit is precisely that it opens up an unconnected sphere of comparison. Though the domain of the occidental comparatist is very broad and incomparably rich, it is necessarily circumscribed; it remains, for better and worse, what Professor Brandt Corstius—in his modest and sensible guide—terms "a community of literatures." Its elements, however varied, are the related products of cultural and linguistic diffusion, and are influenced by one another indirectly if not directly. Whereas a literature of totally disparate origin offers us a body of forms and themes to compare, in the most far-reaching sense, with our own. If we learn what the Noh play has in common with Greek tragedy, we can generalize about organic processes.

We cannot but agree with M. Etiemble that it would be valuable for any European comparatist to become acquainted with a non-European language. But to insist upon this as a requirement is a counsel of perfection—as he must certainly realize, if his interest in China has brought him into contact with sinologues, who regard an acquaintance with Chinese literature as an exacting life-work in itself. More practical is his recommendation for fostering such contacts and helping to develop Asiatic comparatists. Yet, though I am pleased to learn that South Korea now has a Society for Comparative Literature, I do not feel culturally deprived because of my inability to read its transactions. I do feel some concern lest, in undiscriminating sympathy for unfamiliar cultures, we relax the requirements for European comparative literature, succumbing to our occupational hazard and spreading ourselves too thin. What shall it profit our students to gain Swahili and have no Latin? It would be parochial to revert to the ethnocentric stance of Tennyson: "Better fifty years of Europe than a cycle of Cathay." But it is only prudent to recollect, with due respect for Asia and Africa, the epigraph from Marvell that the late Erich Auerbach placed on the title page of his *Mimesis:* "Had we but world enough and time . . ." Let us make sure that we do justice to those parts of the world of letters which definitely lie within our range.

M. Etiemble's subtitle, *Crise de la littérature comparée,* echoes the title of Professor Wellek's challenging communication to the international congress at Chapel Hill in 1958, an occasion which may be said to have dramatized America's coming of age in comparative literature. Professor Wellek used it to criticize the cumbersome and restrictive methodology associated with Baldensperger and Carré—both of whom, as it happened, died that year. Most of the older comparatists everywhere, including the United States, had employed that methodology, usually with less distinction than its exponents at the Sorbonne. Nevertheless the critique was viewed, in certain quarters, as an attack against a *ci-devant* French school and a manifesto on behalf of a *soi-disant* American school. It would be not only ironic but tragic, if a movement aimed at uniting the hemispheres should end by breeding opposition between them. We already live with too many social and political crises. The crisis in comparative literature, far from being a Franco-American conflict along nationalistic lines, has been a methodological issue between two generations—and, as such, a manifestation of growth. A decade of discussion has brought out signs of a realignment in France, which parallels some of the shifts that we have been undertaking. Our problems are the same, and we must continue as partners in seeking solutions.

Yet I sadly suspect that we have not heard the last of such divisive talk about two schools, or of attempts to tar us on into controversy with the French. Some of our Japanese colleagues have been misled into volunteering as our allies. Henri Peyre, who is a living symbol of Franco-American concord, has described the outlook of the comparatist as supranational. His irenic description has been angrily attacked by Irina Neupokoeva, a Russian delegate to the conference on comparative literature called by the Hungarian Academy of Sciences in 1962. Since the Americans—who were not represented at Budapest—had been singled out as a school, this polemical lady, seizing the tactical opportunity, went on to inveigh against them. She even went so far as to defend the obsolescent standpoint of Guyard. What is known as comparativism in Russia had been officially frowned on, like cosmopolitanism or formalism or other germane points of view. In moving halfway toward comparative literature, the Russians have not given up their commitment to nationalism or, at any rate, to Pan-Slavism, Anti-Westernism, and propaganda. Madame Neupokoeva is involved in a Soviet history of world literature, the Russocentric principles of which she has expounded in a discourse before the International Comparative Literature Association at Belgrade in 1967.

Some of the hostility of the Marxists toward ourselves seems to derive from an oversimplified impression of New Criticism, which they take to be antihistorical. A firsthand look at our critical output should assure them that historicism is still preponderant, and that some of us pay serious attention to sociology, to ideology, indeed to Marxism. We try to locate our comparisons within the context of history. But Madame Neupokoeva, rejecting the term *comparative,* prefers to talk about "the study of the interconnection and interaction of literature." That is no more than literary history à la Guyard and Van Tieghem, with a shift in priorities to the Slavic and eastern spheres. For the process of comparison, so essential to any formal analysis, she would substitute a second type of history. It would be diachronic instead of synchronic; stated otherwise, instead of viewing simultaneous phenomena in chronological sequence, it would work from prearranged models of historical development applying to different periods in different countries. The prearrangement would, of course, be determined by Marxist doctrine. Methodologically, this is very like what she reprehends in the cultural typologies of Arnold Toynbee. Though she speaks pretentiously of science, the scientific method—being empirical rather than dogmatic—cannot operate within a closed system of ideas.

Marxist studies in literature seem to be taking a more flexible and pragmatic turn in Hungary, under István Sötér and his colleagues. Their approaches have an immediate bearing for us, since we have been invited to collaborate on a history of literature in European languages, an international project to be coordinated by the Literary Research Institute of the Hungarian Academy. Preliminary outlines have suggested ways of reducing the massive subject to manageable proportions by dividing it horizontally into movements and vertically into genres. This would have the effect of enclosing formal considerations within a historical checkerboard, a framework so discontinuous that it might discourage the tracing of forms and some of the comparative strategies. It is proposed to start *in medias res* with the romantic period, an area not immune from national self-consciousness. I shall be curiously watching what transpires when we arrive at the realistic movement—having gathered, to my discomfort at Belgrade, that our comrades from the Soviet Union still cling desperately to that unhistorical concept of Socialist Realism which they inherited from Gorky, Zhdanov, and Stalin. Scholarly cooperation which crosses ideological boundaries is a prospect we should like to further. But will our collaborators be asking us, as the Communists did last summer, to accept their ideological dogmas?

If we cannot begin by agreeing upon the definition of terms, we shall be building another Tower of Babel. On the *bureau* of the International Comparative Literature Association, I confess, there were moments when one felt like a member of the Security Council of the United Nations. Yet there should be hope for the long run, as well as intermittent frustration, in that analogy. Possibly we can derive some reassurance from the dictionary of terms now being compiled under the sponsorship of the I.C.L.A., which should put our critical usage on a solid semantic foundation. Such disjointed compilations can be more satisfactory than the diffusive syntheses of semi-anonymous teams; for, though our literary lexicons are palpably uneven, they contain many articles whose worth is guaranteed by the signature of the individual author. Comparative literature affords frequent occasions for teamwork, for the meeting of minds in dialectical interplay, albeit not in *Gleichschaltung*. But since it remains a humanistic pursuit—"La littérature comparée, c'est l'humanisme," says the emphatic M. Etiemble—its achievements must be those of individuals. The works to be compared must, in each case, be encompassed by an individual mind. Admittedly, *comparatist* is an awkward term; but it gains momentum when we use it to designate a Lukács, a Curtius, a Brandes, or a Croce in spite of himself.

I have deliberately cited examples of incontestable stature, standing at some temporal and geographical distance from ourselves. It may be that the conditions we face do not engender such polymaths. Yet an association of comparatists is not in its nonage, when its members have erected such monuments in the world of scholarship as the *Motif-Index of Folk-Literature, A History of Modern Criticism, A History of Literary Criticism in the Italian Renaissance,* or *The Singer of Tales.* Modern learning has not been free from distempers: would that we had a Bacon to diagnose them! Instead we have a William Arrowsmith, who has abandoned humanism for obscurantism, taken up the practice of antischolarship, and sought the plaudits of the philistines by indiscriminately denouncing the activities of his fellow humanists, in a rhetoric as loose as his own translations. Most of us are not less conscious than he of the pettifoggery that has too often trivialized research in the philological fields. We have reacted against it in our time, and have opposed it with constructive criticism at intramural gatherings of the profession. What is of greater importance, we ourselves have turned from the more specialized disciplines to comparative literature because of the possibilities for enlargement, integration, and revitalization that it holds out for the humanities.

That we first must set our house in order, that we have been rethinking our concepts and centering our focus—this is what I take to be the meaning of our so-called crisis. It has won us freedom to move forward in directions hitherto avoided or ignored. In the past comparatists were sometimes justly blamed for working at too far a remove from the esthetic object. Two preeminent *Romanisten* who spent their later careers in America, Leo Spitzer and Erich Auerbach, inevitably gravitated to comparative literature and brilliantly demonstrated the use it could make of the *explication de texte.* Their interpretations, so exemplary in their very differences, have done much to bridge the gap between stylistics and linguistics. That *rapproachement* should also help to sharpen the scrutiny of comparative metrics. Translation, which had long been taken for granted, has been rediscovered as a tool for bringing out stylistic and

cultural traits. Poets have been bringing fresh inspiration to the translator's craft. Comparatists have a special responsibility for seeing that it
is scrupulously practiced. In the recent instance of Mikhail Bulgakov's
Master and Margarita, they should have decisively distinguished between
the scrupulousness of Mirra Ginsburg's translation and the carelessness
of Michael Glenny's, which showed up the reviewers who did not show
it up.

The most common ground between history and criticism has been
largely occupied by the history of criticism. More broadly, the history of
ideas, the study of literature as a means of philosophic expression, has
reoriented our understanding of guiding currents and artistic *-isms.* The
method characterized by E. E. Stoll as "historical and comparative" has
richly illuminated the changing forms and persisting conventions of
drama. Though it is less readily applied to so polymorphous a genre as
the novel, we have been consolidating and systematizing our insights into
the techniques of narrative. Folklore, once excluded from the purlieus of
polite literature, now seems to be its model, nay its matrix. The habit of
fabulation may yield us a key to the processes of the imagination. Claude
Lévi-Strauss envisages a progression, which we could illustrate, "du
mythe au roman." If our quarterly critics have been promiscuous in their
reducing of everything to myth, or too eagerly amateurish in tracking the
symbol down to its tenebrous lair, then it is for the comparatist to propose
and uphold higher standards of interpretation. New modes of critical
thinking are daily pressing upon us, some of them wide in their external
sweep, others seeking to probe internal depths. To comparative literature
they offer an extension of outlook, in exchange for the methodological
rigor they clearly require.

Under the somewhat confusing slogan of *Néo-critique,* these tendencies have been manifested in France, possibly by way of reaction
against the *Paléo-critique* they attribute to the Sorbonne. Their key word,
structure, seems to borrow some of its currency from linguistics and
anthropology. It may suggest, but does not promise, a morphology of
literature; it is concerned, not with form, but with what used to be dismissed by formalists as content. *Stoffgeschichte,* which was all but dismissed from comparative literature, has been revived with thematics, and
can look forward to a bright future. Taking motifs, *topoi,* or images as
the distinctive components of imaginative structures, we can observe
how they are put together or can differentiate the meanings they convey
in varying contexts. The pitfall is the psychoanalytic temptation to in-

dulge in subjective biography; the aim is an organic analysis of a writer's works and of the code whereby he communicates with us. To consider these potentialities is to recognize the obsolescence of instruments which have served their useful turn: in particular, the Baldensperger-Friederich bibliography. Though its listings can be updated indefinitely, its categories no longer cover the subject pertinently. Having taken all literature for our province, we need special bibliographies rather than an *omnium gatherum*.

Only the Recording Angel could be the perfect bibliographer; and if she registers our publications and actions, I fear she will notice a certain imbalance. We spend too much of our energy talking—as I am now—about comparative literature, and not enough of it comparing the literature. We have too many programs and not enough performances, too many drum majors and not enough instrumentalists, too many people telling us how to do things they have never done. We put too much stress on setting up, or knocking down, apparatus. We debate endlessly over such purely schematic problems as periodization, while periods lie fallow, awaiting investigation. Hours that might better be devoted to reading and contemplation are expended, like this one, at meetings and conferences. In short, the substance of our common pursuit is jeopardized by an overemphasis on organization and methodology. I shall be sorry if my candor sounds like disregard for much necessary effort. I am aware that new departures have to be organized, and that sound results cannot be achieved without discussing methods. A discipline still working out its relations with more established disciplines will normally engage in critiques and self-criticism. It will take on the aspect of a cause, enlist revivalistic sentiments, announce itself with heraldic fanfares, and promote its interests with self-advertisement.

All of this is wholly understandable. Furthermore, the nature of our subject is excursive and gregarious; it stimulates us to travel and to forgather; and we should be ungracious if we shied away from the kind of social and intellectual exchanges that have been arranged so auspiciously here. Yet Messrs. Pichois and Rousseau, in speaking of congresses, hold out an epigrammatic warning, together with an etymological pun: "Se faire carrefour . . . ne va pas sans une certaine trivialité." If comparatists would resist the danger of becoming organization men, they must realize that they are well past the organizing stage, and must cease to preoccupy themselves with the trivia of Paracomparatism. I am not even sure that we should be congratulating ourselves upon the growth of the American

Comparative Literature Association. After all, we are not the Rotary International. Our colleges and universities, which Thorstein Veblen likened to department stores, compete with one another by installing new brands of popular goods. So it is with the current expansion of comparative literature. Whether an institution actually ought to have such a department unless it has a strong group of language departments, a number of thoroughly experienced scholars, and a large library—that was the question put to you by the report of our committee on professional standards three years ago.

It is doubtful whether our recommendations are being consistently followed, and we have no authority to enforce them beyond an appeal to good will and common sense. Again at the risk of playing the spoilsport, I doubt whether the exfoliation of periodicals is a sign of progress in itself. The Hegelian maxim could prove to be applicable in reverse: an increase of quantity could mean a decrease in quality. If comparative literature promises any advance beyond the neighboring disciplines, that is because it is more demanding than they are; it presupposes more preparation than they do; and to dilute its demands would endanger its essence. Its practitioners must continue to be specially qualified and, what is more, to have a sense of vocation. One hesitates to broach the mere notion of an elite, in a democracy where the worst are so full of passionate intensity. The precedent of Henry Adams is not altogether encouraging, since—despite his considerable accomplishment—he assessed his scholarly career as a failure. And yet he handed on a timely precept to us, in his *Education,* when he entitled the final chapter "Nunc age." After all the preliminaries, the propaedeutics, the estimates, the surveys, and the self-questionings, after reassessing the state of our union, the comparatist should advise himself: *Nunc age.* Now proceed: compare the literature.

THEMATICS AND CRITICISM

This article was written as a tribute to appear in the *Festschrift* for René Wellek, *The Disciplines of Criticism: Essays in Literary Theory, Interpretation, and History*, edited by Peter Demetz, Thomas Greene, and Lowry Nelson, Jr. (New Haven, 1968). It is a kind of prospectus for a fairly new method, which I myself have tried to utilize in *The Power of Blackness* and *The Myth of the Golden Age in the Renaissance*—and which has something in common with what is called structuralism, though it has a more historical orientation. I have since undertaken a more precise and systematic treatment of the same approach in connection with an article on Motif, which is scheduled for publication in the forthcoming *Dictionary of the History of Ideas*.

A book which tried to simplify its problems by talking down to its readers was paraphrased by one of its critics in French: "N'ayez pas peur, petits enfants; le sujet n'existe pas." Possibly I could allay a well-grounded suspicion which may greet my title by pointing out that my subject has only very lately come into existence. But in a broader sense— the sense in which Monsieur Jourdain talked prose before he studied rhetoric—it has always existed, insofar as it is nothing more nor less than the subject matter of literature. Laymen have always recognized this, and amateurs practised it whenever they wrote books about the women of Shakespeare or gave lectures illustrated with slides on the highways and byways of the Thomas Hardy country. On the other hand, men of letters single-mindedly devoted to craftsmanship have deprecated such an approach since Flaubert, who wanted to write a book without a subject and claimed that the rhythms of his sentences came to him before the words. Formalism has been a predominant trend, sharpening and narrowing the focus of our literary critics, ever since John Crowe Ransom published his manifesto, *The New Criticism,* a generation ago. The contribution of René Wellek has been a connecting link between the earlier Slavic formalists and the American school, as well as between a strictly formalistic and a more broadly historical vantage point.

The comparative novelty of New Criticism, at least to us, and the common ground amid its diversity of approaches lay in its concentration upon the object as a work of art. That, in turn, had been a salutary reaction against an old-fashioned kind of scholarship which was so concerned with background, with externals of biography, history, sociology, that it all but ignored the foreground, the esthetic texture of the works themselves. The leading critics of the nineteenth century could be psychologists like Sainte-Beuve or moralists like Matthew Arnold, and there are distinguished continuators of those respective traditions, notably Edmund Wilson and Lionel Trilling, who properly reach a much wider and more general public today than their colleagues whose concerns are more technical. We are also aware that the other half of the world, the hemisphere that professes allegiance to Marxist philosophy, regulates its criticism by ideological standards and regards a critical formalist as a traitor to the working class. Indeed there has been a heavily documented polemic by an East German scholar, Robert Weimann, *"New Criticism"* *und die Entwicklung bürgerlicher Literaturwissenschaft* (Halle, 1962), which views an undue concern with form as a symptom of bourgeois decadence. The self-limiting criterion of the New Critics, internal coherence, has been as extreme in its way as those polar criteria which the Marxists derive from external conditions.

Yet there have been indications of late that some members of the American school are allowing more leeway for the role of personality and for the context of society. W. K. Wimsatt, its most serious theoretician, has produced an impressive antiquarian monograph on the portraits of Alexander Pope. Cleanth Brooks, its most accomplished explicator of poetic texts, has brought out an illuminating study of William Faulkner which explores the highways and byways of Yoknapatawpha County. The open-minded critic cannot afford to be too much of a purist, since literature has a habit—which he must follow—of absorbing so much else, of involving itself in so many extraneous matters, of extending its purview farther and farther. Much of what interests readers most is connected with what formalists might regard as literature's impurities. A poem is a verbal artifact, yes, more obviously than some of the freer forms; but its arrangement of signs and sounds is likewise a network of associations and responses, communicating implicit information and incidentally touching off value judgments. The programmatic survey of René Wellek and Austin Warren, *Theory of Literature,* which has so widely and helpfully influenced graduate studies since its publication in 1948, is sharply subdivided between what it labels "intrinsic" (style and structure and various formal devices) and what it considers "extrinsic" (the social, the psychological, and the philosophical aspects of literary art).

This would seem to be turning inside out the old mechanical dichotomy between form and content, offering the inside position to factors that used to be looked upon as outer embellishments, mere decorations —all that Sainte-Beuve dismissed when he spoke of *rhétorique*. The notion of content, of that which is contained, has its parallel in the German *Gehalt;* it presupposes form as a sort of container, a superficial holder for emotions or ideas, which constitute the substance to be imparted. But, as Plato suggested and Spenser affirmed, "soul is form and doth the body make." Hence form gets metamorphosed into content: "the medium," as Marshall McLuhan puts it, "is the message." One of our central terms, which we have had to borrow from the French, is *genre;* yet genre painting is the kind that subordinates the portrayal to what is portrayed; the picture itself counts for less than the anecdote it tells. When we speak of epistolary novels, we have a formal category in mind; but when we speak of Gothic novels, we seem to be dealing with subject matter. The novel's inherent dependence on the latter, its use or abuse as a convenient vehicle to convey a segment of actuality, has been recently underlined by the appearance of the so-called nonfiction novel—to say nothing of such self-contradictory compounds as the *anti-roman*. Fortunately the categories of modern fiction have found their Polonius in Wayne C. Booth, who can be as exacting over point of view as the neoclassicists were over decorum.

We continue to think of novels in terms of what they are about: a picaresque novel is about a picaroon, a rogue, and it exploits the opportunities that his misadventures present for a rambling inspection of low life. But the very nature of that ramble, easygoing and loose as it may seem, is by no means formless. On the contrary, it incarnates a structural principle which has successfully adapted itself to the purposes of most of the major novelists at one time or another. Therefore the term "picaresque" implies not merely an antihero, with all his capacity for disillusionment, but a linear movement which is both episodic and comprehensive, which can linger by the wayside or take the highroad to town. By contrast, the epic presents a narration more formally composed, more implicated with such conventions as the invocation to the Muse, which can be traced back—through the studies of Milman Parry and Albert Lord—to the circumstances of oral delivery. Different epics narrate different stories; yet usually they contain certain analogous episodes which take on a functional significance, such as the journey to the underworld, the conclave of the gods, or the dalliance with a temptress—

whether her name be Circe, Dido, Alcina, Armida, or Acrasia. Thus content gets metamorphosed into form; the selection and disposition of themes becomes an organic part of the artistic process; and Ben Shahn offered a usable hint to writers when he titled his lectures on painting *The Shape of Content.*

Our keyword *theme* may sound somewhat jejune, particularly to those who associate it with required compositions for Freshman English. The original Greco-Latin *thema* simply denoted a rhetorical proposition, the argument of a discourse, what in Jamesian parlance we now like to term the *donnée.* It could be the topic chosen by the orator or assigned to the schoolboy; through the pedagogical influence of the Jesuits the term became equated with an academic exercise; and the French soon specialized it to mean a translation of a given passage into another language. The adjective *thematic* has generally had to do with meaning as distinguished from technique. Though his excogitations have done much to extend its possibilities, our critical anatomist Northrop Frye is quite conservative in his own definition. Thematic modes, as opposed to what he calls fictional modes, are dependent upon their conceptual interest; they are roughly equivalent to what Aristotle called *dianoia,* the thought of the poem. Stephen Gilman discriminates further, in his monograph on *La Celestina,* between thesis and theme, between the directive idea and the underlying "sense of life." Gradually, and rather charily, we have been approaching the sphere of thematology. If ever a word was set up to be knocked down, it is that forbidding expression, which no dictionary has yet been broad-minded enough to admit. Presumably it heralds a science of themes, although even a pioneering enthusiast might hesitate to describe himself as a thematologist or to attend a thematological congress. Perhaps its ablest pioneer was the Italian comparatist Arturo Graf, whose nineteenth-century monographs examined such phenomena as the Devil and the Earthly Paradise.

Thematology would seem to be a pseudoscientific approximation of the German *Stoffgeschichte,* literally the history of stuff or fabric—an underlying conception at once more solid and less pretentious. However, it came to stand for the less imaginative researches of Germanic philology, its plodding accumulations of medieval legend or oriental lore on its pedantic quest for sources and analogues. Wilhelm Dilthey assigned an important place in his poetics to the study of motifs, *Motivenlehre;* but all too many investigations bogged down at the level of source hunting, *Quellenforschung.* The method was severely condemned by Benedetto Croce, who felt that it was extraliterary because it established no inner relationship among the differing treatments of the same theme. It was viewed with something like a nationalistic suspicion by the official French exponents of comparative literature, Fernand Baldensperger, Paul Hazard, and Paul Van Tieghem. Latterly the Institut de Littérature Comparée at the Sorbonne, in delayed reaction to the changing methods of literary history (which it envisaged for so long as a chronicle of French authors traveling abroad or of foreign books translated into French), has begun to relax its pursuit of fortunes and influences and to concern itself more seriously with *thèmes et structures*. Thematics was incorporated into poetics by the Russian Formalist, Boris Tomashevsky. Meanwhile the masters of the twentieth-century novel had been enlarging and elevating the usages of the thematic.

Realizing that narrative is—like music—a temporal medium, and deeply preoccupied with time itself as a theme, they emulated Wagnerian *Leitmotiv* and worked out controlling designs through the repetition and recognition of identifying phrases. Literature may not have needed to borrow from music such effects as it had previously gained through the epithets and formulas of some of its earliest genres, but it could now orchestrate them with a complexity which was psychological as well as musical. Thomas Mann explicitly described the style and structure of his own writing as "thematisch." Marcel Proust expressed the modulating relations of his lovers in a "little phrase" from a sonata by his imaginary composer Vinteuil. James Joyce brought home the self-reproach of his young artist by intermittently echoing a monkish byword for remorse of conscience, "Agenbite of Inwit." Some of these techniques have been carried farther by the contemporary practitioners of *le nouveau roman*. Echoes, frequently in the guise of quotations from music and literature, play a strategic part in any attempt to recreate the stream of consciousness. Their resonance would be more clearly registered in a thematic index than in the dramatis personae. We seek guidance through Proust in Raoul Celly's *Répertoire des thèmes,* just as we look up Mozart's works in Köchel's catalogue. Here again there seems to be a tendency for a substantive element to turn into an instrumental device. The message (*pace* Mr. McLuhan) becomes the medium.

Psychology, too, has added a deeper dimension to the critical examination of themes. Not that the Freudians have contributed much beyond the reduction of everything to the same old sexual allegory, any more than the Frazerians have greatly enlightened us by imposing on every conceivable story the composite outlines of a blurred monomyth. By hypothesis, the Jungian archetypes are ungraspable in their fullest primordial force; but Maud Bodkin has traced their emergence through certain poetic patterns, such universals as Rebirth or Paradise/Hades. What is known as the Thematic Apperception Test confronts its beholder with a set of ambiguous pictures, which he is asked to interpret in his own fashion, thereby disclosing his personal configuration of traits. The originator, Dr. Henry A. Murray, who is a literary man as well as a clinical psychologist, has pointed out some of the implications of the test for the creation of literature in "Personality and Creative Imagination," a paper read to the English Institute and published in its *Annual* (1942). The situation of the writer is not subject to such controlled observation; yet culture provides him with a sequence of themes to which he responds according to his imaginative bent; and when we are fully aware of them and can trace their projection through the minds of other writers, we may then be in a position to gauge both the individual quality of that response and the functioning of the collective imagination.

When Tonio Kröger dedicates himself to his calling, in Thomas Mann's parable of the writer's vocation, he speculates: "I gaze into an unborn world of phantoms, which must be ordered and shaped; I look upon a swarm of shadows of human figures, who beckon me to conjure them up and redeem them." Without attempting to enter that private underworld, to catch its embryonic forms before they have been summoned from their matrix, or to accompany Faust on the subterranean stages of his exploratory descent, we still have some degree of conversance with those disembodied spirits through their transmigrations into literature. We can take stock of this stuff (to repeat a good Shakespearean word), we can gain a rough impression of the repertory, as it were, on the rudimentary plane of bibliographies, dictionaries, and handbooks. The *Bibliography of Comparative Literature* (Chapel Hill, 1950) is a well-meaning catchall which has probably outlived its usefulness. Initiated by Louis Betz (1897) and augmented by Werner Friederich, it was edited principally by Fernand Baldensperger (1904), whose schematic framework during many years virtually comprised a methodology for the field. The section headed "Literary Themes (Stoffgeschichte)" includes subsections covering "Fables and Fabliaux," "Legends," and "Literary Types," but only as "Generalities." Specific themes are listed alphabetically under "Individual Motifs" and categorically under "Collective Motifs."

Individual motifs include not only Hiawatha, Mary Magdalene, and Robert the Devil, let alone Chicago or Clocks and Bells, but also War and Peace subsumed in a single category, Love (though it laughs at locksmiths, it toes the line for bibliographers), and Humor—which Professor Frye would not be alone in regarding as a mode rather than a motif. Why are such broad abstractions not classed as collective motifs, if indeed they be motifs at all? That other heading proves to be even more of a taxonomic jumble. Under it we encounter the subheading "Characters and Types," which seems to overlap "American Types and Trends" on the one hand and "Ecclesiastical Characters and Localities" on the other. Evidently the problem is the logical one of discriminating substance from accident. There ought to be room for everyone under "Men, Women, Children"; yet, rather arbitrarily and narrow-mindedly, there is a special compartment for "Foreigners, Barbarians, Gringos," while "Virtues, Vices, Crimes" are lumped together with a truly ecumenical tolerance. The sole conclusion we are led to is that the editors of our bibliography have not decided what they mean by a theme. It could be a geographical setting (the Alps), a cultural order (Chivalry) or a fundamental idea (the Problem of Evil). Professor Friederich explains that certain lists are necessarily selective; manifestly Nature or Utopia would warrant a bibliography by itself.

In defining their scope, the compilers of the *Dizionario letterario* published by Bompiani (Milan, 1947-1950) were faced with a much simpler task. Seven of their handsomely illustrated volumes, after an introductory review of intellectual movements ("movimenti spirituali"), deal with *opere,* the works themselves, such as *Giuseppe Andrews* and *Signora Bovary.* To reread them here in synopsis is like following the libretto of an opera. The obstacle for the non-Italian reader is comparatively slight when he must guess that Scott's *Heart of Midlothian* has been retitled *Le Prigioni di Edimburgo;* it is somewhat more opaque when Whittier's *Snowbound* figures as *I Prigioneri della neve,* so that we must look them both up under the P's, although the latter imprisonment is purely metaphorical. The eighth tome of this fascinating work of reference has been reserved for *personaggi* from Gilgamesh to Superman, and the modern figure is neither the hero of Nietzsche nor the heroine of Shaw—neither a bird nor a plane—but the prodigy of the comic strips. Such personages, as Shakespeare could teach us if Clark Kent did not, have a way of stepping out of their contexts and leading lives of their own. Some characters, like those of the Commedia dell'Arte, exist independently of the many scenarios wherein they perform the same roles. New Comedy often changed its scene, but never its cast. Errant youths and heavy fathers, parasites and pandars, et cetera, were invariable with Plautus:

> haec urbs Epidamnus est, dum haec agitur fabula;
> quando alia agetur, aliud fiet oppidum,
> sicut familiae quoque solent mutarier:
> modo hic habitat leno, modo adulescens, modo senex,
> pauper, mendicus, rex, parasitus, hariolus.

Literary characterization, as distinguished from allegorical personification, is most fully embodied in individuals rather than fixed types. Such individuals, however, may come to typify some of their outstanding characteristics: the idiosyncratic Don Quixote becomes the generalization "quixotic." Indeed we might assume that a theme is a genus, handed down through impersonal tradition, and that the author stamps his individuality on the species. The book that deals most directly with our subject—with the subject matter of literature thematically conceived— is the compact and up-to-date lexicon of Elisabeth Frenzel, *Stoffe der Weltliteratur* (Stuttgart, 1962; revised, 1966, 1970). Herein the themes are presented as *Längschnitte,* longitudinal sections of literary history, printed under the names of their protagonists from Theodoric the Ostrogoth to Billy the Kid, with summaries of their successive incarnations in poems, plays, and books. The fact that Byron is represented and Homer is not reminds us of the increasing extent to which, over the centuries, poetry has become subjective and authors have confounded themselves with their characters. Though Venice is accorded a listing for the conspiracy that inspired Otway's *Venice Preserved* and one or two other writings (it was both the place and the subject for the 1955 congress of the International Comparative Literature Association), there is no entry for Rome—in spite of all the sentiments, ephemeral and eternal, which it has elicited from generations of poets and which have been recounted in Walter Rehm's *Europäische Romdichtung.*

Normally the assumption seems to be that a theme is identifiable by, if not completely interchangeable with, some particular hero. Such is the argument of Raymond Trousson, whose recent pamphlet bears the ballast of a triple title, *Un Problème de littérature comparée: les études de thèmes—essai de méthodologie* (Paris, 1965). In a substantial monograph, *Le Thème de Prométhée dans la littérature européenne* (Geneva, 1964), he has demonstrated how rewarding such a pursuit can be if its mythical protagonist holds as rich and varied a significance as Prometheus did for Aeschylus and Shelley, Tertullian and Shaftesbury, Hesiod and Gide. Another Belgian scholar, Robert Vivier, in *Frères du ciel* (Brussels, 1962), has broadened the issue by pursuing, rather more selectively and suggestively, the parallel and yet dissimilar flights of two classical prototypes for *hubris,* Icarus and Phaeton. M. Trousson would delimit a theme to a single figure, though he would pursue it through all its explicit phases. Yet Faust himself, ample and significant as his own manifestations have been, can also be treated as an extension of what E. M. Butler entitled *The Myth of the Magus.* (And the individualism of the romanticists can be universalized, as Ian Fletcher and his collaborators show in *Romantic Mythologies* [London, 1967].) M. Trousson's delimitation offers a practical alternative to the all-embracing categorization of Baldensperger and his disciples, and it receives some support from the influential handbook of Wolfgang Kayser, *Das Sprachliche Kunstwerk:* "Theme is always related to certain figures; it is more or less fixed in time and space."

But most of our thematologists would be interested in significant places as well as persons, not to mention ways of getting there, namely voyages. The *voyage imaginaire* is one of those genres determined by themes, and it ranges from fantasy to satire. Both are reflected, along with the ever-developing background of science, in Marjorie Nicolson's *Voyages to the Moon;* elsewhere, in *Mountain Gloom and Mountain Glory,* Miss Nicolson has shown how man's sense of infinitude has been affected by his fluctuating attitudes toward the landscape; while W. H. Auden, in *The Enchafèd Flood,* has focused his poetic insight on "The Romantic Iconography of the Sea." There seems to be a point, exemplified by Hardy and the naturalistic novelists, at which the setting of some works takes on a thematic aspect. In an epoch of unheroic modernity, when people must struggle with things, certain objects—notoriously the machine—have become crucial subjects: witness Leo Marx's instructive study of its impact on American writers, *The Machine in the Garden: Technology and the Pastoral Ideal in America* (New York, 1964). Frederick J. Hoffman has not flinched before the ultimate encounter of "Death and the Modern Imagination" in *The Mortal No* (Princeton, 1964). The meeting of lovers at dawn—surely one of the universals of culture—is the theme of *Eos,* a compilation latterly issued by experts working in some fifty languages. Sigmund Skard provided access to another branch of thematics in his bibliographical survey, *The Use of Color in Literature.* A study just published by Robert Martin Adams, *Nil: Episodes in the Literary Conquest of Void during the Nineteenth Century,* addresses itself to the *ne plus ultra,* the theme of nothingness. At the other extreme, literary accounts of the creation and its consequences, as analogous to *Paradise Lost,* are catalogued, translated, and reprinted by Watson Kirkconnell in *The Celestial Cycle.*

Dr. Frenzel has increased our debt to her with a little manual, *Stoff-, Motiv-, und Symbolforschung* (Stuttgart, 1963). We can take the symbology for granted in this connection, since it involves interpretations of *Stoff* and *Motiv,* whether they be patristic or psychoanalytic, and ask her how she discriminates between those other two concepts. Very simply, albeit she is conscious of more complex and confusing definitions: themes are primary, the raw materials of the writer's craft, while motifs are the basic situations as he begins to shape them. If in our tentative gropings we turn to the plastic arts, where criticism usually enjoys the benefits of more concrete perceptions, we find that usage diverges considerably. Motif seems to signify what is depicted—let us say a hillside in Provence—while theme means the manner of treatment, as it would differ between Cézanne and Van Gogh. So Erwin Panofsky's *Studies in Iconology* discusses the separation of themes and motifs during the Middle Ages and their reintegration during the Renaissance, which Jean Seznec illustrates by showing classical Virgins and Gothic nymphs in his *Survivance des dieux antiques.* Ernst Robert Curtius seems to come closer to the art historians than to his literary colleagues, when he pauses to define our terms in his essay on Hermann Hesse. "Motiv" is the objective factor for Curtius; it approximates the objective correlative of T. S. Eliot; it sets the plot in motion and holds it together. Whereas the "Thema" is the subjective component, the personal coloration, an endowment rather than a discovery, lyrical where the *Motiv* inclines to be epical or dramatic.

Note that Curtius, classicist that he was and Romance philologist, makes no use of *Stoff.* It is far from my purpose to quibble over terminology, even when some critics reverse the meaning that words have had for others, so long as their intentions are perfectly clear. The formulation works for Curtius as a distinction between subject and treatment, between what the artist draws out of the public domain and what he contributes out of the depths of his unique personality. To the concept of theme it adds a psychic charge which should be relevant in other connections. Its use of *Motiv* can be construed as a literary application of the module commonly used by the folklorists, which has its monument in Stith

Thompson's *Motif-Index of Folk-Literature*. Therein some 40,000 tales, myths, fables, romances, jestbooks, exempla—the corpus of nonliterary fiction—are categorized under twenty-three letters of the alphabet (three having been omitted to avoid typographical confusion). Naturally the letter A stands for accounts of the Creation; not surprisingly D, which is the rubric for stories involving magic, brings in the largest quantity of entries. Now there is nothing magical about the number 23, and there is something arbitrary in any system of taxonomy when it is applied to the irreducible factors of human behavior. There are about 800 types of fairy tales in the classification of Antti Aarne. More pertinently for us, his Finnish school, through its sustained endeavor to classify them, has been able to chart their migrations and metamorphoses.

Count Gozzi, the playwright, declared that there were just thirty-six plots for the stage—a declaration subsequently questioned by Schiller and confirmed by Goethe. A contemporary esthetician, Etienne Souriau, has refined the analysis with his book, *Les 200,000 Situations drama-tiques.* It does not very seriously matter how many there are; and, as potential spectators who would rather be surprised than bored, we really ought to prefer the larger figure. What matters are the natural ties that relate a twice-told tale to its archetypal source, the recognizable store of possibilities to which the world's fictions can be retraced, the continual recombination and ramification of traditional features to meet the onset of fresh experience. The universal custom of fabulation repeats itself in cross-cultural paradigms. How deeply the iceberg of culture itself sub-tends beneath the surface we have been coming to realize more and more. The sophisticated processes of a self-conscious literature do not differ as much as we used to think from the subliminal processes of folklore. The true cultural function of the nineteenth-century novel, as formulated by Mircea Eliade in *Images et symboles,* has been, "despite all its scientific, realistic, and social slogans," to comprise "the great reservoir of down-graded myths." What may seem detritus to a specialist in comparative religion, like Professor Eliade, may well seem refinement to a student of comparative literature. One man's notion of decadence is another's idea of progress. What matters, in such a circumstance, are the continuities.

The Sicilian storyteller Euhemerus has not left us much besides his name, which we invoke when admitting our predisposition to convert human beings into myths. Needless to add, this predisposition is dan-gerous, howbeit fundamental. The cause of enlightenment has been better served by the effort to demythologize. Friedrich Gundolf, whose thematic studies set the posthumous fame of Julius Caesar above the actuality of his historic career, ended by giving aid and comfort to one of the most heinous expressions of twentieth-century Caesarism, the imperial theme of Mussolini and Hitler. In our time we have watched history downgrading itself into legend. Nonetheless we must agree with Professor Eliade that mythopoeia continues from age to age, adapting itself to the exigencies of change for better and worse; and when the ancient demons go underground, their avatars are likely to reappear in the mass media. The most persistent continuity has been that of the classical pantheon. It was already scoffed at in the era of Lucian, yet the skeptical André Gide could take Theseus as the protagonist of his fictional testament. Iphigenia had as much vitality for Goethe as for Euripides; Antigone has been no less contemporaneous to Anouilh than to Sophocles; and the Agamemnon of William Alfred will not conclude the line that commenced with Aeschylus. The wanderings of Odysseus go far beyond Homer, as W.B. Stanford has retraced them in *The Ulysses Theme*. It follows that these protagonists must be polyvalent—that is to say, they embody values that vary from drama to drama and from period to period.

Myth is bound to be colored by the mythographers: consider the varying viewpoints of Hesiod, Ovid, Natalis Comes, Lemprière, Bulfinch, W. H. Roscher, Robert Graves. Those of us who were introduced to the Greeks by *Tanglewood Tales* may have grown up with unduly puritanical notions about them: Hawthorne's Hecate, for instance, when dazzled by the radiance of Phoebus, suggests that he ought to be wearing a black veil. Thanks to humanistic education, the retired Olympian gods and the unemployed Greek heroes have maintained their prestige in the West, though it has been challenged by their chthonic counterparts from the Norse Valhalla. By the device of *figura,* which Erich Auerbach has done so much to illuminate, Christendom was enabled to absorb Jewish prophets and even pagan demigods into its typology of saints. The Fathers of the Church reinterpreted episodes from the Old Testament—and, in carefully selected cases, the classics—as prefigurations of the Gospels. But this did not obliterate the sharp line between revealed truth and poetic fable. Milton was sternly criticized by more rigid classicists for composing an epic about the Christian revelation, and for personifying Sin and Death allegorically, rather than drawing his cast of characters from legend or romance. Dante intermingled mythical, legendary, and historical figures, but each of them was allotted an orthodox place in his afterworld. The point is that they all preexisted somewhere in the racial memory; except for personifications, it would have been inconceivable for him to invent a character.

Medieval literature drew upon a syncretic and secular mythology, epitomized by the canon of the Nine Worthies: "Three paynims, three Jews, and three Christian men." Equally triadic was the body of material that lay at the disposal of the romancers: the matter of France, the matter of Britain, and that of Rome the grand—still grand enough to include some relics of Greece and, above all, Troy. The utilization of those three matters in poetry was not limited to the countries they represented. King Arthur and his Knights served as heroes for Chrétien de Troyes and Hartmann von Aue; Charlemagne and his Paladins evolved the rallying cries for Italian heroic romance. Our understanding of Shakespeare is somewhat beclouded by a failure to appreciate his relation to his thematic material, to the stuff that dreams and dramas are made of. We are now ready to concede, on the internal evidence of what he managed to write, that he was a cultivated reader; we can conscientiously reread the British chronicles, the Greco-Roman biographies, and the Italianate *novelle* that furnished the eclectic grist for his unexampled mill; but we are still embarrassed by naïve presuppositions about artistic originality, or else intimidated by labored reductions of art to its sources and influences—whereas to see the problem as one of selection from the available narratives and adaptation to the dynamics of the theater is to gain insights into Shakespeare's dramaturgy. What he left out can be quite as meaningful, in this light, as what he concentrated upon or interpolated.

The marriage of the Ovidian enchantress Titania to the gnome king of Germanic lore, Oberon or Alberich, attended by the thoroughly English Puck or Robin Goodfellow, is a characteristic *discordia concors,* a harmony produced from the very disparity of its components. We may not award Shakespeare the palm when we remember what Homer and Chaucer did with the two plots he reworked in *Troilus and Cressida,* yet the conjunction raises some major critical questions. Corneille was attacked by the formalistic critics of his day, who invidiously compared *Le Cid* with models of neoclassical tragedy. A thematic criticism, by contrasting the play with Spain's national epic about the same hero, might have widened the whole esthetic perspective. The extensive scrutiny that has been accorded to Shakespeare's imagery, when it has not been sidetracked by psychological or biographical curiosity, may afford further encouragement for thematics. An image may be too slight to constitute a theme; but, as a verbal and visual unit, it can carry a theme by association; and, in a cluster, it can help to organize that coordination of speech and action which fulfills the dramatic design. A case in point would be the sequence of images relating to horses and serpents, which are respectively associated with Anthony and Cleopatra. Indeed the image has become so pervasive a part of our lives, and we are such an image-conscious society, that the economist Kenneth Boulding has proposed it as the nucleus of a new science—or, at any rate, a means of unifying the social sciences—to be known as Eiconics.

To be sure, it is the plastic arts that display the most tangible icons; and art history has developed a discipline for revealing the ideas that are symbolized in its painted or sculptured images. To follow Edgar Wind's interpretation of "The School of Athens" is to realize how vast a train of philosophical thought lies behind the sensuous brush strokes of a Raphael. In order to profit from the stimulating example of the iconologist, the would-be thematologist must be comparably well informed in the history of ideas. Here he may have learned some clarifying lessons from the philosopher-historian Arthur Lovejoy, whose work has conjoined so fruitfully with literary studies. Some of those key ideas, which he and his colleagues and students have signalized and tracked down, were diffused in the guise of literary themes, such as the attitude of primitivism so closely related to the pastoral mode. Lovejoy's Great Chain of Being itself might be viewed as a gigantic image, an unchanging outline for speculations which have altered with the intellectual climate, from the spiritual hierarchy of the Neoplatonists to the Darwinian struggle for existence. The theme is thus the avenue for a progression of ideas, whose entrance into literature it invites and facilitates. For those who like their great ideas made easy, authorities from the University of Chicago have fixed them at a definite number, derived them from a set of books they happen to sell, and indexed them in what is loudly advertised as a "Syntopicon."

Their enterprise, for all its self-promotion, has about it a quirk of medievalism. During the Middle Ages, when high culture was regulated by a Latin canon whose forms were static, when living authors were frankly derivative and readers depended heavily on excerpts, abridgments, and compendia, ideas tended to crystallize into set topics or commonplaces. Those *topoi*, as Curtius has magisterially demonstrated in *Europäische Literatur und lateinisches Mittelalter,* were links that ultimately transmitted the remote past of Greece and Rome to the awakening

Europe of Dante's vision. A *topos* is a theme in the most expressly rhetorical sense: it may be a purple passage from an oration, a standardized description of a locality, or an elaborately protracted metaphor—such as the stock comparison of nature to a book, which is as old as the Phoenicians and as modern as Shakespeare. The rise of scientific empiricism would discourage such an analogy, just as the more naturalistic viewpoint of the Renaissance and subsequent epochs would foster an augmenting individualism, a mentality less receptive to the typical than to the original, more impatient with received ideas and prone to dismiss *topoi* as mere clichés. This does not mean that themes would not persist, but that they would take on more protean shapes. Charles Mauron pointed in a cyclic direction when he collected his interpretations of certain moderns under the title, *Des Métaphores obsédantes au mythe personnel* (Paris, 1963).

A personal myth, of course, is a contradiction in terms. In moving away from the traditional and the general, the cycle has moved toward the particular and the autobiographical, since when the writer rejects his inherited stock of subjects, he is forced back upon the innermost resources of the self. Then, half-consciously, his state of mind is projected through a series of obsessive metaphors, almost as if an artist were inscribing his signature. Along with the obsessions that have been transposed into myths by the artistry of French writers, in M. Mauron's account, we might adduce Poe's claustrophobia, Hawthorne's secret chambers, or Melville's feelings for blood brotherhood. English critics long have recognized the detection of fervors and recurrences as a way of bringing out a writer's distinctive pattern. When I tried to sketch a critical profile of Christopher Marlowe's shaping spirit, my poet—individualist though he was—led me back recurrently and fervently to the classic myth of Icarus. The *psychocritique* of M. Mauron, which is based on subtle perception rather than amateur psychoanalysis, should be differentiated from such procrustean undertakings as J.-P. Wéber's *Domaines thématiques* (Paris, 1964). M. Wéber, after surveying an author through the totality of his work, reduces it rigidly to a single theme, e.g. a clock for Vigny. Jean-Pierre Richard has labeled this type of criticism with the unhappy adjective *totalitaire,* and Raymond Picard has polemicized against it in *Nouvelle critique ou nouvelle imposture* (Paris, 1965).

The most far-reaching effort to probe the poet's consciousness—if not to fathom the collective unconscious—has been the suggestive investigation of the late Gaston Bachelard. Professor Bachelard, the Sorbonne philosopher, shifted in midcareer from science to poetry in order to come to terms with "l'imagination matérielle," with nothing less than the mind's direct response to the universe, with matter itself in its pristine reduction and the attempts of man's imagination to grasp it through the four elements: fire, water, air, earth. His introductory volume, *La Psychanalyse du feu,* is at once more and less than it claims to be. To be precise, material things cannot be psychoanalyzed, nor is the analyst trying to set his couch on fire; this is "a psychoanalysis of subjective convictions relating to our awareness of the phenomena of fire." Drawing upon mythology like Freud, Bachelard diagnoses "the Prometheus complex" as "the Oedipus complex of intellectual life." Proceeding mainly by free association, and illustrating richly by quotation from the more intuitive and surrealistic poets, he has completed his elemental scheme with additional books on *l'eau, l'air, la terre,* and the several kinds of revery that they respectively stimulate. A more discriminating and systematic inquiry is promised by Bernhard Blume's articles on islands and rivers in German poetry. An overambitious venture, subjecting the imaginative faculty to historical and even statistical analysis, has been made by Jacques Bousquet in *Les Thèmes du rêve dans la littérature romantique: essai sur la naissance et l'évolution des images* (Paris, 1964).

To apprehend and characterize the mental landscapes of individual authors, to distinguish their lights and shades, their recognizable contours and sensory attributes, is the aim of an enlarging school which has sometimes been adventurous enough to describe its approach as phenomenological. Its most intrepid proponent, Georges Poulet, with his *Etudes sur le temps humain,* perceptively explored the sense of time in Proust and others less overtly immersed in it. With a companion study, *La Distance intérieure,* Professor Poulet turned from the temporal to the spatial dimensions of literature. Mallarmé was his principal warrant there; some of his other subjects seem less amenable to the sort of abstraction he strove to impose upon them. Isolated lines from Marivaux ("I am lost, my head whirls, I know not where I am!") may be quoted to lend a facile impression of metaphysical pathos or existential vertigo. But in their contexts they express no more than the age-old confusions of comedy, and can be vulgarly paralleled up and down the history of the stage. Jean-Pierre Richard gets farther, in *Littérature et sensation,* because his measuring rod is stylistics, not metaphysics. All close reading entails a certain amount of impressionistic subjectivity, not less so when it looks at interiors than when it looks at surfaces. When the reader is

Virginia Woolf, commenting on the Brontës' love of red carpets, or
Proust, discerning Stendhal's fixation on heights, then the intuition is
worth our while. But when J. Hillis Miller traverses "the inner space" of
Yeats's or Eliot's poems, the result is a heavy-footed superimposition.

That, by stressing distance, duration, coloring, or tactile values, a critic
actually penetrates to the interior of a writer's mind, alas, is merely another metaphor. Such concerns fill in our comprehension of the thematic
texture; but, like those famous *nouveaux romans,* they leave us lonely
in a world from which the humanity seems to have been abstracted.
After all, it was the threatened disintegration of character that prompted
modern novelists, in the wake of Joyce, to seek mythic prototypes. The
prototype for Leopold Bloom is Ulysses; yet unofficially he seems to have
more in common with the Wandering Jew; and there are moments
when he would like to imagine himself as Mozart's Don Giovanni—
who in turn, was one of more than 500 reincarnations of Don Juan
Tenorio in song and story. (Actually, Bloom's operatic stand-in is less
distinguished and more vulnerable: the jealous peasant Masetto.) Where
the authorities disagree so completely, there is not much hope of reaching
a consensus; but, so far as the disagreement is verbal, it may point the
way to a critical redefinition. If there is any agreement that a theme
should be identified with the name of a personage, then it may be said
that the theme of Don Juan has occasioned some 500 variations. We are
accustomed to evoke him as the very model of a single-minded amorist,
and that impression is amply corroborated by Leporello's statistics in
the opera. Yet no human personality is ever reducible to a single trait;
even the Marquis de Sade occasionally had other matters than sex upon
his mind.

Don Juan's original role, in the play by Tirso de Molina, was that of
an all-round trickster, whose seductions were simply one of his many
engaging tricks. His greatest part, in Molière's sinister comedy, was that
of a sardonic iconoclast, a libertine in thought as well as love. The constant feature of his variable legend is the dénouements, when the statue
drags him down to hell. This is a fate which he shares with his northern
contemporary, Faust, who paralleled his career in other spheres. However, the version of the Faust theme that we accept as the greatest,
Goethe's, softened by the romantic cult of womanhood, overturns the
somber Lutheran object lesson and replaces damnation by salvation.
Thus a theme may veer from one extreme to the other. The infernal
ending of both legends is classifiable as a motif; for if themes are linked

to characters, motifs are segments of plot. The tale of Romeo and Juliet is one theme, and that of Pyramus and Thisbe another; but they share the same motif, the tryst in the tomb, which also has some relevance for Tristram and Iseult. When Shakespeare burlesqued Pyramus and Thisbe in *A Midsummer Night's Dream,* he retained the thematic story-line while transforming the emotional charge. A comic theme may have a serious purport. The comedies about Amphitryon are so numerous that Giraudoux numbered his version 38, and the professional thematologists have multiplied that reckoning. An earlier, more fragmentary treatment, the Reformation interlude of *Jack Juggler,* exploits the confrontation of the twin Sosias, when Mercury assumes the body of Amphitryon's servant, to satirize the doctrine of transubstantiation.

Themes, like symbols then, are polysemous: that is, they can be endowed with different meanings in the face of differing situations. This is what makes an inquiry into their permutations an adventure in the history of ideas (see Don Cameron Allen on Noah or George K. Anderson on the Wandering Jew). Our knowledge can be enriched by finding out why certain themes have been chosen at certain periods (the Wagnerian resurrection of the *Nibelungenlied*) or in certain localities (the Vergilian linkage of Rome with Troy) or by certain authors—why should the saintly figure of Joan of Arc have impressed such skeptics as Mark Twain, Bernard Shaw, and Anatole France, while failing to win the sympathy of Shakespeare? Themes, like biological entities, seem to have their cycles, phases of growth, of heyday, and of decline, as with Troilus and Cressida. It is not surprising, in our latter day, that so many of them seem to have reached a state of exhaustion. Audiences get tired of hearing the same old names, and writers find it harder and harder to compete with their illustrious forerunners. But motifs seem inexhaustible. As long as man's aspirations and limitations are what they have been, his journey through life will be envisioned as an intercepted quest, like that of *Moby-Dick.* He will sooner or later find himself located somewhere, and place will be sublimated by dream. His ego will invoke its alter ego, its double or *Doppelgänger,* whether in reflection of the author's intimate bond with his protagonist or with his reader ("mon semblable, mon frère") or by the sort of optical illusion that projects a fabric for our fantasies.

If a theme itself can be so concretely pinned down, particularized into a local habitation and a name, the speculative area of thematics remains much wider and more flexible: witness the timely study of Eugene H.

Falk, *Types of Thematic Structure: The Nature and Function of Motifs in Gide, Camus, and Sartre* (Chicago, 1967). What is called thematism, in Bernard Weinberg's introduction, embraces much of what used to be set aside as having to do with the externals of literature. We are now willing to admit that a writer's choice of a subject is an esthetic decision, that the conceptual outlook is a determining part of the structural pattern, that the message is somehow inherent in the medium. The scenery and the ideology are not less basic to the main design than the accepted constituents of plot and character. Ideas play their roles by appearing in the garb of images. Whatever the writer undertakes to describe, by the act of his description, becomes a contributing feature of the final arrangement. It emanates in large part from his powers of observation and his years of experience, but perhaps in larger part from a common store of associations and memories which—vast and varying as they are —tend nonetheless to assume familiar guises and to display recurrent characteristics. Criticism must teach itself to recognize them, to discriminate between their more and less creative embodiments, to place and relate them all within the continuous order of those things which men have imagined. Thereby we may come to understand what the imagination is, how it works, what it needs to work upon, how by selecting and arranging it modifies and transforms, how it enhances life by endowing it with meanings and with values.

TWO *ROMANISTEN* IN AMERICA:
SPITZER AND AUERBACH

What is exemplified here through two related figures, with whom I had the good fortune to be in contact, is the unique contribution that the forced exile of European intellectuals brought to our culture during the middle years of the twentieth century. This, in its academic aspect primarily, was the theme of the second annual *Perspectives in American History,* edited by Bernard Bailyn and Donald Fleming, and sponsored by the Charles Warren Center for Studies in American History, Harvard University. Entitled *The Intellectual Migration: Europe and America, 1930–1960,* it was supplemented with biographical listings and republished between hard covers by Harvard University Press the following year (1969). The volume comprises a series of brief surveys and personal testimonials, ranging through many fields from theoretical physics to art history— *mémoires pour servir* toward the more compendious account that some day should do fuller justice to the historic shift and the intercultural adjustment. The special problems of the situation, as they affect the literary expatriate, form the subject of my essay, "Literature and Exile" (*Refractions*).

I

The literary event to which I owe my acquaintance with Erich Auerbach happens to have been the birth of Cervantes. In the fall of 1947, four hundred years afterward, it was being commemorated at Harvard University by a series of lectures and conferences. Américo Castro, whom I likewise had the pleasure of meeting on that occasion, was naturally among the presiding spirits. One of the private receptions took place at the home of Amado Alonso, who himself had twice become an émigré. As a young Spaniard, trained at the Centro de Estudios Históricos in Madrid, he had emigrated to Buenos Aires, where he had been placed in charge of the Institute de Filología. As a leader in the academic opposition to Perón, he had just been compelled to leave Argentina a year before. His decision to settle in the United States signalized a revival of Hispanic studies at Harvard—though his leadership of it would, alas, be cut short by his premature death in 1952. From the hospitable Don Amado I gathered that Auerbach, of whose work I then had barely heard, was present by a happy accident. He had just come for the first time to America, where he would be spending the rest of his career, and was here in Cambridge to visit a son who was studying chemistry at the Harvard Graduate School.

The man I met was slight and dark, gentle to the point of diffidence, yet lively and engaging in conversation, speaking mostly French at that time, and looking not unlike one of those kindly ferrets in the illustrations of children's books. Though he had recently published *Mimesis,* and would shortly have his Swiss publisher send me a copy, he was not sanguine about its impact on either side of the Atlantic. Though he was on leave of absence from his chair of Romance Philology at the Turkish State University in Istanbul, he spoke with candor and modesty about his possible willingness to accept an American professorship. Finding that we had much to talk about, both on a theoretical and on a practical plane, we agreed to lunch together a few days later. Our lunching place deserves at least a footnote in the annals of cultural migration. The Window Shop was started during the nineteen-thirties, by a group of Harvard faculty wives, as a means of finding employment for German and Austrian refugees. Having flourished, it had moved along into a well-known habitat on Brattle Street, which had formerly been a New England tea-room and had originally been the smithy of Longfellow's Village Blacksmith. Where the spreading chestnut tree had stood, *Sacher Torte* was now the specialty of a Viennese menu.

Regularly favored by the patronage of the stately Hellenist, Werner Jaeger, and of other scholarly expatriates, this was our local Cantabrigian symbol of the great American melting pot. Auerbach seemed pleased to be taken there, and our dialogue opened with a polite exchange about the tenor of life in Cambridge, Massachusetts. Prompted by his questions, I found myself repeating an old byword about the Galata Bridge at Istanbul: that, if you sat there long enough, all the world would pass by. Auerbach, whose penetrant eyes had been inspecting the situation, did not immediately respond. Instead he rose, excused himself, and walked to a neighboring table. Its occupant, who warmly greeted him, was—as Auerbach explained on his return—an American with whom he had been acquainted in Istanbul. Coincidence had reinforced my groping parallel. In the ensuing discussion he made it clear why he no longer wished to sit and wait at his Turkish bridge. Whether, by crossing the seas, he had come to another Byzantium, worthier of Yeats's ideals for a holy city of the arts, might well have been in doubt. But America, at any rate, had niches ready to be filled by wandering sages. Belatedly yet wholeheartedly, Auerbach joined that throng of European intellectuals who passed by the transatlantic bridge, to the vast enrichment of our culture.

Born in 1892 at Berlin, Erich Auerbach had proceeded through his earlier studies to a doctoral degree in law at Heidelberg. After his military service, he shifted his interest to Romance philology, taking a second doctorate at Greifswald in 1921 with a thesis on the Italian and French *novella* of the early Renaissance. For several years thereafter he was employed by the Prussian State Library, while publishing a number of translations from the Italian—notably a German version of Vico's *Scienza Nuova,* which was to be a main guidepost in the development of his own thought. In 1929, when he was named professor at the University of Marburg, he brought out his compact study of Dante, which characteristically emphasizes the earthly aspects of the *Divina Commedia.* After six years, he was forced out of his appointment by the Nazi government. Like so many German intellectuals, he took the path of exile that led to Turkey. He was appointed to his new university post in 1936, and served for the next eleven years. One of the by-products of his teaching was a small handbook, prepared for the orientation—or, perhaps we should say, the occidentation—of his Turkish students.[1] This introductory sketch of the Romance languages and literatures offers no hint of those special insights which he was even then beginning to generate.

One of his anecdotes casts a comic light upon the sense of disconnection from which he must have suffered. On taking up his official duties at Istanbul, he was introduced to various Turks with whom, it was presumed, he would have much in common. One of them, understandably, was the Turkish translator of Dante, whose rendering of the *Commedia* had been accomplished in less than two years; indeed it would have been completed sooner, he boasted, had he not also been translating potboilers during the same interim. When Auerbach congratulated him on his presumable grasp of the language, this colleague blandly confessed that he knew no Italian at all. His brother did; but that was scarcely a help, since the brother had been away at the time. To Auerbach's obvious question, his informant replied that he had worked from a French translation. Auerbach, doing his best to keep his eye-

---

1. Erich Auerbach, *Introduction aux études de philologie romane* (Frankfurt, 1949). This is the original text of which a Turkish translation was published at Istanbul in 1944. The English translation by Guy Daniels, *Introduction to Romance Languages and Literature* (New York, 1961), is abridged and not entirely accurate.

brows from twitching, asked which one. "I don't recall the name," said the Turk, "but it was a large brown book." What could be expected, under these circumstances, from so highly qualified a *Gelehrter* as Auerbach? He would be working, as he liked to put it, "dans un grenier." After he had used up his backlog of notes, he would have to suspend his medieval researches. In the absence of learned journals, compilations, and commentaries, how could one continue to be a scholar?

To be sure, there was a fair collection of the major authors of the West. And it is true that, in countries where seminars were grinding out professors and bibliographical tools were being multiplied, critics had begun to wonder whether all the philological apparatus was not obscuring the literary artistry. A certain correlation was suspected between the short-sightedness of footnote-scholarship, *Anmerkungswissenschaft,* and the acquiescence of the German universities to the Hitler regime. Auerbach, at all events, could never be deprived of his own learning and training. His artistic perceptions, innately keen, had been broadened by historical perspectives acquired from Vico and from Vico's modern apostle, Benedetto Croce. He found himself perforce in the position of writing a more original kind of book than he might otherwise have attempted, if he had remained within easy access to the stock professional facilities. There is not a single footnote in the English edition of *Mimesis,* and the only ones in the German edition are simply Auerbach's translations of the texts already cited in foreign languages.[2] Each of these is the theme of a chapter devoted to its stylistic interpretation. But the sequence of twenty chapters also comprises an anthology— or, better, an imaginary museum—of European civilization extending, across three millennia and eight languages, from Homer to Virginia Woolf.

Ever since Aristotle expostulated with Plato over the imitation of nature, *mímesis* has been the central and most problematic concept of esthetics and criticism. Auerbach's subtitle pins it down to the representation of reality by means of words, so that textual explication becomes the key to a concrete understanding of the occidental past. Realism in the explicit sense, as practised by the French novelists, is telescoped

2. Erich Auerbach, *Mimesis: Dargestellte Wirklichkeit in der abendländischen Literatur* (Bern, 1946). The excellent English translation by W. R. Trask, *Mimesis: The Representation of Reality in Western Literature* (Princeton, 1953), contains an additional chapter on *Don Quixote,* originally written for the Spanish edition.

into two dense chapters toward the end of the book.[3] Equally real, for Auerbach, are a mob scene under the Roman Empire and the stream of Mrs. Ramsay's consciousness in *To the Lighthouse*. The selection of passages to be chronologically analyzed is always interesting and often surprising. The recognition of Odysseus by Euryclea, Eve and the serpent in a mystery play, Manon Lescaut and her lover at supper, Pantagruel's mouth viewed as a microcosm—these are privileged moments if not epiphanies. We are plunged into particularity without any introduction. Auerbach shies away from generalization, though a brief epilogue draws together the guiding threads of his approach.[4] His starting point is the canonical assumption of traditional rhetoric, the separation it maintained between grand and humble styles, plus the subsequent conditions of their intermixture, so deliberate in the Bible and elsewhere, with an effect of elevating the commonplace which has social as well as esthetic implications.

His other key idea, which more peculiarly bears the stamp of his thinking and derives from his work as a medievalist, is the exegetical device of *figura*. That rhetorical term of the ancients had been utilized by the early Christians, when they saw the personages and events of the Gospels prefigured in the narratives of the Old Testament. In the Middle Ages it was invoked to show how a particular manifestation could express a transcendental reality. Thus it illuminates the vivid concreteness of Dante's otherworldly allegory. Auerbach had traced and formulated this conception through an article first published in Italy at the outset of the Second World War.[5] (A decade afterward I sat next to him at a meeting of the Modern Language Association, watching his weary smile and hearing his wry comment, as an American colleague made effective but unacknowledged use of his method.) Since *mimesis* is realistic by definition, and *figura* is a symbolic mode, one of the contributions of Auerbach's book is to demonstrate precisely how they conjoin and enmesh. He wrote to me that his European reviewers, though they were friendly, looked upon *Mimesis* as no more than "an amusing series of analyses (in?) of style."[6] Having hoped that his integrating ideas would

3. Cf. the remark of René Wellek, "Auerbach's Special Realism," *Kenyon Review*, XVI, 1 (Winter, 1954), 301: "it concerns not realism but man's attitudes toward the world in general."
4. Auerbach found occasion to amplify and clarify his position in "Epilegomena zu Mimesis," *Romanische Forchungen*, LXV (1954), 1/2, 1–18.
5. Erich Auerbach, "Figura," *Archivum Romanicum*, XXII (October–December, 1938), 429–489; reprinted in *Neue Dantestudien* (Istanbul, 1944) and translated into English by Ralph Manheim in *Scenes from the Drama of European Literature* (New York, 1959).
6. Letter from Erich Auerbach to Harry Levin, December 15, 1951.

be noticed and discussed, he transferred his hopes to the English edition, which was laboriously being prepared under the sponsorship of the Bollingen Foundation.

Meanwhile he had received his first American appointment from Pennsylvania State College, where—in addition to his teaching in Romance languages—he taught a course in Goethe for the German department. After a mutually satisfactory year he would have been given tenure, but for a technicality which arose when the prerequisite medical examination revealed a heart condition. He was enabled to spend a congenial interlude at the Institute for Advanced Study in Princeton, where he also gave one of the Christian Gauss Seminars. In 1950 he was called to Yale, and he passed his last years on that distinguished faculty which includes such cosmopolitan figures as Henri Peyre and René Wellek. His position there he described as "almost ideal."[7] He had occupied the transitional years in "filling up the enormous lacunae in bibliography, and western life in general, caused by the eleven years in Turkey—adaptation to academic and literary life in USA . . ." He was delighted to have generous hours for reading and writing, along with a few courses wholly devoted to medieval subjects. His essay applying the stylistic theories of *Mimesis* to Baudelaire and modern poetry, he declared, would be his farewell to modernity.[8] My feelings of loss were all the more poignant, when he died in the fall of 1957, because he had accepted an invitation to teach the course in Dante at Harvard that year. "Had we but world enough and time . . ."

Marvell's line is quoted on the title page of *Mimesis,* whose dates of composition are also given on the verso: "Mai 1942 bis April 1945." Partly to fill in temporal gaps from the resources of American libraries, Auerbach's later investigations were again specialized and concentrated on more distant periods. They are vivified by a percipient reader's concern with the nature of the reading public, manifested earlier through a study of the role the audience had played in French classicism.[9] His illumination of the dark ages before the invention of printing should counterbalance the postliterate sociology of Marshall McLuhan. The introduction to Auerbach's final volume harks back to his earliest men-

---

7. Letter from Erich Auerbach to Harry Levin, October 21, 1951.

8. Letter from Auerbach to Harry Levin, January 12, 1949.

9. Erich Auerbach, "La Cour et la ville," in *Vier Untersuchungen zur Geschichte der Französischen Bildung* (Bern, 1951), a volume dedicated to Leo Spitzer. Manheim's English translation of this article appears in *Scenes from the Drama of European Literature.*

tor, Vico, and reaffirms the commitment to historicism they shared.[10] In
contrast to the medievalism of Ernst Robert Curtius, Auerbach stresses
changes rather than continuities. History, as he conceives it, is recorded
consciousness, to be interpreted by continual scrutiny of the surviving
records. For the questionable absolutes of *Geistesgeschichte,* he would
substitute a relativistic perspective, which seeks realities in those different places where our differing predecessors have found it.[11] What con-
fers a unity on this outlook is a vision of Europe intensified by successive expatriations to the east and west. A posthumous collection is
entitled *Scenes from the Drama of European Literature.* Now and then
an elegiac tone hints to us that the drama is a tragedy which has entered its last act.

2

One of Leo Spitzer's favorite words—which, of course, he brilliantly
elucidated—was *ambiente.* Though I was more casually acquainted
with him than with Auerbach, I had the chance to meet Spitzer in his
American ambiance, at a time when he had comfortably settled into it.
The scale of the Johns Hopkins University, and its emphasis on its
graduate program, evidently brought out the personalities of its professors in a way which must have been comparable to the German
universities before the war. I had been invited in 1950 to read a paper
to the Hopkins seminar in literary criticism. To my surprise and embarrassment I perceived in my audience the very man to whom I should
have been listening, probably the greatest living virtuoso of the *explication de texte.* I felt some slight protection in the fact that my subject
was a contemporary American writer, though I was unprepared for
Spitzer's analogy between Ernest Hemingway's metaphors and those
of the Church Fathers. Still, it was flattering to have a commentator
who had produced so impressive a body of commentary himself; and,
on the whole, he was much kinder to me than I deserved. As it hap-

10. Erich Auerbach, *Literatursprache und Publikum in der Lateinischen Spätantike und im
Mittelalter* (Bern, 1958); translated into English by Ralph Manheim as *Literary Language and Its
Public in Late Latin Antiquity and the Middle Ages* (New York, 1965), with a full bibliography of
Auerbach's writings.
11. For a differing opinion on this point, registered by a close colleague, cf. René Wellek,
"Erich Auerbach (1887–1957)," *Comparative Literature,* X, 1 (Winter, 1958), 94. See also Dante
Della Terza, "Erich Auerbach," *Belfagor* XVIII, 3 (May, 1963), 306–322, and W. B. Fleischmann,
"Erich Auerbach's Critical Theory and Practice: An Assessment," *Modern Language Notes,*
LXXXI, 5 (December, 1966), 535–541.

pened, he had only one criticism to offer, and he offered it with some urbanity. But, as those who knew him better could have predicted, it was sufficient to cast doubts on whatever I had been attempting to demonstrate.

Though the substance of my remarks proved somehow acceptable, I had been proceeding in methodological error. Having started properly enough by analyzing a passage, I had then gone astray, and had sought to illustrate the range of my author's style with brief quotations gathered here and there throughout his work. Spitzer fervently believed, and I should have remembered, that the explicator's task is to extract the quintessence of an author from a single text, selected with care for the purpose. Thus the choice is the strategic step, and the process is like plucking the flower in the crannied wall, whose immanent secret could teach us the knowledge of God and man. That this was a highly mystical conception Spitzer admitted, when he summed up explication as "a theodicy in a nutshell."[12] There was something rabbinical, an austerely patriarchal dedication, about the truly leonine figure he cut. His mode of writing reveals him as a secular Talmudist, sometimes almost a Kabbalist, a high priest amid the hieratic mysteries of literature. In any case, after scoring his point and setting me straight, he showed his warmly sociable side. We had a long walk and a good talk next day. I got a glimpse of his Faustian study—described by his gifted colleague, the Spanish man of letters Pedro Salinas, as an alchemist's laboratory.[13] Its emblem was a portrait of the philologist's patron, Saint Jerome, with the lion very much in evidence.

Leo Spitzer was born in Vienna in 1887. He took his doctorate at the university of his native city in 1910, working chiefly under Wilhelm Meyer-Lübke, the redoubtable etymologist of the Romance languages. Spitzer was fond of recollecting his master, with praise for his rigor and blame for his rigidity. So vivacious a pupil was bound to rebel against a positivistic philology, which altogether divorced linguistics from literature. Moreover, he had another Viennese master, more dynamic if unofficial, in Freud; Freudian psychoanalysis was to have a marked influence on Spitzerian stylistics, which in turn would help to bridge the gulf between linguistics and literature. For a trial lecture that he was asked to give, in qualifying for the post of *Privatdozent,* Spitzer haz-

---

12. Leo Spitzer, *Linguistics and Literary History: Essays in Stylistics* (Princeton, 1948), p. 128.
13. Pedro Salinas, "Esquicio de Leo Spitzer," printed as an introduction to Spitzer's *Essays in Historical Semantics* (New York, 1948), p. xvii.

arded the disapproval of his medievalistic seniors by holding forth upon a contemporary novelist, Matilde Serao. This avid interest in the present would not decline with his own advancing years; one of his unfinished projects was to have been devoted to *le nouveau roman*. He was always intensely concerned with the word—not merely *la langue* but *la parole*—as the vital link in the chain of human intercourse. Out of his experience as an Austrian censor during the First World War came a study of circumlocutions for hunger among Italian military prisoners. Again, a mother's pet-name for a child provided him with material for a psycholinguistic inquiry.

He managed to bring his solid training in *Wortbildungslehre* to the service of literary art at its most creative, by centering his doctoral dissertation upon the techniques of word formation used by Rabelais. The contributions that came after this one in such dazzling profusion, and on so ubiquitous a variety of subjects, assured him quick advancement in the hierarchy of learning. He taught at the University of Bonn from 1920 to 1925, when he was appointed to the professorship at Marburg. Auerbach succeeded him in that chair, when Spitzer was called to Cologne in 1930. Three years later National Socialism began to decimate the German faculties, and—again preceding Auerbach—Spitzer found a temporary position at Istanbul. The relative inadequacy of the Turkish libraries—which would turn out to be a blessing in disguise for Auerbach—made a long sojourn unthinkable for Spitzer, who gladly accepted the call from Johns Hopkins in 1936. The two scholars kept in touch from a distance, and followed each other's work with mutual esteem. They would be brought into closer relations when Auerbach eventually came to America, and one of his later volumes is dedicated to Spitzer. But Istanbul represents a parting of the ways, insofar as its lack of scholarly paraphernalia drew a sharp line between the two approaches within the same field: the infra-scholarship of Spitzer and the para-scholarship of Auerbach.

Both men were aware of their divergence. Spitzer considered Auerbach's emphasis, in contrast with his own, to be sociohistorical rather than strictly stylistic.[14] Auerbach, while praising Spitzer for his tenacious pursuit of individual forms, acknowledged a more general intention: "My purpose is always to write history."[15] Spitzer had begun by

14. Leo Spitzer, "Les Etudes de style et les différents pays," in *Langue et Littérature: Actes du VIIIe Congrès de la Fédération Internationale des Langues et Littératures Modernes* (Paris, 1961), p. 28.

15. Auerbach, *Literary Language,* p. 20.

reacting against an old-fashioned school of literary historiography, based narrowly upon biographical data, in favor of an esthetic and psychological approach. Since style is the unique use that the individual makes of a common language, it discloses itself in deviations from norms; hence its analyst, emulating the psychoanalyst, looks for verbal tics and tries to account for them. Spitzer's monograph on Henri Barbusse, for example, lays bare the persistent imagery of violence in the vocabulary of that ardent pacifist. "The Style of Diderot," under Spitzer's investigation, appears to be regulated by sexual rhythms. The diction of Charles Péguy reflects his assent to the metaphysics of Bergson. In the slang of Charles-Louis Philippe, an obsessive repetition of one phrase, "à cause de," betrays a subconscious determinism. But Spitzer was no less concerned with form than with psychology, and some of his critical concepts are useful tools. The concept of chaotic enumeration clarifies the structure of Claudel's poems—or, for that matter, Whitman's. The principle of linguistic perspectivism helps to explain the oscillations of viewpoint in *Don Quixote*.

Problems of meaning were ultimately philosophical, to one who believed in speech as a reflection of *Weltanschauung*. Social tensions were illuminated when Spitzer traced such expressions as *Schadenfreude* or *Gentile*. His arrival in Baltimore brought about a stimulating conjunction, since the Hopkins—through the learned and lucid endeavors of Arthur Lovejoy—had become a center for the history of ideas. Insofar as that discipline might reduce literature to a handmaid of philosophy, Spitzer had and voiced his reservations.[16] But the intellectual cross-fertilization inspired him to his farthest-ranging studies in semantics: the related pair of monographs on the terms *milieu* and *ambiance* and on the long tradition of cosmic order subsumed by *Stimmung*. Auerbach's reorientation was limited by the circumstance that he spent hardly more than a decade in the United States, whereas Spitzer lived among us for twenty-four years. René Wellek reports a conversation in which Spitzer complained that he was now "echolos";[17] yet his writings reverberated when they were published in English; and, furthermore, his adopted country had some impact on him. Along with elucidations

16. Leo Spitzer, "History of Ideas versus Reading of Poetry," *Southern Review*, VI, 3 (Winter, 1941), 584–609.

17. René Wellek, "Leo Spitzer (1887–1960)," *Comparative Literature*, XII, 1 (Fall, 1960), 310, an admirable appraisal with a selective bibliography. See also the well-informed tribute of Spitzer's co-worker Helmut Hatzfeld, "Léon Spitzer et la littérature française," *Etudes Françaises*, II, 3 (October, 1966), 251–253.

of Poe and Whitman, his English essays include the acute and amusing *tour de force,* "American Advertising Explained as a Popular Art," which explicates a pictorial advertisement for Sunkist Oranges.[18] The second sentence of his first American book reads as follows:

I dedicate this first book of mine printed in America, which is to continue the series of studies in stylistics previously published in Germany—*Aufsätze zur romanischen Syntax und Stilistik,* Halle (Niemeyer) 1918; *Stilstudien,* I–II, München (Hueber) 1928; *Romanische Stil- und Literaturstudien,* I–II, Marburg an der Lahn (Elwert) 1931—to Assistant Professor ANNA GRANVILLE HATCHER who is an outstanding American scholar in the too little cultivated field of syntax—which in her case, is expanded into stylistic and cultural history—and who could thus teach me, not only the intricacies of English syntax and stylistics, but some of the more recondite features of American culture and of its particular moral, logical, and aesthetic aspirations: a knowledge without which all endeavors of the philologist to explain poetry to an American public must fail completely.[19]

To explicate this remarkable piece of syntax would require the insight of Spitzer himself, plus a self-detachment to which he laid no particular claim. Stripped of its relative clauses and appositions, of what a classical rhetorician would call *epergesis* and *anacoluthon,* and of an almost Shandyan sequence of dashes, it would be a simple gesture of gratitude and acknowledgment to that colleague who would become his successor at Johns Hopkins. But the personal declaration is rounded out, to the extent of 135 words, by professional afterthoughts at both ends. At his end a bibliographical footnote, parenthetically assimilated into the sentence, advertises the continuity with his publications in German. At her end the professional compliment leads, through a moving personal excursus, into an affirmation of scholarly faith and an attestation of national loyalty. Editors who received his manuscripts can recall the visible traces of how he wrote: the accumulation, the stratifiction, the interlineation, addenda, and more last words. Footnotes were his *genre par excellence,* sometimes outrunning the text in Venetian fashion, and containing observations on everything in the manner of Montaigne. The intensive focus he brought to bear on an abstruse point, the polyglot outpouring of related facts and ideas, did not leave

18. Leo Spitzer, *Essays on English and American Literature,* ed. Anna Hatcher (Princeton, 1962).

19. Spitzer, *Linguistics and Literary History,* p. v.

much room for a sense of proportion. On a paper read at a meeting and subsequently printed in *Comparative Literature,* Auerbach commented:

Et ce que Spitzer a dit sur la Peregrinatio est peut-être en peu trop poussé, comme tout ce qu'il fait—mais au fond c'est tellement vrai et neuf que vous ne vous repentirez certainement d'avoir pris l'article pour Compar. Lit.[20]

This tendency to overstrain the evidence at times, to hinge his arguments on supersubtleties which no one else had ever noticed, was calculated to draw more vocal and sharper criticisms. His reading of *Phèdre* stressed the key word *voir* in the concluding monologue of Théramène; but Jean Hytier has pointed out that the word was unavoidable at that moment in any neoclassical tragedy since the offstage dénouement had to be reported by an eyewitness.[21] In such interchanges, which were the breath of Spitzer's life, he was the challenger more often than not. He met a Hopkins colleague in English on his own ground, by challenging his interpretation of Keats's "Ode on a Grecian Urn." The consequent overreading is too erudite to be quite convincing; it mainly proves that Spitzer knew more than Keats about Greek archeology. His polemical stance was robed in righteousness. Not for nothing did his name mean "sharpener." Fellow scholars, especially younger Americans, had to be castigated for their own good. He was here to set an example, to teach us a lesson. One of his most punitive review-articles, on Stephen Gilman's *Art of "La Celestina,"* concludes (though Spitzer characteristically appended a postscript, eulogizing the late Ernst Robert Curtius):

I have often been asked why I devote so much of my efforts to "destructive criticism." The answer is that I believe that, in the discipline of Philology as in the sciences, the ultimate goal, however more arduous in its attainment or approximation, must be Truth; and that the failure to expose contentment with half-truths or non-truths would amount to a conspiracy of silence against that noble discipline.[22]

Professor Gilman could scarcely be expected to accept this pharisaical answer, since every scholar seeks the truth according to his lights and few today believe themselves so uniquely privy to it. A rejoinder, in

20. Letter from Erich Auerbach to Harry Levin, January 1, 1949.
21. Jean Hytier, "La Méthode de M. Leo Spitzer," *Romanic Review,* XLI, 1 (February, 1950), 42–59.
22. Leo Spitzer, "A New Book on the Art of 'The Celestina,'" *Hispanic Review,* XXV, 1 (January, 1957), 24.

probing for the animus that had carried the reviewer so far beyond the legitimate occasion of the review, suggested that Professor Gilman's sin —in Spitzer's eyes—had been to write a book. Spitzer, for all his penetrating intelligence and formidable learning, had never come to grips with the problem of synthesis.

His sharp-edged atomistic mind, a mind which has divided Juan Ruiz into his sources, his own "*obra*" into a thousand and one articles, and his articles into a myriad of footnotes, has been baffled by the fact of composition itself.[23]

It would be hard to compile an exhaustive bibliography of Spitzeriana, written as they were in five different languages and scattered across the world in periodicals of limited circulation. There would be at least a thousand entries; and, if we did not count miscellaneous collections, monographs, or pamphlets, there would be no books among them. Many, which are not explicit reviews, were touched off by the efforts of other writers to discuss subjects about which Spitzer had deep knowledge and strong opinions. If he needed to be provoked into writing, perhaps it is fortunate that he was so infinitely provokable. His reaction to six pages by Grace Frank on a Provençal poem took the form of a seventy-four-page monograph.[24] Increasingly and somewhat defensively, during his American period, he would talk about his methodology. It was more easily demonstrated than formulated, with autobiographical cross-reference to earlier demonstrations. Whenever he directly confronted the literary object, he was more interested in beauties than faults, believing as he did that the details he scrutinized were organic parts of a perfect whole. His critics accused him of knowing well in advance what he claimed to arrive at empirically. Spitzer replied that such reasoning was inherent in "the philological circle," the continuous movement of the interpreter's mind from the text at hand to the contexts of widening awareness and back again.[25] His hypotheses might be no more than shrewd hunches, but so were the scientist's.

In a politely devastating critique of the phenomenological critic, Georges Poulet, Spitzer maintained that the "chameleonic" approach of the philologist was more germane to literature than the systematic

23. Stephen Gilman, "A Rejoinder to Leo Spitzer," *Hispanic Review*, XXV, 2 (April, 1957), 120.

24. Leo Spitzer, *L'Amour lointain de Jaufré Rudel et le sens de la poésie des troubadours* (Chapel Hill, 1944).

25. Spitzer, *Linguistics and Literary History*, pp. 19ff.

approach of the philosopher.[26] Spitzer's own procedures resisted formulation because, in the last analysis, they were based upon a rare combination of intuition and erudition. One of his attempts to set them forth takes its departure from a dictum of Friedrich Gundolf, "Methode ist Erlebnis," and repeats a scholastic adage which Spitzer loved to quote, "individuum est ineffabile."[27] His method was his very exceptional self. An essay of mine had the good luck to please him because it cited an instance where the lifelong devotion of a single humanist had done more to clarify certain exacting problems than the heavily organized enterprises of a modern team. In this connection he wrote:

> Choosing from your own words, I would say that the '*new* frontiers of knowledge' consist in the gigantically increasing *information* we get in our times while a unified Weltanschauung or wisdom, is disappearing. Just open any of our journals and you witness the anarchy of values while the learning displayed is (sometimes) stupendous.[28]

In September 1960, two weeks before his sudden death at the Italian resort he frequented, I spent a week in close contact with Spitzer at Liège. As the two Americans invited to address plenary sessions at the congress of the Fédération Internationale des Langues et Littératures Modernes, we were lodged at the same hotel and took a number of walks and meals together. Only once, when we had to climb a steep hill on a visit to a local professor, did he show the hesitations of age. But I found him constantly mellow and sparkling, benign and fatherly. What was to be his farewell address, "Les Etudes de style et les différents pays," appropriately terminated the congress and received a standing ovation. Possibly because he was speaking in urbane French, which lends itself less readily to polemics than German or even English, he seemed to have come to terms with himself, his fellow men, and his field. His final statement was a proclamation of open-mindedness, a far cry from the doctrine he had been propounding at Baltimore ten years before:

> Ainsi beaucoup de chemins mènent vers la Rome de la stylistique, et la stylistique elle-même n'est pas la porte d'accès unique au paradis de la bonne critique littéraire.[29]

26. Leo Spitzer, "A propos de la 'Vie de Marianne,'" *Romanische Literaturstudien, 1936–56* (Tübingen, 1959), pp. 248–276.
27. Spitzer, *Linguistics and Literary History,* pp. 1, 11.
28. Letter from Leo Spitzer to Harry Levin, August 17, 1951.
29. *Langue et littérature,* p. 38.

Shortly before we parted, he agreed to give some lectures at Harvard the following year. That my own university so narrowly missed the opportunity of hearing both Spitzer and Auerbach is one of my lasting regrets.

3

Conversing with Auerbach at—of all places—the site of the Village Smithy, I had been reminded of Longfellow walking down Brattle Street from his home to the Harvard Yard a hundred years before. He had been the first professor of modern languages at his alma mater, Bowdoin College, and one of the first in the country. During his undergraduate days, the college had offered no instruction in that area. He had picked up some French from a church organist at Portland, and he prepared himself for his teaching duties by a grand tour of Europe which lasted three years. Another such *Wanderjahr* preceded his arrival at Harvard, where he held the Smith Professorship of the French and Spanish Languages from 1836 to 1854. When he resigned, in order to devote full time to his literary activities, notably his verse translation of Dante, he broadened his role as a cultural mediator between the hemispheres. His predecessor, the first Smith Professor, George Ticknor, belonged to that early and eager band of American students who had sought to quaff the cup of knowledge at its German academic source. After studying at the University of Göttingen and traveling widely in Spain and elsewhere, he had laid out the program of instruction in the modern languages at Harvard. His resignation widened his scope by permitting him to concentrate upon his pioneering history of Spanish literature.

Longfellow's successor, James Russell Lowell, was also a respected man of letters rather than a professional scholar. Yet it should not be forgotten that, at the fourth meeting of the Modern Language Association of America in 1886, Lowell—whose teaching career had been interrupted by his ministries to Spain and Britain—was elected president. During the next generation the MLA, reinforced by the establishment of graduate schools and the introduction of the Ph.D., saw itself consolidated into a citadel of philological scholarship. By and large, it emulated the methods of Germany, with a special American zeal for the sheer accumulation of facts; and, since it was farther removed from the springs of its subject matter, it was even drier than its model. Its standard products were textbooks of historical grammar. English studies were allowed somewhat more leeway, since they had long functioned within the framework of rhetoric and have always attracted the part-time writer. But there too the history of literature hardly looked beyond the Middle Ages, while the language requirements were overburdened with such extraneous matters as Gothic. In the departments of foreign languages, so much of the pedagogical effort went into elementary chores that advanced research was the exception more often than the rule. By the opening decades of our century, the severance between philology and *belles-lettres* was all but complete.

Of course, it is the exceptions who prove worth remembering, particularly among scholars, and we have had our share. If C. H. Grandgent seems more typical of the MLA than his forerunners at Harvard in Romance Languages, he must be credited with what is still a standard edition of the *Divina Commedia*. But it is significant that, before Grandgent took over the course in Dante at Harvard, it had been taught by Charles Eliot Norton, whose prose translation is so frequently cited; for Norton, though he pointed the way to more technical approaches in the history of art and archeology, prided himself on remaining a gentlemanly amateur. By the nineteen-thirties the *Publications of the Modern Language Association* had become such a catchall for encrusted professionalism that a younger generation of college teachers was able to stage a successful revolt. This was the New Criticism proclaimed by John Crowe Ransom. Though its strategic exponents had come from southern states, they recognized two Anglo-American forerunners: T. S. Eliot, a British subject since 1927, and I. A. Richards, who was translated from Cambridge University to Cambridge, Massachusetts, in 1939. The consequent rediscovery of literature as an art, through emphasis upon its structures and textures, had a wholesome influence in the classroom. A concomitant disregard of historical and linguistic contexts threatened serious misconstruction at the scholarly level.

There was some danger lest the pendulum swing too far in the new direction: toward a concern with texts which lacked the background to understand them fully, an assumption that the critic's and the scholar's interests were mutually exclusive. This attitude had been exacerbated by the dryasdust philistinism of a good many elder scholars, who made a point of choosing detective stories when they were reading for pleasure. Such, then, was the impasse which the example of Europe could resolve and the European migration would help to correct. The traditional *explication de texte* had been reduced to a perfunctory exercise since Gustave Lanson, but it could be reanimated by informed perceptivity on the part of the *explicateur*. Poets like Andrey Bely, critics like Victor Shklovsky, and philologists like Roman Jakobson had joined forces under the aegis of Russian Formalism. The Centro de Estudios Históricos at Madrid, the Cercle Linguistique de Prague, the *Idealistische Philologie* of Munich—what these varying schools had in common was a focus on stylistics as the middle ground between linguistics and literary criticism. The timely presence in the United States of Spitzer and Auerbach—the one so active a controversialist, the other so influential through his book—was a reassurance, for some of us caught in the crossfire, that our discipline embraced both erudition and esthetics.

When the history of the twentieth-century diaspora is fully chronicled, we should be able to test the parallel it implies with the fifteenth-century influx of catalytic knowledge to western Europe after the fall of Constantinople. Meanwhile, given the scale of events precipitating the latter-day exodus, the number of countries whence the refugees took flight, the brilliance of their talents and the variety of their fields, we make a modest start wherever we can by trying to follow the fortunes of those whose paths have crossed our own. Those losses to European faculties, which have meant such gains for ours, have completed the maturation of American higher learning. A touch of the medieval Sorbonne, with its "nations" of students, has been internationalizing our universities. To be sure, they had previously imported some of their professors, especially for the purpose of language teaching. Witness such colorful figures as Mozart's librettist, Lorenzo da Ponte, who was briefly the first professor of Italian at Columbia University, or the Norwegian-born novelist, H. H. Boyeson, professor of Germanic literatures at Cornell and Columbia. But, until so many distinguished *savants* were expatriated by the political conflicts of our time, the majority of our foreign-born college teachers of languages were what Dr. Johnson would have termed harmless drudges, who would not have achieved substantial positions by staying at home.

Within the more recent movement, the pattern of adaptation has varied according to nationality. Thus the French have tended to be emissaries rather than expatriates. Their viceroy among us, Henri Peyre, admits that his compatriots "have proved more stubborn than most other Europeans in withstanding assimilation."[30] However, they have thrown light on Franco-American relations, notably through the contributions of Gilbert Chinard. The Spaniards, moving to a hemisphere still rich in Hispanic associations, turned their exile into a perspective on the historic uniqueness of Spanish culture. Spitzer, who waxed impatient over what he called "national tautology" ("die irgendweise implizite Behauptung, dass ein spanisches Kunstwerk gross ist, weil echt spanisch, und echt spanisch, wenn gross"), provoked a controversy with Américo Castro over that battleground.[31] In the widespread dispersion of Russian intellectuals, comparatively few were accomplished literary scholars, among whom Gleb Struve stands out as the historian of Russian émigré literature. The American undertakings of Roman Jakobson have combined more effectively with Slavic and general linguistics than with literary studies. Some of the most adaptable émigrés have been those who were trained, in their homelands and by earlier travels, to be experts on culture other than their own. The Slavicist from Italy, Renato Poggioli, and the Anglicist from Czechoslovakia, René Wellek, arriving almost simultaneously at Harvard and Yale, guaranteed a realization of the protracted American hopes for comparative literature.

It is worth noting that the *Journal of Comparative Literature,* undertaken by G. E. Woodberry at Columbia University in 1903, did not survive that year; whereas the journal sponsored by the University of Oregon with the cooperation of the MLA, *Comparative Literature,* has been appearing regularly since 1949, and there are now three additional periodicals in this sphere. A glance at their tables of contents will reveal the extent to which they have thriven upon the collaboration of our European-American colleagues. To the first six volumes of *Comparative Literature* Spitzer contributed five articles. Auerbach had promised an article; but, since he never wrote directly for publication in English, he decided to publish it elsewhere in German; and he did contribute three reviews. It could be reciprocally said that such contributors were happy to find so close at hand "a forum for those scholars and critics who are engaged in the study of literature from an international point of

30. Henri Peyre, "The Study of Literature," in *The Cultural Migration: The European Scholar in America,* ed. W. R. Crawford (Philadelphia, 1953), p. 37.

31. Leo Spitzer, "The Mozarabic Lyric of Theodor Frings," Comparative Literature IV, 1 (Winter, 1952), 1–22. Cf. Américo Castro, "Mozarabic Poetry and Castille: A Rejoinder to Mr. Leo Spitzer," *Comparative Literature,* IV, 2 (Spring, 1952), 188–189. The quotation is from Spitzer's review of Dámaso Alonso's *Poesía española* in *Romanische Forschungen,* LXIV (1952), 1/2, 215.

view."[32] Spitzer had continually chafed against the barriers set by specialization and departmentalism: "The splitting up of a field which knew in former times of no international boundaries is, to say the least, anachronistic."[33] Auerbach acknowledged a sense of European "mission," which he attributed to his own formation—not as a Romance philologist nor indeed as a German, but as a combination of both, a *Romanist,* with the good German's feeling for the civilizing traditions of that Latin world which stretched from the Rhine to the Mediterranean.[34]

Similarly Ernst Robert Curtius would affirm: "Ich wusste mich gebunden an die *Roma aeterna.*"[35] That vision of the monuments attesting the continuity of Europe itself, systematized by the monumental investigations of Germanic scholarship into Romanic matters, made the *Romanisten* more consistently humane than their more nationalistic colleagues, the *Germanisten.* The doyen of their last great generation was Karl Vossler, friend of Croce and founder of idealistic philology, who studied Dante as a mirror of medieval culture and the French language as a mirror of French civilization. A liberal, he was morally fortified by his trans-European outlook; a study of the poetry of solitude in Spain is characteristic of his work during the Nazi period; and he was enabled to resume the rectorship of the University of Munich during the postwar occupation.[36] Curtius, at Bonn, had been undertaking his own internal migration. Hitherto he had best been known as a searching and sympathetic interpreter of modern French literature. Motivated by his "concern for the preservation of Western culture," he returned to medieval Latinity, retracing its tropes and conventions from Vergil to Dante in his magnum opus.[37] To judge from his conversation with Stephen Spender in 1946, he felt that the war had not left much worth preserving.[38] On his brief visit to America, for the Goethe bicentennial in 1949, he seemed gracious but quite incurious.

Whether Spitzer and Auerbach would have produced comparable

---

32. From the editorial statement appearing on the inside cover in each issue of *Comparative Literature.*

33. Spitzer, *Essays in Historical Semantics,* p. 11.

34. Auerbach, *Literary Language,* p. 16.

35. E. R. Curtius, *Kritische Essays zur Europäischen Literatur* (Bern, 1954), p. 439.

36. See Helmut Hatzfeld, "Karl Vossler (1872–1949)," *Comparative Literature,* I, 2 (Spring, 1949), 189.

37. E. R. Curtius, "Author's Foreword to the English Translation," *European Literature and the Latin Middle Ages,* tr. W. R. Trask (New York, 1953), p. viii.

38 Stephen Spender, "German Impressions and Conversations," *Partisan Review,* XIII, 1 (Winter, 1946), 7–13

works of synthesis, if it had been possible for them to go on working in Germany, is a question which does not lend itself to belated speculation. As Jews, they had no choice but to emigrate; possibly they adjusted more readily to a new environment because of their migratory ancestry. But other *Romanisten,* coming for other reasons, have brought with them their skills and talents. Helmut Hatzfeld, who was a pupil of Vossler, is now their dean. Teaching at the Catholic University of America, he has focused his researches upon literary manifestations of the baroque and of mysticism and upon comparative stylistics. Herbert Dieckmann, once a student of Curtius, may be the youngest of the tribe. Having taken his doctorate at Bonn in 1933, he came to the United States via the Turkish detour, and has taught at Washington University, Harvard, and Cornell. Though his intellectual range is wide, his discovery of important manuscripts has centered most of his energies on the reediting of Diderot. By the midcentury, with the reconstruction of Europe, it was clear that fewer and fewer émigrés would be candidates for our professorships. Much is to be hoped for, however, from a younger generation of European-born scholars trained in America, such as Paul De Man, Peter Demetz, Victor Erlich, W. B. Fleischmann, Claudio Guillén, Juan Marichal, Georges May, Alain Renoir, and Walter Strauss.

Spitzer summed up his unstinting advice to young American scholars with an address at a general meeting of the MLA in 1950, "The Formation of the American Humanist." Reminiscing about the ideals and rigors of his Viennese education, he reaffirmed his commitment to scholarship as a way of life. He was unsparing in his censure of those distractions and pressures which make it something less than a *modus vivendi* for most of us. His twin targets were administration and overproduction, and he aphoristically footnoted: "The telephone of the organizer is the deadly enemy of the desk of the scholar."[39] The broad solution he proposed was the establishment of a scholarly elite, which— he urged in his concluding plea—should not be incompatible with the highest aims of a democracy.

You may have decided that, given my criticism of the life actually led by our young scholars in our university system, a system so intimately connected with national ideals, I am criticizing these ideals themselves and that, consequently, as the phrase goes, "I should go back where I came from." But I do not wish to

39. Leo Spitzer, "The Formation of the American Humanist," *Publications of the Modern Language Association of America,* LXVI, 1 (February, 1951), 44n.

go back, I wish to stay in this country which I love. Is it not understandable that a relationship deliberately based on choice may inspire, at the same time, more passion and more criticism than an inherited relationship? It is just because I find in American democracy the only air in which I could breathe, because I am convinced that the average American is more decent, less selfish, and more human than the average of any other nation where I have lived, that I would wish the American university system to possess all the advantages of the best systems of the old world![40]

Elsewhere, with the same extra measure of passion and criticism, Spitzer voiced his specific objections to current practices: to the sort of capricious reinterpretations, by ill-informed reinterpreters questing for novelty, that abound in our learned journals as well as our literary quarterlies. He feared lest the Americans outdo the Germans in such willful and subjective misreading.[41] He found himself reverting, on a second recoil, to historicist and positivistic assumptions which he had previously been reacting against.[42] One of his marginal admonitions is a "negative reading-list," a warning against certain thinkers who have befuddled many an aspiring scholar-critic.[43] The full roster includes some *mauvais maîtres* whom he himself had once esteemed more highly: Bergson, Buber, Dilthey, Freud, Heidegger, Ortega, Sartre, Scheler, Spengler, Unamuno. But Spitzer's precepts had less effect than the striking example he set, while Auerbach was content to go his own way, leaving the paperback edition of *Mimesis* to play an exemplary role before an ever-widening audience. The lesson they propounded to us was reading, the most elementary subject in the curriculum pressed to its most advanced stage through the sharp and disciplined perceptions of incomparably well-stored minds. Nor should it be overlooked, in our faltering effort to carry on their endeavors, that—in Spitzerian terms—"they are the results of talent, experience, and faith."[44]

40. Ibid., p. 47.
41. Spitzer, "The Formation of the American Humanist," p. 23.
42. "History of Ideas versus Reading of Poetry," p. 608.
43. Spitzer, "A New Book on the Art of 'The Celestina,' " pp. 19, 23.
44. Spitzer, *Linguistics and Literary History*, p. 27

A DIALOGUE WITH ARTHUR LOVEJOY

To review Lovejoy's *Essays in the History of Ideas,* as I did for *Isis: An International Review Devoted to the History of Science* when the book was published (February, 1949), and to have criticized as well as praised it, seems in retrospect to have been an act of temerity as well as appreciation. Fortunately, the author responded with characteristic large-mindedness, thereby casting further light on his method. With the kind encouragement of his literary executor, George Boas, I have appended his letter, along with my reply.

This volume celebrates a double occasion: the twenty-fifth anniversary of the History of Ideas Club of the Johns Hopkins University, and the seventy-fifth birthday of its originator, Arthur Lovejoy. Out of a widely scattered body of subscribers and readers, few will question Don Cameron Allen when, in his foreword, he salutes his colleague as "the chief inspirer of the modern study of the history of ideas." And many who have found their own endeavors illuminated or integrated by Professor Lovejoy's articles, as they have appeared over the past generation in various scholarly periodicals, will welcome this chance to have them in a book. Here he has gathered together sixteen of them, whose relation to the totality of his work is made clear in an appended bibliography. There is reason to hope that an additional volume, especially valuable to students of the history of science, will comprise his studies in pre-Darwinian conceptions of evolution; and there might well be a third, devoted to his more technical contributions within the history of philosophy. Meanwhile the principles set forth in the opening essay "On the Historiography of Ideas," and supplemented by the latest afterthoughts of the author's preface, are characteristically and strategically exemplified by the other essays reprinted in the present collection.

Each of them is aimed at the elucidation of a single idea, as defined by philosophy and documented by literature. Though they incidentally cover a vast amount of historical ground, most of them converge upon upon one crucial period: on the late eighteenth and early nineteenth centuries, or rather—to use the pair of critical terms that the author has done so much to elucidate—the shift from neoclassicism to romanticism. Two or three, however, look farther back to the even more crucial shift from classical to medieval culture and pursue through certain Fathers of the Church the inquiry that Professor Lovejoy undertook, with George Boas, in their *Documentary History of Primitivism and Related Ideas in Antiquity* (1935). Thus the current volume compensates, to some extent, for a projected and uncompleted sequel to that undertaking; it is also linked, at many points, to Professor Lovejoy's major historical study, *The Great Chain of Being* (1936). The common denominator of these three books is more easily indicated than attained: it consists of capacities for omnivorous reading and rigorous formulation which all too rarely operate in conjunction today. Too frequently learning accumulates unregulated by conceptual discipline, while thought ramifies unsupported by pertinent research. Professor Lovejoy's leavening example has helped to systematize literary history, as well as to open up the closed systems of metaphysics.

Now ideas are orginated and communicated, elaborated and controverted, for better or for worse, by means of words. Hence semantics plays, in intellectual history, somewhat the role that genetics plays in biology. The appendix to *Primitivism in Antiquity,* which distinguishes more than sixty meanings for the vital word *nature,* thereby traces a rough but significant outline of ancient scientific speculation. The recent volume includes a paper on "Nature as Aesthetic Norm" which continues this process of "analytical enumeration" and surveys the far-ranging applications that critics from Aristotle to Zola have given the term. Within these ten pages are compressed a wealth of reference and a scheme of organization which might have been expanded into a monograph at the hands of another investigator—which indeed have provided both stimulus and material for subsequent investigators. Shakespeare is here but a small item in a large reckoning; yet his constant appeal to nature might itself be the subject of a valued investigation—or, for that matter, his varied and subtle handling of the concept in *King Lear* alone. Professor Lovejoy is at his brilliant best when, having sorted out the relevant particulars, he emerges with the responsible generalizations. In his "Parallel of Deism and Classicism" he demonstrates how the religious views and artistic tastes of an epoch can be derived from its underlying philosophical premises.

However, the philosophy of that epoch happened to be the rationalism of the Enlightenment, which tends to facilitate such demonstrations. Other periods, notably the one that immediately followed, are less susceptible to schematization. Professor Lovejoy is well aware of the complexities and ambiguities of this transition, which he illustrates via the developing theories of Schiller and Friedrich Schlegel. Neatly and efficiently he performs the negative task of disentangling Kant from Coleridge's misinterpretations. Together with a lively sense of paradox, he possesses a keen eye for contradictions and fully realizes that seminal minds are often unsystematic. Rousseau is for him, as for the majority of modern intellectual historians, a dominant influence; but he differs from them by minimizing the primitivism and stressing the progressive trend of Rousseauism. In this respect he also differs from such contemporaneous readers as Voltaire, whose famous letter is relegated to a footnote as a misconception. It is interesting to observe that similar testimony is cited, in other connections, from Dr. Johnson and Herder and Chateaubriand; and while a later essay discusses Schiller's *Über naive und sentimentalische Dichtung,* it pays no attention to the passage where Rousseau is characterized as an elegiac poet. Professor Lovejoy has doubtless read the *Discours sur l'inégalité* more carefully than those on whom its impact depended. The doubt is whether he has gauged— to employ his phrase—the direction in which Rousseau was heading.

Professor Lovejoy is certainly not to be blamed for being more of a philosopher than a historian, for doing greater justice to the fullness and novelty of a writer's thinking than to the possible extent of his influence, for putting stronger stress on incidental distinctions than on broad uniformities. But then, when he talks about such practical manifestations as Chinese gardens and Gothic cathedrals, he manages to abstract them to a theoretical level where the actual constructions seem less important than the misconstructions of another time and place. And when he addresses himself to the very central problem of definition, in his programmatic address "On the Discrimination of Romanticisms," he exposes confusions and isolates attitudes and multiplies categories to the point where his counsel of despair is a skeptical pluralism. This is the point where we are constrained to remember that the diverse phases of romanticism are chronologically—if not always logically— related through dynamic movements and many-sided personalities. Between the different elements of any cultural configuration, there must be continuities as well as discriminations—and who should know this better than the author of *The Great Chain of Being?* But his method, it would seem, is better adapted to tracing a "key idea" down the cen-

turies than to placing a "thought-complex" against its age. Since he nowhere deals with a complete situation, but presents a static exhibit of
eclectic data, he is vulnerable to the kind of critique that functional
anthropologists would level at Frazer.

Furthermore, since meanings shift from one context to another, and
the content of ideas continually changes, Professor Lovejoy's measuring
rod is form. To cite a spectacular instance, the common traits he finds in
the hierarchy of Plotinus and the hypothesis of Darwin could not, of
course, be other than structural. History is more concerned with the
differences; it looks for origins and traditions in order to chart muta-
tions and innovations. Implicit in the concept of the "key idea" is the
antihistorical pseudo-proverb: *Plus ça change, plus c'est la même chose.*
Not that Professor Lovejoy would exclude originality altogether; he
would merely assume that philosophy is the "seed plot" of ideas. He
asserts its primacy with an aggressive dogmatism which may remind
his colleagues in other fields of Molière's *maître de philosophie.* But
assertions *ex cathedra* are not so questionable as professional habits of
mind. In history, though not in epistemology, Professor Lovejoy tends
to be an idealist: that is to say, he regards ideas as animating forces, dis-
regards material factors, and treats intellectual structures as self-sufficient. To explain an inconsistent thinker like Coleridge, he is willing to
appeal from philosophy to psychology. But he seems unwilling to recognize that the explanation for the eighteenth-century garden craze is
connected with the Industrial Revolution; that "nature" is chiefly modified by the development of science; that romanticism was, for its adherents, very largely a social phenomenon.

We may make these qualifications without rushing to the opposite
extreme, as the Marxists have done, and supplanting philosophy by
ideology—that is to say, the rationalization of material interests. Their
economic materialism is the dialectical antithesis of Professor Lovejoy's
historical method, which might well be called philosophic intellectualism. By his very abstraction he avoids their misplaced concreteness; he
invites other students to fill in the outlines he has sketched, or to make
the applications he may have overlooked. In an eloquent paragraph he
suggests that the humanities would profit from the sort of planning and
cooperation that has served to advance the sciences. Among other
specific suggestions, he mentions a full-length commentary on *Paradise
Lost,* and he offers future commentators an admirable model by anno-
tating one of its cosmic themes. Not only his *Journal of the History of*

Ideas, but many historical, philosophical, and philological journals, have for some years been bearing the fruit of his influence. There is, indeed, some danger lest his definitions be taken as labels and mechanically tagged to an increasingly mediocre series of literary documents. But there are no shortcuts to, nor any substitutes for, the thoroughly disciplined knowledge and precisely stated analysis that give Professor Lovejoy's books—including the present volume—unique authority within their sphere. By themselves, they already constitute a benign and clarifying chapter in the history of ideas.

*   *   *

The University Club
801 North Charles Street
Baltimore 1, Md.
April 13, 1949

Dear Professor Levin:

Being a subscriber to *Isis,* I had already read with gratification and—I hope—profit your review of my book of historical *Essays;* but my sense of obligation to you has been heightened by your courtesy in sending me an off-print, with your very kind and generous superscription. An author could hardly hope to have a better—which is to say, a more fair and discriminating and, for the reader, illuminating—review, or from a better qualified reviewer. You even make the book more intelligible, in some respects, than it makes itself; for you have noted explicitly some interconnections between the themes and the theses of different parts of the miscellany (and of the *Great Chain of Being*), which (though not unaware of them) I neglected to point out as definitely as I should have done. I am especially grateful to you also for suggesting that many of the essays are hints, sketches, or intimations, of studies which need to be carried farther, or applied in other fields, by other men. If the book evokes, or provokes, such further investigations or reflections, I shall feel that one of my chief hopes for it has been realized.

That you express dubiety or dissent on some points—and especially on what seem to you some characteristics of the general "method" (as some it call—I have a probably irrational phobia for the word) which the essays exemplify—was to be expected, and your clear statement of them is also a service to the author. Some of them, however, I don't find altogether convincing, and others suggest that I have not made myself altogether clear. I venture, therefore, to inflict on you a few brief comments on two or three of these points.

1. You are entirely just in your observation that, in the things I have published, I have been chiefly occupied with tracing a unit-idea "down through the ages" rather than with "placing a 'thought-complex' against its age." That is a real and a serious limitation in my attempts to contribute to the historiography of ideas. I have not dealt with any *period* as a whole. But this limitation of my published writings does not imply that—or that I think that—the analytical discrimination of ideas cannot be applied to the study of a period. The thing can, *en principe,* be done; indeed, I have made some attempts to do it myself (though not in print). But it is necessary first to catch your ideas—to identify them, to recognize their *intrinsic* implications, to note which of these implications were actually recognized in the period and which overlooked or dodged, and *then* to observe their interactions, alliances or oppositions. (I believe I have already said this more lengthily in a paper not included in the recent volume, on "The Meaning of Romanticism" in *JHI.*) This procedure is, I think, an essential one, if the movement of thought in a "period" is to be really understood; there are some approximations to it in print, but it has not often been adequately exemplified. And it is a very large and difficult task—to be sure of having "caught" all your ideas (or all the important ones) and of having observed fully their interplay in the minds of representative and influential writers or "schools." Some of the major ideas of the mid-18th century, and also of the German Romantic period, have never yet, for lack of thorough analysis, been identified, not to say correlated. (*E.G.,* the distinction of "Reason and Understanding" in the German Romantic philosophers and their English and American echoers still awaits adequate study. I have an unfinished book on "The Romantic Theory of Knowledge" in which I attempt such a study.) In short, until we have more sound *materials* for a synthesis, we shan't, I think, in most cases, be in a position to achieve a true synthetic, or synoptic, understanding of what was going on at a given time. At all events, I have thought it more useful to devote my own efforts to the former and necessary preliminary task. But I don't at all deny that one of the things to be aimed at, and hoped for, is the achievement of the other, larger, and more complex task.

2. It is true, as you say, that I "regard ideas as animating forces" in influencing events or shaping the culture of an age. But I do not think

them the only forces; and I don't remember that I have ever said they are. I don't, on the other hand, think that *they* are shaped by "material factors" anything like so much as some have supposed. They have a "particular go" of their own—partly logical, often pseudo-logical, sometimes mainly emotive;—in short, I am sceptical—though, I hope, open-minded—of explanations of changes in opinion or taste,—outside of certain political changes,—by economic motives. And I am rather confirmed than shaken in this scepticism by the examples which you give of the possibility of such explanation. E.g., "the 18th-century garden craze" was certainly *not* "connected with the Industrial Revolution." For the beginning of the latter can be quite definitely dated; it was the result of the invention of the spinning jenny by Hargreaves in 1767 and its improvement by Arkwright and Crompton in the 1770's; of the power-loom in the late 1780's; and of the steam-engine by Watt in 1769. But by the 1770's the English garden craze had been flourishing for nearly a century. It was, to be sure, economically conditioned; it could not have come about if there had not been numerous country gentlemen having considerable or large estates. But there had been such country-gentlemen in England long *before* the "garden-craze" began. And there was no economic difference between the landed gentry who preferred the Versailles type of garden and those who later became converts to the *goût anglo-chinois.*—Nor (if F. Schlegel was a "Romanticist") *I* don't find in his writings of the early 1790's any evidence that his conversion from classicism to Romanticism in the theory of poetry was in the least for him as "a social phenomenon." I don't deny that economic factors play a part here and there—chiefly, as I have said, in the movement of political opinion (though even there their role can be exaggerated); but there are large and important changes in many provinces of the history of ideas in which I find no sufficient reason for crediting them with any part at all. And I can't but think that you are a little inclined to assume that they are operative where an examination of the relevant evidence does not disclose them—and, in fact, indicates their absence.

3. I think you exaggerate my "intellectualism" a bit—though, doubt-less, if I over-emphasize one part of the picture, it is on that side. But by "ideas" I mean (as I have somewhere explained) ideas accompanied usually by emotions, and often determined by them and by cravings of the imagination and other "psychological," i.e., alogical, factors. But since so friendly and judicious a critic as yourself thinks I don't recognize

them as often as I should, I shall try to amend my ways in this particular.

To impose all this upon you is a poor return for so generous and
gracious a review, for which I am most grateful.

Cordially yours,
Arthur O. Lovejoy

(827 Park Avenue, Baltimore).

*   *   *

Department of Comparative Literature
Harvard University
Holyoke House 15
Cambridge 38, Massachusetts
May 19, 1949

Professor Arthur O. Lovejoy
827 Park Avenue
Baltimore, Maryland

Dear Mr. Lovejoy:

Your letter very graciously continued the valued pedagogical process
which started for me with your lectures and conversations at Harvard
in 1935, and which has been going on since then through your publications down to this last collection. My review of it was intended as an
acknowledgment of that process; and such acknowledgments, I suppose, ought honestly to reflect the variance in respective vantage-points
between the reviewer and the reviewee. If any limitations are thereby
revealed, they are more likely to characterize the former than the latter
—at least they do in the present case.

Since you carry the discussion a stage further by exemplifying two of
them, let me try to reply specifically in both instances. When I spoke of
the garden craze being "connected" with the Industrial Revolution, I
agree that the connection was somewhat loosened by the vagueness of
my phrasing. What I should have said, and could—I believe—have
maintained, was that the garden craze was connected with eighteenth-
century urbanization. As the phrase stands, however, it is an all too apt
example of the sort of generalization that is very properly undermined
by your close historical reasoning.

But if you are willing to assume that romanticism was one movement, and that classicism had been another, I do not believe that the social implications of that particular progression are invalidated by appealing to the personal motivation of such classicists-turned-romantic as Friedrich Schlegel. Social historians of the Reformation have not convinced us that the great religious leaders of that period were motivated by hopes of financial profit; on the other hand, they have well demonstrated how certain doctrines and habits seemed better adapted than others to survive amid changing economic conditions. Some such equilibrium of intellectual and material factors, gauged anew with each new set of ideas and circumstances, would approximate my own rough notion of how history works; and would not, I hope, be too utterly remote from yours.

To these replies I know you could make better ones; but, especially in view of your generosity in answering me already at such illuminating length, I do not wish to trouble you further on the subject. I only wish that before long some opportunity might arise in which we could continue the discussion by word of mouth. With all good wishes,

Sincerely yours,
Harry Levin

MEMOIRS OF SCHOLARS, 1:
MILMAN PARRY

Under the title "Portrait of a Homeric Scholar," and with a short bibliography here omitted, this evocation of Parry by one of his students was published shortly after his death in *The Classical Journal* (February, 1937). His views and methods, here described rather tentatively and then regarded by many elder scholars as altogether heretical, have gained widespread acceptance and universal recognition during the past generation. The principal advances, both in completing the Parry Collection at Harvard University and in interpreting oral literature from the kind of material it comprises, have been made by Parry's former pupil and assistant, Albert B. Lord, who has not only been editing the corpus of Serbo-Croatian heroic poetry but has shown how much light it casts on the epic process in *The Singer of Tales*. All of Parry's writings on the subject—in French as well as English—have recently been collected into a single volume, published by the Clarendon Press in 1971 and edited by Adam Milman Parry, chairman of the Department of Classics at Yale University. Adam Parry, a child at the time of his father's death, lived to become a distinguished Hellenist in his own right. The pattern of tragic fatality repeated itself, when he was killed in an accident at the age of forty-three.

Professors of the classics have reached a point where they spend their time apologizing for their subject. They are apt to promise those who follow their dwindling courses a unique opportunity to undergo a moral discipline, to attain the marks of caste, or at least to assure to themselves a comfortable academic career. Milman Parry disdained such inducements himself and refused to offer them to others. The study of Greek, he had found, is its own reward, and he never attempted to justify it on any but a personal and esthetic plane. He once recruited a cast for the production of a tragedy by holding before them the privilege of memorizing several hundred lines of Sophocles. It delighted him to think that a single year of declensions and conjugations was all that stood between the ordinary individual and the grandest of poems.

An extraordinary individual, he had not delayed for that year of grammatical probation. He had not come upon the language until he left his modest Quaker family in neighboring Oakland to study chemistry at the University of California in Berkeley. The things he valued meant all the more to him because he had not always been able to count upon them. The illumination suddenly shed by Greek on an overburdened adolescence led him through Homer and Hesiod and whatever he could find of the earliest monuments, without other guides. When Professor Herbert Weir Smythe of Harvard visited Berkeley in 1923 to give the Sather lectures, he found a pupil who had qualified himself for stringent graduate studies in Pindar and Aeschylus.

Parry was proud of possessing the oldest and rarest of academic degrees. Although Frenchmen have been known to take fourteen years in achieving it, the Sorbonne awarded him its doctorate in four, and he defended his theses with the highest success before a jury which reads like a bibliography of modern classical scholarship: Victor Bérard, Alfred Croiset, Antoine Meillet. Even more than the University and its methods, perhaps, French thought and life had their effect upon so suggestible an intelligence as his. There he must have acquired that feeling for tradition which continued to haunt him, that ability to deal with the past through association of ideas, that same sense of the cultural continuity of Mediterranean civilization, from the Trojan War to our own day, which is present in the thought of Paul Valéry, the critic with whom he was most in sympathy.

Against this cosmopolite background, his return to America contrasted unsatisfactorily. Parry was capable of meeting fully civilized or definitely uncivilized people on their own ground, but not of reaching his level on the faculty of a small middlewestern college. The souvenirs of that year which he was happiest to take with him to Harvard were a pair of handsome white dogs, the larger worthy of the name of Argos. He used to wash them in Fresh Pond until a policeman abruptly informed him that it also served as the Cambridge reservoir, whereupon he was forced to stride home after two lathered and shivering animals. That was not the only occasion on which he reminded his friends of another connoisseur of heroic lore, Don Quixote.

It is easy to recall the exhilaration of a Harvard freshman when, after an anticipated routine of parsing and scanning, Parry would dismiss Terence and introduce Molière and Sacha Guitry, or further illustrations from comic supplements and burlesque shows. In those days there was still an aura of the Latin Quarter about him; it may have been the black hat, or the beard he wore for a while, or his collection of drawings by Marie Laurencin, or his relish for such unclassical poets as Laforgue, Apollinaire, Eliot, and Cummings. Literal-minded graduate students sometimes complained that they would carefully collate a passage in Tacitus and be greeted with a lecture on its use by Racine, or that those who wanted to know the history of textual criticism of Thucydides were asked to criticize Spengler's theories of history. But significant technical matters were treated with ingenuity and detail. To clarify some of the perplexities of ancient versification, he even invented a device for reckoning meters on a graph.

The scholar's mind was not, so far as Parry was concerned, a warehouse to be stocked up with job lots of assorted erudition and prefabricated opinions. It was an instrument to be kept sharp and bright by constant and skillful use. As a confessed disciple of Erasmus and of Renan, he preferred dialectic to dogma. He had a knack of sweeping through any field of learning that lay near his venturesome path. It was impossible to be exposed to him during those periods of assimilation without catching a little of his enthusiasm for an unexpected variety of subjects. There was method in his excursions; music, Slavic, ethnology, mnemonic psychology were exploited for the benefit of Homer; his articles, his teaching, his casual conversation tended insistently in a direction that critics and general students of literature may find it profitable to pursue.

The problem to which Milman Parry devoted the best efforts of his short career has been a subject of learned inquiry for more than two millennia. Such subjects need to be approached again with extreme wariness, and Parry was not in the habit of taking things for granted. He never really solved the Homeric Question; he demonstrated that it was irrelevant. He had suspected, and experience afield confirmed his suspicion, that it is more difficult to frame the right questions than to find the right answers. What we know about literature is based largely on the personalities of writers, on the originality of their expression and the realism with which they reflect the interests of their times. These critical concepts, filled out by the facts about Vergil and Milton, adequately account for the *Aeneid* and *Paradise Lost,* but they bring us no nearer the secret of the *Iliad* and the *Odyssey.*

The peculiarities of the epic, as practised by "literary" poets, are readily explained by pointing to the example of Homer. But why did Homer, with presumably no one to imitate, choose to confine himself so strictly and to adapt the telling of his tales to a particular set of conventions? Parry's way of finding out was to examine the texts, to keep his eye on the object, to scrutinize the form for a clue to the function. He studied first the language, or the words available to the poet, then the diction, or the words selected, and finally the style, or the way in which the poet used them. Scholars had long surmised that the Greek epic must have been recited before it was written, but his statistical and philological analyses showed exactly how and why it had been composed.

He seized upon the distinctive units of Homeric style in its repetitions, so that he was able to tabulate the traditional epithets, the fixed metaphors, and the other recurrent ways of describing a situation. Early singers—and verse is originally song—may well have been able to draw upon this body of formulas for the purpose of rounding out their hexameters, just as the rhythm itself helped to make the story memorable. Parry's theory presupposed more than guilds of professional poets, illiterate and often blind, but skilled in a technique of oral narration that had been elaborately developed and continued to be rigidly controlled; it implied communities that knew what to listen for, whose traditions had fashioned these poets and were in turn refashioned by them.

Had Parry been content to confine his researches to the classics, his views, however cogent, would have remained a hypothesis. But his broad training and his concern with method carried him beyond that stage, since he regarded himself as primarily an anthropologist of literature. By that he did not mean that he looked upon his subject as an amorphous mass of documents out of which the history of custom and ritual could be conveniently reconstructed. He considered literature itself the richest and most sensitive of human institutions—not a two-dimensional page in a book, but a rounded organism embracing the people by and for whom it was created. He foresaw the possibility of establishing a physiology of literature, of investigating the way it works, the necessities which call it into being, the circumstances under which it flourishes.

Before the development of writing, poetry occupied a universal place, for it taught people how to regard things. Today, after centuries dominated by a line of men of letters who exercised their calling as a medium of self-expression, it might be noted that a school has arisen which again utilizes literature as a means of consciously manipulating the emotions toward a conventional ethic. Glory was not, to Sarpedon, the will-o'-the-wisp that sonneteers and historians and journalists later made of it, but a guerdon which poets had the power to confer and on which the prestige of chieftains depended. By accepting the epic as a phenomenon that occurs under a given series of social conditions, Parry was able to supply himself with a number of parallels for comparative study.

Homer, then, is to be understood not by consulting later classical authors or professed imitations in other languages, but by relating him to a context which includes *Beowulf,* the *Song of Roland,* and the *Eddas,* along with the popular poetry carried on today among the Tartars, the Afghans, or the southern Slavs. Notably in Yugoslavia, where newspapers and mechanical innovations have not quite leveled the patriarchal pattern of living, and where memories of Balkan battles and of Marko, the King's son, are still vivid, a waning generation of oral poets struggles to maintain its art. Here was a laboratory for Parry in which actual observation might determine how the singers built up their repertory and transmitted their craft, or what effect changes of time and place had upon their dialects, verses, and themes.

The fruit of his two South Slavic expeditions—more than a ton of manuscripts, typewritten commentaries, printed matter, photographs, instruments, and phonograph records—is now the property of the Harvard College Library. He had hoped, after completing his collection and transcription, to edit texts and translations of the more representative poems. It was a comprehensive scheme, but Parry was thirty-three. His conclusions would have ripened into a monograph which Homer was to share with Huso, the blind and venerated *guslar* to whom he attributed the best of the Slavic poems he had discovered. First-hand familiarity with the processes of oral literature had increased his estimate of the role a gifted poet can play. Conversely, it had convinced him that no individual is able to stray far beyond the accumulated tradition in which he is writing.

To trace the logical steps that drew Parry's attention to the Balkans is one thing; to characterize the energy that took him there is another. A less confident nature, recoiling as he had done from the tawdriness of California, might have been only too willing to settle into the gentility of New England. With a wife whose sympathetic support had made possible his French training and two children who were fond of listening to his lore, with an international reputation and the admiration of students and colleagues, his future as a Harvard professor seemed obvious to all except himself. There was in him a scholar-gypsy whom no amount of composition papers and committee meetings could tame.

It is clear that he thought of his work less and less in academic terms, that he would have gone on enlarging the scope of his activities. He loved to meet the contingencies of travel, to tinker with his recording machine, to visit the local pashas and exchange amenities, to ply his *guslars* with wine and listen to their lies. He attained native shrewdness in apportioning their pay to the jealous canons of village renown and in detecting stale or contaminated material when it was foisted upon him. He not only spoke the language, he produced the appropriate gestures and inflections. He respected the hierarchical nicety with which his hosts handed out the different cuts of meat. Their outlook seemed invested with an order that he had not encountered among the schools and movements of the civilization that had formed his own.

The mood of primitivism in so cultivated a mentality is not altogether surprising. It was not a romantic aberration; for Parry, slight though he was, had the emotional grasp of one who has supported himself since the age of thirteen. Despite his deftness in argument, philosophy and anything he labeled "critical theory" made him restless; frequently he would cut the knot of abstract discussion by appealing to "reality." In speech he shunned foreign phrases and Latinate words, seeking the simplest and most concrete English. His writing reveals sensibility of judgment, catholicity of taste, a rigorous method, a historical point of view—all the valuable qualities of the modern intellectual, including a distrust of the intellect.

Parry was anxious not to be taken in by the rationalizations and self-deceptions essential to the comfort of most minds. His kind of skepticism derived from an acute perception of uncertainty, of what Sophocles called "the chances of life." Even for hours of fatigue, he chose books about the War or films of action, because he felt that lighter entertainment attempted to soften and glide over the facts of human existence. At one time, he assumed responsibility for turning down a dissertation that seemed to start from false premises, although his elders had already approved and it meant years to some student. He appreciated the dilemma and it distressed him, but he could not let private sentiment or official conformity obscure what he conceived to be the truth.

His Homeric apprehension of the harshness of events was fulfilled by his death. The accident in Los Angeles on the third of December, 1935, was as trivial and pointless as that which killed his hero, Colonel Lawrence of Arabia, a few months before. Lawrence too, like Parry, had been a scholar. Parry, like Lawrence, recognized in an alien people the dignity and magnanimity he had missed in his own world. To him, as to Lawrence, the heroic values were no less real than the unexpected explosion of a loaded pistol. They had given him not only a sense of reality, but an idealistic interpretation of it. He knew that experience was really sudden and violent; he believed that it could also be noble and tragic.

The moment he cherished most occurred toward the end of one of his earliest days in the Serbian hills, during the summer of 1933. They had settled at an inland village and at length come across a *guslar,* the first epic poet Parry had ever known, an old man who claimed to have been a warrior in youth and to have cut off six heads. All afternoon he sang to them about his battles. At sunset he put down his *gusle* and they made him repeat a number of his verses. Parry, very tired, sat munching an apple and watching the singer's grizzled head and dirty neck bob up and down over the shoulder of Nikola, the Hercegovinian scribe, in a last ray of sunlight. "I suppose," he would say, in recalling the incident, with crisp voice and half-closed eyes, "that was the closest I ever got to Homer."

This closeness to the object is the best measure of his achievement as a Homeric scholar, and as a technician who reached literary criticism from an independent and profound approach. "How can we seize the physiognomy and the originality of the early literatures if we do not enter the moral and intimate life of a people, if we do not place ourselves at the very point in humanity which it occupied in order to see and feel with it, if we do not watch it live, or rather if we do not live for a while with it?" This question, from Renan's essay on the future of science, he had asked himself at the outset. The years at his disposal he spent in answering it, in bringing his own vitality and the apparatus of science and scholarship to bear upon the nature of the literary process, in penetrating dead languages, extinct traditions, and scholastic encrustations to the life at its core.

MEMOIRS OF SCHOLARS, 2:
FERNAND BALDENSPERGER

The official necrology known as a minute on the life and services of a colleague, to be spread upon the records of the Harvard faculty, is a collaborative endeavor. That is to say, it is drafted by the chairman after consultation with his committee, and rewritten after it has been submitted for their criticisms and further suggestions. Thus I must acknowledge gratefully that the present memoir benefited from the collaboration of John H. Finley, Jr., Marcel Françon, and Francis M. Rogers. It appeared in the *Harvard University Gazette* for February 21, 1959.

The village where Philippe-Jules-Fernand Baldensperger was born, Saint-Dié-en-Vosges, was an augury of his far-ranging career; for from its early printing press had been issued a cosmographical tract which, as it happened, gave the name of America to the western hemisphere. More to the immediate point was the year of his birth, 1871, when his corner of France was victimized in the aftermath of the Franco-Prussian War. Like his older friend and fellow native of Lorraine, Maurice Barrès, Baldensperger was first of all a patriotic Frenchman; but his ultimate mission was to interpret between French and German culture. In his poems and stories, published under the transparent but gallicized pseudonym of Fernand Baldenne, he would keep returning to his region. After *lycée* his technical training at Zurich was designed to prepare him for the management of his family's textile factory. But the Swiss landscape evoked a poetic response; he came to feel completely at home in the German language; and in the fiction of Gottfried Keller he found the subject to which he later devoted his principal doctoral thesis. His secondary dissertation in Latin, on the Danish poet Öhlenschläger, would be suggested by a subsequent visit to the Scandinavian countries, where he was given example and encouragement by that most cosmopolitan of critics, Georg Brandes.

In the meanwhile, Baldensperger had begun his graduate studies at Nancy and continued them at Heidelberg and Berlin, before completing the doctorate at Paris in 1899. He had mastered the third of his professional languages through a series of visits to England and Scotland, where he studied at Edinburgh and lectured at Glasgow. In 1900, upon the premature death of Joseph Texte, the pioneering incumbent of what was then the single chair of comparative literature in France, Baldensperger was his logical successor at the University of Lyons. Baldensperger's reputation as the most promising figure in the developing field was solidified in 1904, when he published both his exemplary monograph, *Goethe en France,* and his systematic revision of the standard bibliography, initiated by Louis Betz and recently continued by Werner Friederich. Hence, when Louis Liard—whom he had encountered through his provincial examinations—was reorganizing higher education in 1910, Baldensperger was called to a new professorship at the Sorbonne. There he founded the Institut de Littérature Comparée and —with his former pupils, Paul Hazard and Jean-Marie Carré—the influential *Revue de littérature comparée.* After the First World War, when the University of Strasbourg became French again, he took a leave of absence to establish its strategic chair of comparative literature.

Paris, in the years between the wars, was truly the clearing-house of world literature; and Baldensperger's institute became the polyglot center for scholars and students from every literate country. From the substructure of literary history, so firmly reared by Gustave Lanson and his school, Baldensperger traced the international ramifications, particularly the influence of French authors abroad and the impact of foreign works in France. This presupposed a centripetal interest attested by his studies and surveys of French literature, along with an edition and a biography of Alfred de Vigny. But there were many side-interests, notably music, which inspired a life of César Franck and a study of musical sensibility among the romanticists. Baldensperger's historical scope, expanded by his feeling for the interconnection of all cultural phenomena, was as broad as his geographical range; but he tended to concentrate on romanticism, conceived as the intellectual revolution that shaped the Modern epoch. Among his innumerable contributions in this area, perhaps the largest is *Le Mouvement des idées dans l'émigration française, 1789–1815.* But, as is evident from his handbook, *La littérature,* and from his four volumes of collected *études,* he was interested in esthetics and critical theory as well as in more strictly historical problems. In 1930 his achievement was appropriately signalized with a two-volume *Festschrift* containing sixty-two articles by colleagues and disciples of eighteen different nationalities.

Though he was widely honored, he never gained the honor he sought most eagerly: election to the Académie Française. His characteristic reaction was to publish a good-humored article, describing his unsuccessful candidacy. In 1935, upon becoming *professeur honoraire,* he wrote his memoirs, modestly entitled *Une Vie parmi d'autres.* A less productive scholar, a less determined internationalist, might have then been content to retire in the Vosges. Instead, Baldensperger embarked upon a second career in the United States. His constant travels, which encompassed Russia and the Far East, had taken him on five previous occasions to this country, where his clear-cut features and his vivacious manners had made a strong personal impression. He had come first to Harvard in 1913, as exchange lecturer under the terms of the Bacon-Hyde arrangement with the Sorbonne. As a captain in 1917–18, a tour of duty brought him to many American universities; and during the nineteen-twenties he returned to lecture at Columbia and elsewhere. Harvard had offered courses in comparative literature since the eighteen-nineties; a department, conferring graduate degrees, had been organized in 1906; its original chairmanship had been held by W. H. Schofield, the medievalist, whom Baldensperger had known in Berlin. However, the leading exponent of the subject was actually a professor of French, Irving Babbitt, whose concern for the history of ideas was imparted to undergraduates through his course in the romantic movement.

Thus it was especially fortunate that Baldensperger, who had been in close touch with Babbitt, consented for a brief period to become at once his successor and Schofield's. That period, 1935–1940, was not a propitious one for cosmopolitanism; and it was further saddened, for Baldensperger, by his wife's death and separation from his three children. But his authority kept the field alive; he personified Europe in America at a stage when contact was difficult; he foresaw and stimulated that efflorescence of comparative literature which would take place in American universities after the Second World War. He was increasingly concerned with what he would have called general literature, offering a sequence of six half-courses in the literary history of the world. He also taught a course in Goethe for the Department of German. Under his editorship, six volumes of the Harvard Studies in Comparative Literature appeared. Prompted by his sojourn, he translated Anglo-American poetry into French and brought his penetrating curiosity to bear on the enigmas of Shakespeare's sonnets. After his retirement from Harvard, he spent five more energetic years as visiting professor at the University of California in Los Angeles. Back in Paris from 1945 until his death in 1958, he liked to welcome the numerous friends he had made in America. They will remember him as a gracious host, a generous mentor, an indefatigable exemplar, a citizen of the Third Republic who proved by his very survival—into other times and other places—that the frontierless Republic of Letters was not quite dead.

MEMOIRS OF SCHOLARS, 3:
RENATO POGGIOLI

Another minute for the Faculty, this was printed in the *Harvard University Gazette* on November 7, 1964, and reprinted in a pamphlet entitled *Lives of Harvard Scholars* issued by the University Information Center (1968). The committee included Herbert Dieckmann, John H. Finley, Jr., A. B. Lord, and Wiktor Weintraub. A less formal and more expressive portrait has been admirably sketched by Gerald Fitzgerald, as a preface to his translation of *The Theory of the Avant-Garde* (Cambridge, Mass., 1968). The principal manuscript left by Renato Poggioli, *The Oaten Flute,* is currently announced for publication in 1973 by Harvard University Press.

The interrupted career of Renato Poggioli was one of those gains to American academic life which came about in our time through Europe's losses. Happily, in his case, he never lost active contact with his native land. He managed to pursue two fruitful careers simultaneously: one as a man of letters in Italy, the other as a scholar-teacher in the United States. Combining poetic gifts with linguistic skills, he made a durable contribution to Italian literature in the form of a series of standard translations, chiefly from Russian poetry but also from prose fiction and from many other languages, ranging from Novalis to Wallace Stevens. Starting young, he continued to publish regularly as a reviewer, critic, and essayist; with his lifelong friend Luigi Berti, who survived him by less than ten months, he later founded and edited the quarterly *Inventario,* which dedicated itself particularly to the mission of cultural interchange. The news of his premature death on May 3, 1963, was widely lamented in the Italian press and occasioned warm tributes from such literary figures as Eugenio Montale and Tommaso Landolfi. The twenty-five years of his American residence, which are of most concern to his Harvard colleagues, were enriched by the continuity of his European associations.

Poggioli's antecedents were deeply rooted in Tuscan soil. The treasures of the past were as much a part of his boyhood experience as a swim in the Arno. Born in Florence on April 16, 1907, he took the classical curriculum at *liceo* and specialized in modern languages at the University of Florence, receiving his doctorate *summa cum laude* in

1929 for a thesis on the poetry of Alexander Blok. For a brief period he was a lecturer on both Russian and Italian literature at his alma mater, and he was granted the teaching degree of *libero docente in filologia slava* from the University of Rome in 1938. Having gone to Prague as an exchange fellow at the Charles University in 1931–32, he returned there as executive secretary to the Italian Institute in 1934–35. The next three years were spent as lecturer in Italian at Polish universities, first at Wilno and subsequently at Warsaw. In 1935 he married Renata Nordio of Venice, whom he had come to know when they were fellow students, and who was to share his peregrinations and interests with the fullest devotion and understanding. Their daughter, Silvia, was to be born at Providence, Rhode Island, in 1946.

Very much the twentieth-century intellectual, Poggioli was more interested in new worlds than in the museum world of his immediate background. By conviction a socialist, he was too well versed in Russian culture to be much attracted toward the Soviet regime. His political mentor was Gaetano Salvemini, whose last lectures at Florence he had heard as a student, and whose family friendship he was to cherish during the last Harvard years of the exiled historian. In his consistent disapproval of Fascism, Poggioli too had come under the suspicion of Mussolini's police, and America loomed as a haven upon his horizon. The opportunity came through an invitation from President Neilson of Smith, who made a policy of welcoming a brilliant succession of émigré scholars. To finance the journey Poggioli translated a recent Polish novel in two weeks, only to discover that funds were blocked. After somehow arriving and teaching Dante at Northampton in 1938–39, he accepted an assistant professorship at Brown University, where he spent several engrossing years, taking a leave of absence to serve in the United States Army during the war. After commuting to Cambridge as visiting professor of Romance languages in 1946–47, he was called to Harvard the following year as Associate Professor of Slavic and Comparative Literature.

Both departments were then being reorganized, having previously led a somewhat marginal existence. To their expanding pedagogical needs he could respond with characteristic ambidexterity. Out of his large repertory of courses, many undergraduates favored the one on Russia's two greatest novelists, popularly known as "Tolstoyevsky." Graduate students were dazzled and disciplined by a sequence of seminars in Romanticism, Symbolism, and other esthetic theories, which he always pinned down firmly by textual explications. He became a professor in 1950, and Curt Hugo Reisinger Professor of Slavic and Comparative Literature in 1960. Acting chairman of the Slavic Department in 1952, he was chairman of the Department of Comparative Literature from 1952 to 1963. As a member of the Dumbarton Oaks Board of Scholars (1951–1953), a Syndic of the University Press (1953–1958), and a Senior Fellow in the Society of Fellows (1953–1963), he genially put his immense reading and his traveled judgment at the service of his colleagues. He collaborated in more than the usual number of organizations and publications here and abroad; he taught on occasion at various other universities, notably Rome in 1953–54 and the Sorbonne in 1961. But, despite some tempting overtures from Europe, he was naturalized as an American citizen in 1950, and his commitment to Harvard University was complete.

Much of his published work was devoted to the interpretation of Slavic literature—a particular *tour de force* for an Italian writing in English. His principal books in this field are *The Phoenix and the Spider* (1957), a collection of critical essays on Russian prose writers, and *The Poets of Russia: 1890–1930* (1960), which won the Faculty Prize of Harvard University Press. His training as a Slavicist, joined to his Latin inheritance and reinforced by his international tour of duty, made him a living personification of comparative literature. His cosmopolitan insight into the dynamics of artistic change and development was formulated in his theoretical study of modernist movements, *Teoria dell' Arte d'Avanguardia* (1962), hailed as a landmark in Italy and currently being translated. During his sojourn at the Center for Advanced Study in the Behavioral Sciences at Palo Alto in the spring term of 1963, he was bringing other promising projects to completion, above all a monumental treatment of the pastoral as a genre and a mode of thought, *The Oaten Flute*. Further studies in the idea of decadence and in utopianism, along with a volume of collected papers, are in the process of being edited. Hence Poggioli's scholarly achievement, already so considerable, should be greatly amplified by his posthumous influence.

Yet printed words, however eloquent, will never quite convey the unique vivacity of his teaching. His delicate sense of form drew substance from his vigorous sense of history. His passion for ideas was tempered by the playfulness of his humor. He sought to awaken students to alternatives, rather than to superimpose a doctrine of his own. With all the warmth of his generosity, he could be stern toward intellectual dishonesty; he could react volcanically against academic intrigue. To see him leaving the library, juggling books and gestures with both hands, his Etruscan face illuminated by a wide smile and a dangling cigarette, answering a band of questioners with quotations in half a dozen languages, was to feel that—for the moment at least—the steps of Widener had become the terrace of a Latin Quarter café. Nonetheless his ways had been Americanized; he was fond of covering the country on long motor trips with his wife and daughter; and it was on one of these, near the Oregon border of California, that they met with the brutal collision that cost him his life. It may not be amiss for us to recall his favorite passage from Dante, which tells how Ulysses refused to stay comfortably at home, but traveled forth again westward and encountered his end while continuing the quest for virtue and knowledge: *virtute e conoscenza.*

MEMOIRS OF SCHOLARS, 4:
PERRY MILLER

This memoir, for which I must take full responsibility, was published in the *American Philosophical Society Year Book* for 1964. Again I am painfully conscious of the disparity between a *curriculum vitae* and the life that energized it. Some day I may possibly return, in a less official vein of reminiscence, to some of the personalities with whom I have studied and taught. Since the occasion of writing, two of Perry Miller's books have been posthumously published, edited by Elizabeth Williams Miller: *The Life of the Mind in America, from the Revolution to the Civil War* (New York: Harcourt, Brace, and World, 1965), and *Nature's Nation* (Cambridge: Harvard University Press, 1967).

If Perry (Gilbert Eddy) Miller was not a New Englander by birth, he was one by both works and election—in the fullest sense of the Calvinistic phrase—and by ancestry as well. His mother, a solid Yankee, came from Wallingford, Vermont, as did the parents of his father, a middlewestern physician who was more of a latterday Transcendentalist than a worldly success. Miller himself was born in Chicago on February 25, 1905, attended public schools in his native city, and earned his undergraduate and graduate degrees at the University of Chicago. His years of adolescence coincided with the brief decade known, until its leading exponents gravitated to New York, as the Chicago Renaissance. A brilliant youth with literary aptitudes, growing up in its provocative atmosphere, was bound to be affected by its Bohemian coloring, its iconoclastic attitudes, its espousal of critical realism as against the Genteel Tradition. Miller always remained a middlewesterner in his hearty manner, his outgoing temperament, and his immense avidity for a culture which was not to be taken for granted at any point. This was the very impetus that rounded the family cycle, conveyed him eastward to his spiritual home, and elicited dynamic ideas from the arid preserves of antiquarians and genealogists. On vacations from school with his head full of *Walden,* he had first hitchhiked to New England, where he looked up great-aunts and visited ancestral graveyards. The fresh eyes, the romantic ardor, the youthful vigor, and the ambitious drive that he brought to a field which seemed overworked—which seemed indeed, to some lively contemporaries, exhausted—ended by turning a personal rediscovery into a monumental endeavor.

After a restless freshman year, he dropped out of college in 1923. For the next three years he knocked about the world, satisfying a boy's appetite for adventure on a literal plane. He started by wandering westward to Colorado, fraternizing with tramps and I.W.W.'s; then he worked his way east and confirmed a latent histrionic flair by picking up small jobs in the entourage of the theater. Finally, having taken to sea with the merchant marine, he arrived at the Belgian Congo, where he found himself "supervising, in that barbarian tropic, the unloading of drums of case oil flowing out of the inexhaustible wilderness of America." It was there, on the edge of the central African jungle, that he suddenly experienced his vocation: "to have thrust upon me the mission of expounding what I took to be the innermost propulsion of the United States." In retrospect, and with due qualification, he was fond of comparing that experience with the famous vision of Gibbon, sitting among the ruins of the Capitol and conceiving *The Decline and Fall of the Roman Empire*. Miller was well aware that the contrast would prove at least as striking as the comparison; but he amply justified the assumption that he too had sat at a historiographical crossroad. If the Roman pattern was decadence, the American theme was development, and the Christian religion could be historically conceived as the principal agent of both. The America that Miller returned from Africa to study, in order to expound it from its origins, was not the materialistic exporter of oil but a visionary explorer whose most decisive adventures had taken place in the sphere of intellect.

Thus he had already set his goals when he reenrolled in the University of Chicago, where he proceeded to take the Ph.B. in 1928 and the Ph.D. in 1931. American literature was accorded little attention from English departments anywhere at the time; but he was encouraged by the sympathetic counsel of Percy Holmes Boynton; and he also profited from the courses of the colonial historian, William E. Dodd. In 1930 he married Elizabeth Williams, a fellow graduate student who was to be his devoted collaborator in the research for and the writing of all his books. The couple spent the following year in Cambridge, where Miller used the local libraries to complete his thesis and entered into his fruitful association with Samuel Eliot Morison and Kenneth B. Murdock. After obtaining the doctorate, he was to spend the whole of his teaching career as their colleague on the Harvard faculty. Advancing from the post of instructor and tutor in History and Literature, he was promoted to tenure in 1939; designated as Harvard's first Professor of American Literature in 1946, he was appointed to the newly established Powell M. Cabot Professorship in 1960. His introductory course in American literature, originally offered in stimulating conjunction with two gifted and short-lived friends, F. O. Matthiessen and William Ellery Sedgwick, became his own uniquely effective vehicle for undergraduate instruction. His graduate seminars in various aspects of colonial and nineteenth-century thought were keystones of an expanding program in American studies. Ranging widely from the Department of English, he likewise taught under the departmental rubrics of History, Philosophy, General Education, and the Theological School.

The adventurous zest that animated all his intellectual undertakings expressed itself more directly in the Second World War, wherein he served with the Office of Strategic Services as captain and major in the army of the United States from 1942 to 1945. Afterward, when the European universities were discovering American civilization, he inaugurated a special chair at Leyden. Later he played a similar part in a seminar at Tokyo University. Returning to his own researches, he spent two congenial terms as a member of the Institute for Advanced Study at Princeton. He lectured widely through the United States and Europe; he was actively associated with many professional organizations and scholarly publications; he garnered more than the usual meed of distinctions, including five honorary degrees and a prize from the American Council of Learned Societies for Distinguished Scholarship in the Humanities. In 1956 he became a member of the American Philosophical Society. A sociable man with no children of his own, and with strong feelings of gratitude toward his own teachers, he in turn became a proudly paternal mentor for his former students who went on to distinguish themselves. Like other intellectuals of the self-conscious generation that came of age during the twenties, he cultivated a mettlesome life-style, in spite of some fragility in health. Tall, bespectacled, pink-faced, prematurely gray, perennially boyish, originally slender, he put on bulk with the years, and his sensitivity was insulated by his camaraderie. Usually jovial, he could sometimes be brusque—and even, on one or two occasions, aggressive to the point of using his fists. More and more his nervous energies sought the relaxation of alcohol, which clouded his last years and hastened his death on December 9, 1963.

That Perry Miller should have given us our fullest understanding of

Puritanism was a sheer triumph for the historical imagination, for a liberalism catholic enough to embrace an antithetical orthodoxy. At a moment when the word itself meant hardly more than a popular target, he had been drawn to the subject by his resolve to begin at the beginning. On a higher level he had to fight for the history of ideas against the prevailing vogue of economic and social history. His doctoral dissertation, *Orthodoxy in Massachusetts, 1630–1650* (1933), constitutes the indispensable preface to his further inquiries. His major achievement, *The New England Mind,* comprises two volumes, separated in their composition by the war, but unified in their artistic construction, dramatic presentation, and massive documentation: *The Seventeenth Century* (1939) is a systematic "anatomy of the Puritan mind," *From Colony to Province* (1953) is an absorbing narrative of the Puritan experiment. The impact of the first volume was registered soon after its appearance when the Modern Language Association devoted a discussion meeting to it, while some of Miller's incidental findings—such as his appendix on the influence of Petrus Ramus—opened up new areas for subsequent scholarship. Though he did not continue his full-scale account of the New England mind, the story reaches its eighteenth-century climax with his authoritative biography of Jonathan Edwards in the American Men of Letters series (1949). His central concern for the powerful theologian of the Great Awakening led him to edit an unpublished manuscript, *Images or Shadows of Divine Things* (1948), and helped to initiate the Yale edition of Edwards' complete works. A collection of Miller's important articles was published under the apostolic title of *Errand into the Wilderness* (1956).

Since he was constantly digging up documents, sifting over half-forgotten tracts, and digesting voraciously sermons long unread, his editorial activities were a vital contribution in themselves. The fruits of his industrious and percipient reading were shared through a sequence of rich anthologies: especially *The Puritans* (1938), compiled in original collaboration with Thomas H. Johnson, and *The Transcendentalists* (1950). His selection from Roger Williams' writings was framed by a challenging reinterpretation of Williams' doctrines (1953). The essay with which he introduced the text of Thoreau's lost journal, *Consciousness in Concord* (1958), provoked some controversial reverberations. In the final decade of his life, Miller shifted his chronological interests to the period between the American Revolution and the Civil War. Though he never finished the large work he planned, he produced a number of interesting offshoots, notably *The Raven and the Whale* (1956), a study in the backgrounds of Poe and Melville. From the completed chapters he left on religion, law, technology, and the esthetic crosscurrents of "Romantic America" it is hoped that two posthumous books will emerge. Miller's broadening geographical focus was consistent with his emphasis, from the very first, on the continuities between the Bay Colony and the European past. Despite a humorous article about his exasperations as an academic Innocent Abroad, he was anything but a nationalist or a provincial. Nothing could be farther from provinciality than his gift for entering doctrinaire minds, for dramatizing lost causes without undue sentimentality, for reconstructing in their own terms the issues our world has displaced. To exercise it he had to be that rare hybrid, in Reinhold Niebuhr's phrase for him, "a believing unbeliever." Such a fusion of erudite sympathy with critical detachment should assure Perry Miller his place among America's foremost intellectual historians.

THE JUDGMENT OF POSTERITY

The train of speculation and citation that engaged me here was prompted by a panel discussion of literary historiography, under the chairmanship of Paul De Man, during the fourth triennial meeting of the American Comparative Literature Association at Yale University, April 2, 1971. Afterthought nearly doubled the length of my short paper—and much increased its density, I fear—when it was rewritten for publication in *Arcadia: Zeitschrift für Vergleichende Literaturwissenschaft* (1. Heft, 1972). I now see that what the subject calls for is really a monographic treatment, which I can only hope that these suggestions might help some future student to carry out.

Living in a literary rhythm set by weekly best-seller lists, Books of the Month, annual awards, and last year's remainders, we might find it salutary to look back toward a time when writers looked farther ahead. Writing came into being for the sake of the record, so to speak, for the transmission of current or recent experience to successive generations. In the past men have shown much concern for the fate of their distant progeny, as well as for the repute of their ancestry, and literature has been the time-binding testament that existed to reinforce such ties. Its tribal memories and oral traditions, originally, had not even depended upon the written word. Poets from Pindar to Shakespeare have claimed the authority to commemorate a name, and upon occasion to share the fame of the heroes they have celebrated. Ovid could invoke, as a familiar convention, such poetic intimations of immortality ("vatum praesagia").[1] But it was Petrarch, above all others, who envisioned the poet's highest reward as an enduring reputation: "vitae finis principium est gloriae."[2] Though he cannot be said to have discovered posterity, any more than he can be said to have discovered mountains, he projected strong feelings about both. In his early letter to Tommaso Caloiro on the desire for premature praise, he argued that true *fama* does not begin until death. Accordingly, he addressed his writings to future readers, hoping to reach in them the wisest and fairest judges. His autobiographical epistle, *Posteritati,* lay perforce unfinished at his demise. Yet, in some of his letters, he likewise attempted

1. *Tristia,* IV.x.129.
2. *Epistolae familiares,* I.2.

to establish communion with noble Romans like Cicero; for timelessness was his ultimate frame of reference; and high commendation, as he wrote to a resurrected Varro, must come not from one's own era but from all the centuries.[3]

Horace has rested his claim to have built a monument *aere perennius* on an explicit innovation, on having first successfully adapted Aeolian song to Italic verse (elsewhere he seems willing to settle for an aftermath of a hundred years).[4] And if a lesser poet like G. R. Derzhavin could repeat *non omnis moriar,* that courtly pioneer could maintain that he had used Russian meters to sing the praises of Catherine the Great and to enlighten the Tsars.[5] When Derzhavin's great inheritor Pushkin came in turn to compose his *exegi monumentum,* he could make a much bolder assertion: that, in a cruel age, he had glorified liberty and spoken out on behalf of the proscribed.[6] That was indeed too outspoken a vaunt to be printed during his lifetime, but the poem concludes by expressing a stoical indifference to the censure of fools. The corollary to this state of mind was, of course, full trust in an infallible posterity, which would understand and appreciate what one's short-sighted contemporaries had overlooked, distorted, or suppressed. Thus the neglected Stendhal could console himself by projecting a series of posthumous dates for his critical vindication.[7] His most hopeful expectation, 1880, turned out to have been justified by the enthusiasm of Taine and an élitist cult at the Ecole Normale Supérieure. His most belated projection—a century after his death in 1842—also proved to be worth waiting for, since it tested the significance of his novels for the Resistance during the Second World War. Another writer ill at ease with his time, Henry Adams, seems to have been less fortunate in concluding his autobiography with the hope that, if his centenarian shade returned in 1938, he "would find a world that sensitive and timid natures could regard without a shudder."[8]

The actual menace that world held for timid and sensitive natures had been all too prophetically apprehended by Kafka, the bulk of whose work would be published after his death in 1924. Like Vergil and Chaucer and others, he had expressed deathbed doubts as to

3. *Ibid.,* XIX.16; I.9; XXIV.6.

4. *Odes,* III.xxx.12; *Epistles,* II.i.39.

5. G. R. Derzhavin, *Pamiatnik,* ll. 14–16.

6. A. S. Pushkin, *Ia Pamiatnik . . .* , ll. 15–16.

7. See Harry Levin, *The Gates of Horn: A Study of Five French Realists* (New York and London, 1963), p. 85.

8. *The Education of Henry Adams* (New York, 1928), p. 505.

whether his literary remains, in their more or less fragmentary condition, should ever be presented to the public. That melancholy Jacobean, John Marston, had gone further in his gesture of self-obliteration; having in midcareer abandoned the theater for the church, he had ended by requesting that he be buried under the anonymous inscription, "Oblivioni Sacrum." This cryptic epigraph can be glossed by the concluding poem, dedicated "To euerlasting Oblivion," in his satirical sequence, *The Scourge of Villanie:*

> Let others pray
> For euer their faire Poems flourish may.
> But as for mee, hungry *Obliuion*
> Deuoure me quick, accept my orizon.[9]

But, though these lines may deserve the Nirvana they ask for, Marston still occupies a modest place on Parnassus. (As it happens, his is one of the many names inscribed on the granite façade of the Boston Public Library.) Worthy of special note are those works which were never motivated by any prospect of publication and have consequently been given to the world with the heightened excitement of an archeological discovery. Such introverts as Emily Dickinson and Gerard Manley Hopkins took no steps to see their poetry into print, regarding it primarily as a mode of mystical self-communion not unlike prayer. Even more striking was the situation of Mikhail Bulgakov, because the barriers that prevented him from publishing were externally superimposed by government censorship. Cut off from an audience while he lived, he went on writing his books with a courage and a conviction that have been finding their warrant at last.

To these inheritors of unfulfilled renown, the idea of posterity has functioned as a court of appeal, reversing the fallible judgments of contemporary critics more often than not. The irony of such reversals could be excruciatingly bitter, as it was with Keats's own anonymous epitaph ("Here lies one whose name was writ in water"), so soon to be controverted by the train of appreciation and admiration heralded in Shelley's "Adonais."[10] English literary history would recognize both poets, along with Byron, as the major talents in the second generation of that movement which it so expressly characterizes as romantic. Yet the term was quite unfamiliar to them, or to the elder generation of

9. John Marston, *The Scourge of Villanie*, ed. G. B. Harrison (London, 1925), p. 119.
10. See W. J. Bate, *John Keats* (Cambridge, Mass., 1963), p. 694.

Wordsworth and Coleridge—who in their heyday were placed in a marginal category, rather derisively nicknamed the Lake School. None of them had the widespread circulation or the general approbation that was then accorded to Samuel Rogers or Thomas Moore, while Blake had so minor and tangential an impact that it was left for the Pre-Raphaelites to rescue his reputation from underground. With the passage of years and with the growth of a retrospective tradition, some of the last have moved forward in the unending procession, while some of the quondam first have been falling behind. Though we still may have some trouble in defining the concepts of Romanticism, its connotations have become such touchstones that we judge its predecessors by them, conveying our approval with the teleological label of Pre-romanticism. What Diderot prescribed for history at large may well be particularly applicable to literary history: that we study it backwards.[11]

The gaps between immediate reception and eventual recognition, between how it strikes a contemporary and the revenges of time's whirligig, are measured by the span that originality must traverse in order to make its breakthrough and gain acceptance. Its coevals are more likely than not to misunderstand it; therefore, Du Bellay counsels, echoing Petrarch, "entrust the fruit of thy labor to an incorruptible and unenvious posterity"; and Mathurin Régnier takes it for granted that "Le juge sans reproche est la postérité."[12] (One of the strongest presuppositions here is a belief in progress and human perfectibility.) Music proposes the cardinal example of Johann Sebastian Bach, who was esteemed in his day as a performer, though he was barely noticed as a composer until he was rediscovered by Mendelssohn. The fortunes of Melville furnish our literary historians with their most flagrant miscarriage of critical justice and their most triumphant rectification. (Melville's own discovery of Hawthorne was weighted by the claim: "I am Posterity speaking by proxy."[13]) The curve of Henry James's prestige has mounted to such vertiginous heights that it may be in some danger of toppling downward. Whether the contemporaneousness of the subject was an advantage or a limitation for the critic, Sainte-Beuve could

11. Denis Diderot, *Oeuvres complètes*, ed. J. Assézat (Paris, 1875), III, 492f. (*Plan d'un université pour le gouvernement de Russie*).

12. Joachim Du Bellay, *La Deffence et illustration de la langue françoyse*, ed. Henri Chamard (Paris, 1904), p. 246 (ch. V); Mathurin Régnier, *Oeuvres*, ed. Edouard de Barthélemy (Paris, 1862), p. 197 (*Satyre* XV).

13. "Hawthorne and His Mosses," in *The Shock of Recognition*, ed. Edmund Wilson (New York, 1943), pp. 187–204.

never make up his mind; but he himself seems distinctly more at home in the seventeenth or eighteenth century than he is with Flaubert or Baudelaire. *The Oxford History of English Literature,* by rule of thumb, excluded living authors from its twentieth-century volume.[14] Appearing in 1963, it was outdated as soon as T. S. Eliot died just two years afterward. At the other extreme a survey of American fiction, which prided itself on dealing with no novelist over forty, reads like an anachronism just ten years afterward.[15]

Put off by small-minded parochialism or high-handed interference in his homeland, like the exiled Joyce or perhaps the muted Solzhenitsyn, the writer may come to feel that the foreign response to his work is a manifestation of "cette postérité vivante." Joyce translated that consolatory phrase in his notebooks, attributing it to Chamfort, through whose succinct writings I long searched for it in vain.[16] Much later I stumbled across it in a speech by Mirabeau, who had been defending the French Revolution by appealing to the sympathies of democratic nations.[17] Given such antithetical responses as those of Edmund Burke and Thomas Paine, we could not attest that the international verdict on this event was unanimous—nor will it ever be. Could opinion ever be unanimous in reacting to anything as kinetic as an important book, except to the extent that its very survival might be defined as an index of its importance, with due allowance for the fact that reactions continue to differ? Nietzsche has commented, apropos of the French Revolution, that the interpretation has obscured the text and hence the past is bound to be misunderstood by posterity—or rather, since we ourselves have become posterity, we must admit that its hour is already past.

Wie es zuletzt noch, in aller Helligkeit der neueren Zeiten, mit der französischen Revolution gegangen ist, jener schauerlichen und, aus der Nähe beurteilt, überflüssigen Posse, in welche aber die edlen und schwärmischen Zuschauer von ganz Europa aus der Ferne her so lange und so leidenschaftlich ihre eignen Empörungen und Begeisterungen hinein interpretiert haben, *bis der Text unter der Interpretation verschwand:* so könnte eine edle Nachwelt noch einmal die ganze Vergangenheit missverstehn und dadurch veilleicht erst ihren Anblick erträglich machen.—Oder vielmehr: ist dies nicht bereits

---

14. J. I. M. Stewart, *Eight Modern Writers* (Oxford, 1963).

15. Ihab Hassan, *Radical Innocence: Studies in the Contemporary American Novel* (Princeton, 1961).

16. Quoted by Herbert Gorman, *James Joyce* (New York, 1939), p. 136.

17. H. G. Riqueti, Comte de Mirabeau, *Collection des travaux,* ed. Etienne Méjan (Paris, 1792), III, 196.

geschehen? waren wir nicht selbst—diese "edle Nachwelt"? Und ist es nicht gerade jetzt, insofern wir dies begreifen—damit vorbei?[18]

The notion of welcome abroad as the final decision of a living posterity presupposes that distance lends a clarifying perspective, which transcends ephemeral detail and local allusion. Yet the best-known American authors in other countries, such as Fenimore Cooper and Jack London (neither highly honored by his compatriots), have been admired by foreigners for their regional colorations and their national stereotypes. The Nobel Prize has demonstrated that the Swedish Academy is quite as fallible as any other circle of critics. Some of the rarest wines do not travel well; some of the cheapest do. Addison held that the test of genuine wit was whether or not it would bear translation.[19] That is the sort of test we would scarcely dare put to some of the world's greatest poetry.

The argument that time must be the arbiter of value, and that endurance through it will be the best criterion, tends to be somewhat circular, inasmuch as it brings us back to the question of what determines this perdurability. Dr. Johnson begged that question when, paraphrasing Boileau, he recommended "books which have stood the test of time, and been admired through all the changes which the mind of man has suffered from the various revolutions of knowledge, and the prevalence of contrary customs."[20] But Johnson was not one to let other critics resolve his responsibilities; in his monumental *Preface* he himself assumed the mantle of posterity and proceeded to confer "the dignity of an ancient" on Shakespeare—in other words, a classical status.[21] The acknowledgment of Shakespeare's preeminence had not offered, at least since Dryden, any peculiar novelty. Johnson's unique contribution lay in his enabling arguments against the prescriptions and the constrictions of neoclassical dramatic theory. However, the underlying principle that led him to the canonization of Shakespeare was grounded upon the very bedrock of neoclassicism: "Nothing can please many, and please long, but just representations of general nature." During the previous century and a half, the fugitive and accidental features of Shakespeare's art had faded out or fallen away, and what now loomed so large were its timeless and universal contours. It had been abstracted

---

18. *Jenseits von Gut und Böse,* sec. 38.

19. Joseph Addison, *The Spectator,* ed. D. R. Bond (Oxford, 1965), I, 263 (No. 61).

20. Samuel Johnson, *The Rambler,* ed. W. J. Bate and A. B. Strauss (New Haven and London, 1969), II, 122 (No. 92).

21. Arthur Sherbo, ed., *Johnson on Shakespeare* (New Haven and London, 1968), I, 61.

and sublimated to the plane of Imlac in *Rasselas,* where the poet "must disregard present laws and opinions, and rise to general and transcendental truths, which will always be the same; he must therefore content himself with the slow progress of his name; contemn the applause of his own time, and commit his claims to the justice of posterity."[22]

But Imlac's program is greeted with raised eyebrows by Rasselas; Johnson's footnotes bear witness to the persistence of Shakespearean particularities; and it could hardly be said that his own works came to fruition within a temporal vacuum. In noting that the emergence of poetic excellence was "not absolute and definite, but gradual and comparative," he opened the way for a relativistic outlook: a realization that so-called universality must be reckoned on a finite scale, that every object worthy of being respected had its quiddity, and that breadth of interest might be obtained for a wide variety of reasons. "Time," he admitted, "has sometimes co-operated with chance"—a precept which could be supported by countless examples.[23] Vergil owed his preferential standing throughout the Middle Ages partly to the coincidence that allowed his Christian readers to interpret the *Fourth Eclogue* as a religious prophecy. Galsworthy has lately undergone a revival because his family chronicles seem to accord with the conventions of B.B.C. soap opera. Inevitably the passage of time has its winnowing effect; while most things are predestined to be buried, a few others come to light as the soil is sifted; but, so long as the years continue to succeed one another, there can be no escape from the new contingencies that they bring with them. Every age is thereby an age of transition from the preceding one to the next, and its version of literary history is the sum of its critical decisions as to what it wishes to hand on. These in due course are reversible by the succeeding ages, so that the last word can never be much more than a temporary consensus.

Literary history can never be definitive for the simple reason that—like its subject matter, like the concept of posterity itself—it exists in the Heraclitean flux of ever-changing time. We are misled by naïvely primitive metaphors when we think of it as a settled afterworld *sub specie aeternitatis* where everything has finally come out right. Shakespeare himself, our leading candidate for eternity, was seriously preoccupied with mutability. He too could echo the Horatian challenge:

---

22. Samuel Johnson, *The History of Rasselas, Prince of Abyssinia* (Oxford, 1927), ed. G. B. Hill, p. 51 (ch. X).

23. *Johnson on Shakespeare,* I, 59.

> Not marble nor the gilded monuments
> Of princes shall outlive this powerful rhyme.[24]

But he was profoundly conscious, and could trenchantly demonstrate, that mere human beings were the fools of "envious and calumniating time" and that no one was exempt from the ravages of "cormorant devouring time."[25] Swift's *Tale of a Tub* is dedicated "To his Royal Highness, Prince Posterity," who is conceived as an illiterate infant under the tutelage of Father Time. It is Swift's conceit that nothing contemporary will last long enough to be read when that illustrious pupil has learned his letters. Blackened paper will meanwhile have been utilized for more ephemeral needs. Dryden will have gone the way of Tate, Durfey, Rymer, Dennis, and Bentley.

What is then become of those immense Bales of Paper, which must needs have been employ'd in such Numbers of Books? Can these also be wholly annihilate, and so of a sudden as I pretend? What shall I say in return of so invidious an Objection? It ill befits the Distance between *Your Highness* and Me, to send You for ocular Conviction to a *Jakes,* or an *Oven;* to the Windows of a *Bawdyhouse,* or to a sordid *Lanthorn.*[26]

More reverently, in the old library of Westminster Abbey, Washington Irving paused to meditate on "The Mutability of Literature." The vaunted imperishability of art is, at most, contingent and relative; it is not a matter of living forever, but of outlasting the artist's mortal life, of creating something which—as Ernest Hemingway expressed it, more modestly than Horace—will not "go bad afterwards."[27] It brings out a crucial difference between the short term and the long run, but continuance does not necessarily mean perpetuity.

A creeping obsolescence is inherent in the nature of the materials, in the words and forms that writers use, and this is one of the reasons for the existence of literary historians. The belief in immortality was, to Ernest Renan, no more than an invincible confidence in the future of humanity. Holding such a confidence himself, he furthermore believed that the advance of literature ran parallel to the development of science. Consequently, it was enough to have made one's contribution to this progressive march of intellect during one's epoch. It was an illusion to expect anyone, except for specialists, to read one's work in future

24. *Sonnets,* LV.1–2.
25. *Troilus and Cressida,* III.iii.173; *Love's Labours Lost,* I.i.4.
26. Jonathan Swift, *A Tale of a Tub,* ed. Herbert Davis (Oxford, 1957), pp. 21–22.
27. Ernest Hemingway, *Green Hills of Africa* (New York, 1935), p. 27.

generations. The greatest writers would survive primarily as names, and the reading of literary history would in the main replace the reading of what they had written.

Nous souhaitons que notre nom reste bien plus que notre livre. Notre immortalité consiste à insérer dans le mouvement de l'esprit un élément qui ne périra pas, et en ce sens nous pouvons dire comme autrefois: *Exegi monumentum aere perennius,* puisque un résultat, un acte dans l'humanité est immortel, par la modification qu'il introduit à tout jamais dans la série des choses. Les résultats de tel livre obscur et tombé en poussière durent encore et dureront éternellement.[28]

Reducing Renan's humane skepticism to pseudopedantic absurdity, Anatole France went so far as to claim "that the professors and scholars constitute the whole of posterity all by themselves."[29] France was commenting upon a session of the French Academy, an institution he would later join, whose forty members are known as the Immortals during their lifetimes, though most of them are forgotten soon after their deaths. His overstatement could be documented by the instance of Terence, whose comedies were not very well received by their original Roman audiences, but have enjoyed an enormous fortune during the subsequent centuries because their Latin style and edifying *sententiae* fitted them so conveniently into the curriculum of the secondary schools.

The Longinian discernment of certain qualities that should "please all and always" may have seemed attainable to the ancients.[30] It is tantalizingly ironic that so many examples of this broad appeal have survived only as they were fragmentarily quoted in the pseudonymous treatise *On the Sublime.* Sappho, whose most famous poem was preserved by that means, seems to have counted heavily—and, as it turns out, justifiably—on such an eventuality, when she announced that her blessing from the golden Muses would keep her from being forgotten after she died.

> ἀλλ' ἔμ' ὀλβίαν ἀδόλως ἔθηκαν
> χρύσιαι Μοῖσαι οὐδ' ἔμεθεν θανοίσας
> ἔσσεται λάθα.[31]

---

28. Ernest Renan, *L'Avenir de la science: Pensées de 1848* (Paris, 1890), pp. 223, 225–226.
29. Anatole France, *La Vie littéraire* (Paris, 1897), I, 113 (*Sur le Quai Malaquais*).
30. W. Rhys Roberts, ed., *Longinus on the Sublime* (Cambridge, 1907), p. 57.
31. Reconstructed by J. M. Edmonds, *Lyra Graeca* (London and New York, 1922), I, 192; see also p. 237.

The manuscripts of the classics, extant or lost, need merely be mentioned to indicate the role of accident in shaping our canons of ancient literature. Academies have traditionally been better at stabilizing and preserving the cultural heritage than at contributing to it. The unlikely presumption that a modern writer could somehow become a classic, which had its landmark in Johnson's reappraisal of Shakespeare, developed into an eclectic pantheon with Sainte-Beuve and the nineteenth century. T. S. Eliot's conception of an ideal order, wherein each new masterpiece affects the interrelation of all the preexisting works, is counterweighted by what W. J. Bate has recently termed "the burden of the past," the problem of the writer's cumulative awareness of all that has preceded his modernity.[32] Both conceptions stress the dynamic, but increasingly difficult, continuity between tradition and innovation, which could be further illustrated by the points of connection between Eliot's poetry and his critical revaluations. The intensive reconsideration of the Metaphysical poets during the present century has, I trust, brought us closer to an understanding of their own period; it has unquestionably reflected ours. Far from having little to do with criticism, as suggested by R. S. Crane a generation ago, literary history is committed to a continual process of selection, revaluation, and self-revision.[33]

Wissensoziologie has alerted us to the ulterior motives working within any discipline; and we know that historicism itself, as an offspring of romanticism, has been concerned with establishing national identities, with the quest for whatever can be called the usable past. The masterly *Storia della letteratura italiana* of Francesco De Sanctis was, among various other things, an expression of the Risorgimento. Comparable literary histories have sometimes been undertaken in a spirit of liberal opposition to a status quo, as with the *Main Currents* of Georg Brandes or V. L. Parrington. At other times an authoritarian state has controlled the reinterpretation; Heine became a nonperson under the Nazis; and the intermittently revised editions of the Soviet Encyclopedia register the retroactive changes of the ideological line. But, though historical objectivity is an approximation to a goal rather than an achievable certainty, legitimate revision operates through the progressive correction—rather than the studied perpetation—of distor-

32. W. J. Bate, *The Burden of the Past and the English Poet* (Cambridge, Mass., 1970).
33. R. S. Crane, "History versus Criticism in the University Study of Literature," *English Journal*, XXIV (1935), 645–667.

tions, misconceptions, and errors. The congenital bias of the observer in favor of his own viewpoint, after all, may be neutralized by a widening of perspectives. An unhistorical critic like Boileau, with a condescending nod to antecedents ("Enfin Malherbe vint . . ."), could envisage the past as an evolution toward the refinements of his particular moment.[34] His cavalier insensitivity to the French masters of the Renaissance stands in significant contrast to the English retrospect of Dryden, who professed a comparable set of neoclassical principles, yet could view comparatively the strengths and weaknesses of "the last age" and the limits of his own.

> Our Age was cultivated thus at length,
> But what we gain'd in Skill we lost in Strength.
> Our Builders were with Want of Genius curst:
> The Second Temple was not like the first.[35]

Dryden was viewing that First Temple from the vantage point of the second, as Johnson would be from what Professor Bate has so very aptly described as the third. That is to say that each was acutely aware of his contemporaneous situation, then of the age of Shakespeare, and again of his own posterior relationship to that age, and that the exercise of his critical judgment was based upon a kind of dialectical interplay. Who else could have pronounced so authoritatively, speaking with the voice of Shakespeare's posterity? For ourselves, coming so much later and with so little reassurance for counting upon an indefinite future, this displacement shifts the emphasis to the past. We shall never know how posterity will react, but we can learn a certain amount from the way it has already reacted. Through the study of *Überlieferungs-geschichte* we can trace the impacts and the vicissitudes of literary history: its ups and downs, discoveries and demotions, revivals and rustications, probations and canonizations—in short, those continuing shocks of recognition which relate it organically to the lives and minds of all who have participated in it. As for posterity in the millennial sense, perhaps it can most meaningfully be treated as a heuristic myth like that of Utopia, which has accomplished much by setting unattainable goals.[36] The viable path is not from contemporaneity to posteriority

34. *L'Art poétique,* I. 131.
35. "To my Dear Friend, Mr. Congreve, on his Comedy called *The Double Dealer*," ll. 11–14.
36. See Henri Peyre, *Writers and Their Critics: A Study of Misunderstanding* (Ithaca, 1944), pp. 250–268.

but from anteriority to contemporaneity. This is why Croce could remark that all true history was contemporary history ("ogni vera storia
è storia contemporanea").[37] When, in the theatrical prelude to Goethe's
Faust, his poet voices the conventional hope for a delayed reward from
the *Nachwelt,* he is recalled by the professional clown to the earthy
immediacies of the *Mitwelt* here and now.[38] Nevertheless the issue remains problematic, as this counterstatement from *Torquato Tasso*
would seem to imply:

> Und wenn die Nachwelt mitgeniessen soll,
> So muss des Künstlers Mitwelt sich vergessen.[39]

But, though the Princess would thus absolve the artist from the claims of
immediacy by pointing to his higher engagement with futurity, in the
next scene we watch her crowning Tasso with a laurel she has snatched
from the bust of Vergil. And while we are seeking for wisdom from
Goethe on our theme, we should also remember the tag-line of *Goetz von
Berlichingen,* the curse upon a mistaken posterity: "Wehe der Nach-
kommenschaft, die dich verkennt!" Expressing himself in his own
person elsewhere, he speculates on the psychological basis of the whole
notion, the satisfaction of immortal longings by a subjective appeal
from a smaller to a larger venue of opinion.

> Der Appell an die Nachwelt entspringt aus dem reinen, lebendingen Gefühl,
> dass es Unvergängliches gebe und, wenn auch nicht gleich anerkant, doch
> zuletzt aus der Minorität sich der Majorität werde zu erfreuen haben.[40]

Christian eschatology had met that perennial urge by holding out the
vista of a spiritual afterworld. But Dante, while professing to write *De
monarchia* for the benefit of posterity, had declared that he was thereby
simply paying his debt to prior generations; he was animated rather
by duty and gratitude than by a neopagan love of worldly fame.[41] Later
and more secular centuries would relocate heaven on earth, seeking it in
the material future through the idea of progress. "La postérité pour le
philosophe," maintained Diderot, "c'est l'autre monde de l'homme

---

37. Benedetto Croce, *Teoria e storia della storiografica* (Bari, 1943), p. 4.
38. *Vorspiel auf dem Theater,* ll. 73, 77.
39. *Jubiläums-Ausgabe,* XII, 103; ibid., X, 126.
40. Ibid., XXXVIII, 256–257 (*Maximen und Reflexionen*).
41. *De monarchia,* I, i.

religieux."[42] In his correspondence with the hardheaded sculptor Falconet, who held that posterity was no more than a dream or a lottery, Diderot saw it as an ethical principle taking the place of religion. Men would be consoled for their sorrows and inspired to noble deeds by the posthumous esteem of their fellow men. Diderot's invocation is almost a prayer: "O postérité sainte et sacrée!" This goddess would become a patron saint of the Religion of Humanity and an ideological herald of the French Revolution. "Every age would be the posterity of all preceding ages," Carl Becker has summed it up, "and as the eighteenth century, in the light of two thousand years of human experience, had vindicated Socrates and Regulus against the erring opinion of their time, so generations yet to come would vindicate the Voltaires and Rousseaus, the Robespierres and the Rolands."[43] Robespierre himself would apostrophize a posterity still in the throes of birth:

Doux et tendre espoir de l'humanité, postérité naissante, tu ne nous es point ètrangére; c'est pour toi que nous affrontons tous les coups de la tyrannie; c'est ton bonheur qui est le prix de nos pénibles combats; découragés souvent par les objets qui nous environnent, nous sentons le besoin de nous élancer dans ton sein; c'est à toi que nous confions le soin d'achever notre ouvrage, et la destinée de toutes les générations d'hommes qui doivent sortir du néant.[44]

And Robespierre concluded his speech to the Jacobins, on the question of war in 1791, by urging a nascent posterity to inaugurate new days of equality, justice, and happiness. Revolutionary ethics, torn between conflicting authorities, still appeals to posterity as its final authority. In his courageous "Letter to the Fourth Congress of Soviet Writers [1967]," Alexander Solzhenitsyn criticized the Russian censorship for usurping posterity's function: "Of fleeting significance, it attempts to appropriate to itself the role of unfleeting time—that of separating good from bad."[45] That he has found an audience outside Russia, where all but one of his books are banned, strengthens the case for foreign contemporaries as a living posterity. That he should be able to go on writing, in the face of such blank opposition within his homeland, bears witness to the

---

42. *Oeuvres complètes,* ed. J. Assézat and Maurice Tourneux (Paris, 1876), XVIII, 99–102. See Herbert Dieckmann and Jean Seznec, *Diderot et Falconet: Les six premières lettres* (Frankfurt, 1959), *Analecta Romanica,* VII, 10–18 and *passim.*

43. Carl Becker, *The Heavenly City of the Philosophers* (New Haven, 1932), p. 142.

44. Charles Vellay, ed., *Discours et rapports de Robespierre* (Paris, 1908), p. 155.

45. "Letter to the Fourth Congress of Soviet Writers, May 16, 1967," in *Cancer Ward,* tr. Nicholas Bethell and David Burg (New York, 1969), pp. vii, xii.

influence of posterity as a source of moral inspiration. Thus he confirms the transcendence of the written word over the individual life:

I am of course confident that I will fulfill my duty as a writer under all circumstances—even more successfully and more unchallenged from the grave than in my lifetime. No one can bar the road to truth, and to advance its cause I am prepared to accept even death. But may it come about that repeated examples will finally teach us not to stop the writer's pen during his lifetime.

FROM TERENCE TO TABARIN:
A NOTE ON *LES FOURBERIES DE SCAPIN*

An issue of the *Yale French Studies* (1967) was dedicated to Henri Peyre, in honor of his sixty-fifth birthday, and was devoted to the central theme of French Classicism, which Professor Peyre has done so much to illuminate. Though the instance I have presented is somewhat marginal, I am glad to see the paper back in print for two reasons. The first is the chance to correct a text badly garbled by editorial mishap, so that my quotations from Latin verse somehow came out in prose. The second is an interest in comedy which I have long pursued through my teaching, but which as yet has not led to such writing as I had planned—and continue to plan.

If some grove in the Elysian Fields were frequented by the shades of comic playwrights, Molière and Terence would doubtless have fore-gathered to discuss the vicissitudes of their critical reputations. They had been already brought together, in the company of a vulgar mounte-bank, by one of the most famous—not to say patronizing—criticisms ever launched at Molière. Boileau, in the third canto of his *Art poétique,* had been hesitant in awarding his personal accolade because he felt that Molière, too avid for public approval, had

> Quitté, pour le bouffon, l'agréable et le fin,
> Et sans honte à Terence allié Tabarin.

We know that Molière, like a respectable classicist, had previously imitated the Latin playwright; we even have the word of his fellow actor La Grange, in the preface to *L'Ecole des femmes,* that this play had been modeled upon the *Adelphoe.* Editorial footnotes and doctoral theses can be trusted to have made the most of such borrowings and to have worked out parallels by summarizing plots. But the gravamen of Boileau's critique was that Terence's eclectic borrower, incorrigibly tak-ing his property wherever he happened to find it, had turned aside from his impeccable source to dally on the Pont Neuf, as it were. For it had been there, in the previous century, that the Italianate mountebank Tabarino had set up his trestles and offered his songs and gags as an inducement to the public for buying his nostrums and embrocations. Molière indeed reflected that situation in the *entr'acte* of *L'Amour médecin* where the quack doctor advertises the therapeutic virtues of *orviétan,* and several of his other plays present us with our best evidence of how deeply the roots of comedy are intertwined with the medicine show.

Now if the shade of Molière could complain about Boileau's stricture, the shade of Terence could respond by complaining about his treatment at the hands of so redoubtable a critic as Julius Caesar. Caesar's qualifying verses, which are cited no less often than Boileau's, occur in an epigram which salutes Terence rather ungraciously as half a Menander ("o dimidiate Menander"). The Roman poet is pronounced the equal of his Greek predecessor as a devotee of pure style ("puri sermonis amator"). But Terence is accused of lacking that central quality without which any writer of comedies would seem to be fatally deficient, nothing less than comic energy ("vis comica"). In other and cruder words, Terence may not have been funny enough for Caesar, whereas Molière may have been all too funny for Boileau. Here the disagreement is not between the playwrights but between the critics and their respective standards. Caesar seems to have been judging by the comic spirit, Boileau somewhat less relevantly by the *esprit de finesse,* and Molière's departure from the neoclassic criterion ended by making his own work into a model, which has been described as "the *Hamlet* of farce." Terence, as we learn from his prologues, had not been on very congenial terms with the audiences of his day. His survival down the centuries has been a highly literary phenomenon. If he is the vital link in the chain of New Comedy extending from Menander to Marivaux and beyond, he may well owe his unique position to the fortuitous disappearance of most of his master's works.

Much of his continuing prestige may stem from two incidental qualities, which endeared him to schoolmasters and secured the tenure of his plays as a staple of the curriculum. The first was the one that Caesar had singled out for praise, the exemplary lucidity of his Latin. The second, which may not be unconnected, was his flair for *sententiae.* Though the dramatic situation might not prove uproariously comical, he could always bring it to a point with some tersely worded moral precept, so that the mild frivolity of the context could be subsequently ignored and his works could be regarded as a grand repository of wise saws and quotable aphorisms. Hence it was specified in the Elizabethan statutes of Westminster School that the Queen's Scholars should perform a play by Terence each Christmas, in order to cultivate good speech ("bene loquendi") and to hear good advice ("consilia"). That annual performance still goes on, just as it did in the school days of Ben Jonson or of John Dryden, for whom it may well have constituted their earliest association with the great comic tradition. Since there are only six plays in the Terentian canon, among which the *Phormio* has been perhaps the most popular, every school generation has witnessed it at least once. In the old dormitory theater a round of applause has gone up every time a self-conscious schoolboy has stepped to the footlights and solemnly voiced a *sententia:* fortune favors the brave ("fortis fortuna adiuvat"), a word to the wise ("dictum sapienti sat est"), or as many minds as men ("quot homines tot sententiae").

There remains the usual disparity between such pedagogical generalizations and the far from exemplary behavior of the pair of youths who are so admonished on the stage. "When the cat's away the mice will play" is not a Terentian adage, but it helps to indicate the kind of suspense that hangs over New Comedy. Inevitably its playboys go a-wenching; their holiday is over when their heavy fathers return; then monetary obstacles are placed in the way of amatory objectives; and it becomes the role of the clever servant or parasite, aiding the lovers by duping their elders, to find a way out and resolve the conflict between generations. The interest of the plot is bound to focus increasingly on this strategic role and on the increasing ingenuity of its repertory of stratagems. The title of the lost Greek play on which *Phormio* was based, *The Claimant (Epidicazomenon),*—not by Menander, as it happens, but by Apollodorus—may offord some hint as to the characterization. Terence's adaptation of it develops symmetrically; each of his *adulescentes* gets into trouble with a girl; one of them gets married against his father's wishes, though paternal opposition will melt away at the end when the orphan is identified as a long-lost niece. The other *adulescens* has not quite such honorable intentions; he is in love with a cithern-player, a slave who must be purchased from a bawd; and the legalistic ruse of the title character is to procure the money as a dowry from one *senex* by pretending to be a suitor who will take the unwanted daughter-in-law off his son's hands.

The double intrigue is unified by the domestic circumstances that the old men happen to be brothers and the young men must therefore be cousins. The perennial *agon* between crabbed age and flaming youth flares up with the successive disembarkations of the two *senes,* returning home from their journeys to be confronted by the misrule that has prevailed during their absences. Demipho, under the impact of rumors about the marriage, soliloquizes bitterly but philosophically. Such meditation ought to prepare us for the worst when things are going best. The homecoming traveler should think about risks and losses, his son's crime, his wife's death, or his daughter's illness. Since these are all too common experiences, he should not be too surprised if they happen to him. Anything better than what he then expects should be counted as clear gain.

> quam ab rem omnis, quom secundae res sunt maxume
> meditari secum oportet quo pacto advorsum aerum nam ferant:
> pericla, damna, peregre rediens semper secum cogitet,
> aut fili peccatum aut uxoris mortem aut morbum filiae;
> communia esse haec, fieri posse ut ne quid animo sit novom;
> quidquid praeter spem eveniat, omne id deputare esse in lucro.

By means of a familiar Terentian device, this moralistic soliloquy is overheard by the *fallax servus* Geta, who counters with a certain amount of moralizing from his own point of view. He remarks to the lover Phaedria that the servant's wisdom is ahead of the master's; for Geta has been reflecting upon the misfortunes that such a return could bring him: whippings, fetters, drudgery at the mill or on the farm— the lot that slaves are constantly threatened with. Since none of these retributions would surprise him, he will count anything better as clear gain.

> o Phaedria, incredibile quantum erum ante eo sapientia.
> meditata mihi sunt omnia mea incommoda, erus si redierit:
> molendum usque in pistrino, vapulandum, habendae compedes,
> opus ruri faciundum. horum nil quicquam accidet animo novom.
> quidquid praeter spem eveniet, omne id deputabo esse in lucro.

It is illuminating to watch Molière, as he adapts this passage to the prose of *Les Fourberies de Scapin*. Terence has shown the master and the servant vying with one another in the mournful interchange of edifying commonplaces; the single humorous element is supplied by the line of verse that Geta echoes from Demipho. Molière's transposition allows the old man, Argante, to be greeted by the protagonist, Scapin himself, whose stature is thereby enlarged. In their direct confrontation without asides, it is the greeter and not the voyager who painfully enumerates the hazards of homecoming, under the guise of quoting a text from the ancients. Each of these has the effect of an additional blow, shrewdly administered by Scapin to the suffering Argante. Consequently the scene takes on a dimension of irony; and when Scapin continues—as Geta did—by imaging the discomforts that he may encounter in his own person, we sympathize with him and feel a certain *Schadenfreude* over the imagined calamities of Argante. (Though we are no longer living under a regime of slavery, the prospect of a beating seems as much of a menace as ever.) What was merely didactic has become dramatic; and though the two speeches are given to one interlocutor, they give the other one more of a psychological opportunity to register a characteristic reaction:

Que pour peu qu'un père de famille ait été absent de chez lui, il doit promener son esprit sur tous les fâcheux accidents que son retour peut rencontrer: se figurer sa maison brûlée, son argent dérobé, sa femme morte, son fils estropié, sa fille subornée; et ce qu'il trouve qu'il ne lui est point arrivé, l'imputer à la bonne fortune. Pour moi, j'ai pratiqué toujours cette leçon dans ma petite philosophie; et je ne suis jamais revenu au logis, que je ne me sois tenu prêt à la colère de mes maîtres, aux réprimandes, aux injures, aux coups de pied au cul, aux bastonnades, aux étrivières; et ce qui a manqué à m'arriver, j'en ai rendu grace à mon bon destin.

This leads into a passage, barely adumbrated by Terence, where the possible redresses of the law are seen as an even more vivid series of tortures. The episode that follows provides an occasion for Silvestre, the *valet* of Argante's son, to masquerade as a professional bully by whose horrendous threats the reluctant father is blackmailed into inadvertently subsidizing his son's romance.

One of the theatrical conditions that differentiates Molière from Terence most strikingly, and comes closer to Meredith's emphasis on the feminine influence in comedy, is the utilization of charming actresses. The shrewish *matrona* drops out, though the indispensable *nutrix* survives, since recognition scenes could hardly take place without the old nurse's identification of strawberry marks. But, where both of Terence's heroines merely subsisted offstage, both of Molière's play dynamic parts; and his counterpart for the cithern-player, a heroine stolen by gypsies, is no less insistent on marriage than his other heroine. The symmetry of the parallel intrigues has thus been intensified, since both fathers must now be mulcted to set up the two young couples. That step entails still further responsibilities for the arch-schemer dominating both plots. The original trickster, Phormio, was self-confident enough ("homo confidens"), and—as a *parasitus*—he was ostensibly more of a free agent than his successor, Scapin. The latter is a servant, albeit the very cleverest of clever servants and by no means a Roman *servus* or slave. Considerable freedom of action is promised by his listing among the dramatis personae as "valet de Léandre, et fourbe." We may view him as a crowning figure in the brilliant sequence of valets, whose comic possibilities Molière had sounded by playing many of them himself. Yet, since the rogue in Scapin outplays the domestic, he becomes a picaresque hero in his own right. The interplay is brought out when Léandre testily calls him "Monsieur le coquin" and he jauntly acknowledges the salute: "Monsieur, votre serviteur."

We should recognize that we are dealing with neither a Mascarille nor a Sganarelle, but with Molière's one and only Scapin. He had been clearly inspired by the Scappino of the Commedia dell'Arte, though the Italian comedian had hailed from Milan, while Molière has set his scene at Naples to fit in with the classical convention of a Mediterranean seaport. The name itself has the overtones of escape: from *scappare,* to get away, to make one's getaway, to get away with some mischief or other. In Callot's incisive delineation, sharply differing from the mask of the gentler servingman Harlequin, the archetypal Scapin has a beak-like nose and warlike moustaches; wearing loose garments and a rakish hat, he carries a flat wooden sword which looks more suitable for the bastinado than for the duello. Handyman, factotum, jack of all trades ("Laissez-moi faire!"), he is above all a well-meaning busybody who practices his *fourberies* benignly when it is a question of young people in love ("homme à m'intéresser aux affaires des jeunes gens"). When it is a question of older people harboring contrary motives, he deploys the rich resources of his basic malice. Consciously he manipulates human beings, in terms which might have suggested Bergson's theory of laughter: "La machine est trouvée!" The scheme for blackmailing Argante was hinted by Terence; the machination against Géronte, one of Molière's most illustrious plagiarisms, was lifted from the otherwise forgotten comedy of Cyrano de Bergerac, *Le Pédant joué.* There it may be significant that Corbineli, who employs the ruse to deceive the pedant Granger on behalf of his wayward son, is characterized as "valet du jeune Granger, fourbe."

Corbineli's trumped-up tale is more absurd than Scapin's, since it avers that young Granger has been kidnapped by Turkish pirates who have somehow navigated the Seine as far as Paris. Consequently the repeated outcry of old Granger, "Que Diable aller faire dans la galère d'un Ture?" makes slightly more sense when its echo becomes the *mot de caractère* so indelibly associated with Géronte. "Que diable alloit-il faire dans cette galère?" has come to serve as a byword for going out of one's way to get into trouble. It can also stand for the sticking-point of an unlikely story which nonetheless finds acceptance. The obtuse Géronte perceives that it is far-fetched without perceiving that it is false, as his gullibilities—played upon by Scapin—overcome his avarice and other conflicting emotions. Could there have been no other place for Léandre to walk? Disastrous curiosity! Géronte's own stupidity is later brought home when his son's fiancée, the laughing Zerbinette, recounts the joke on him to him; since she is unaware of his identity, the playback is at once more ironic and more good-humored than its precedent in *Le Pédant joué*. The victim's realization of his plight is exacerbated, at this point, because he is smarting from Scapin's last and latest trick: a revenge which has been motivated by Géronte's initial reaction to the swindle involving the Turks. He has mortally offended Scapin by proposing that, in lieu of a ransom, it would be "l'action d'un serviteur fidèle" to offer himself as a hostage for his young master. And Scapin, vowing to get even, has perpetrated his culminating deceit solely for his own satisfaction.

Molière had used up most of his material from the five-act *Phormio* during the first two acts of *Les Fourberies de Scapin,* and had eked it out by borrowing the gag of the Turkish galley from Cyrano de Bergerac. Having more or less settled the affairs of the lovers, Scapin is operating on his own in the third act; it is his cadenza of roguery; and, since everything else has been built up to it, it is not calculated to let him down. The *lazzi* of the sack, which seems to have been borrowed from the Commedia dell' Arte, possibly through the dubious Tabarin, lends Scapin his definitive opportunity to play the virtuoso of mischief-making. Since Géronte is not financially mulcted here but physically chastised, he is reduced to the lowest level as a comic butt; and he reacts to his castigation as he did to the earlier deception, with the same ambiguous combination of suspicion and credulity, low cunning and high indignation. The bag on Scapin's back, into which Géronte must crawl, might also be viewed as a distended version of his professional attributes, moneybags. The indignity that he undergoes within it, like that of Sancho Panza tossed in a blanket, is the predicament of a human being who gets treated as if he were a thing. Having frightened Géronte into hiding where he cannot look out, Scapin is enabled to act out three bullying roles in as many dialects, and in each case to deliver some exploratory blows, just to prove that there is nothing in the bag worth taking seriously. Finally, at the very moment when he is carried away by his impersonations, they are exposed by the reemergence of Géronte like a jack-in-the-box.

Less audacious, the other valet Silvestre has expressed his occupational fear of *coups de bâton* from the very first scene of the play. Impersonating a *spadassin* in his turn and swaggering "un peu en roi du théâtre," according to Scapin's instructions, Silvestre has taken obvious pleasure in threatening to beat his old master, Argante. *Serviteurs fidèles* indeed! In the introductory catechism that defines Scapin's relationship with Léandre, assault and battery are among the sins to which the servant confesses: under the covering darkness, it now comes to light, he has attacked his young master. He escapes due punishment because Léandre is so helplessly dependent upon his officious services. The latent aggressions that reach the surface, in such reversals, foreshadow that critical moment when Figaro will denounce Count Almaviva. Phormio, who boasted that he had almost beaten men to death with impunity, ended by shaming the errant pantaloon Chremes into condoning the peccadillos of youth. Scapin's final blackmail, which effectively silences the fuming Géronte, is his muffled attempt to apologize loudly and publicly for subjecting his elder master to his *coups de bâton*. His gesture of retaliation falls into perspective as a deliberate stroke of poetic justice. For Boileau it was a crude anticlimax, coming as it did after Molière's most serious comedy:

> Dans ce sac ridicule où Scapin s'enveloppe,
> Je ne reconnois plus l'auteur du Misanthrope.

In Englishing this reductive couplet *mutatis mutandis,* Sir William Soames transposed the examples from Molière to Ben Jonson:

> When in the Fox I see the tortoise hissed,
> I lose the author of the Alchemist.

But the parallels are inexact; *The Alchemist* is more farcical than *Volpone,* taken as a whole; when Sir Politick Wouldbe fatuously climbs into his tortoise shell, he invites the thumping that he duly receives, whereas the sack is a triumph of Scapin's contrivance. Nor is it Scapin himself or Molière that the sack envelops, as Boileau misleadingly suggests. After all, it is Géronte who receives and deserves that fitting retribution who fulfills the traditional definition of the clown as "he who gets slapped." It was not for nothing that the sword of Scappino looked more like a *bâton*. Slapstick may not be recognized in the classical *ars poetica;* but it is an art in the theater, notwithstanding; and *Les Fourberies de Scapin* is its assailing and unassailable classic.

AN INTRODUCTION TO BEN JONSON

In 1937, just three hundred years after Jonson's death, there was no compact selection of his best works in print. The monumental Herford-Simpson edition, which had started to come out in 1925, had yet to reach its halfway point. In an interchange of correspondence and conversation with the late Bennett Cerf of Random House, I suggested that Jonson be included in their series of single volumes mainly devoted to the English masters, most of which had originated under the British imprint of the Nonesuch Press. Mr. Cerf surprised me, not by being generously responsive to the suggestion (from a man of his catholic enthusiasms I had rather expected such a response), but by asking me to be editor of the volume. It was a rash decision on both sides, since the American publishers had no experience in that kind of fussy editing, and the proof corrections were numerous and expensive. For my part, I was interested in Jonson, had been directing and acting in amateur performances of his plays, was assured of access to his quartos and folios through the Harvard College Library, and had the time to spare from my Junior Fellowship. On the other hand, I was not well versed in editorial and bibliographical procedures (then not so highly refined as they are today), and whatever I learned about them I found out the hard way, through the trials and errors of collation and correction. The resulting version was very imperfect, but it was closer both to the original text and to modern usage than the one available reprint, which was largely based on the early nineteenth-century Gifford edition. An attractive format assured it a friendly reception in the United States (1938) and later in England (1940), where it was kindly welcomed by Evelyn Simpson, now continuing the great edition. In reprinting my introduction here after much hesitation, I shift the responsibility to Walter Kaiser and other friends who wanted to see it resurrected. Clearly this essay was written a long generation ago, and belongs to another period as well as another author—one at whom I would look askance. If I could, I would qualify his sweeping generalizations and modify his impressionistic and allusive style. He had been encouraged by John Livingston Lowes to write a book about Jonson; and this, plus one or two specialized articles, was as far as he would get. Consequently, he would take particular satisfaction in Jonsonian books by former students: Jonas Barish, John Enck, Stephen Orgel, Wesley Trimpi. Four preliminary paragraphs, relating to the original context, are omitted from the text that follows.

1. TRADITION

In the history of literature, Ben Jonson has gone down as a figure, rather than as a writer. Critics call him by his first name upon very slight acquaintance. The strength of this impression is a testimony to the malice of one of his friends, William Drummond of Hawthornden. The eighteenth century contributed to the confusion by producing a Johnson whose opinions were quite as emphatic and even more influential. The nineteenth century, with its preference for personalities above achievements, put the final stamp on what was left of Ben Jonson's reputation. His unique personal prestige, the extraordinary number of his articulate friends and enemies, the fact that we know more about him than we need to know—these are the accidents that constrain him into playing the part of eccentric. What is actually eccentric is the development of English literature. By the standards of his time, Jonson never deviates from his defined intentions and assured techniques, which constituted the nearest approximation that England had yet made to an organized culture and an academic style. Saint-Evremond expressed the mind of the Restoration when he singled Jonson out for the select company of Aristotle, Horace, Corneille, Boileau, and other literary law-givers. A succession of revolutions has impaired their authority.

For most of the last two centuries Jonson's principal function has been to serve as a stalking-horse for Shakespeare. Others abide our question, Shakespeare transcends it; and if you would understand, point for point, the limitations he transcends, go read Jonson. Often an attempt is made to settle the problem on a quantitative basis—Shakespeare's characters are considered three-dimensional, Jonson's are reproached with incorrigible flatness. The retort to this kind of criticism is a stubborn insistence that, strictly speaking, no literary creation has any dimensions at all. Another chapter in the history of taste and of studies has been compiled since the days when Jonson was damned by the canons of Shakespearean pantheism. Scholarship talks less about nature and more about the theater. Esthetics requires a measure of abstraction. The old impatience with limitation has been replaced by a new appreciation of convention, which we take to be not only the form but also the essence of art.

No dramatist could have strayed very far from the crude psychology and constricting conditions that hedged in the Elizabethan stage. It is true that Shakespeare had an artifice against artifice, an unequaled capacity for conveying the impression that he was not subject to such limitations. So successful are his occasional touches of nature that we are still surprised when his personages act according to the exigencies of the plot, and not according to motives which we ourselves should acknowledge in their place. But this trick of transcendence is not to be reckoned with; all that can be said is that it succeeds sporadically, even in Shakespeare. Webster catches it now and then, Dekker and Heywood handle it rather inexpertly, and if Jonson is really responsible for the painter's scenes in *The Spanish Tragedy,* he had mastered it too. There is no reason to condemn his usual method of characterization for dealing with encounters instead of experiences and appealing to judgment instead of sympathy. Jonson's characters move in the same world as those of Marlowe and Middleton, Nashe and Donne, lampooning courtiers and pamphleteering journalists. In this as in other respects, Jonson is closer than Shakespeare to the literature of his day, and by no means preoccupied with the literature of the past.

Jonson is commonly conceived as a man who wrote comedies because he had a theory about why comedies ought to be written. This formidable misconception is buttressed by Jonson's own words, in a tireless series of prefaces, prologues, and asides. To accept them is to take an author's rationalizations about his own work too seriously and to ignore the historical circumstances that they were designed to meet. The comedy of humors was not arrived at as a descriptive formulation for purely critical purposes; it was seized upon as a polemical weapon to answer the Puritan attacks on the stage. Jonson, Chapman, and other dramatists were exploiting a psychological novelty which had appeared at the turn of the sixteenth century, in order to ward off popular resentment against the satirical sharpness of their "wormwood comedies." The induction to *Every Man out of his Humour* sets forth the full argument for comedy as a social purgative. It is perhaps as relevant to Jonson's work as psychoanalysis is to the dramas of Eugene O'Neill.

Like Aristotle's doctrine of catharsis, which it strikingly resembles, Jonson's theory of humors is less analytic than apologetic, less a system of literary criticism than an exercise in ethical justification. Had Jonson regarded it as more than a convenient metaphor, he would have become entangled in the contradiction that brought the Spanish philosopher Huarte before the Inquisition. If you undertake to reform society by confronting it with its own picture, and that picture is so darkly deterministic that it precludes all possibility of reform, what then? Do you curb your reforming zeal? Do you moderate your behaviorism? Are you obliged to choose between philanthropy and misanthropy? Or are you simply a hard-working playwright, with a hard-headed and somewhat doctrinaire view of humanity, trying to protect your vested interests by beating the moralists at their own game? O cursèd spite!

If Jonson's too ample protestations can be construed to show him as a reformer, he does nothing to discourage the assumption that he is a pedant as well. Here the incentive may be a private one. We must bear in mind the bricklayer's apprentice who lived to receive an honorary degree from Oxford, the second-rate actor and patcher of second-hand plays who forged for himself the position of *arbiter elegantiarum* in English letters. Jonson was a dramatist before he was a scholar. Poetry was too literally its own reward, and he envied the status of acquaintances who had fallen back on the church or the law—Donne and Bacon, for example. The wars of the theaters, his repeated retirements from the loathèd stage, and the petulance and paralysis of his old age left him no solace but his books. As his audiences grew smaller, his own orientation widened; he improved his relations with the ancients and began to invoke posterity. Practical disappointments could only confirm him in the theoretical principles of a self-made humanist.

Gathering manuscripts and accumulating commentaries, enjoying the friendship of scholars like Camden, Cotton, Savile, and Selden, he sought to fit into a better regimen for a literary life than the Bohemian purlieus of the theater afforded. The *Discoveries* are chiefly remarkable as an evidence of this phase of Jonson's activity, as an armory of maxims and a storehouse of ideas, as a link between Jonson and his masters in rhetoric, Seneca and Quintilian, Vossius and Heinsius. The very titles of his occasional collections of verse and prose—*Underwoods, The Forest, Timber*—glance at the *Sylvae* of the polymaths of humanism. His failures, never clapperclawed by the palms of the vulgar, were dressed up in annotated editions to catch the eyes of the learned. The thin quarto of *Sejanus,* with its marginal freight of Latin citations, must have formed a curious item on an Elizabethan bookstall. Derisive echoes make us wonder at Jonson's presumption in daring to gather his plays into a folio volume and publish them under the self-confident designation of *Works.*

The cultivation of these outward and visible marks of erudition accomplished far more than its calculated effect. It persuaded readers that the *Works* smelled exclusively of the lamp and desensitized their perception against a swarm of other odors—fragrant, pungent, savory, and rank, as the case may be. Jonson does speak with much conviction when he is paraphrasing the classics, but it is doubtful if an indefinite number of hours in a library could have taught him to sketch in his detail so casually as this:

Ha' not I
Known him, a common rogue, come fiddling in
To th' ostería, with a tumbling whore,
And, when he has done all his forced tricks, been glad
Of a poor spoonful of dead wine, with flies in't?

It would be strange if signs of Jonson's vast reading had not crept into his writing; it would be stranger if the Tyburn brand on his thumb, his military career in the Low Countries, his religious conversion, his dubious activities as a spy, and all his duels and amours had not given him opportunities for observation that are assimilated in the things he wrote. Next to extreme bookishness, undue realism is the quality for which Jonson has been most bitterly censured. At Saint John's College, Cambridge, he was looked down upon as "a meere Empirick, one that getts what he hath by obseruation, and makes only nature priuy to what he indites." He put down everything he read, according to one side, everything he saw according to the other.

These vicissitudes of opinion are resolved by a single consideration —Jonson, first and last, was preeminently a craftsman, planning and constructing his verse and prose as solidly as he had learned to lay bricks. That is why he has been mistaken for both a pedant and a reformer, why he has been miscalled an arrant translator and a mere empiric. The fact is that, like a good workman, he felt the weight of literary tradition while remaining within the current of contemporary life. He differs from his fellow writers not in aims and methods, but in being more conscious of the task of adaptation they jointly performed and in going about it more systematically. England had, for the first time, a legislator of Parnassus, to sit in the chair later occupied by Dryden and Samuel Johnson. All of a sudden, it had seemed, there were not enough forms and concepts, not enough phrases and words, in the native stock, to express all the possibilities of which people were becoming aware. There had ensued a stage of borrowing and engrafting, of translation and experiment. What was now needed, and what Jonson definitely represented, was a vernacular classicism.

In this light, we are struck by the straightforward and pragmatic nature of Jonson's classical program. The efforts of scholars at the universities, lawyers in the Inns of Court, and friends of the Countess of Pembroke had failed to revive tragedy in its pristine purity; schoolmasters, critics, and divines united to deplore the way in which Paul's

Churchyard flouted the rules of rhetoric; English poets had abandoned the chase after the chimera of quantitative meters. Ben Jonson entered the field as a professional man of letters. As one who thoroughly grasped and had extensively practised most of the bastard forms that had sprung up, he knew how they could be clarified and made supple. As the first of a line of neoclassicists, he wanted not to surrender to Greece and Rome but to rival them, to wed ancient form to modern substance. He had hoped to achieve a perfect embodiment of this ideal in the fragmentary pastoral *The Sad Shepherd,* where his proclaimed purpose was to garner

> ... such wool
> As from mere English flocks his Muse can pull,

and therewith to fashion

> ... a fleece
> To match or those of Sicily or Greece.

It is characteristic of the culture of the Renaissance at its ripest that it should seek to give classical precedent a local habitation and a name. Horace's *fons Bandusiae* is transformed into Ronsard's *fontaine Bellerie.* The tropes of Catullus,

> Quam magnus numerus Libyssae harenae
> lasarpiciferis iacet Cyrenis,
> oraclum Iovis inter aestuosi
> et Batti veteris sacrum sepulcrum;
> aut quam sidera multa, cum tacet nox,
> furtivos hominum vident amores,

suffer a sea-change, in Jonson's paraphrase:

> All the grass that Rumney yields,
> Or the sands in Chelsea fields,
> Or the drops in silver Thames,
> Or the stars that gild his streams,
> In the silent summer nights,
> When youths ply their stol'n delights.

Sedate dignitaries from the pantheon of Natalis Comes are jostled out of Jonson's masques by English worthies from Captain Cox's library; the same blend of refined commonplace and homely folklore tinctures the lyrics of Jonson's disciple, Herrick. The tribe of Ben was responsible for fastening his favorite measure, the heroic couplet, upon English poetry, where it prevailed with the tenacity of neoclassicism itself until, further straitened by an enforced sojourn in France, it become the cell in which Pope was condemned to pace out his existence, five steps down and five steps back.

We can distinguish between what is classical and what is native in the traditions available to Jonson, but we have no means of measuring the extent to which they make themselves felt in his work. It would be futile to try to determine the preponderating element or to weigh them both in the clumsy balance of form and content. The norms of dramatic structure, in comedy and in tragedy, Jonson had obviously generalized from Latin models, more precisely from Plautus, Terence, and Seneca. For the profound significance of the Roman satirists to the late Elizabethan mentality, particularly after downright imitation had been prohibited and the pent-up gall had burst forth on the stage, Jonson's "comical satires" are our main witness. Yet more than the materials of his plays is indigenous. The conventions of the English morality are respected in Jonson's casts and plots, in the charactonyms of his personages, in the beast-fable of *Volpone* or the gaping Hell-mouth of *The Devil is an Ass*. And beneath his writing runs a broad substratum of journalism, of all the tracts, broadsides, and jestbooks that had granted literary recognition to the London underworld before Jonson came along.

Finally, there is a plane upon which these opposing forces reach an equilibrium. The extremes of rhetoric and pamphleteering, the old and the new, foreign and domestic, and erudite and popular meet in an illusory half-world, wherein the *fallax servus* borrows the lath dagger of the Vice and Cato shakes his finger at Til Eulenspiegel. The whole farrago of types and themes becomes intelligible, from this distant vantage-point, as the outside of a large, heterogeneous cultural movement. Across Europe, along the drift from Renaissance to Reformation, from Italy to Germany, stride two gigantic protagonists, the rogue and the fool. In the conflicts of humanistic learning and empirical experience, the war between theology and science, a literature is evolved which has the expansiveness of the picaresque and the inclusiveness of satire. It is the age of Erasmus, Brant, Rabelais, and Cervantes. It is time for Shakespeare's Jaques to cry "Ducdame" and to call all fools into a circle.

Against the background of the Reformation, then, rather than that of the Renaissance, Jonson may be seen at his best. He was by birth and apprenticeship an Elizabethan, but the succeeding years are those he dominates, and the elegies of his lamenting "sons" would have been more impressive if they had not been issued in the year of the Bishops' War. For it is Jonson's career which most strongly marks the transition in English literature from sonnet to satire, from comedy of the court to comedy of the city, from poets who celebrated imaginary mistresses to poets who dedicated themselves to detraction, from the virtuous conduct of Castiglione's Courtier to the gross etiquette of Dedekind's Grobian. Jonson is the legitimate heir of the Renaissance, of the Elizabethan age, and of Christopher Marlowe—it took a third poetic craftsman, T. S. Eliot, to discern that. When we come to examine the texture of Jonson's verse, we shall be grateful for this discernment. We must recognize the formal continuity, if only to appreciate how sharply it reserves its intellectual bearing. Marlowe belongs to one century and Jonson to another, and their respective attitudes toward human nature are as far apart as More's *Utopia* and Hobbes's *Leviathan*.

2. SATIRE

The richness of the Renaissance, about which so much has been said, is more than a metaphor. In what was, after all, the heroic age of mercantile enterprise, it should not astonish us to find a luster reflecting the influx of wealth from the Indies and of gold from the Americas. We breathe the glittering atmosphere of the Mediterranean, ever the center of fashion and luxury, in *The Jew of Malta, Othello,* and *Volpone,* while *Eastward Ho, The Tempest,* and *The Fair Maid of the West* have in them something of the saltier air of British adventure. Economic expansion, in England, was accompanied by an intensely universal feeling of nationwide participation, which finds cultural expression in the collections of the voyagers, in the Tudor translations, in the chronicle plays, in the idealized figure of the Virgin Queen. This exaltation and confidence, which suggests comparison with the American Dream, seems to lose its bloom in the last decade of Elizabeth's reign, just as the freshness of our own national ideals withered after the Civil War.

In the latter half of the sixteenth century, there was time for a new English aristocracy to grow up, and for a popular monarchy to leave off fostering democratic notions and assume more or less absolute pretensions. By the turn of the century, a mercantilist economy had dammed up the enormous flow of resources, and it was no longer easy to believe that all things were possible to any man. Patents and monopolies still changed hands; the great companies were setting out to establish the new plantations; projectors flourished and made the court a hotbed of promotion and intrigue. Step by step, through the literature of these crucial years, we can watch the sentiment of expectation change to a sense of wariness, depression, and disillusionment. With increasing introspection, everything is anatomized. Newer and more analytic forms, such as the character and the essay, are devised; ancient modes, like satire and epigram, are borrowed to fit modern instances. The native hue of Elizabethan resolution is sicklied over with the pale cast of Jacobean melancholy. Nature, it is felt, is in decay; the times are out of joint; *difficile est satyram non scribere.*

That Ben Jonson should have viewed this change in the light of the historic contrast between the Roman Republic and the Roman Empire was inevitable. Exasperated by the demands of the groundlings, exhausted by the rivalry of Marston, Dekker, and other poetasters and professionals, he was led to adopt the idiom of the Silver Age and to address himself, in the tone of Martial and Tacitus, to the imperial theme. *Sejanus,* with its acid depiction of the caprice of princes and the folly of favorites, greeted the accession of the leading apologist for the divine right of kings, the future patron of Somerset and Buckingham. Small wonder that it brought Jonson to the Star Chamber. It is no accident that Shakespeare, in his Roman tragedies, and Chapman, in his French histories, were dwelling upon the problem of authority, or that the issues of *Coriolanus* and of *Sejanus* seem even more rife today. The concentrated indignation of Jonson's Roman elders, the glimpses of espionage and repression, the epsiodes of judicial murder, the mood of flattery and fear evoke as many echoes in our ears as the cry, "Lictors, resume the fasces!"

Significantly, both of Jonson's tragic heroes are villains, so confirmed in their villainy that they need no motive; Sajanus resolves to debauch Livia before her husband has struck him, and Catiline does not wait for the election of Cicero to hatch his plot. If their efforts do not achieve the fullness of tragedy, it is Jonson's fault, for failing to counterweight them with anything but appeals to principle and exercises in rhetoric. Cicero, not Catiline, is remiss. It would be rash to conclude that the satiric spirit is hostile to tragedy. On the contrary, Jonson's tragedies come most to life when his courtiers are fawning or when his women, whose psychology is never more than cosmetic-deep, are gossiping. The very satire that called the story of Sejanus to Jonson's attention, Juvenal's tenth, is almost medieval in its stress upon tragic reversal of fortune. The tragedian of an age of satire, Seneca, had been the unavoidable model for every Elizabethan dramatist who aspired to the buskin. Shakespeare himself was forced to describe the Trojan War and Homeric heroes as "Nothing but lechery! all incontinent varlets!" His Cleopatra gives more than a hint of how Jonson might have treated her:

> ... the quick comedians
> Extemporally will stage us, and present
> Our Alexandrian revels. Antony
> Shall be brought drunken forth, and I shall see
> Some squeaking Cleopatra boy my greatness
> I' the posture of a whore.

The genius of tragedy is essentially the same as that of comedy, as Socrates mumbled through a haze of wine fumes, very early one morning in the house of Agathon. Of the tragedy of the Renaissance, disposed as it was to leave so little to fate, this is particularly true. Tragic suffering can be, and in the more remote past has been, blind and passive; comic matters notoriously involve some human agency. The slings and arrows of an outrageous fortune are not to be endured, revenge is sweet, revenge ripens into conspiracy, conspiracy passes over into intrigue, and the gap is bridged; the Elizabethans have proved at least that a similar dramatic technique will serve for tragedy and for comedy. Thus Tiberius and Sejanus, the Jew of Malta and his blackamoor, the arch-plotter Volpone and the parasite Mosca, hunt down their prey in parallel couples.

If tragedy can scoff, comedy can scorn. The comical satires are of the "biting" variety, not the "toothless." Professing to sport with human follies, not with crimes, Jonson too often took it upon himself to dispense poetic justice, to regulate his comical satires by a more rigorous ethic than life itself ever provides, to conjure up an inferno of punishments for his personal enemies. Some high-minded malcontent—an Asper or a Crites—like the melancholy Jaques, and not unlike the sort of madman that Hamlet pretended to be, figures as Jonson's accredited representative and is entrusted with the responsibility of scourging vice, untrussing affectation, and reconciling humors all around. Jonsonian comedy invariably tends in the direction of an arraignment; it must enact a trial and achieve an official resolution of the comic knot, whether by royal Cynthia or imperial Augustus, by court or Senate, or merely by a nonchalant interloper or humane jurist of the Bridlegoose breed.

In the riper comedies, the rules become more flexible. The final court room scene in *Volpone,* it is true, reverses the venal decision of the fourth act, but by that time our faith in lawyers and judges and Venetians and human beings has become corroded, and we sense the hollowness of the categorical imperative. In *Epicene,* the pretense is acknowledged, and we are invited to hear a false canon lawyer and a mock doctor of divinity hold a sham disputation. This discrepancy between law and life is the condition that governs *Bartholomew Fair.* "Think to make it as lawful as you can," pleads Dame Purecraft, and Rabbi Busy discovers scriptural sanction for the eating of pig. The bumpkin Cokes, while being edified by a ballad on the wretched end that befalls pickpockets, is robbed of his purse. In this select company of gamblers and bawds, only the half-witted Troubleall would insist upon warrant for what is done; in the very sink of enormities, the pompous Justice Overdo can find no one to expose but his own wife; in the topsy-turvy jurisdiction of Pie-powders, it is the reforming element—Overdo, the puritan Busy, and the angry man, Wasp—who land side by side in the stocks. Jonson could go no farther in reducing his own legalism to absurdity, except by haling into *The Staple of News* that trial of dogs which Aristophanes had originated and Racine would improve. These names are worth recalling, if they convey the generalization that parody of justice has always been a premise for comedy.

His object all sublime Jonson gradually relinquished to the genuine doctors and divines. With a more incisive perception of the conflict between interests and ideals, "the space between the breast and lips," he gave up the attempt to discipline his characters and they profited by their freedom. His uncompromising attitude toward his fellow men persisted, but he no longer described them as good and bad; they were simply fools and knaves or, in Elizabethan parlance, gulls and coney-catchers. The eschatology of *The Alchemist* is based on this simplified scheme; after the three knaves have cozened their victims, one of them outwits the other two, who thereupon assume the status of fools, while the arch-knave is pardoned and permitted to baffle the one honest man of the piece. *The Devil is an Ass,* as its name implies, is a study in comparative ethics, demonstrating that what is religiously regarded as the absolute in evil can only bungle along by contrast with what goes on above ground. "Hell is a grammar-school to this!" exlaims the chastened fiend, and departs on the back of the Vice, setting off an ineffectual fire-cracker, and leaving the field to Protagoras and Jeremy Bentham.

Because Jonson was enough of an Aristotelian to rank knowledge above virtue, and enough of a Machiavellian to delight in ingenuity for its own sake, it does not follow that he ever succeeded in banishing morality from his stage. In comedy, as well as tragedy, there must be a context of good and evil, but it can be defined socially rather than theologically. Pity and terror, accordingly, give way to insouciance and curiosity, and sometimes to contempt and cynicism. Comic writers start by making certain devastating assumptions about human nature, by questioning every man's honesty and every woman's virtue, even though they seldom push them to such drastic conclusions as *Mandragola, The Country Wife, Turcaret,* or *Volpone.* "Interpreteth best sayings and deeds often to the worst," says Drummond of Jonson. These assumptions inhere in the tradition of classical comedy, as part of that perfectly Euclidean realm where there are so many coincidences and no surprises, where old men exist to leave legacies, clever parasites to get around them, beautiful orphans to be shipwrecked, and young men to go a-whoring.

Jonson had assimilated the latent antagonisms of this early comedy—fathers versus sons, philistines against poets, the city as opposed to the universities. When he came to print *Every Man in his Humour* in folio, he heightened the asperity of the elder generation by assigning Old Knowell a speech out of Juvenal on the depraving of youth through luxury and trade, and weakened the position of the younger generation by omitting Lorenzo Junior's defense of poetry. The Ovid of *Poetaster* becomes virtually the "marked man" of later romanticism, condemned first by his father to the study of law, and then by the Emperor to banishment. When Jonson came to composition with his audience, however, in *Epicene* and *Bartholomew Fair,* youths could expect indulgence and pantaloons or serious asses might tremble in apprehension of the fate of Malvolio. His scholars, dropping their academic accent, set up for wits; the city became the town, and they found their way around it without difficulty. It might have comforted the banished Ovid to learn that he had furnished the very language for this elegant new coterie of Truewits and Clerimonts.

Epicene, the most brittle of Jonson's comedies, was the most likely to win Pepys' plaudits and fit Dryden's canons. Frankly a thing of veneer, explicitly discouraging attempts to glance beneath its polished contours, it stands at an interesting halfway point between Plautine and Restoration comedy. Its courtly air and its emphasis on the relations between the sexes remind us that it was written for the boy actors who had performed Lyly's plays, whereas Jonson's apprenticeship was served with the troop that had employed Marlowe, while *Sejanus* and *Volpone* were produced by Shakespeare's company. But the action of *Epicene* is not presided over by any Meredithian comic spirit. If it were not farce, it would be pathology. Was there ever a more disillusioned cavalier than Sir Dauphine Eugenie, setting out to win the collective favors of a bevy of women he totally despises? And in the attitude of the wits toward their monomaniac victim, there is more than a touch of sadism, of the "comedy of affliction."

For all its artificiality, *Epicene* was definitely set in London. From that time forth, Jonson cast aside the *fabula palliata* and took up the *fabula togata.* The change is merely a matter of nomenclature, since Jonson always followed the standard comic practice—from Menander to Minsky—of conceiving the comic stage as an intersection of city streets. Within this convention there is dramatic unity, as well as room for considerable movement. All that is needed are a few doors and windows, which Jonson, revising *Every Man in his Humour,* had no trouble in labeling "Moorfields" and "The Old Jewry." He never returned to the "fustian countries" where he had dallied before, or to the Rome that he had tried to use as a looking glass for England. Italy, to an English eye the prime breeding-place of corruption, had seemed the appropriate setting for *Volpone.* It is a grim chauvinism which insists on laying the scene for *The Alchemist* at home:

> Our scene is London, 'cause we would make known,
> No country's mirth is better than our own.

The demands of realism are most fully satisfied by *Bartholomew Fair.* Although the most meticulously local of Jonson's plays, it is also the most broadly universal; for is not all the world a fair—paraphrasing Seneca, Jonson develops the conceit in his *Discoveries*—and do not men seek gilded roofs and marble pillars, even as children are attracted to cockleshells and hobbyhorses? Under this more genial dispensation, humors diffuse into vapors, and vapors evaporate *in fumo*. Like a pilgrimage, a fair forms a comprehensive natural background against which all types and classes may be exhibited; like Chaucer, Jonson allows his characters to step out of the proscenium. Ursula, the pigwoman, challenges an odorous comparison with the Wife of Bath herself, let alone Elinor Rumming or Marion Tweedy Bloom. Here as always, realism thrives upon the implicit contrast between the way things are presented and the way literature has been in the habit of presenting those same things. What, then, could be a crueller falling-off than for Leander, having swum the Hellespont from Sestos to Abydos, to let a foul-mouthed ferryman row him across the Thames from the Bankside to Puddle Wharf?

The plots of *Eastward Ho, Volpone,* and *The Alchemist* are more highly wrought, but not so farfetched as we might believe. Amid the traffic and speculation of the Renaissance, treasure trove, legacy hunting, and alchemy were considered legitimate alternatives in the general pursuit of riches. If this crass afterthought robs Jonson's comedies of their fantasy, it binds them much more firmly to the life of their time. For they have a single theme, which may be underscored as the leading motive of Jonsonian drama, and which is enunciated by its most authoritative spokesman in the magic words, "Be rich!" Even through the disembodied parables of his final period, Jonson was playing with such subjects as the pursuit of the Lady Pecunia; and in the projector Merecraft, he created a prototype for the Mr. Micawbers and Robert Macaires and Mulberry Sellerses of bourgeois literature.

Gold is the core of Jonson's comedy, getting and spending are the chains that bind it together, and luxury furnishes the ornaments that cover its surfaces. It is further stipulated, by Volpone himself, that such gold must not be the reward of any productive endeavor. Both *Volpone* and *The Alchemist* hinge upon some monstrous device, a will or the Philosophers' Stone, but Jonson can bring to bear upon almost any situation a suspiciously circumstantial familiarity with all the ruses of craft and quackery. Insofar as it would be the nature of Volpone or Subtle to plot, whether on or off the stage, the motive of chicane becomes the determining factor in the strategy of Jonson's plays. In *Volpone,* perhaps even more than in *The Alchemist,* he has erected his most imposing hierarchies of collusion. In the later play he relaxes the two-edged ironies of fathers who disinherit sons and husbands who prostitute wives, in order to admit a procession of more earth-bound appetites, starting from the petty desires of a lawyer's clerk to cut a figure and culminating with the intransigent gluttony of Sir Epicure Mammon.

This fat knight is a Falstaff who has suddenly begun to babble like a Faustus. Hankering after fleshpots, his lordly talk is "all in gold"; "Silver I care not for." Out of the boundless opulence which his insatiate libido has already summoned up, he is even prepared to make an occasional benefaction—"And now and then a church." The limit of his lust is only measured by his gullibility; he observes Hapsburg and Medici traits in Doll Common, and addresses her in the language that Faustus reserved for Helen of Troy. 'Tis pity she's a whore! Before he takes her upstairs, he is warned not to arouse her fanaticism by introducing topics of biblical controversy. "We think not on 'em," he succinctly replies. And their departure gives Face and Subtle the excuse to bring experiments to a fiasco and blame it upon Sir Epicure's impatient sensuality. "O my voluptuous mind!" he cries.

Marlowe consistently presented the voluptuary as a hero; to Jonson, he is always either a villain like Volpone or a dupe like Sir Epicure Mammon. Taking up, at Eliot's suggestion, Sir Epicure's moist-lipped recital of the delights he hopes to enjoy, and placing it alongside Gaveston's announcement of the entertainments he has prepared for Edward II, we can observe in each case a texture woven with equal richness and a comparable barrage of sensuous appeal. Jonson's accumulation of images is even denser and more various than Marlowe's, and its effect is utterly subversive. Jonson could not have expressed his reservations more explicitly, nor hit upon a more elaborate contrivance for turning to dust and ashes all the lovely fruit of the Renaissance imagination. Nothing has been neglected, but the intonation has changed, for he is consciously dealing in illusion. Marlowe to Jonson is as Hyperion to a satyr. Sir Philip Sidney had pimples, Jonson told Drummond, and advanced a clinical explanation of Queen Elizabeth's best-known trait.

The luxurious trappings of Jonson's verse are to be viewed, but not touched; they will either vanish away or taint whoever is brash enough to reach out for them. The limping jig of Volpone's deformed chorus rehearses the tale of Lucian's cock, whose crowing awoke its indigent master from dreams of banquets and visions of riches. The plague hangs over the house in which *The Alchemist* operates; brightness falls from the air. Sooner or later, of course, Jonson would rally to the cause of the expiring Renaissance, and the Ghost of Dionysius would bawl down Zeal-of-the-Land Busy in Leatherhead's puppet show. He would have *Pleasure Reconciled to Virtue* in a masque, at any rate. Perhaps Jonson's asperity was due to the fact that he was a satirist by vocation and a Stoic by philosophical inclination. But vocation and inclination are the result of temperament; if Jonson had not been a scholar, he might have called himself a Puritan. And if he had never existed, there still would have been the Puritans, and other poets would have found it difficult not to write satire. Sir Toby Belch's question was a little beside the point. Malvolio was virtuous precisely because the cakes were stale and the ale was running thin.

Jonson raised one question which neither Mandeville nor Rousseau would settle. Like his author, the miser of *The Staple of News* is a disciple of Seneca:

> Who can endure to see
> The fury of men's gullets and their groins?
> What stews, ponds, parks, coops, garners, magazines,
> What velvets, tissues, scarfs, embroideries,
> And laces they might lack? They covet things
> Superfluous still, when it were much more honour
> They could want necessary. What need hath Nature
> Of silver dishes or gold chamber-pots?
> Of perfumed napkins, or a numerous family
> To see her eat? Poor and wise, she requires
> Meat only; hunger is not ambitious.

Here, in his Stoic doctrine of nature, he is at variance with King Lear:

> O' reason not the need; our basest beggars
> Are in the poorest thing superfluous.
> Allow not nature more than nature needs,
> Man's life is cheap as beast's. Thou art a lady;
> If only to go warm were gorgeous,
> Why, nature needs not what thou gorgeous wear'st,
> Which scarcely keeps thee warm.

Jonson takes more for granted than Shakespeare does. He presupposes that life is fundamentally a compact, rational affair, needlessly complicated by impulse and artifice. To Shakespeare, all experience, however variegated is of the same baseless fabric. The two poets, who worked so closely together, were as far apart as Heraclitus and Parmenides. Jonson adopts the attitude of society, Shakespeare the viewpoint of the individual, which is finally more real to us. Jonson's instrument is logic, Shakespeare's psychology; Johnson's method has been called mechanical, Shakespeare's organic. That is why we must criticize Shakespeare in terms of movement and warmth, Jonson in terms of pattern and color.

3. RHETORIC

It was an inescapable irony which compelled Jonson to spend his last twenty years as a purveyor of magnificence to the court. It was ironic that a Stoic should be a party to such an extreme form of conspicuous consumption as the masque; that a poet should be forced into competition not only with Inigo Jones but—as *Neptune's Triumph* dramatizes the issue—with the cook, and at a far lower stipend than the dancing-master; that Ben Jonson should be called upon to provide what he himself ruefully brands

> ... the short bravery of the night,
> ... the jewels, stuffs, the pains, the wit
> There wasted, some not paid for yet!

But it was inescapable, because Jonson had been overlooked by popular success; because he had to get what comfort he could from his official position as poet laureate; because his talent for decoration, his penchant for symbolism, his command of poetic convention, his play of allusion, his knowledge of the classics, and his interest in folklore needed an occasion to converge upon. Shakespeare's career proceeded, according to Edward Dowden's formula, out of the workshop into the world; Jonson's career went in the other direction.

All of his conscientious craftmanship was insufficient to impose coherence on so synthetic a medium. To gather some slight conception of what it was all about, we find ourselves trying to envisage an aristocratic revue or an erudite animated cartoon. Spain and France, in the persons of their ambassadors, quarreled over invitations, precedence, and the King's right ear; Lanière and Ferrabosco contributed galliards and corrantos; the Queen, the Prince, the Lady Arabella, and other mummers disguised themselves as gipsies or heathen deities or parts of speech, and mounted the musicians' gallery to descend in some grandiose machine. From state papers, *viola da gamba* scores, and architects' elevations, we emerge as confused as Pocahontas must have seemed, when John Smith took her to the performance of *The Vision of Delight*. Thumbing through Jonson's part in these evanescent entertainments is like visiting a costumer's shop strewn with a musty assortment of bent farthingales, second-hand armor, faded wigs, and limp dominos.

If there is any special significance in the masque, it is apparent in the frequency with which a pastoral note is sounded, with which golden ages and happier eras are restored, or we are whisked away to unreal Arcadias and remote Hesperides. Behind the frivolity and superficiality of the genre lay at least one meaning—that the court and the city no longer shared any literary conventions, that there was less and less of that community of interest which had permitted the Globe and Blackfriars to present the same plays. Structurally, the relation between Jonson's masques and comedies is close, too close to have pleased the spectators of his last comedies. Yet Jonson's comedies, from first to last, have a tendency to crystallize, whenever opportunity offers, into a series of games, ceremonies, shows, songs, litanies, orations, and every sort of masque-like invention. The rites conducted by Sejanus, Volpone's medicine show, Morose's invective against his barber, Dapper's interview with the Queen of Faery, Justice Clement's merry assizes, Littlewit's redaction of *Hero and Leander*—these episodes, besides fulfilling their dramatic function in the plays to which they belong, are independently reducible to formal pattern.

Looking beyond these internal harmonies, Jonson invites our scrutiny as an engineer of plots. We have noticed that the recurrent trials point a moral; we must recognize that they also adorn a play, by supplying an external framework for the action and a ritual for some of the scenes. If we admit the parallel between promoting a confidence game and spinning a comic intrigue, we can appreciate the way Jonson utilized the get-rich-quick motive and the scheme of a hoax in his most successful comedies. His others are less so because they sacrifice situation to character. The lists of dramatis personae, in *Every Man out of his Humour* or *The New Inn,* read like pages out of Earle and Overbury. The stage becomes so overloaded with sharply defined, carefully delineated supernumeraries, who have been called into being only to have their legs pulled, that it becomes all but impossible for a plot to get under way.

The difficulty of introducing his characters in a natural sequence of encounters was met by Jonson with a great deal of ingenuity. The plan of *Volpone,* turned to account again in *The Alchemist,* enables them to make their entrances one after another, without monotony or stiffness. The opening scene of *The Alchemist,* wherein the thieves, having fallen out, bespatter each other with abuse until the spectators have learned the past history, crimes, misdemeanors, and unendearing foibles of all three, is a triumph of exposition. The complicated intermarriages, the awkward progresses from house to house, and the Mephistophelian servants that comic dramatists allowed themselves in order to hold their plots together, Jonson was never quite ready to give up. But he did devise, in *Bartholomew Fair,* a new unity, which incorporates the three old ones into a more manageable partnership, based solely upon local color. The critical dialogue in which he sought warrant for his innovation in Horace's *Art of Poetry* did not survive the conflagration of his library, but we have today in the films ample evidence of the breadth and diversity of this method. Particularly in the journalistic milieu of *The Staple of News,* with his gift for recreating an atmosphere, Jonson seems to be striving toward a comic institution around which to build his play—like the thinking-shop of Aristophanes or Sheridan's school for scandal.

Occasionally the hand of the puppeteer appears, the situation is obviously manipulated, and we smell a device. If Jonson had been less fond of those who are witty in themselves, he might have done more convincing portraits of those who are the cause that wit is in others. There are not enough fools positive and too many fools contingent. The dramatist relies upon the assistance of his characters to bring off his practical jokes. It is the difference between Socrates' basket and Falstaff's; Socrates is made a fool by Aristophanes, Falstaff by Mistress Ford and Mistress Quickly. It would not have occurred to Jonson to let well enough alone, as Molière did, and let circumstances force Sganarelle to practise medicine. Jonson's ironies must be overseen by his personal representatives, ever alert to persuade the jealous Corvino to lend his wife to another, or to stir up a reluctant duel between Sir John Daw and Sir Amorous La Foole. Sometimes his fools are conscious of their folly and have good reasons for persisting. Captain Otter, as a creature of humors, is a palpable fraud; he is a realistically drawn, thoroughly unpleasant broken-down gambler, who affects certain mannerisms which we have come to associate with the name of Jonson's pupil, Dickens, to ingratiate himself with his rich wife and her fine friends.

Because Jonsonian comedy can only succeed by subordinating parts to whole, its cast of characters is not its outstanding feature. Each has only his characteristic move, as in chess, and the object of the game is to see what new combinations have been brought about. Between the abstract idea of the plot and the concrete detail of the language is a hiatus. Nothing is lacking, but the various components can be distinguished without much trouble. In Corvino's phrase, it is too manifest. After the large masses have been sketched out in baroque symmetry, decoration is applied to the surfaces. What is said, frequently, does not matter, so long as something is said, and then Jonson is at special pains to make what is said interesting for its own sake. Surly's school-book Spanish and Doll's memorized ravings are simply blocked in. But when Mosca reads the inventory, or when Subtle puts Face through the alchemists' catechism, they too are saying something where—in the dramatic economy—they mean nothing, and their speeches take on the aspect of incantation. It is a trick which reaches its logical limit in *Epicene,* where everything spoken has a high nuisance value and the words themselves become sheer filigree. Beyond that point, they have the force of Molière's comic refrains. Lady Wouldbe's uncontrollable flow of recipes, prescriptions, literary opinions, and philosophical speculations, at cross-purposes with Volpone, demonstrates how conveniently this talking-machine technique bears out Bergson's theory of laughter.

To linger over the elements of pure design in Jonson's dialogue is to ignore its expressiveness as representation. The language itself is completely idiomatic, uninhibited by the formality of plot and characterization or the complexity of scenes and speeches. Because "Spenser writ no language," Jonson withheld his admiration, and he could spare Marston nothing but a prescription to purge unnatural diction. His own occasional verse moves, like his drama, on the social plane and speaks in the familiar tones of human intercourse. Even self-communion, with Jonson, takes the form of a public address. Ode, epigram, elegy, epistle —nearly every poem is composed on something or to somebody, brandishing precepts and eliciting examples in the injunctive mood of Roman poetry. A poetic style suitable for these purposes had to be fittest for discourse and nearest prose. Whatever the restraints Jonson chose to accept, his handling of words never lost its flexibility; throughout the most tortuous stanzas his phrasing remains as English as Purcell's.

It would be hard to derive an inference about Jonson's dramatic verse from the comedies he wrote in prose, since *Epicene* and *Bartholomew Fair* are farther from one another than each is from the remaining plays. Neither the enameled elegance of the one nor the rough-and-ready realism of the other accomplishes anything that Jonson has not been able to achieve in meter with the help of two fertile resources, enjambment and the broken line. He is so unwilling to pause every time five iambs have elapsed, that he now and then revives the classical stratagem of concluding a line in the midst of a word. And he is so fond of crisp dialogue that he often divides a single pentameter among three speakers, as in the staccato asides that punctuate the harangues of Tiberius or Voltore. Longer speeches strike up a syncopation between the shifting colloquial rhythms and the sustained stresses of blank verse. Face's praise of Spaniards is rendered in a string of four-foot clauses, so that the iterated phrase leaps across the page and then creeps back again:

> Ask from your courtier to your inns-of-court man,
> To your mere milliner. They will tell you all,
> Your Spanish jennet is the best horse; your Spanish
> Stoop is the best garb; your Spanish beard
> Is the best cut; your Spanish ruffs are the best
> Wear; your Spanish pavan the best dance;
> Your Spanish titillation in a glove
> The best perfume. And for your Spanish pike
> And Spanish blade, let your poor Captain speak.

The cadence is individualized to catch the breathlessness of Celia's appeal for mercy or reverberate with the finality of Volpone's revelation.

It is typical of Jonson, as of Dryden and the baroque in general, that rhythmic arrangement should take precedence over actual sound. High, astounding terms are relatively rare. Already a rationalistic bias is perceptible; writers seem less eager to use words for their own sake and more anxious to employ them for what they signify. Jonson had the custom of setting down everything he proposed to say in prose and versifying it in a subsequent operation. Hence his poetry is primarily pictorial and only then musical, it addresses the visual rather than the auditory instincts, it appeals—as the writing of a poet who gave up the stage for the printing-press—to the eye instead of the ear. Like his personifications of Fancy and Wonder in *The Vision of Delight,* Jonson's eye had the power to summon up an infinite variety of vistas. Like a good apothecary, he was never without an ounce of civet with which he might sweeten his imagination at will. "He hath consumed a whole night in lying looking to his great toe,"—if we are to believe Drummond—"about which he hath seen Tartars and Turks, Romans and Carthaginians, fight in his imagination."

Graphic speech is the generic trait with which even Jonson's ugliest ducklings are well endowed. The stolid Corvino indulges in unsuspected flights of conceit and the sullen Ananias reveals a flamboyant strain of polemical eloquence. Kitely's jealousy of his wife prompts him to deliver an exhaustive survey of the wiles of amorous deception. To dismiss the threat of punishment, Voltore invokes a swarm of luridly ridiculous tortures upon the prostrate person of his client. In introducing Drugger as an honest tobacconist, Face cannot resist the temptation to add a dozen lines covering the various sharp practices of dishonest tobacconists that Drugger utterly eschews. Dramatic action is supplemented by the potential drama of these three speeches. In each instance a set of images picks up the situation where the business leaves off and projects it to the most extravagant bounds of possibility. Uniformly Jonson's style is stamped with the brilliance of his iconoplastic talents.

The imagery surprises us by being so tangible, by presenting its objects not as fanciful comparisons but as literal descriptions. They are seldom glimpsed through the magic casement of metaphor, through the intervention of rhetoric. The rich jewel in the Ethiop's ear belonged to Juliet only by metaphysical parallel; Jonson would have slashed off the ear, conveyed the jewel to Volpone's coffers, and dangled it before Celia as the price of her virtue. Heaping up sensuous detail in thoroughgoing Elizabethan fashion, he ordinarily contrives to bring it within the immediate grasp of his tantalized characters. The result is that the theme of his plays and their poetic realization are more closely knit together. Examining the content of Jonson's images, Caroline Spurgeon has discovered that the largest single category is drawn from the usages and conditions of society and that he returns more consistently than any of his rivals to the subject of money. A further consequence of this restriction of materials is a kind of heightening of the commonplace, more proper to the humorous than to the lyrical imagination. Deprived of other figures of speech, Jonson relies much on hyperbole. That is not the only quality of style he shares with Aristophanes and Rabelais.

The poetry of misplaced concreteness and solid specification is an instrument of the satirist; he is adept at mastering the tricks of a trade and enumerating technical data; his swift, disintegrating glance takes in all the ingredients of Goody Trash's gingerbread. A profusion of images is not the best way to communicate feeling. Selection is more likely to produce the poignant response; accumulation bewilders at first and invites analysis in the end. When Jonson's intention is not satirical, his "wit's great overplus" dilutes the effect of his verse. Into one line,

> Ditch-delivered by a drab,

Shakespeare can concentrate an impact that Jonson labored through the long and learned *Masque of Queens* without quite attaining. Ultimately his facility at image-making becomes self-conscious and, as it were, poetical. It carries him into the region of the conventionally beautiful and leaves him among the curlèd woods and painted meads. It ominously foreshadows the time when poets will work with a repertory of standard items and critics will ponder the distinction between imagination and fancy.

Satirists are well aware that appearances deceive, yet it is with appearances that satirists are chiefly concerned. Jonson delights in exhibiting façades, because they both impress us and make us uneasy about what lies behind them. Every once in a while a masochistic fascination leads him to explore the obverse of beauty, to give way to the fly-blown fancies of *The Famous Voyage,* to betray a revulsion worthy of Swift.

> Though art's hid causes are not found,
> All is not sweet, all is not sound.

It is never simple for literature to report the senses directly. In the Renaissance especially, it was hard to reconcile perceptions and principles; attempts oscillate from the sheer apprehension of Marlowe to the sublimated allegory of Spenser. Between these poles there is room for voluptuousness, scientific curiosity, asceticism, prurience—all the degrees and mixtures of intellectualized sensibility that we see in *Ovid's Banquet of Sense, The Metamorphosis of Pygmalion's Image, Nosce Teipsum,* or *The Ecstasy.* As an Elizabethan, Jonson too had been perplexed by the problem. As a Stoic and satirist, he was able to make his own rejection. As a professional man of letters, he had to keep on writing through a period when immanent emotions and confident attitudes were being reduced to questions of literary technique.

In his fecundity and in his artificiality, in his virtues and in his faults, Jonson remains the craftsman. When he appraises the wayward apprentice Shakespeare, he speaks with the authority of a fellow craftsman, and—after a few precise couplets of prefatory remarks, acknowledgments, and qualifications—deliberately turns on the lyric strain:

> I therefore will begin. Soul of the age!
> The applause, delight, the wonder of our stage!

And he proceeds to a workmanlike and reasonably impassioned estimate. Because he was in the habit of discussing his craft concretely, he could not fail to be interested in Plutarch's comparison of poetry and painting. It is no mere chance that any effort to describe his own work falls repeatedly into the vocabulary of the fine arts. If we are looking for a single impression of Ben Jonson, it is of the Flemish painters that we are finally mindful—of crowded street scenes and rich interiors, of sharp portraiture and lavish ornament, of the gloss and the clarity and the tactile values that are the tokens of mastery.

ON THE EARL OF ROCHESTER

During the early nineteen-forties the avant-garde publishing firm of New Directions, under the creative editorship of James Laughlin IV, sponsored the Poet of the Month, a handsomely printed series of pamphlets which originally could be subscribed for or purchased at thirty-five cents apiece. Some of the best early work of new poets then emerging —Dylan Thomas, John Berryman, Richard Eberhart, Delmore Schwartz, Josephine Miles, among others—first appeared in that format. Occasionally the monthly sequence would be varied by including a foreign poet in translation or some neglected older English poet. For one such occasion I undertook to edit a selection from the poetry of John Wilmot, Earl of Rochester. Under the title of *A Satire against Mankind and Other Poems,* it was published and dated as of June, 1943, elegantly hand-printed in two colors after the Restoration style by Victor Hammer on his press at Wells College. The distinguished printer—a professor of art, who had found a happy avocation in printing—was also a devout Roman Catholic, who customarily terminated his colophons with the initials for the Latin motto of the Jesuits: *Ad majorem Dei gloriam.* After some correspondence with me and a thoughtful rereading of the text, he agreed that this particular typographical effort could not be appropriately dedicated to the greater glory of God. The subject offers a standing invitation to verbal paradox, which—I see as I reread my introduction— I did not have the moral strength to resist.

Rochester's paradoxes and problems—which began when he was born, on April 1, 1647, the only child of a Cavalier father and a Puritan mother—did not end until he died, on July 26, 1680, in the torments of venereal disease and the comforts of religious conversion. Within those thirty-three years he had pursued, to their logical limits, a rake's progress of the body and a pilgrim's progress of the mind. Hence, in the memoirs and tracts of his time, he cuts a conspicuous but always elusive figure: his life is full of scandals and his death is matter for sermons. Yet it is Rochester himself who remains the most shameless scandalmonger and the most desperate moralist of a period which is equally distinguished for its scurrilous gossip and its eloquent preaching. It was Rochester who most acutely perceived the widening distance between preaching and practice, and who first sought to bring them together within the ambiguous yoke of satire.

His apology for himself and his period was an orthodox assumption that human nature is equally compounded of vice, "that seed of originall sin," and virtue, "that sparke of primitive grace." For Rochester, as for André Gide, "Les extrêmes se touchent." No other age except our own, perhaps, has been so painfully conscious of those extremes, or so bent upon realizing their conflicting possibilities. The seventeenth century, obsessed with the fall of man, could take nothing for granted that happened since. Once the bitter fruit of new philosophy had been digested, religious doctrines could be doubted, moral codes flouted, social orders disrupted, economic systems attacked, and political hierarchies overturned with impunity. Nor was the Restoration what its name implies. It was a precarious façade, masking the wreckage of fire and plague and civil war. In that vain effort to keep up appearances, the court became a school of realistic thinking and ironic writing.

Rochester, as a courtier, found his example in the libertine monarch, "Scandalous and Poor," Charles II; as a thinker, he found an even more scandalous preceptor in the materialistic philosopher, Thomas Hobbes. He found his vocation in "this gibing, gingling knack, call'd *Wit*," his medium in "dang'rous Poetry." The direction of English culture, between Shakespeare and Newton, was being determined by a strategic series of encounters between poetry and science. In Rochester's student days, the last days of the Commonwealth, he had attended the most advanced of the Oxford colleges, Wadham, while it was still fostering the germs of the Royal Society. Later, when his lampoons had brought him into momentary disgrace with the king, he assumed the role of a mountebank and burlesqued the scientific pretensions of his contemporaries.

His was a more ruthless empiricism than theirs. Religiously, he devoted his exhaustive investigations to the delimited sphere of women and wine: "*Cupid* and *Bacchus* my Saints are." The favor of those saints is notoriously evanescent, and as his devotion increased, their blessings tended to diminish. But that was precisely the demonstration for which Rochester had volunteered. He had made the libertine's calculation of pleasures and pains with the fatalistic accuracy of the mathematician. He had proposed to follow no guide except his appetites, to live by "the Light of Nature, Sense." He fully realized that time was against him, that " 'tis Nature's Law to change," that—though pleasure may prove illusory—"Pain can ne'er deceive." Thus "The Imperfect Enjoyment" is his characteristic theme. And warmth and vigor, his most substantial qualities, are overshadowed by the paler abstractions of insipidity and impotence.

Even his love lyrics show the pale cast of thought, and his drinking songs have the harsh sobriety of a hangover. "The true veine" proved to be neither anacreontic nor pastoral, but philosophical and satiric: Rochester—for the metaphysical Marvell, who could also wax satirical —was "the best English satirist." Satires were identified with satyrs in the Restoration mind, and satyrs enacted the afterpiece to a tragedy. Because the tragedy had been universal, the satire was all-inclusive. Its protagonist, like Hamlet, directs his sharpest scorn against himself, and dies a martyr to his own intelligence. "A Satire against Mankind" is Rochester's critique of pure wit. Although it follows Boileau's eighth satire most of the way, by the end it has gone much farther. Thomas Rymer, the first critic to suggest the comparison, considered the French poet "little better than a man of straw." The French poem had also stressed man's bestial attributes and minimized his intellectual achievements:

> Mais l'homme, sans arrêt dans sa course insensée,
> Voltige incessament de pensée en pensée.

But Boileau merely complains that this rational animal is often unreasonable, whereas Rochester attacks the reason itself. Boileau, like a scholar, thinks that other men are unlike himself and therefore fools. Rochester, the man of the world, knows that other men are like himself and therefore knaves. While Boileau—with the traditional ironies of the humanist—is praising folly, Rochester, in all seriousness, is castigating knavery. Of the two, he is the intransigent moralist, who observes that duchesses and kings can be prostitutes and stallions; the uncompromising rationalist, who thence concludes that all men and women must be irrational yahoos and beasts that want discourse of reason. The only subject he can wholeheartedly praise is, literally and figuratively, nothing. The sweeping negations of his satire against himself and mankind are corroborated by the brittle nihilism of his panegyric "On Nothing."

If he believes in anything, it is not in the positive materialism of the Epicurean but the skepticism of the Stoic. Now and then he may be transported, by the penetrating curiosity of Lucretius, beyond "the flaming Limits of the Universe"; but he always returns to the calm despair of Seneca in the absolute face of death. Death and life, flesh and spirit, thought and poetry, are finally reduced to words—to one of his favorite words which finds no Latin counterpart in Seneca's tragic chorus on mortality, "Whimsies." Honor—by the demonstration of one of his favorite characters, Sir John Falstaff—is annihilated with a final breath. On the field of so-called honor, his contemporaries allege, Rochester practised what Falstaff preached. With respect to the code of gallantry, they tell us, his satire was consistent with his behavior. At all events, posterity will never forgive the bluntness of his attack upon a rival satirist, the callousness that could hire professional bludgeons to confute John Dryden.

Though heroism is no longer possible to such a state of mind, its very impossibility remains a challenge and a torture. Dryden sounded metallic and hollow when he tried to drum up an epic out of the commercial war with the Dutch. Rochester, who lived down his youthful elopement by honorable service in that war, was free to commandeer Dryden's heroic quatrains and make them serve his ironic intentions:

> I'll tell of Whores attack'd their Lords at home,
>   Bawds Quarters beaten up, and Fortress won;
> Windows demolish'd, Watches overcome,
>   And handsom Ills by my Contrivance done.

The narrator, Rochester's "Maim'd Debauchee," masquerades as a retired admiral who, "being good for nothing else," offers the wisdom of reminiscence. His alternative, the life of action, offers military glory in metaphor, sensual indulgence in reality. It is a brutal answer to the expectations of the Renaissance, to the sensuous idealism of Thomas Campion:

> Then wilt thou speake of banqueting delights,
> Of masks and reuels which sweete youth did make,
> Of Turnies and great challenges of knights,
> And all these triumphes for thy beauties sake ...

Here the Restoration satire sounds like a mocking echo of the Elizabethan lyric. At every stage, Rochester's rakish escapade seems to hark back to Campion's chivalric pageantry. Yet the earlier imagery has been coarsened and the easy rhythms have been agitated. Between the two poems lies, more heavily than years of wars, the consciousness of heroic ideals that have been violated.

In paradoxical contrast to the immediacies of earlier poets, or to the unambiguous concreteness of Rochester's peculiar themes, his diction tends to become abstract and intellectualized. Donne will talk familiarly of philosophic speculations; Rochester will speculate philosophically on vulgar matters. The mixed effect is one of fascination and revulsion, as expressed in the chilling endearments of the "Song of a Young Lady to her Ancient Lover." A careless irregularity of poetic form, running to half-finished lines and ill-sorted rhymes, matches the deliberate unconventionality of Rochester's mind. His method of composition runs particularly to paraphrase, and he is diabolically fond of citing scripture for his purpose. By changing half a dozen words, he can convert the sacred ejaculation of Quarles, "Why dost thou shade thy lovely face?," into a profane appeal to the poet's mistress.

Rochester is never more completely in his element than when he is transmuting the gold of other poets into baser metals. He rarely refines upon his originals; instead, he reinvigorates them—in "An Allusion to Horace," as in his allusions to Boileau and Seneca and others. The Roman poet's satire on satire becomes one of the points of departure for English classicism, and Rochester makes a place for himself among Dryden and Wycherley, Pope and Swift, among the masters of the mock-heroic style. We hardly expect to find him in that place, however, for we must admit that his poetry is a rather special sort of fare, like the banquet to which Don Giovanni invited the Commendatore. It is a tempting banquet, but perhaps the guests are too distracted by the presence of the statue to derive the fullest enjoyment from the conversation of beautiful women and the flow of good wine. And though their host continues to provide both wit and luxury, his mind is preoccupied with a pressing appointment.

FROM *GUSLE* TO TAPE-RECORDER

Questions involving the decline or impending death of the novel have been raised so often during the past generation that they must be taken quite seriously. Yet the implicit prediction is not so gloomy as it sounds, when viewed in the full perspective of the novel's origin and history to date and of its relationship to other narrative modes. This was common ground for a symposium on narrative under the auspices of the Department of Comparative Literature at the University of Illinois, Urbana, on November 9, 1967, moderated by A. Owen Aldridge and published in that department's journal, *Comparative Literature Studies* (September, 1969). When, in looking for current signs of transition, I made some mention of William Styron's *Confessions of Nat Turner,* the critical storm that developed around it had still to brew. The presupposition of its most extreme critics—that only a black writer could write with any authority about the black experience—is certainly arguable; but it reinforces my emphasis on the increasing reduction of fiction to factuality.

In the year one thousand nine hundred and thirty-three a gray falcon flew from the fair land of America. He flew over lands and cities, until he came to the shore of the sea. There a steel ship was waiting for him. The falcon flew into the ship and rested its heroic wings. His ship was called the Saturnia, and it was as swift as a vila of the mountains.

I venture to begin on an epic note by quoting an oral poem, a heroic lay translated from the Serbian. You will observe that the traditional formulas have taken on certain overtones of modernity. The falcon has become a stowaway on a transatlantic luxury liner, which in turn is compared with another indigenous bird. The falcon itself, as the poem continues, becomes a metaphorical epithet for its hero—who happens also to have been its translator.

That was not a gray falcon, but Professor Milman Parry, the glorious. Our history will tell of him and remember him for many generations. He was a man of fine character, adorned by wisdom and uprightness, one of good heart and of blessed mien. Our history was dear to him, and he had come to like our poems. It was because of them that he had traveled here to our heroic fatherland. . . . Swiftly he flew over the ocean until he arrived at the Adriatic Sea. A short while later he came to Split, and there rested for a time. Thence he continued until he arrived safely at Dubrovnik. There the Saturnia stopped and cast its anchor.

But this is only the beginning of an epical itinerary.

Milman Parry departed from the harbor and went to Hotel Imperial. There he stopped and rested, and drank his fill of cool wine; and there he found a companion for himself, a keen Hercegovinian young man, by name of Niko Vujnović. The following day they departed to travel throughout our heroic homeland, to seek out our bards, for they were interested in our Serbian *gusle*...

The *gusle,* with its single string and its crude carving, is a far more primitive instrument than the lyre. Yet it formed the sing-song accompaniment to a sequence of chanted epics which provided a young American scholar with a solution to the Homeric problem. Parry, who lost his life just two years afterward, was able to demonstrate the processes of oral composition, as they were then still practised in Yugoslavia by pre-literate bards or *guslars.* The poem from which I have quoted was improvised in his honor by one of them, as a farewell to him after his first round of field trips; and this little epic, in which the singer of tales pays his tribute to the collector of songs, sounds appropriately elegiac. It might almost be the lay of that last minstrel, Macpherson's Ossian or Yeats' Oisin.

Parry and Albert Lord, his pupil and successor, found their informants a generation ago, and gathered the bulk of their monumental collection at perhaps the latest possible moment; for, even in the Hercegovinian mountains, the coffee houses now resound with electronic forms of entertainment. Thus the Yugoslavian demonstration has confirmed the sociocultural insight of W. P. Ker: that a given mode of narration is organically related to the way of life it bodies forth. Conventions, repetitions, and stylistic devices, which played a functional part when the epic was originally sung, have tended to lose their significance after it has been written down. There is a sharp point about literary epics in Horace Walpole's sweeping remark: that every epic poet has failed, with the sole exception of Homer, the inventor of the genre.

Walpole himself was being somewhat retrogressive, when he sought to revive not only Gothic architecture but likewise Gothic romance. It is neither Strawberry Hill nor *The Castle of Otranto,* but his letters that comprise his living monument. These, in their interplay of opinions, their observation of manners, and their gossip about personalities, reveal him preeminently as a man of his time. Nor was it any accident that eighteenth-century fiction had hit upon the epistolary novel as its characteristic vehicle. The fact that Richardson had started as a printer and a guide to letter-writing made him a bourgeois spokesman no less typical than Franklin, and Richardson's novels may be viewed as landmarks to the full attainment of literacy on the part of the enlarging middle classes.

"O Richardson! in spite of ourselves, we take part in thy works, we join in the conversation, we approve, we blame, we admire, we grow irritated or indignant," exclaimed Diderot in his widely reverberating eulogy, which might be said to mark the arrival of the novel as a dominant form.

...In the course of a few hours I had run through a larger number of situations than the longest lifetime is likely to offer. I had heard the true discourses of the passions; I had seen the springs of self-interest and self-respect touched upon in a hundred different ways; I had become a spectator at a multitude of incidents; I felt I had acquired experience.

We have grown so used to our peculiar relationship with a book of fiction that we take for granted this extension of minds, which enables us vicariously to share in the experiences of others. Nowadays, when auditory and pictorial means of communication are encroaching upon our book-culture, there are even scholars like Marshall McLuhan who uproariously welcome that encroachment. I am not sure how far we can apply Mr. McLuhan's invidious distinction between hot and cool media, and I find it even more confusing that the adjective *cool* is currently used for what we considered hot stuff in the days of my youth. Surely the psychic temperature of the younger generation is as calorific today as it ever was.

Yet, insofar as such terms can be usefully employed, print is the hottest medium that mankind has ever devised. Since its messages are absorbed in private, it sets up a special intimacy between the reader and the writer. Whereas the epic developed out of a public performance, and consequently has something or other in common with the audio-visual arts, a novel can be as personal as a letter from Clarissa Harlowe to Miss Howe. In addition, it is a material object, sitting as it were upon the reader's lap, and—as we need hardly be reminded—a negotiable commodity, from which the writer hopes to gain a living. All novels are self-conscious, from *Don Quixote* to the newest *nouveau roman*. But *Tristram Shandy* owes its unique position to its insistent awareness that it is a book.

Its blank or blackened or marbled pages, its misplaced chapters, its typographical tricks, and its lascivious asterisks are merely the external symptoms of a deep complicity and an inner tension. Sterne may affirm that writing is "but a different name for conversation." He himself can write as if he were speaking to a listener: "I need not tell your worship, that all this is spoken in confidence." However, we cannot speak back, and he is continually pressing his advantage over us: "But courage! gentle reader! I scorn it—'tis enough to have thee in my power—but to make use of the advantage which the fortune of the pen has now gained over thee, would be too much—No—!" As usual, Sterne protests too much; he is drunk with novelistic power. The endless prenatal digression of Tristram Shandy was as much of a psychological experiment as those explorations of the ego by Montaigne and Proust.

On the other side, we novel-readers are by no means passive. The printed word conveys more data than Mr. McLuhan's other media, and it may define itself more sharply, as he suggests. But since the alphabet is a symbolic—rather than a representational—system, the author encodes his images for us into words which we decode by referring to a different set of images, our own. In order to meet his imagination halfway, we must reconstruct his verbal descriptions out of our experience, visual and otherwise. Even when we collaborate in this fashion with so graphic an expositor as Dickens, we are making our own mental pictures; no wonder his illustrators have varied so much. Readers are continually engaged in projection and participation, and every reading is bound to differ slightly from the reactions of any other reader.

"Has the reader ever fallen head over heels in love?" asks Stendhal. "Has he had the good fortune to spend a night with the most adored mistress of his life?" Then, at the inviting and exciting climax of *The Life of Henry Brulard,* he puts us off with rhetorical questions. "Really, I cannot continue; the subject surpasses the speaker . . . ," he apologetically concludes. "One spoils such tender sentiments by recounting them in detail." D. H. Lawrence would disagree emphatically. Our contemporary novelists would feel that they were shirking their moral duty, if they did not take their readers into the bedrooms of their characters. Yet Stendhal was the least puritanical of men, and the sexual aura of Madame de Rênal or the Duchesse de Sanseverina is far more potent than that of Lady Chatterley.

Stendhal's willingness to concede that some things might prove inexpressible is at odds with his insistence elsewhere on getting "the little

true facts" with complete exactitude. But he never loses his grasp on—
what is the novelist's most important asset—the reader's confidence,
probably because his manner is so confiding. The novel being what it is,
a comprehensive register of human individuality, all the great novelists
have been extreme individualists—not least Stendhal, whose *persona* is
as variable as his repertory of pseudonyms. That double identification,
which links the reader to the writer through their mutual involvement
with the protagonist, has become more rigorous during the past century.
In our era of suspicion the narrator, once so omniscient, tends to be regarded as unreliable.

Sophistication has meant circumscription. First-person narrative—
simulated letters, memoirs, confessions—forced him into an impersona-
tion, which was stretched to the breaking point by Proust's eavesdrop-
pings and coincidences. It was turned within by Joyce's interior
monologue, but externalized all over again by his intervention through
so many other voices and techniques. The prevailing alternative has
been the Jamesian method, an impersonal presentation depending on
one character's center of consciousness. Though Flaubert has generally
been credited with initiating the modern stress upon point of view,
that master began his masterpiece in the first person plural. For all his
vaunted objectivity, he occasionally allows himself to express his sympathies, as he does with the old peasant woman, or to pass moral judgments, as when he tells us that Emma Bovary has been prostituting
herself.

The myth of the invisible artist paring his fingernails, after having
refined himself out of existence, originated in Flaubert's intensely human correspondence and reached its apogee in the esthetic theories
of that young exhibitionist, Stephen Dedalus. The novelist's current
place of retreat is behind a camera, where he takes trick shots from
cinematic angles with Alain Robbe-Grillet. The disappearance of the
narrator, according to the late Wolfgang Kayser, would foreshadow the
end of the novel itself. Although other critics would differ in their
diagnoses, an increasing number of them have struck this apocalyptic
attitude. The story, be it incident or anecdote, has long since ceased to
be a determining feature, except for certain limited subspecies like the
murder mystery.

The continuity of the story-line has always been open to interruption
from flashbacks, prognostications, and other deliberate shifts of the time
scheme. Now we have the novel—or so it is designated—of Marc

Saportas, *Composition No. 1,* printed on pages which are unbound and unnumbered, so that the reader can shuffle them for himself into random sequences. Meanwhile experiments with time have been undermining the concept of duration. William Burroughs would randomize the very process of composition by "folding in," as he puts it, irrelevant material clipped out of his casual browsing in magazines and catalogues. Plot, which was so primary for Aristotle in dealing with epic and tragedy, obviously cannot stand the strain of indefinite discontinuity. Its subordination to character may indeed be that aspect of the novel which has differentiated it from the other species of narrative.

But characterization, so apparently solid and central in nineteenth-century fiction, seems to disintegrate under the analysis of twentieth-century psychology. The issue came to a head in the controversy between Arnold Bennett and Virginia Woolf. It may well be, as Nathalie Sarraute has subtly argued, that after we read Proust we mentally put together those personages which he has been at such pains to take apart. Let us hope so; for, with the author out of sight, the plot in eclipse, and the characters on the verge of dissolution, we feel consigned to a limbo from which there seems to be no exit. On the other hand, we need not be too much disturbed by the slogan *l'anti-roman,* when we recall that Sorel coined it three hundred years before Sartre, and that the novel came to life with Cervantes as a protest against the romance.

Nor can it be affirmed that the antihero is the particular denizen of our time, since he is at least as old as Don Quixote. The masculine protagonists of novels, by definition, could never be heroic in the truly epical sense: witness Captain Osborne and Captain Dobbin in *Vanity Fair, A Novel without a Hero.* It is true that the formation of character, the education of the self in the school of experience, and the cultural strivings and struggles of the individual, have shaped a major novelistic mode in the *Bildungsroman.* It might seem that latterly, with Beckett and Genet, the Goethean formula of self-development has been reversed; that what we are invited to contemplate, mirroring that disheveled life-style which has come so conspicuously into view, is rather a novel of deformation, an *Entartungsroman.*

Changing styles reflect conflicting values. By the seventeenth century, it should have been perfectly clear that the old heroic apparatus was obsolete. Even Milton, while sustaining the grand style, nodded once or twice. Into his description of the luscious repast tendered by Adam and Eve to the Archangel Raphael, he inserted a touching parenthesis:

"No fear lest dinner cool." Momentarily that half-line transports us from the innocence of primal Eden to a latterday world of petty domestic cares. The disparity between his lofty diction and the trivialities of every day was the ground for a once-famous parody of Milton by John Philips, *The Splendid Shilling*. The obvious potentialities of this kind of mock-heroic treatment for the purposes of satire were realized by Dryden, Pope, and others before and afterward.

The mock-epic, which exalted the commonplace for ironic effect, was turned upside down by another hybrid genre, the travesty, which vulgarized the noble themes of tradition. One of the ambivalences of Joyce's *Ulysses* is whether to take it as a mock-epic or as a travesty, whether to stress the apotheosis of Bloom or the comedown of Odysseus. Most popular of all travesties was Scarron's burlesque of Vergil's *Aeneid*. It is worth citing, despite its studied vulgarisms, because it highlighted a crisis in the art of storytelling. You will remember that, after the banquet at the close of the first book, Dido heaves a long sigh— which the parodist reduces to a belch. Thereupon, in succinct Latin, the lovelorn queen requests Aeneas to rehearse his tale from the beginning: the treachery of the Greeks, the misfortunes of his comrades, and his own wanderings.

His response will constitute the second and third books, possibly the most influential narration in the secular literature of the West. It is anticipated in Dido's amplified speech, which I quote here not from Scarron but from his English imitator, Charles Cotton, who has rendered it in Hudibrastic doggerel:

> Quoth she, "Aeneas, out of jesting,
> Thou needs must tell, at my requesting,
> All the whole tale of Troy's condition
> Since first you troubled was with Grecian;
> Hector's great frights, and Priam's speeches,
> And eke describe Achilles' breeches,
> How strong he was when he did grapple,
> And if Tydides' horse were dapple;
> Tell me, I say, of Paris' lech'ry,
> The Grecians' quarrel, and their treach'ry,
> Your challenges, your fights and battles,
> And how you lost your goods and chattels."

Here the antiheroine of Cotton exhibits a curiosity which ranges far beyond Vergil. Much of what she wants from a story is characteristically feminine, especially details about the scandal that instigated the Trojan War. She is not interested in the shield of Achilles; she would like to find out, rather anachronistically, what he was wearing. Scarron's Dido, speaking somewhat less inelegantly through indirect discourse, is even more inquisitive about such matters as cosmetics:

> Si Dame Hélène avait du liège,
> De quel fard elle se servait,
> Combien de dents Hécube avait,
> Si Paris était un bel homme . . .

Women, though they had little to do with the epic, would exert a decisive influence over the novel, and the emphasis of Anti-Dido's questioning is decidedly novelistic. Fights and battles look backward to Homer, yes; goods and chattels look ahead to Balzac. It is easy to understand how Scarron, after the crudity of his *Virgile travesti,* could go on to become a pioneering novelist with his *Roman comique*—or, for that matter, how both Cervantes and Fielding after him could formulate their intention as "a comic epic in prose." It would remain for their successors, particularly the Russians, to show that prose could be tragic. Meanwhile fiction was sloughing off the conventional trappings of narrative verse, often treating verse itself as an archaic survival, prose being so much closer to the language of ordinary life.

This commitment to immediacy makes, in some degree, for a repudiation of structure. The novel is notoriously a chameleon, in its continuous adaptation to new intellectual climates and social environments. Conversely, it has been the pace of growth and change in the modern period, the advance of the empirical outlook stimulated by the sciences, the successive liberations undertaken in the name of democracy—not to mention the contributions of technology to material welfare—which have brought out that adaptability. The storied past of mythology is unrecapturable; it happened once upon a time, long ago and far away, when giants walked the earth and heroes slew dragons and men lived in the hazy light of magic and miracle. The novel inhabits the domain of the prosaic here and the recognizable now—or, in any case, some chronological junction to and from which we can easily return.

It seeks to satisfy our appetite for reality. Hence the fascination of Clarissa's letters, which we might be reading over the shoulder of her correspondent, or else the stratagems of Defoe to palm his fictions off as authentic documents: *A Journal of the Plague Year, Memoirs of a*

Cavalier, The History and Life of Captain Jack. Significantly, it was late in his prolific career as a journalist that Defoe became an early realist. But, though the very word *novel* is cognate with the word *news,* he and his contemporaries did not call themselves novelists. They maintained their plausibility by pretending that they were historians or biographers, not to say autobiographers: *The Life and Opinions of Tristram Shandy, The History of Tom Jones, a Foundling.* The realistic novel has coexisted and interacted with journalism through the greater part of its evolution.

Writers scanned the newspapers for their subjects, and frequently discovered them—as Dostoevsky did—among reports of the most sensational crimes. For others, as for Dickens, every book was an opportunity to expose the inequities and the absurdities of another obnoxious institution. Zola failed to impose scientific methods on the novel, but he did set exacting standards of documentation for it. Factual approaches seem to have driven out mythical world-views; myths can be construed, in retrospect, as conceptual substitutes for the facts; and the documentary trend has been mounting in recent years. The so-called "nonfiction novel" of Truman Capote is not a novel at all, though it utilizes the perceptive eye and the trained ear of the fiction-writer to exploit a morbid job of reporting.

No other novel published this year is likely to make a wider or deeper impact than William Styron's *Confessions of Nat Turner.* Mr. Styron derives his topic and title from a twenty-page pamphlet about the slave revolt, which he has eked out with further research and imaginative talent. This would seem to fulfill—more richly than our previous instance—the paradox of the nonfiction novel, in the sense of being a *vie romancée;* but so does *The Betrothed* or *War and Peace.* The striking effectiveness of Mr. Styron's book is due in large part to its sympathetic historical reconstruction, but probably in even larger part to its topical timing, its emergence at an hour of crisis in the nationwide movement for civil rights. Its actuality has repercussions of *actualité* or timeliness.

This tendency of truth to outstrip fiction is carried farthest by my third example from the bookshops, *La Vida* by Oscar Lewis. Professor Lewis is by profession a sociologist rather than a novelist, and I am not sure he would be flattered at seeing his book reviewed among recent fiction in a new periodical. Having previously investigated Mexican family life on the basis of recorded interviews, he has more recently taken his tape-recorder to Puerto Rico. His happy faculty for persuading his subjects to speak for themselves—and, presumably, for translating from a highly colloquial Spanish—contrasts oddly at times with the jargon of his profession. Yet the result is a story of human interest, not only more authentic than any novel, but more moving and more readable than most.

Our wheel has come full circle from oral culture, with its reliance on folk memories and on the generalized patterns of legendary lore. Our highly developed organs of information have given us direct access to other people's lives, on such a scale and with such particularity that the artistic imagination can scarcely compete; there seem to be so many other ways, more exact and thorough, of satisfying the appetite for reality. The novel, though more informative than the *guslar,* turns out to be less efficient than the tape-recorder. Preoccupation with fact, fact, fact—the Gradgrind System—may turn out to be self-defeating for fiction in the long run. Those omens of decline, which the critics have variously noted, are symptoms of technological obsolescence. This is not to assert that the novel is disappearing, but that its quality has fallen off.

A comparative glance at the publishers' lists of fiction and nonfiction would find much more of both immediate interest and lasting value in the latter category. A writer like John Hersey has clearly done better work in his reportage than in his journalistic novels. Let us not be confused by the cultural lag into thinking that nothing has changed. The pseudo-novels of Louis Auchincloss might have been meaningful, if they had been written fifty years ago under the pseudonym of Edith Wharton. So long as Hollywood needs scenarios, there will be a market for novels. That ultimate consumer, understandably, has become an inspirer or initiator. A New York syndicate has recently been tightening this profitable connection by prefabricating best-sellers: dreaming up subjects, more or less scandalous, selling the film and paperback rights in advance, and—at the final stage—calling in a non-novelist to write a book which will claim to be fiction only to protect itself from the libel laws.

If Madame Bovary were alive today, it is doubtful if she would read so many novels. She would be surrounded by other temptations; she would be seduced by other addictions; she would escape by taking other trips. To admit that the novel is slightly outdated need not be a pessimistic assumption. On the contrary, it is a more hopeful stance than to set one's back against whatever innovations may be in store. When Daguerre invented photography, it was gloomily predicted in some quarters that the art of painting would soon be killed off by its mechanical rival. Conceivably it might have been, if its sole aim had been literal reproduction. Instead it was forced to reconsider its aims, to reexamine the nature of its medium, and—with some stimulus from Daguerre's invention—to engender one of its most brilliant schools, the Impressionists.

In the spacious house of fiction, Henry James has reassured us, there is room for many mansions. Who will build the new structures, what they will look like, how we shall live with them—that is still another story, which I am not prophet enough to foretell. But the parallel with the plastic arts is suggestive, inasmuch as photographic realism has already been replaced in the novel by more impressionistic modes of apprehension, along with more lyrical modes of expression, whether we term them epiphanies or *tropismes*. Relieved from the naturalistic requirements of field work, the novelist should be free to pursue his investigations inward—where he may encounter other pitfalls, to be sure, in the danger of subjective fantasies or the indulgence of autobiographical impulses.

Proust, Joyce, Mann, and Kafka—great masters of the last generation, which may have been the last great generation of novelists—were searching for transitional solutions in essayistic speculation, in thematic prototypes, and in the rediscovery of myth and fable. Some of the most interesting fiction published after them has been bursting forth from those countries which had been politically bottled up, notably from Germany since 1947. From Russia too, where official pressure tried to revive the epic under the misleading label of Socialist Realism, a clandestine literature has been emerging, powerful in its satire and in its grotesquerie. Lately there have been signs that grotesquerie and satire are not dormant in the land of Poe and Mark Twain, where the principal genre of nineteenth-century narrative was not the novel but the romance.

The habit of fabulation, as Bergson described it, is instinctive and therefore must be universal. Its function, as he saw it, is to mediate between the ego and society. More explicitly to our purpose, it preserves continuities; it envisages possibilities; it projects ideals; it sums up conditions; it determines man's conception of himself. Though its basic materials are unchanging, they have been and will be subjected to endless permutations. Every story that has ever been told is a chapter in a chronicle which is to be continued, world without end. "Shall we for-ever make new books," Tristram Shandy inquires, "as apothecaries make new mixtures, by pouring out of one vessel into another?" If I may conclude by responding to a rhetorical question, I would answer in the affirmative.

THE QUIXOTIC PRINCIPLE:
CERVANTES AND OTHER NOVELISTS

Some of my students have said that *Don Quixote* is my King Charles's head, since it keeps turning up whenever I talk about fiction. I believe that it is bound to turn up, because of the paradigmatic role it played in the gestation and development of the novel. My first exposure to it, in translation, was rather perfunctory; but then, after agreeing to put it on the syllabus of a course in Great Books, I set out to read it in Spanish, with generous encouragement and constant enlightenment from my Spanish colleague, Amado Alonso. Much of what I understand about it I owe to him. Of course I was particularly interested in its catalytic effect, especially upon French literature, and even more in isolating the principle that conduced to that effect. Hence, when I was asked to write a chapter on the book's influence for a new Spanish manual on Cervantes, edited by J. B. Avalle-Arce and E. C. Riley, I was glad to make this reconsideration. The original English version has been published in the first volume of *Harvard English Studies,* edited by Morton Bloomfield (Cambridge, 1970). Two closely related studies appear in my *Contexts of Criticism,* "The Example of Cervantes" and "*Don Quixote* and *Moby-Dick.*" What is here called the Quixotic principle was clearly a major theme in *The Gates of Horn,* but perhaps it emerges more strikingly when disentangled from the dense context of modern realism.

Our paradox is that a book about literary influence, and indeed against it, should have enjoyed so wide and decisive a literary influence. However, no one writes a book without hoping to influence his readers, even if his hope is to dissuade them from reading certain other books. Cervantes is by no means as obsessive as his monomaniacal protagonist, yet the writer returns to his proclaimed crusade in his final sentence: "I never desired any other thing, then that men would utterly abhor the fabulous impertinent and extravagant bookes of Chivalries: And to say truth, they begin already to stagger; for, undoubtedly, such fables and flim-flam tales will shortly faile, and I hope never rise again."[1] They were failing already, to be sure; there had been actual legislation to curb them; and he must have realized, with advancing commitment to his task, that he was not just dismissing an obsolescent genre; he was inventing a new one. Like any great invention, it had its forerunners and its congeners. Something like it had come out of the train of epic degeneration that produced the earlier Italian poems about the paladins

1. *The History of Don Quixote,* tr. Thomas Shelton (London, 1896), IV, 278.

of Charlemagne, notably that of Pulci. Rabelais had taken off from a folk tale to satirize not only the pedantries of scholasticism but the Arthurian quest for the Holy Grail. Classical mythology, reconsidered in sophisticated retrospect, had been fair game for the mocking commentary of Lucian and many others.

More specifically, the Cervantistas have pointed to a dramatic skit, which seems to have adumbrated *Don Quixote* a few years before: *El Entremés de los Romances,* the interlude of the ballads. Here the prototype is merely a dim-witted peasant whose head has been turned by the lore of the *Romancero* so that he identifies himself with some of its heroes. Could he have caught this disease as readily by listening as by reading? A number of the lines he quotes will be echoed by Don Quixote, who—like his predecessor Bartolo—will blame his horse for one of his discomfitures. Now Cervantes was himself a playwright, who has left us eight vivacious interludes. But, as Yeats commented: "No playwright has made or will make a character that will follow us out of the theater as Don Quixote follows us out of the book, for no playwright can be wholly episodical."[2] Yeats's generic distinction may not always prevail; for instance, Shakespeare's characters have ways of getting into extradramatic involvements, yet none of them has led so autonomous a career in other minds than that of their creator. Moreover, we cannot identify ourselves so intimately with a personage on the stage, where he is corporeally represented by an actor—who, in a manner of speaking, gets between us and the part he is playing—as we can with some vicarious ego into whose existence we have entered through the pages of a novel.

This is the very essence of the novelistic relationship, that covenant between the story and the reader of which *Don Quixote* is at once an exemplification and a critique. Since there are innumerable readers with endlessly varying attitudes, they are bound to vary widely in their conceptions of their common hero. That variance, well attested by the range of critical interpretation and of pictorial illustration, seems again to have been deliberately cultivated by the novelist, who leads us into an atmosphere of perspectivism, as commentators have noted, both in stylistic detail and in philosophic generality.[3] Yet, through all the dizzy-

---

2. William Butler Yeats, "Discoveries," in *Essays and Introductions* (London, 1961), p. 273.

3. See Leo Spitzer, "Linguistic Perspectivism in the *Don Quijote*," in *Linguistics and Literary History* (Princeton, 1948), pp. 41ff.; also Claudio Guillén, "On the Concept and Metaphor of Perspective," in *Comparatists at Work,* ed. S. G. Nichols and R. B. Vowles (Waltham, Mass., 1968), pp. 60–64, 69–71.

ing shifts of vantage, Don Quixote never loses his vivid albeit dual identity; and Sancho Panza is equally his inimitable self, playing a reciprocal and indispensable role in the grand design; for, without the squire to accompany the knight, one could not imagine him faring forth a second time. Though the iconography is so varied, we immediately recognize them both in any visual depiction—partly because of their inseparable conjunction, we must admit. The Don could serve as well as any character ever conceived to answer Melville's question, "What is an original?"[4] Nevertheless, no purely literary creation has more solid standing as a type. Even the crotchet that sets him apart from his fellow men turns out to have a well-nigh universal application.

His unchivalrous compatriot, Don Juan, might seem to have had comparable fortunes in literature. But, though Tirso de Molina deserves the credit for having created the latter, there is at least a figment of legend behind him; and the original play has since been equaled or outmatched by more than one of the many subsequent treatments of the same material; whereas, despite that callow interlude suggesting the basic device, Cervantes holds a patent upon his characterization which no other novelist could conceivably infringe. His imitators, of course, are myriad; I shall glance at some of them in passing. But my focal interest will be his emulators—those who, not content with exploiting his discovery, pushed on to make advances of their own—and, above all, with the imaginative process that he developed and that his peers continued and renewed. The integrity of his concept was tested by imitation, not to say plagiary, even before he had completed the second part of the novel. The popularity of the first part seems to have inspired a continuation of the knight's adventures by an apocryphal hack who signed himself Alonso Fernandez de Avellaneda. Cervantes must have been well along with his own sequel, for the news of the false Don Quixote does not catch up with the true one until the fifty-ninth chapter. He responds by changing his announced destination, whither his rival has already gone.

Thereafter the plagiarized author finds several occasions for a retaliatory thrust at his plagiarist. He introduces a character out of Avellaneda's book, and makes him swear that there is no resemblance whatsoever between the two Dons. He takes particular pains to arrange

---

4. See Harry Levin, "*Don Quixote* and *Moby-Dick*," in *Contexts of Criticism* (Cambridge, Mass., 1957), p. 104.

a conclusive death for his hero, so that he can never again be exhumed by the ghouls of the literary marketplace. Avellaneda had really done Cervantes a favor, by showing how ineptly the knight and the squire could be treated at other hands. Such caricatures could be retitled, à la Pirandello, *Two Characters in Flight from an Author*. What is more significant, Cervantes was past master of a somewhat Pirandellian method which might be termed the book-within-the-book. It is a dangerous method for an immature or a pretentious writer, since it can result in disclosing his innate literariness. But Cervantes is so secure in his use of it that he can make the Bachelor Sampson Carrasco, in the second part, wonder whether there will ever be a second part. Sampson's role, at the outset of Part Two, is to announce that Part One has been published. Some 12,000 copies are now in print; Don Quixote will soon be boasting of 30,000. Consequently he will be recognized wherever he goes. "To conclude, he is so gleaned, so read, and so knowne to all sorts of people," says Sampson in their preliminary discussion of the new book, "that they can scarse see a leane horse passe by, when they say, 'There goeth Rosinante.' "[5]

During the decade that had passed between the publication of the two parts, Cervantes' figures had stamped themselves as types upon the popular consciousness. In contrast then to Part One, where the Don meets with misunderstanding on all sides, most of his interlocutors in Part Two are prepared to play his game. In fact, they go so far out of their way to cater to his madness with practical jokes that—and the invidious comparison is repeatedly drawn—they seem madder than he. Sampson, dressing up as a knightly challenger, finds himself swiftly unhorsed. The Duke and the Duchess, with their stately pranks, virtually turn their castle into an inn, and so complete the pattern of reversal. Don Quixote and Sancho Panza, as Thomas Mann reminds us, "would never have got to the ducal court, if the dignitaries there had not already known the remarkable pair so well from reading about them, and been delighted to see them personally 'in reality' and to entertain them as a princely amusement." And Mann goes on to comment: "That is wholly new and unique; I do not know anywhere else in world-literature where a fictitious hero lives upon his own frame, as it were upon the reputation of his reputation."[6] The framing work, the

---

5. *Don Quixote*, tr. Shelton, III, 36.
6. Thomas Mann, "*Meerfahrt mit Don Quijote*," in *Leiden und Grösse der Meister* (Berlin, 1935), p. 230.

book-within-the-book, is now *Don Quixote* itself, to which Cervantes can afterward juxtapose the falsification of Avellaneda. What could better substantiate Cervantes' declared purpose of underlining the difference between true and false history?

His fictive chronicler, the Cid Hamete, though he has been an ambiguous source of authority, gradually seems to become what recent critics would term a more reliable narrator. Cross-reference to his Arabic manuscript forms an important part of the shifting perspective. So does all the literary apparatus: the classical echoes and mock-epic flourishes and high-flown episodes, the inquisition in the library, the manuscripts uncovered at the inn, the critical debate with the Canon of Toledo. Don Quixote's first internal monologue is a wishful projection of his story as it might be celebrated by posterity. The glimpse that we are given of a printing press at Barcelona may be viewed as a kind of author's acknowledgment, for the cultural change that is being registered has as much to do with the invention of printing as with the decline of chivalry. But if the printed romance was by now a contradiction in terms, an indulgence in cultural lag, it was no less appealing for that nostalgic reason. *Don Quixote* has been called, by Albert Thibaudet, "le roman des romans."[7] That epithet, which suggests its central status among other novels, likewise indicates the duality of its substance, since there is no word in French to distinguish the novel from the romance. Moreover, according to Thibaudet, it is likewise "le roman contre les romans." As distinguished from the *roman d'aventures,* the romance of chivalric adventure, the novel was emerging through picaresque fiction, the confession of roguery.

Cervantes knew his rogues as well as did Alemán or Quevedo, and he had the ingenuity to test the fading pretensions of *Amadís of Gaul* —or, to a lesser extent, the *Orlando Furioso*—by shrewdly realistic criteria. There are no supernatural wonders in his comic world, though there are plenty of tricks to delude the unwary. He is careful to explain the mechanical workings of his oracular brazen head. Life is made up of useful and tangible objects, commonplace more frequently than not, such as the Barber's basin. The only enchantment is Don Quixote's paranoid fantasy that it must truly be a magical helmet, which the wicked sorcery of enchanters has reduced to this humble shape. Thus enchantment and disenchantment have exchanged their traditional roles, as they do with a vengeance when Sancho Panza undergoes a

7. Albert Thibaudet, *Le Liseur des romans* (Paris, 1925), p. xv.

series of lashings in the earnest effort to transform a husky peasant wench into the noble and beauteous and invisible Dulcinea del Toboso. The *donnée* is not much more complex than the primitive farce about the blockhead whose daily round has been bemused with snatches of balladry. Cervantes made his vital innovation when he elevated this mock-hero to a sphere of excessive literacy. In one of his exemplary tales, *The Glass Licentiate,* he briefly sketched the peregrinations of a scholarly monomaniac who replies with brittle sagacity when baited and regains the light of reason just before his death.

In the Knight of the Rueful Countenance we behold a full-length portrait of a single-minded reader for whom reading is believing, and whose consequent distortions of reality help to sharpen our apprehension of it. His malady, from which many have suffered during the five hundred years between Gutenberg and McLuhan, has been diagnosed by Ernest Renan as *morbus litterarius.*[8] Professor McLuhan seems to think that he has discovered a cure for it. Don Quixote's biography is the classic case of what Herman Meyer has named *das zitathafte Leben,* the quotation-oriented life.[9] All of our lives are more or less oriented to precepts and allusions. Sancho Panza relies on folk wisdom and pungent proverbs, in contradistinction to the book-learning and the rhetorical speeches of his master. The contrasting textures of the language contributed to that intermixture of high and low styles which, as Erich Auerbach has shown, provides the textual basis for realism. It was a brilliant stroke for Cervantes to have settled upon his subject, to have tried it out in his first six chapters, to have launched his knight and brought him back in battered pride to his endangered library. But Cervantes manifested even greater brilliance by sustaining his theme through the second sally that takes up the rest of Part One, and thereafter through the third expedition which constitutes Part Two, without unduly repeating himself and with so resourceful a sequence of variations.

In spite of his expressed misgivings about translation, he has transcended barriers as far as any writer can, and Spaniards have rejoiced in the international scope of his ubiquitous appeal. Pérez Galdós has observed that *Don Quixote* had more readers than the other masterworks of the West because it could be enjoyed by the old and the young,

8. See Harry Levin, *The Gates of Horn: A Study of Five French Realists* (New York, 1963), pp. 5off.

9. Herman Meyer, *Das Zitat in der Erzählkunst: Zur Geschichte und Poetik des Europäischen Romans* (Stuttgart, 1967), p. 62.

the wise and the ignorant, "the cultivated Frenchman" and "the crass Yankee."[10] But he also claimed that "only Spain, fertile in talents, in heroes, in saints, and in monsters, gives us such hybrids of reason and unreason, of mystical faith and martial pride, fused within a single soul."[11] It is possibly a mark of corroboration that this statement echoes a conceited phrase from a romance parodied on the first page of *Don Quixote,* "la razón de la sinrazón," and that this oxymoron would furnish a title for Galdós' last novel. Such bywords function in a frame of reference which is the legitimate heritage of every educated Spaniard. For him, no doubt, there are rich pleasures of recognition which a foreigner is not qualified to feel. My old teacher, Irving Babbitt, liked to cite a pseudo-proverb: "There is something Spanish in the Spaniard which causes him to behave in a Spanish manner."[12] Clearly, I cannot pretend to penetrate into that arcanum of *Españolismo;* and such nationalistic tautologies, though they are sometimes propounded by Hispanists, leave the question opaque. Substitute another nationality, and you have the same *petitio principii.*

But an outsider can pick up a good deal at second hand from the observation, fully accredited by his countrymen, of Cervantes—or, for that matter, Galdós. As a late nineteenth-century novelist, Galdós was very much a man of his time: a liberal and a modernist, looking forward rather than backward, during a period when the clericals and the reactionaries seemed to be practising some sort of collective Quixotism in a conspiracy to keep the clock turned back. Their comparative success, as he depicts it in his novels dealing with social problems, makes Galdosian irony more bitter than Cervantine. His standard-bearers of science and rationalism, like the earnest young protagonist in *La Familia de Léon Roch* or Pepe in *Doña Perfecta,* are frustrated and defeated by the vested interests of tradition. The latter story is located in the heart of Spain, in as arid a region as La Mancha, in a miserable village known as Orbajosa after its main crop, which is garlic (*ajo*). Characteristically and quixotically, the local antiquarian would prefer to derive the place name through a grander Roman etymology from the Latin *urbs-augusta.* "Everything here is irony," as Pepe so tragically

---

10. Benito Pérez Galdós, *Crónica de la quincena,* ed. W. H. Shoemaker (Princeton, 1948), p. 114.

11. Galdós, *Amadeo I,* in *Obras completas,* ed. F. C. Sainz de Robles (Madrid, 1941), III, 1047. See also J. C. Herman, *Don Quijote and the Novels of Pérez Galdós* (Ada, Oklahoma, 1955).

12. Irving Babbitt, *Spanish Character and Other Essays* (Boston, 1941), p. 1.

learns. "The people of this land live by imagination."[13] Cervantes, like all great writers, has acquired an extra dimension within his native culture, since he has done so much to delineate its patterns. But if he loses that quality when his work is exported, something else may have been gained by its adaptation into another milieu and by the emulation it has stimulated.

The problem of adapting—or else of not adapting—must be instanced as our hero's predominant trait; and he remains himself, a Spanish tourist, in Fielding's roughhewn comedy *Don Quixote in England*.[14] But elsewhere we soon hear of *Le Don Quichotte français*, of *Der deutscher Donquixott*, and even of a Pomeranian Don Quixote in *Siegfried von Lindenberg* by J. G. Müller,[15] a novel of *Junkertum*. Our hero has been submitted to the vicissitudes of history as well as geography, and has championed new causes as well as old. A minor Russian poet, Prince Odoevsky, projected a *Don Quixote of the Nineteenth Century*.[16] It is characteristic of Kafka that he should want to have the story retold as an existential parable, visualized from the viewpoint of the downtrodden Sancho Panza. Contemporary crazes, *mutatis mutandis,* took the place of the old fixation upon knight-errantry. *The Spiritual Quixote* of Richard Graves lampooned John Wesley and the Methodist movement. *The Romantic Quixote* of William Combe, illustrated by Thomas Rowlandson and satirizing the vogue of the picturesque, was the first volume in the once-famous trilogy of Dr. Syntax's tours. The cycle of translation had commenced during Cervantes' lifetime with Volume One: first into English by Thomas Shelton in 1612 and then into French by César Oudin in 1614. Writers acquainted with Spanish did not have to wait for translations. Jacobean playwrights borrowed plots from the episodes of *Don Quixote* and from the *Exemplary Novels*.

Francis Beaumont followed a traceable course in *The Knight of the Burning Pestle* when he allowed a grocer's apprentice to climb onstage and to take over the mock-heroic and mock-romantic proceedings on behalf of the middle class. Samuel Butler applied the formula to the

13. Galdós, *Doña Perfecta*, in *Obras completas*, IV, 437, 409.

14. See E. B. Knowles, "Cervantes and English Literature," in *Cervantes across the Centuries*, ed. Angel Flores and M. J. Benardete (New York, 1947), pp. 282ff. and *passim*.

15. See Lienhard Bergel, "Cervantes in Germany," in Flores and Benardete, ed., *Cervantes*, p. 312 and *passim*. See also J. J. A Bertrand, *Cervantes et le romantisme allemand* (Paris, 1914).

16. See L. B. Turkevich, "Cervantes in Russia," in Flores and Benardete, ed., *Cervantes*, pp. 350–351 and *passim*.

Puritans, from a Cavalier point of view, in the rocking-horse tetrameters of his *Hudibras*. Don Quixote's unfulfilled notion of turning shepherd and reenacting a classical pastoral was worked out by Charles Sorel in *Le Berger extravagant,* which generalized the whole situation with an alternative title, *L'Anti-roman*—an expression which Sartre could do no better than borrow, when he wrote his preface to the first *nouveau roman* of Nathalie Sarraute. One of Marivaux's earliest experiments in prose fiction, *Pharsamon,* bears two alternative titles: *Les Folies romanesques* and *Le Don Quichotte moderne,* both of which reverberate to the line of inquiry that I have been pursuing.[17] Le Sage, who went so far as to translate Avellaneda along with Cervantes, was one of the many Frenchmen, including Beaumarchais and Mérimée, who sought romance in the peninsular birthplace of the picaresque. Tapping the same vein, Smollett not only translated the authentic *Don Quixote* into English but also modeled his own *Sir Launcelot Greaves* upon it, even to the point of the heroic agnomen—inasmuch as a greave, like a *quijote,* happens to be a piece of leg armor.

The most robust of the English offshoots is the one that subscribes itself, on the title page, *The History of the Adventures of Joseph Andrews and His Friend Mr. Abraham Adams, Written in Imitation of the Manner of Cervantes.* Here the protagonist and the deuteragonist have changed places, since the Quixote is truly Parson Adams, no less absent-minded than high-minded, who can solace his discomfitures by rereading Aeschylus in Greek. In place of chivalric romance, the book in the background is *Pamela,* which Fielding has no trouble in reducing to absurdity. The maidservant Pamela, who has fended off her master in order to marry him, is now endowed with a brother, the manservant Joseph, who lives up to his forename by virtuously resisting the advances of his lady. Richardson was not among those amused by what he considered "a lewd and ungenerous engraftment."[18] Parson Adams disentangles himself to join Parson Primrose, from *The Vicar of Wakefield,* among the good-hearted enthusiasts and well-meaning eccentrics who could trace their descent to La Mancha. So could my Uncle Toby, as seconded by Corporal Trim; Sterne's Yorick expires "with something of a Cervantic tone"; and even Walter Shandy is said to speak with "Cervantic gravity."[19] Critical discussions of the

17. See Maurice Bardon, *"Don Quichotte" en France au XVIIe et au XVIIIe siècle* (Paris, 1931).
18. John Carroll, ed., *Letters of Samuel Richardson* (Oxford, 1964), p. 133.
19. Laurence Sterne, *Tristram Shandy,* book I, ch. 12; book III, ch. 10.

English humorists ordinarily center upon these worthies, not excluding Don Quixote. He became so lovable a figure that the critics devoted their best efforts to glossing over the characteristics that had made him a comic one, just as Maurice Morgann tried to do with Falstaff.

Henry Brooke, digressing from a long-winded fable significantly titled *The Fool of Quality,* singled out Don Quixote as "the greatest hero among the moderns."[20] Now, when an antihero becomes a hero, as contemporaries of Saul Bellow and Samuel Beckett and Günter Grass do not need to be reminded, it is a sign that values have been undergoing an overturn. A mounting veneration for an erstwhile laughing-stock might indicate a falling off in the general sense of humor. It could also mark a rise of individualism, plus a sympathy which supplanted ridicule when an individual displayed his idiosyncrasies. Romanticism gloried in the good fight for the losing cause, *unus contra mundum* if worst came to worst—or best came to best. Erasmian folly was no longer a laughing matter, if it proceeded from a set of principles which did not seem less noble for being far-fetched. Don Quixote was discussed and revalued on the same plane of moral seriousness as Prometheus or Antigone. At a widening distance in time and space, the contrasts stressed by Cervantes had been blurred together: a Spanish inn seemed hardly less romantic than a genuine castle, and an ineffectual gesture was somehow finer than a doughty deed. In the long run, the impact of any book is the sum of its various readings; and when these differ from the author's purposes, they reveal the readers' special concerns.

The German romanticists claimed Cervantes' work as their own and, with the Schlegels, regarded it as pure poetry.[21] The punctilious hidalgo was regarded as a rebel against society like the Plutarch-reading Karl Moor, who is compared with him in Schiller's preface to *The Robbers,* his first play. To the mind of the Enlightenment, Don Quixote had personified that sentimental gush or *Schwärmerei* which would be more highly esteemed by a succeeding generation. Goethe had purged himself of such tendencies by writing *The Sorrows of Young Werther,* where his self-pitying surrogate finds temporary solace in the epos of Homer and preeminently in the pseudo-epic of Ossian. In Goethe's self-mocking skit, *The Triumph of Sensibility,* a quixotic prince finds his

20. Henry Brooke, *The Fool of Quality* (London, 1906), p. 44.
21. See René Wellek, *A History of Modern Criticism,* 1750–1950 (New Haven, 1955), II, 28, 51.

Dulcinea in a doll, which proves to be stuffed with books, among them *Werther.* The point of departure for Goethe's Faust, as for Don Quixote, is a book-lined study; but the two explorers, each of them measuring *das Wort* against *die Tat,* accumulated theory against the practice of life, take opposite courses. Both the autonomy and the universality of Cervantes' creation were acknowledged by Turgenev, when he coupled Don Quixote with Hamlet in a well-known essay. Hamlet had been romanticized for the worse, as Don Quixote had been for the better, signally in *Wilhelm Meister's Apprenticeship;* and on Goethe's misconception of a weakling who cannot make up his own mind Turgenev based his short story "A Hamlet of the Shchigri District."

In the essay he contends not only that Hamlet and Don Quixote are polar opposites, but that every man has his archetype in the one or the other: on the one hand, the hesitant and introspective skeptic; on the other, the activist fanatically dedicated to the fulfillment of certain philanthropic ideals. However this simplistic dichotomy may deviate from the intentions of either Shakespeare or Cervantes, it could be related to the physiognomies of Russian literature. As between Tolstoy's heroes in *War and Peace,* for example, Prince Andrey could be considered a Hamlet and Count Pierre a Quixote. Turgenev, whose own temperament inclined him to be more Hamlet-like, envisioned a self-conscious follower of Don Quixote in Rudin, who dies at Paris on the revolutionary barricades; and, though Bazarov in *Fathers and Sons* is an up-to-date nihilist, he imposes his dogmas on situations with a truly quixotic zealotry. In the broad typology of Russian nineteenth-century culture, the so-called Westerners—like Turgenev—were the Hamlets, while the Slavophils were the Quixotes—especially Dostoevsky, who found Cervantes a recurrent source of inspiration. His cherished project of writing about "a positively good man" found its problematic fufillment in *The Idiot.*[22] There the ultimate emulation was nothing less than the *imitatio Christi.* But the literary exemplar was *Don Quixote,* which in his *Diary of a Writer* Dostoevsky called "the last and greatest word of human thought, the most bitter irony that man can express."[23]

In his notes for *The Idiot* he linked the Don with Mr. Pickwick, duly noting some diminution of stature in Dickens' benevolent humbug. Both of these unlucky philanthropists held a peculiar interest by being comical. A terse notation referring to Don Quixote and the acorns (pre-

---

22. See E. J. Simmons, *Dostoevsky: The Makings of a Writer* (New York, 1940), p. 210.
23. Ibid., p. 211.

sumably those which inspired the knight's discourse to the goatherds on the Golden Age, and thereby symbolized the humane ideal he was seeking to recapture) seems to suggest that Dostoevsky may have been attempting a parallel in some of the idealistic speeches he put into the mouth of Prince Myshkin. The closest analogy seems to be the discussion prompted by a recitation of Pushkin's rather Cervantine poem "The Poor Knight." This is not comic but all too serious; and Myshkin, though charming, is tragic; his noble outbursts culminate, alas, in a state of all too literal idiocy. Comparably, his higher model, Jesus, is rebuffed and rejected by this world in Ivan Karamazov's parable of the Grand Inquisitor. Thus the gradual sublimation of Cervantes' intention across the centuries—which commenced with his own elaborations and afterthoughts, and was carried to metaphysical heights in the reinterpretations of the Romantic Movement—reaches its point of apotheosis with Dostoevsky, when the Foolish Knight takes on an aspect of the Fool in Christ.[24] At the other extreme, he could be Sovietized in a play by Lenin's cultural commissar, Anatol Lunacharsky.

No book has had a more spectacular fortune than the one whose relations with others I am considering. Since it assumed so prominent a place in the canon of European classics, and stood so near the beginnings of the novel, it was destined to figure in the formation of nearly all the other novelists. It was almost certain to be a milestone in their development; Stendhal testifies that his first encounter with it was "perhaps the greatest epoch of my life."[25] The all but countless imitations that it invited and sanctioned, the quasi-Quixotes adapted by other writers to other contexts, some of which we have been glancing at, have been systematically catalogued and amply documented in a number of studies. What should concern us rather more centrally is not so much the direct line of Cervantes' impact as the basic process he discovered and its wider employment, which I shall venture to call the Quixotic principle. Bernard Shaw, in one of his prefaces, berates the critics as usual—this time for attributing his technique of disillusionment to the influence of Ibsen or Nietzsche. Actually, he tells us, it was from a forgotten novel, *A Day's Ride, a Life's Romance,* by a minor novelist, Charles Lever, that Shaw learned "the tragicomic irony of the conflict between real life and the romantic imagination."[26] What he diagnoses

24. See Walter Nigg, *Der christliche Narr* (Zurich, 1956), pp. 221ff.
25. Stendhal, *Vie de Henry Brulard,* ed. Henri Martineau (Paris, 1927), I, 152.
26. G. B. Shaw, *John Bull's Other Island and Major Barbara* (New York, 1908), p. 158 (preface to *Major Barbara*).

as "Pott's" disease (for Lever's hero boasts that unromantic name) is the very malaise that had affected Don Quixote and Mr. Pickwick.

But Shaw did not gain his awareness of it from Cervantes, though he suggests that Lever might have got something through Stendhal; and we know well enough where Stendhal got it. In *The Counterfeiters* of André Gide, the novelist Edouard is writing a novel which will be entitled *The Counterfeiters*. What could be more appropriate, since fiction by definition is no more than a fabricated semblance of the truth it sets out to convey? The subject of this book-within-the-book is formulated in terms which come so close to Shaw's as to imply that each writer had independently come across the quixotic principle: "the rivalry between the real world and the representation that we make of it for ourselves."[27] That representation tends to be inherently romantic in the bookish sense of the word: *romanesque*. It has been argued—not to say overargued—by Denis de Rougemont that romance in the amatory sense, the cult of love between the sexes as we conceive and practise it, was superimposed upon the modern world by courtly troubadours and medieval romancers and sonneteering Christian Platonists.[28] Rougemont's thesis could be epitomized by La Rouchefoucauld's maxim that some people would never fall in love if they had not heard about it. The passion of Paolo and Francesca was set aflame by a book they were reading together, the romance of Lancelot and Guinevere, which Dante curses as a go-between. Dante meanwhile has narrated the romance of Paolo with Francesca, and has revivified it by placing it in the contrasting context of a book-within-a-book.

Romances did not cease to exist when *Amadís* was put down, or when the Curate and the Barber burned Don Quixote's books. The Romantic Revival could be said to have suffused this spirit into all phases of human behavior. We should remember that the novel of its leading exponent, Rousseau, evokes another medieval love story; and if his Julie stands in the shadow of Héloïse, then her Abelard, Saint-Preux, might have been christened after some chivalric predecessor. The starting point for Scott—which means the starting point for Manzoni, Cooper, Balzac, and the nineteenth-century novel—was the library at Waverley Honour, where the quixotic young Edward indulged in "Castle-Building."[29] Scott has his realistic side, his lowlands as well as his highlands,

27. André Gide, *Les Faux-monnayeurs* (Paris, 1925), p. 261.
28. Denis de Rougemont, *L'Amour et l'occident* (Paris, 1939).
29. Walter Scott, *Waverley*, ch. iv.

his Hanoverian allegiance along with his Jacobite nostalgia. Yet he remains at heart a romanticist because, quite unlike Cervantes, he was less interested in exposing reality than in embellishing it. As daily life became more drably urbanized and uneventfully uniform, much of fiction came to serve the desire to escape through fantasy into distant regions where the scenery was more picturesque and the prospect of adventure could still be held out. Many Anglo-American novelists, such as Hawthorne and the Brontës, expressly looked upon their works as romances, in order to claim more imaginative latitude. This Quixotism on the part of the author has its *preux chevalier* in the whimsical person of Lewis Carroll's White Knight.

It was the professed intent of Dickens to romanticize familiar things, but increasingly he comes out among the realists. The *donnée* of his first novel, *Pickwick Papers,* with its paunchy middle-class knight and its boot-shining cockney squire, is decidedly Cervantine. Don Quixote himself was not more chaste in resisting Maritornes during the bedroom farce at the inn than is Samuel Pickwick, Esq., when he blushes at being seen in his nightcap by the lady with the curling-papers at the Great White Horse in Ipswich. If he beams and bumbles his way toward an escape to the countryside and to the sentimentalities of Christmas, he comes back to London with a vengeance and to the terrain of future Dickensian satire, the lawcourt and the prison. Remote as Cervantes stands from the ground of Dickens' later writings, the two great caricaturists are linked by their common gifts of mimicry and powers of invention. I trust that the categories I have been using, for the sake of convenience, are understood to be relative rather than absolute. All narration involves some degree of interaction between realistic and romantic elements. Realism presupposes romanticism, and makes its sharpest points in juxtaposition with it, as I have been trying to demonstrate here and elsewhere. The novelist as we have known him, from Cervantes to—but not through—Joyce, and as contrasted with other storytellers working within the other narrative modes, has been primarily a realist.

This has not been the rule with the classic American tradition. One exception, H. H. Brackenridge in *Modern Chivalry,* made an amusing local extension of Cervantes' formula. But the primary emphasis has fallen upon the Gothic, upon the search for a past, or upon the exploitation of regional color. Melville hailed Cervantes as one of his personal demigods, associating him with John Bunyan and Andrew Jackson in a moving apostrophe. Yet the elaborate procedures of *Moby-Dick* are aimed at dignifying and amplifying a humble set of conditions, at conferring the honors of knighthood upon a crew of fishermen. A humorist must by nature be more of a realist, since his business is the perception of incongruities; and Mark Twain not infrequently seems to pursue the course of Cervantes, most straightforwardly with his *Connecticut Yankee in King Arthur's Court*. As an innocent abroad he played Sancho Panza, refusing to recognize the Old World's marvels and equating America with a modernity before which storied castles could do nothing but crumble. Whereas at home the romance-ridden South, spuriously gothicized by too long an immersion in the Waverley novels, was one of his principal targets. Its faded glories and its declining legends are intermingled with brute force and earthy cunning in Faulkner's darkly variegated chronicle of the Compsons and the Snopeses. It is not surprising to learn that he reread *Don Quixote* every year, as if it were the writer's Bible.[30]

With Hemingway, the revolt against literariness became a major stylistic premise. Its manifesto is his famous description of the retreat at Caporetto in *A Farewell to Arms,* where all the rhetoric of abstraction has been exploded on the battlefield. The experience of war has always tended to sharpen the edges of realism, as it must have done for Cervantes at Lepanto. It was crucial for Tolstoy at Sebastopol, and the quixotic principle can be seen at work throughout *War and Peace*. Consider the sturdy general Kutuzov, shrugging aside the complicated strategies of the military theorists and biding his time for the Battle of Borodino by dozing over a pallid historical novel of Madame de Genlis. The running contrast with Napoleon is highlighted by histrionic gestures and grandiose announcements. Even the frequent use of French in the novel, which underscores the artificiality of court circles, focuses attention on the immediacies of the Russian homeland, just as Pierre's dabblings in freemasonry pale before his initiation into the comradeship of battle. As for Napoleon himself, having realized his mad wishdreams and entrammeled Europe in misadventure, he was in no position to appreciate the irony of Cervantes. Afterward at Saint Helena, after dinner with his small entourage, we are told by his chronicler Las Cases: "He finished by reading to us from *Don Quixote,* stopped at several jests, and, putting down the book, remarked that it

---

30. William Faulkner, in *Writers at Work,* ed. Malcolm Cowley (New York, 1958), p. 136.

surely took courage to laugh in that moment at such trivialities."[31]

But, even as his youthful dreams of grandeur had been nourished by literature, so his private legend—as set down by Las Cases in the *Memorial of Saint Helena*—would stir the ambitions of the next generation. What *Amadís of Gaul* was to Don Quixote the *Mémorial* would be to Julien Sorel. When we first encounter Julien he is poring over it, astride a beam in his father's sawmill whence it is roughly knocked into the millrace. No matter, for he has virtually memorized it; and, as he ascends the social scale in *The Red and the Black,* he patterns himself on two additional and somewhat contradictory models: Rousseau's *Confessions* and Molière's *Tartuffe*. In *The Charterhouse of Parma* Fabrice del Dongo has a more urbane upbringing, yet it begins in the bedazzlement of the Napoleonic image and the baptism of fire at Waterloo—the pioneering treatment of war in modern fiction —which teaches him that being in the army is not like being a hero of Ariosto. The official biographer of the Napoleonides, those little would-be Napoleons whose quixotic aspirations so often culminated in mercenary defection and political compromise, was naturally Balzac. His catchphrase, *Lost Illusions,* might aptly stand as a generalization to cover all the instances that I have been reviewing, beginning with Don Quixote on his deathbed and extending far beyond the sentimental education of Frédéric Moreau. The case history that Balzac so designates, that of Lucien de Rubempré, is the object lesson of literary talent selling out.

The undergrowth of chastened romanticism, out of which such realism develops, is still fairly obtrusive in Balzac. It is more disciplined, though by no means absent, in Flaubert. When Kierkegaard in 1843 called for a feminine version of *Don Quixote,* he was unaware that this hiatus had been filled at least twice: in the mid-eighteenth century with *The Female Quixote* by the American-born Englishwoman Charlotte Lennox, and in 1800 with *Female Quixotism* by an American who sounds like an old-fashioned schoolmarm, Tabitha Tenney.[32] Kierkegaard's suggestion was, at any rate, well taken; for the typical gentle reader, to be addressed and served and swayed by the novelist, would be a woman. The fictional heroines—Clarissas, Corinnes, and Consuelos—had all exhibited quixotic symptoms. The girlish reveries of

31. Comte Emmanuel de Las Cases, *Le Mémorial de Sainte-Hélène,* ed. Jean Prévost (Paris, 1935), p. 369.
32. Søren Kierkegaard, *Either/Or,* tr. D. F. and M. L. Swenson (Princeton, 1944), I, 210.

Tatiana, in *Evgeni Onegin,* had been bibliographically footnoted. Through the interplay of sense and sensibility, Jane Austen had criticized Mrs. Radcliffe and Fanny Burney. E. S. Barrett, whose early pseudonym was Cervantes Hogg, had presented a paradigm in *The Heroine,* where a farmer's daughter sallies forth into a picaresque world, armed with no more than misleading assumptions about it, nurtured by the circulating libraries. "I sat down and read Ossian, to store my mind with ideas for conversation," she confides to us on one occasion, and on another: "Being in such distress, I thought it incumbent on me to compose a sonnet."[33] Ultimately, but not before she has impulsively and repeatedly placed her virtue in danger, she is cured by reading *Don Quixote.*

The usual habits of novel-reading, of course, tended to spread such infections rather than cure them. Homeopathy could be efficacious only if the restorative book was molded in the Cervantine tradition. This particular delusion of grandeur, the self-portrait of the housewife as a heroine, was given the definitive stamp of Flaubert in *Madame Bovary.* Flaubert's Emma, like Jane Austen's, is "an imaginist."[34] Putting so much of himself in the part, while transposing the sex, he stresses her sentimental education: girlish readings, the idyll of *Paul and Virginia,* the religiosity of Chateaubriand. She loves literature "pour ses excitations passionnelles."[35] A scene is set at the opera for her affair with Léon —a performance of *Lucia di Lammermoor,* appropriately derived from a Waverley novel. (Similarly, an operatic setting lends itself to the attempted seduction of Natasha in *War and Peace.*) The female counterpart of Quixotism, or self-deception incited by literature, is known as *Bovarysme;* its ending can be tragic when not bathetic; but Flaubert, while modernizing the initial concept of Cervantes, vastly broadened it. M. Homais can be just as much of a *Bovaryste* as Emma, and the fads and slogans that he projects are the vulnerable presuppositions of bourgeois society. That reduction is carried to encyclopedic extremes in *Bouvard et Pécuchet,* where a pair of conscientious clowns pushes its quixotries into many successive fields of blundering endeavor.

Cervantes and Flaubert, then, rank together as the alpha and omega of the quixotic principle. In view of the span between them, perhaps we could generalize further by adapting an aphorism from Pascal. He

33. E. S. Barrett, *The Heroine,* ed. Walter Raleigh (London, 1909), pp. 170, 21.
34. Jane Austen, *Emma,* ch. xxxiii.
35. Gustave Flaubert, *Madame Bovary,* ch. vi.

was speaking of eloquence, which faces a similar problem: whenever words are used, they are abused, so that, if one genuinely seeks to carry conviction, one must begin by discrediting the verbal medium. Accordingly we could say: "Le vrai roman se moque du roman."[36] The true novel flouts the novel—or, to catch another nuance, the *romanesque*. Such mockery, focusing as it does on literary material, tends to take the form of parody. Fielding thus began by parodying Richardson, in "the Manner of Cervantes"; Jane Austen with divers parodies, memorably that of the Gothic novel in *Northanger Abbey;* Thackeray with his burlesques in *Punch* of Bulwer, Lever, Cooper, Disraeli—not to mention *Rebecca and Rowena,* subtitled *A Romance upon Romance.* It is not for nothing that we speak in this connection of a "takeoff," or that so many novelists have started as parodists and played, in Stevenson's phrase, "the sedulous ape" to their forerunners.[37] Proust took off with a series of pastiches in *Le Figaro,* recounting a topical scandal *à la manière de* Balzac, Flaubert, Sainte-Beuve, Goncourt, and others. Through the posthumous fragment *Against Sainte-Beuve,* we now know that the *Remembrance of Things Past* (which contains purported excerpts from the Goncourt *Journal*) was helped into life by the midwifery of *The Human Comedy.*

Joyce's *Ulysses* constitutes a parody of parodies, both in its reductive relation to Homer's *Odyssey* and in such excursions as Gerty MacDowell's into the mawkish sphere of schoolgirl magazines, let alone the episode that stylistically recapitulates the evolution of English literature. But Joyce goes deeper, since he enters the minds of his leading characters so completely; he shows how consciousness is pieced together by reminiscence and how thought is patterned by echoes, whether these be Molly's songs or Bloom's advertisements or Stephen's scholastic formulations. By this stage, and in the mature fiction of the writers I have been citing, the novelist has taken us far beyond mere parody. But he had to make his breakthrough at the level of stylistic precedent. Through the parodic he moved on to the satiric, starting from a critique of literature and ending with a criticism of life. Hence Cervantes' explicit attack on books of chivalry can be read as an implicit renunciation of feudal institutions—or, better still, a salutation to the Renaissance. As historical circumstances changed, the central

36. Blaise Pascal, *Pensées,* pref., 24. The original formulation is: "La vraie éloquence se moque de l'éloquence."

37. R. L. Stevenson, "A College Magazine," in *Memories and Portraits.*

mechanism could be continually enlarged and rendered more flexible in meeting those changes. It was, after all, no more than some *idée fixe* which needed to become unfixed again and sharply detached in the light of fuller experience. It was, indeed, like falling out of love; and the infatuation that had preceded it could be likened, in Stendhal's terms, to the crystallization that dazzles the lover.

The overriding idea might assume the guise of an ideology to be challenged, of a doctrine that turned its believers into doctrinaires, or a frame of reference that proves inadequate for the phenomena it was intended to cover. The quest may take its hero to different regions in search of dissimilar objects, and yet still serve as a vehicle for testing hypotheses and breaking down preconceptions. Systems like that of Tristram Shandy's father or—more tragically—that of Richard Feverel's father, *-isms* and *-ologies,* hobbyhorses and mental constructs of all sorts, must be verified and rectified by facts. And, since facts are not the same as words, our best means of gaining contact with actuality through them is to dramatize the processes of verification and rectification. The record is always having to be corrected in some particular. "Systems of metaphysics are to philosophers," wrote Voltaire, "what novels are to women . . . I have ventured to let the air out of some of those metaphysical balloons."[38] We watch this habit of deflation as it works through chapter after chapter with Candide, who is so naïve that it takes a war, an inquisition, an earthquake, a tidal wave, and a disastrous tour of the world to disabuse him of his faith in the Leibnitzian optimism of Dr. Pangloss. Yet it would be a mistake to believe that the quixotic principle is a negative one, simply because it operates through disillusionment. Rather, it is a register of development, an index of maturation. Its incidental mishaps can be looked back upon as milestones on the way to self-awareness.

Georg Lukács was therefore well warranted, fifty years ago in his *Theorie des Romans,* when he made *Don Quixote* the crucial link in the chain of narrative extending from the ancient epic to the modern *Bildungsroman,* wherein the subjectivity of the individual develops into an ironic overview of life.[39] The path is clear, then, from Cervantes to Proust. Marcel is a young Quixote when he goes questing *à la recherche du temps perdu.* His *Amadís de Gaula* is the *Almanach de Gotha;* and that nostalgic magic-lantern vista of the baronial past, colored with all

38. Voltaire, *Courte Réponse aux longs discours d'un docteur allemand.*
39. Georg Lukács, *Die Theorie des Romans* (Berlin, 1920), *passim.*

the heraldry, the genealogy, and the poetry of latter-day snobbism, is dispelled shortly after his duchess puts on the wrong shoes. His dubieties over his elusive Albertine bear a surprising likeness to the jealousies of Cervantes' Curious Impertinent. But, where Cervantes' book-within-the-book is a thoroughly outmoded document which somehow has the effect of launching Don Quixote into the world, Proust's ultimate book is the one that he will write upon his retirement from the world, the very work that is being created before our eyes. His last appeal is not from art to life but from life to art, an art which justifies life by rounding it out. It seems fitting that Proust should recall Cervantes, along with Dostoevsky and Tolstoy, and likewise Shakespeare and Sophocles, in his poignant memoir, "Filial Sentiments of a Parricide." For the recognition scene and the resolution of a novel must finally be what they were to Alonso Quixano the Good upon his deathbed: as Proust has summed it up, "a belated moment of lucidity."[40]

40. Marcel Proust, *Pastiches et mélanges* (Paris, 1919), p. 224.

ON THE DISSEMINATION OF REALISM

This essay bears witness, in the fullest sense, to the quixotic principle in action. When I announced at the outset that "our subject is beset with controversy at every juncture," I was very far from being prepared for the juncture that even then confronted me. The circumstances of inception and presentation are explained by the postscript that was written to be published with the paper in *TriQuarterly* (Winter, 1968). The paper itself was also published in the *Actes/Proceedings* of the fifth congress of the International Comparative Literature Association (Belgrade, 1969), and—translated into Hungarian and refuted by Professor Köpeczi—in *Helikon* (Winter, 1968).

When the institutions of Japan were opened to western influence a hundred years ago, it was said that the Emperor Meiji wanted to have a British parliament, a German army, and a French literature. France provided a model in the literary sphere, just as Germany did in the military or Britain in the political domain. What appealed to the Emperor, no doubt, and put France in so central a position among the other cultures, was the authority of its classical tradition, which had held a comparable attraction for Frederick the Great. Yet even after monarchy had yielded to revolution, and classicism had been succeeded by romanticism, it was still France that set the pace, through a sequence of artistic movements which ran parallel to its revolutionary upheavals. To view them in historical perspective is to see the romantic movement —with its emphasis on sensation, individuality, and local color—as an anticipation of realism. So Alain Robbe-Grillet can retrospectively tell us: "Literary revolutions are always carried out in the name of realism."[1] The name itself would change with the generations. Champfleury, who did more than anyone else to publicize the label that had first been attached to Courbet's paintings, predicted that *réalisme* would last no longer than thirty years.[2] Zola, the leading publicist for naturalism, saw it as a continuation of realism, but felt that the time was ripe for another catchword. Whereas Georg Brandes used the later expression, in characterizing the English romanticists, not simply for Words-

---

1. Alain Robbe-Grillet, *Pour un nouveau roman* (Paris, 1963), p. 162.
2. Documentation for references not otherwise specified can be found in my book, *The Gates of Horn: A Study of Five Realists* (New York and London, 1963).

worth's cult of nature but for Shelley's radicalism and Byron's raillery.[3]

The school of the midcentury found its reluctant master in Flaubert, that disenchanted romanticist who rejected all catchwords and would not enroll himself as either a realist or a naturalist. Nonetheless the trial of *Madame Bovary* was an event as crucial to realism in 1857 as the premiere of *Hernani* had been to romanticism in 1830. It is significant that this public hearing took the form of a legal prosecution rather than, as earlier, a theatrical performance. The Goncourt brothers and Zola, as well as Baudelaire, would be arraigned in their turn for writings which have since won vindication as an indictment of the regime. Insofar as the issues they faced were recognizable elsewhere, the formulas sharpened in France were adaptable, with due allowance for the cultural lag. Herman Bang applied them to Scandinavian writers; Luigi Capuana launched the campaign for *verismo* in Italy. In England, where George Moore had to brave the boycott of the circulating libraries and Henry Vizetelly was sent to jail for publishing abridged translations of Zola, the very word *realism* carried scandalous undertones. It was popularly associated with all the ills that the realists were seeking to expose, and they themselves were stigmatized by the taboos they had questioned. As for the French, they were looked upon as an immoral people because their authors wrote with such searching candor. Meanwhile there were conservative French critics who, on moral grounds, commended foreign examples to their compatriots. Melchior de Vogüé campaigned for the Russians, as Ferdinand Brunetière did for the English, because their realism seemed to be palliated by a native strain of idealism.

Five younger French novelists, scandalized by *La Terre,* protested that Zola was distorting reality. On the other hand Mark Twain conceded, though not for publication during his lifetime, that the same conditions might be matched in Massachusetts, U.S.A.[4] Thus our subject is beset with controversy at every juncture. If we approach it historically, we can agree that the term originated in France and that the concept was a product of the nineteenth century. Yet realism, as Bertolt Brecht pointed out, is much better suited to a broad than to a narrow definition.[5] Erich Auerbach has perceptively analyzed some realistic passages

3. Georg Brandes, *Hovedstrømninger i det 19. Aarhundredes Litteratur: V, Naturalismen i England* (Copenhagen, 1875).

4. Mark Twain, *Letters from the Earth,* ed. Bernard DeVoto (New York, 1964), p. 173.

5. Bertolt Brecht, *Versuche 31,* sec. 13 (Berlin, 1954), p. 106.

from the *Iliad* and the Old Testament. Two centuries before the Japanese had any intercourse with the occident, they had access to detailed accounts of their merchant class in the lively novels of Saikaku. It behooves us, then, to distinguish explicitly between realism as a modern literary movement and what I shall more broadly venture to call the realistic impetus—the movement being, of course, a more self-conscious and more rigorous manifestation of the impetus. In the broadest sense, we may say with Theodor Fontane: "Realism in art is as old as art itself; nay more, *it is art*."[6] This is scarcely more than a reversion to the Aristotelian *mímesis,* the imitation of nature, or to the neoclassical canon of verisimilitude. But we should not forget that *vraisemblance* means *la semblance du vrai,* that poetry at best is concerned with things like truth. How true to life is a given artifact, whether or not the imitation closely resembles its object—the history of criticism bristles with arguments over such questions.

Whenever we speak of a work as realistic, we are voicing the opinion that it corresponds to known and felt realities. Our criterion is a variable, since it must depend upon the experience of various individuals, more or less like ourselves; it must be subjective in essence, though objectified by the environment and interests they have in common. The colors and the contours of reality will vary from one country to another. To an American reader, *Main Street* and *Babbitt* are caricatures of the commonplace, whereas a Hungarian critic, Jean Hankiss, has testified that he finds Sinclair Lewis exotic.[7] In the former case, the response involves recognition and verification; in the latter it comprehends novelty, estrangement, and the widening of horizons. Both responses play their parts in the gradual consensus that authenticates such works and declares their value. Possibly, if Prosper Mérimée had located *Carmen* and *Columba* in France, we would find him less of a romanticist than a realist. Observation and imagination, like particulars and universals, are fused together by literature in ever-changing proportions. It is the proportion that determines whether the resultant synthesis should be labeled realistic, romantic, or otherwise. Therefore, as Karl Korn reminds us, pure realism has never existed.[8] If the reproduction were completely exact, it would be identical with what it under-

---

6. Theodor Fontane, *Schriften zur Literatur,* ed. H. H. Reuter (Berlin, 1960), p. 4.

7. Jean Hankiss, *La Littérature et la vie: Problématique de la création littéraire* (São Paulo, 1951), p. 163.

8. Karl Korn, "*Le Réalisme dans la littérature,*" Documents, XI, 7 (July, 1956), 732.

takes to reproduce. But, since its means are necessarily limited, the best that skill can make of them is no more than a lifelike impression. That is why Maupassant preferred to regard himself and his colleagues as illusionists rather than realists.

Visual depiction may come closer than verbal suggestion to offering literal facsimiles of its models. Yet even here, as E. H. Gombrich has shown in *Art and Illusion,* a process of stylization intervenes, which the more veracious artists have continually striven to modify. Living in the age of cinema, we are aware that even a photographic slice of life must be cut and angled and composed. Every medium offers its own resistance and thereby shapes its particular conventions. These must be confronted and handled by the artist himself, according to his unique endowments of talent, style, and temperament. Though the mimetic instinct—or what we have called the realistic impetus—is primary in art, it can only work in combination with the impulse toward what Aristotle called harmony. This is the formal aspect, conditioned by the artist's relation to his material, and it ordinarily predominates at the initial stages of any artistic development. Given the differences between the stuff of life itself and the words or pigments we use to represent it, given the reduction in scale, the selection of pertinent data, and the acceptance of an expressive part for an inexpressible whole, it follows that our representations are basically symbolic. They have been induced to approximate nature, at once more comprehensively and more precisely, through a deliberate effort at transcription. Hence realism appears as a somewhat belated phenomenon in the history of literature. Like the scientific attitude or the democratic ideology, with both of which its destinies are linked, it is a characteristic expression of modernity.

The opposite of realism is idealism, in philosophical terms; in critical discussions, it is usually romanticism. But the dialectical antithesis may well be allegory, which is polar in its assumption that transcendental ideas are the true realities and that these are merely exemplified by the objects at hand. The world-view of the Renaissance and its aftermath can be differentiated from that of the Middle Ages by its vivid interest in such objects for their own sake. Implicit disparities between the ideal and the real had not passed unnoted by previous epochs, but appearances could be preserved by the mode of irony. Any explicit description of actual practices, such as Machiavelli's *Realpolitik,* had to be an exposure of those idealized precepts by which men had pretended to live. Machiavelli had acquired his realism through disillusionment in ethics and politics. The literary realist would likewise be a disillusioned idealist, and his method would entail a systematic testing and unmasking of illusions. Here the seminal example is *Don Quixote,* wherein the preconceptions of chivalric romance are so conclusively discredited. Like the rueful knight breaking up the illusory puppet-show, every realistic novelist is a professional iconoclast, bent on shattering the false images of his day. His novels deal, in their own way, with a set of presuppositions which he demonstrates to be unreal, invoking as his touchstone the reader's sense of reality. The peculiar intimacy between writer and reader, made possible by the technology of printing, is a factor which has made prose fiction the vehicle of realism *par excellence.*

Where Shakespeare had spoken of holding the mirror up to nature, Stendhal undertook to put it on wheels and send it traveling down the highway. Both were using a well-worn and oversimplified metaphor in order to repudiate the unnatural: to criticize bad acting, in Shakespeare's case, and artificial writing in Stendhal's. The manifestos of the realists may protest too loudly when they disclaim artifice, which is after all their precondition. There is always an implied comparison with the unrealistic features of what has gone before; not until it is compared with a better likeness will a symbol seem too crude an approximation of what it stands for. Esthetic norms are not absolute but relative, and must consequently be defined by their contexts. In this respect, as in certain others, realism parallels the concept of liberty, which derives its meaning from the specific constraints it has managed to cast off. A realist is made, not born, and realistic novels presuppose a backlog of romances, even as Don Quixote takes its departure from *Amadís de Gaula.* Cervantes' French imitator, Charles Sorel, formulated that principle with his title, *L'Anti-roman*—a formula which Jean-Paul Sartre has revived in prefacing the first *nouveau roman* of Nathalie Sarraute.[9] For, though the novel still comes under the heading of *roman* or something like it in most European languages, it turns its back upon the *romanesque.* Or rather, while presenting its own substance as a guarantee of the factual, it attacks the fictitious for having become synonymous with the untrue. It accuses literature of becoming too literary, of escaping into a sentimental daydream which cannot be dispelled except by shock treatments, sudden contacts with vulgar or brutal mundanities.

This may help to explain why great novelists have so often begun by

9. Nathalie Sarraute, *Portrait d'un inconnu* (Paris, 1948), p. 7.

writing parodies of their predecessors, as Fielding did of Richardson or
Ernest Hemingway of Sherwood Anderson. Beginning with a literary
critique, they have generally moved on toward social criticism. The
classical tradition, being aristocratic, had taken a good deal for granted,
including the rule that epic and tragic heroes must be captains or kings.
Domestic scenes and mercantile transactions have been relegated to the
lower levels of comedy. Medieval romance was a sublimation of the
courtly society in the castles; anti-romance found its outlet in the
fabliau, the bawdy humor of stories exchanged in the towns. Later the
picaresque tale, abandoning the castle for the inn, proceeded townwards
into the precincts of trade. Since realism grew up amid the culture of
cities, its fortunes rose with the prosperity of the middle classes, whose
individualistic style of life it so fully reflected. A side-glance at the evolution of painting in the Low Countries would bear out this correlation
in all its worldly richness and solidity. As for the novelist, he could
hardly be other than what Thomas Mann confessed himself: "ein
bürgerlicher Erzähler."[10] However, by virtue of his artistic vocation, he
was now a burgher with a difference. Like Tonio Kröger, like Mann
himself, he became "ein verirrter Bürger," a townsman who has strayed
beyond his bourgeois origins.[11] As an observer, he was free to detach
himself from the commercial values that dominated his world, to survey
its actions critically, and at times to speak out in opposition.

Yet, as a child of the bourgeoisie, he was a participant in a materialistic society, whose preoccupation with commodities and inventories
materially affected his descriptive technique. This was the purport of
Balzac's famous announcement, in his foreword to the *Comédie humaine,* that the writer had three interacting subjects; men, women, and
things. A special concern for things is the abiding hallmark of realism.
Etymologically, it stems from the Latin *res,* and it has close Gallic and
Germanic counterparts in *chosisme* and *Sachlichkeit.* The subtitle of
Godwin's *Caleb Williams* could have been adopted as a general slogan,
Things as They Are, with the implication that they had never heretofore been so deeply probed or so plainly reported. Man's augmenting
involvement with things, his precarious mastery over them, and the
looming menace of reification could be traced by following the transition from the realistic movement to naturalism. More positively, the
immediacies of physical reality were brought nearer by a shift of focus

10. Thomas Mann, *Lübeck als geistige Lebensform* (Lübeck, 1926), p. 54.
11. Thomas Mann, *Novellen* (Berlin, 1925), II, 86.

from phrases or abstractions to things in themselves. Thus in *War and Peace* the generals are overheard by Prince Andrey as they plan the strategy of the 1812 defense. The theoretician Clausewitz refers, casually in military German, to a certain part of the terrain. What is *Raum* for him is home for Andrey: father, sister, son, ancestral estate. The effect of momentary distance—as with Tolstoy's contrasts beween Napoleon and Kutuzov, or between the French-speaking courtiers and the peasants or foot-soldiers—is to heighten the reader's feeling for the real thing, the land itself.

War is the classic rite of initiation for the realist, as indeed it was for Tolstoy, or—to cite an early instance—for the author of *Simplicissimus*. What is more, it incarnates the ultimate conflict between men and matter, personnel and matériel; it reveals the apocalyptic spectacle of human beings reified. The expansion of modern warfare has increased the universality of its impact, so that narratives from opposite sides of the First World War have, ironically enough, shown substantial agreement. I have been mentioning writers from different countries, eclectically and freely, because it is my assignment to illustrate the international character of our theme, as well as to indicate how similar tendencies in art and thought could emerge from differing circumstances. But, since a circumstantial particularity was a major aim of realism, it was pledged to bring out the distinctive traits of each country that took it up. And, since other cultures were rather less consistently analytic, less socially conscious, and less highly centralized, they differed in their fulfillment of the patterns that France laid down. Already the British, through their innate empiricism, had found their way to realism in the eighteenth century; in the nineteenth they were sometimes diverted from that course by sentimentality, moralizing, and whimsy. The Germans, habitually predisposed to metaphysics, were all the slower to evolve a realistic trend; their typical genre was the introspective *Bildungsroman*. The Russians, all but silenced by a despotic government, discovered their humanitarian conscience in the truth-telling voices of their men of letters.

If realism were a simple vernacular, the spontaneous outcome of a pragmatic situation, then the Americans might have been among its pioneers. Actually, they came to it late in its history and their own, since it is predicated upon a recoil from traditional modes which they had developed belatedly. Most of our nineteenth-century storytellers, from Cooper to James, regarded themselves as practitioners of the romance.

When their successors joined the ranks of the realists, with William Dean Howells, they were consciously emulating European precedents. By the twentieth century, the movement had taken hold everywhere as the most normal way of writing, though it was still resisted intermittently by the censors. The naïve intention of Alfred Nobel, in offering his prize for the advancement of idealistic literature, has been understandably disregarded. National distinctions have been neutralized by the mechanisms of city life, while journalism—abetted by the diffusion and the dilution of literacy—has stimulated the appetite for facts and documents. Dostoevsky's adaptation of *faits divers* and Balzac's rivalry with the *état civil* reached their logical culmination in Joyce's *Ulysses*. The middling size of Dublin, together with the limits of the single day he chose to transcribe, enabled Joyce to reproduce his metropolis with unparalleled completeness. Working in continental exile himself, he denationalized his Irish subject matter by making his protagonist a Jew. His reader would soon get lost in the maze of streets and shops and quotidian details, if the story did not follow the outline of the *Odyssey,* linking each shabby figure or sordid episode with some grand Homeric correspondence.

Joyce's landmark points in two directions: on the one hand, to the most thoroughgoing application of realistic techniques that could be imagined; on the other, to the renewed enthusiasm of recent writers for mythology and its timeless archetypes. Symbolism, for so long in abeyance but never wholly absent, has been reasserting itself. Newer slogans have been coined and movements have been rallied to press beyond mere realism toward superrealism, let alone infrarealism. Yet Louis Aragon, once the noisiest of the *surréalistes,* has subsequently affirmed: "What remains alive today in romanticism, in naturalism, as in all the poetic and literary movements that have come after them, is their element of realism."[12] There have been some interesting countercurrents, which have somewhat deflected but never lessened the flow of the mainstream. Though Kafka seems both more and less than a realist, he may be finally—what Dostoevsky considered himself—"a realist in the higher sense," portraying "all the depths of the human soul."[13] Neither the grim fantasies of Kafka nor the psychological inquests of Dostoevsky would be convincing to us, if they were not presented so realistically. The presentation of actuality, Auerbach's *dargestellte Wirklichkeit,* has

12. Louis Aragon, *Pour un réalisme socialiste* (Paris, 1935), p. 73.
13. See E. J. Simmons, *Introduction to Russian Realism* (Bloomington, Indiana, 1965), p. 104.

changed because reality itself is subject to continual change. Capable of assuming as many shapes as it has interpreters, it has seemed to them increasingly elusive and disturbing. It has even been sought on subjective or mystical planes: witness the *Realidad* of Pérez Galdós. Nevertheless, as M. Robbe-Grillet would still argue, every writer thinks of himself as a realist.[14]

The notion of reality was more stable, more palpable, and less complex when Diderot eulogized Richardson for capturing "toute la réalité possible." More reality than this has seemed possible to every succeeding generation, notably the fact of its own existence. It has tried to justify that existence by exploring territory hitherto uncharted and by bringing the record up to date. By outstripping its forerunners, to some extent, it has outdated their kind of realism with its new kind, which will be superseded by the next generation—and so on, while the cycle continues. Realism, as Proust observed, is reborn from age to age in reaction against an outmoded art, which was considered realistic during its heyday. This insight was hedged with reservations for Proust, in retreat from the esthetics of relativism. Believing that art was the truest reality, he was less interested in its obsolescence than in its recapture of the past. Yet the mainspring of modernism has been its will to surpass itself; its heraldic device has been *plus ultra;* and its recurrent question has been "What next?" After so many themes have been covered, is there a point of diminishing returns? Are there any more worlds to explore? Barriers against the candid treatment of sex have been broken through completely, it would seem, so that virtually nothing has been left unsaid. Céline, Samuel Beckett, Henry Miller, exhibiting their private underworlds, have reduced their readers to that dangerous state wherein they can no longer be shocked. If drug addiction promises a last *nouveau frisson,* it must be an escape from reality to fantasy.

The investigation of such bypaths, which has been a continuous source of notoriety for realism, is probably incidental to the pervasive scope of its curiosity. Since our personal resources for understanding the lives of others happen to be so narrowly circumscribed, it serves us as an instrument for enlarging human knowledge. The analogy with experimental science was overstrained by Zola, but there are qualities in both which may be compared: the skepticism, the discipline, above all the trained observation. Affinities with liberalism, humanitarianism, popu-

14. Robbe-Grillet, *Pour un nouveau roman,* p. 171.

lism, and the historic drives toward social democracy are more fundamental. A progressive course had been set from the beginning, when the
realists had spoken for the middle class, as opposed to a feudal aristocracy. As the lower classes became articulate and literate, it became
necessary to lend them a voice, to extend the literary franchise. The
argument for taking this step was put forward by the Goncourts with
their preface to *Germinie Lacerteux:* in a time of universal suffrage the
masses, too, are entitled to claim their right to the novel. Some years
before, when Harriet Beecher Stowe had published *Uncle Tom's Cabin,
or Life among the Lowly,* she extended *le droit au roman* to Negro
slavery, announcing that her theme had been "hitherto ignored by the
associations of polite and refined society." During the very same year, in
Sketches of a Sportsman, Turgenev did the same thing for Russian
serfdom, with equal effectiveness and far greater artistry. That coincidence underlined the importance of the realistic impetus as a liberating
force.

Similarly, the emancipation of the poor from the oppressions of
industrialism was heralded by their enfranchisement within literature.
Karl Marx, writing in the *New York Daily Tribune,* praised Dickens—
along with the socialistic French novelists, George Sand and Eugène
Sue—for having elevated that "despised class," the proletariat, to the
rank of heroes.[15] Marx paid one of his rare tributes to "the splendid
brotherhood of fiction writers in England, whose graphic and eloquent
pages have issued to the world more political and social truths than
have been uttered by all the professional politicians, publicists, and
moralists put together." If a laissez-faire system ignored its humane
responsibilities, at least it allowed those free lances to assume them.
Realism advances irreversibly, making its breakthroughs and taking up
radical causes whenever the need exists, as long as it operates in an
open society—a society which, whatever its inequities may be, has room
enough to tolerate its critics, even as Victorian Britain tolerated Marx,
or as the United States gave him employment and circulated his views.
Whereas in a closed society, one in which all the organs of opinion must
rigorously be controlled by the state, realism is unable to function. For,
as we have seen, it is iconoclastic by nature; its identifying gesture is
image-breaking. Whereas an absolute monarchy, a religious hierarchy,
or any authoritarian government is—if I may risk the term—icono-

---

15. Quoted by Peter Demetz, *Marx, Engels, and the Poets* (Chicago, 1967), p. 45.

plastic, committed to image-making. Its writers and artists are encouraged to fashion the public images of itself, which are disseminated as propaganda and regulated by censorship.

The arts are not inconceivable under such duress; they were cultivated at the courts of England's Elizabeth I, France's Louis XIV, and the Renaissances Popes, not to mention the dynasties of the East. But there the dominant modes of expression were formalized, rather than realistic. We do not talk about monarchist realism, with reference to Balzac, because his commitment to the lost cause of the Bourbons did not obstruct his freedom to criticize the July Monarchy. Genuine realism has to be realism *tout court,* and anything else ought to go by some other name. Hence the thirty-five-year endeavor of Marxist critics to synthesize a compound known as socialist realism, in the long run, cannot prove acceptable to objective historians of literature. The results have been *Ersatz* products like Bombay duck, which is made of dried fish, or Welsh rabbit, which consists of toast and melted cheese. Now there is nothing wrong with fish or cheese, when we know what they are. Since we are not likely to mistake them for meat, we need not engage in polemics over them. It should help us to understand one another, if we define our terms and distinguish our categories. Please let me make it clear that I have no quarrel with socialism. On the whole, I think its ideals are much nobler than those of capitalism, and I believe that most enlightened nations today are striving to attain them, each in its fashion. But socialism is a creed and realism an art. A writer may well be both a staunch socialist and an authentic realist, like Mikhail Sholokhov. However, as we all recognize more and more, it is not only in nonsocialist countries that creed and art conflict upon occasion.

The doctrine of socialist realism, which goes back to the founding of the Writers' Union in Soviet Russia two years before, was officially promulgated at the first Congress of Soviet Writers in 1934, where it was expounded by the commissar for cultural affairs, Andrey Zhdanov. His directive was the aphorism of Stalin that writers are the engineers of human souls. In retrospect this characterization does not seem very encouraging, either to writers or to human souls; but, since the status of writing was far less certain than that of engineering, perhaps it was the engineers who should have felt belittled. At all events, the writers welcomed the premise that they had a role in the building program of the new society, and they ended their laudatory deliberations by passing the following resolution: "Socialist realism, being the basic method of

Soviet literature and literary criticism, requires from the artist a truthful, historically concrete representation of reality in its revolutionary development. In addition, truthfulness and historical concreteness must be combined with the task of ideological transformation and education of the workers in the spirit of socialism."[16] It is impossible to imagine Tolstoy, Flaubert, Dickens, and the other great realists being convened by a political party and voting on how they should write thereafter. To depict reality truly, it is now generally agreed, is quite another matter than to satisy Zhdanov's conception of truth. The commissar was frank in warning the delegates that Soviet literature should be tendentious. The second sentence of their declaration, leaving all pretensions to realism behind, accepted the mandate to transform their works into engines of indoctrination.

The congress claimed descent from the nineteenth-century masters, whom it designated as critical realists, through the patriarchal presence of Maxim Gorky. He himself, as exile and independent, had unquestionably been one of their heirs. He brought the prestige he had earned, as a champion of the underdog, to the support of Stalin's literary line. Yet, in Gorky's speech, he seemed to shy away from Socialist Realism and to be more at ease with the alternative slogan of Revolutionary Romanticism. His emphasis on myth and wish-fulfillment throws light upon his own proletarian fictions, as well as upon the transition that he was sponsoring. Much earlier, in a letter to Chekhov, he had exclaimed, "To hell with realism!"[17] He had gone on to adumbrate his later position: "Present-day literature must definitely begin to color our life and, as soon as it does, life itself will acquire color." This is the optative mood that would produce an overwhelming number of travel-poster novels, realistic in the reportage of industrial and agrarian detail, romantic in their projection of a collective wishdream. Their exemplar was not Tolstoy, who refused to acknowledge any hero but truth; it was the ideologue Chernyshevsky, who had exhibited a wooden model for their positive heroes in his didactic novel, *What Is to Be Done?* What indeed? *Chto delat'?* The answer would be a blueprint of the utopian future, the compulsory optimism of a happy ending, a heroic idealization of daily labor. Appropriately, the Soviet Encyclopedia connects the

16. *Pervyi vesesoiuznyi s'ezd sovetskikh pisatelei: stenograficheskii otchet* (Moscow, 1934), p. 716.

17. See R. W. Mathewson, Jr., *The Positive Hero in Russian Literature* (New York, 1958), p. 225.

epic with socialist realism. Andrey Sinyavsky has suggested that socialist classicism would be a more accurate phrase.[18] Myths have been propagated, under whatever name.

Yet the realistic impetus, flowing deeply underground, was ready to reemerge with the thaw of de-Stalinization. The second Congress of Soviet Writers, held twenty years after the first, rather than three as originally planned, was permitted to approve a more flexible set of statutes. The second sentence, the ideological proviso, was dropped from the official definition of socialist realism. Though the adjective was still the rubber stamp of bureaucratic approval, at a vociferous conference of the Gorky Institute in 1957, a cautious interest was taken in what the unqualified noun has meant to the rest of the world.[19] Dr. Zhivago's question, "Where is reality in Russia today?," could not have been asked directly in Pasternak's homeland. But younger writers, like Alexander Solzhenitsyn, were soon to raise questions of their own in the penetrating vein of the older realists. Sinyavsky is now in prison for having published abroad, together with his brave and sharp brochure *On Socialist Realism,* certain satirical ventures into what he terms fantastic realism, under the pseudonym of Abram Tertz. His public trial in 1966, with Yuli Daniel, marked a crisis—might we hope a turning point? A picture looks somewhat brighter when its darkest aspects are exposed to the light. It must be ruefully added that, even while socialist realism has been relaxing its coercion in Russia, it has been pushed to fanatical extremes in Communist China, where Mao Tse-tung adopted it as a device for regulating the intellectuals. Some of them, by their dissent, have been living up to the more liberal traditions of critical realism.[20]

I echo this last phrase by way of retreating to the common ground that we can all share with the Marxists, since—from the viewpoint I have tried to sketch—critical realism is a tautology. Furthermore, there may be some ambiguity in speaking of traditions, with regard to a movement whose historical thrust has been outspokenly antitraditional. But, since by now it has traversed a large amount of history, it may have been losing momentum while gathering tradition. When we look back

18. Abram Tertz, *On Socialist Realism* (New York, 1960), p. 77. Cf. *On Trial: The Soviet State versus "Abram Tertz" and "Nikolai Arzhak,"* ed. Max Hayward (New York, 1966).

19. *Probleme des Realismus in der Weltliteratur,* ed. I. Anissimov and J. Elsberg (Berlin, 1962).

20. See Merle Goldman, *Literary Dissent in Communist China* (Cambridge, Massachusetts, 1967).

at it, may tempt us into nostalgia, which is a far cry from its original outlook. So forceful and comprehensive a critic as Georg Lukács, who has been so illuminating on the nineteenth-century realists, turns away from those of the twentieth century—except for the nostalgic Thomas Mann—and polemicizes *Wider den misverstandenen Realismus*. The misunderstanding seems to have set in soon after Balzac, for Lukács as for Marx and Engels. That they should appreciate Balzac, in spite of his reactionary dogmas, is a paradox which meets its match in the Marxist underestimation of Zola, who would have made a devoted fellow-traveler. His willingness to face the implications of empirical science, however naïvely, is incompatible with the dogmatic framework of Lukács' old-fashioned metaphysics. The latter would view naturalism as the degeneration of realism because he moralistically confounds a persisting method with a subject matter which has changed. Though we may sympathize with his desire for turning back the clock to a more Balzacian moment, we cannot deny that we stand closer to Kafka. Inasmuch as the world cannot be static, realism is the dynamic principle that prompts the arts to keep up with it.

POSTSCRIPT

The foregoing observations were presented in Belgrade, on August 30, 1967, at a plenary session of the fifth triennial congress of the International Comparative Literature Association. I should like to emphasize that the subject was not of my choosing. One of the principal themes of the conference was "Literary Movements Considered as International Phenomena." I was invited to consider the topic of realism, I suppose, because I had studied and written about it extensively, both at the theoretical level and with particular reference to the examples of Cervantes, Joyce, the French masters, and certain Americans. This special assignment seemed to require not merely a brief restatement of my general views plus a sketchy evocation of the historical movement, but also some attempt to bring the record up to date and incidentally to pay more attention than I had heretofore done to the role of Russian literature. Hence there was no avoiding—one might wish there had been, in afterthought—the problem of socialist realism so-called.

Since the organization was meeting in the Socialist People's Republic of Yugoslavia, and since the Soviet Union was allowing a group of Russian comparatists to attend for the first time, I broached this part of my subject with considerable hesitation. I was encouraged to proceed, however, by the gradual modifications of the original Stalinist party line, which are documented in my paper, as well as by the increasing number of recent voices raised in the name of free speech within the communist sphere. Though I was not unaware of the controversial potentialities in the situation, I hoped, perhaps naïvely, to stimulate a sincere and mutually clarifying exchange. Consequently, I paid due tribute to the great tradition of the Russian realists; I made as many concessions to Marxist commitments as I could in advance; and I tried to neutralize my approach, so far as possible, by disentangling the literary aspect from the political. Alas, one cannot even take exception to the politicalization of art without setting foot in the domain of politics.

My remarks were delivered in what is known as the Hall of Heroes, the grand amphitheater of the philosophical faculty at the University of Belgrade, where an enormous bust of Marshal Tito gazed sternly down upon the unheroic speaker. Two or three distinguished Russian scholars sat in the audience, flanked by a larger number of Soviet delegates who may well be zealous party members but are unknown for their scholarship in the West. I have been told that they listened with sympathetic interest to the first three-quarters of my address. As I approached my problematic conclusion, their sense of shock and embarrassment sharply counterpointed the expressed approval of my western auditors. A short but spirited protest was lodged by the *doyen* of the Russian delegation, Victor Zhirmunsky. This was ironic for me, since I had long admired his work, exchanged professional publications with him, and looked forward particularly to making his acquaintance. It is a larger irony that his position in Russia has been repeatedly imperiled by accusations of cosmopolitanism.

Under these circumstances, as I now can see, Professor Zhirmunsky's attack was not ungracious. He did not question the facts I had adduced as to the origins of Socialist Realism. Rather, he accused me of failing to understand its productions, which he did not defend in any detail. Indeed, he invited me to visit Russia, the better to learn its language and to appreciate its literature. His two sharpest points made me realize that I had been more provocative than I intended. In the first place, I had used an unfortunate metaphor, casting a mildly humorous light on a matter of intense religious conviction. The homely analogy between Welsh rabbit and socialist realism, though imperfectly understood, was logically exact. In each case, an object is misnamed because its essence is lacking, while the qualifier indicates that there has been a substitution. Realism, by my definition, is nothing if not critical. When the writer's task is not social criticism but the glorification of a regulative society, it is something else again.

My second and more serious challenge, which was more widely deplored, was my mention of Andrey Sinyavsky. Professor Zhirmunsky took the view that the case was purely political, inasmuch as Sinyavsky had committed the crime of publishing his writings abroad without permission from his government. This is a curious judgment, in view of the fact that writers like Voltaire and Victor Hugo could becomes heroes of literature for doing the very same thing, *mutatis mutandis*. I was accused of gratuitously dragging politics into an innocuous cultural discussion. My accuser failed to recognize the relevance of the allusion, since he had no way of knowing the brilliant pamphlet on socialist realism, which was the principal document that led to Sinyavsky's condemnation. Thus we, in our comparative ignorance, have access to sources of knowledge which have been withheld from Russian men of learning. If the Soviet Union has been chary in permitting them to travel, is it not precisely because their encounters with foreign colleagues may put them into contact with such knowledge?

Does this mean that, in order to secure the participation of our Marxist colleagues at international meetings, we should voluntarily subject ourselves to the constraints that have compromised their objectivity? When a gifted writer is imprisoned for his devotion to literature, I asked in my reply to Professor Zhirmunsky, should a body of literary historians and critics simply look the other way? Some of my fellow officers in the International Comparative Literature Association, who had worked hard for the laudable purpose of obtaining Russian cooperation, felt that their efforts had been jeopardized by my tactlessness. One or two of the French representatives linked it with the current blunders of American diplomacy. But, though there was a certain polarization toward the ideological extremes, the middle ground did not give way under our feet, and the dialogue ended with promises to continue. Most striking, to an inexperienced bystander who suddenly found himself at the center of a storm, was the disparity between what had to be publicly professed and what might be privately believed.

I suspect that there was less disagreement than officially appeared, but that the eastern Europeans are not used to speaking frankly at open sessions. A delegate from a socialist republic, which I shall not name because I do not want to get him into trouble, whispered to me in an elevator that none of his compatriots believed in socialist realism. One of our many Yugoslavian hosts confided that socialist realism was a dead horse, although there was still a suspicion that it might kick. I was asked for copies of my article with an eye toward translation and publication, not to mention official refutation, both in Hungary and in one of the Soviet republics. A local newspaper took up the issue, with an emphasis that might have been predicted, and I was warned that it would sooner or later be raked over the coals of the Russian press. One of the Hungarian delegates, Professor Bela Köpeczi of Budapest, courteously challenged me to debate over his communication, "Le Réalisme socialiste en tant que courant littéraire international."

Professor Köpeczi's conception, as distinguished from the Stalin-Zhdanov-Gorky formulation, turned out to be highly sophisticated, and so flexible that it was hard to pin down. Striking a positive note, while disregarding the enforced accumulations of mediocre propaganda, he singled out a few rare talents such as Mayakovsky—rather an equivocal exponent of realism or, for that matter, socialism. I gathered an impression that Hungarian intellectuals have been reacting, not so much against the Marxist doctrines as against the nineteenth-century tastes of their eminent critic, Lukács. Some of them engaged in a gallant endeavor to make room for the avant-garde of the twentieth century within the canon of socialist realism. At this stage, we are arguing not about judgments but about terms. Despite the shady history of the slogan, which should have been discredited with the cult of personality, it is still honorific in socialist nations. Since it signifies the kind of art that is acceptable to the state, relatively enlightened critics now do their utmost to prove that whatever they admire is socialist realism.

Our differences narrow down in practice, but not in theory. True realism, accurately viewed both in its historical and technical orientation, could never have been superimposed by directives. Socialist realism, in attempting to gain control of the realistic movement, tended to suppress the realistic impetus, which presupposes full artistic freedom. It could be demonstrated, in Marxian terminology, that socialist realism is a form of revisionism, a rightist deviation from revolutionary traditions. True realism, like objective criticism, is empirical; socialist realism, like Marxist criticism, is dogmatic. Alternative slogans like revolutionary romanticism, analogies with epic and with myth, turn away from the realistic direction. They seem more appropriate as labels for a genre which idealizes its subject matter. Many great works of literature, after all, have maintained an idealistic tendency. From an analytical viewpoint, *Moby-Dick,* in its ennoblement of the working man, its celebration of his labors and sympathy with his struggles, has much in common with the aims of Soviet fiction. Yet no one would call Melville a realist.

There can be no quarrel with the assumption that a nation's literature should express its aspirations. But aspirations are not the same as actualities. When we speak of idealism, we allow for the difference. But when the term *realism* is applied to a work which presents a falsely harmonious picture of a difficult social reality, then readers are being willfully led astray. Those writers who conformed to Stalin's mandate colluded with him in glossing over the bitter truths since revealed. It is to be hoped that socialist art will find a more auspicious formula, rather than persist with one which has caused such dire confusion. At all events, we must remember that critical catchwords, at best, are no more than pedagogical generalizations. Coined for our convenience, they should not get in the way of our understanding. Realism will have taught us nothing, if it does not teach us how to tell the living realities from the verbal abstractions. We ought not to become the prisoners of our categories—much less the categories of other men, who are quite as fallible as we are.

AMERICA DISCOVERS BOHEMIA

The *Literary History of the United States,* edited by Robert E. Spiller et al. and published by the Macmillan Company (1948), is a characteristic product of its decade, marking as it did a culmination of the endeavor to organize American literature into an academic specialty. I was asked by its editors to write a transitional chapter, linking together four idiosyncratic figures who straddled the nineteenth and twentieth centuries and had been especially conscious of older worlds—and had therefore better be relegated to a comparatist than to a hundred-percent Americanist. Though I could trace but the merest shadow of any movement, this was my yesterday, and it helped me to explain the today in which I first began to read. I was glad to pay a debt of gratitude to Huneker, from whom I first had heard the news about European modernism, as well as to express an appreciation of Bierce, who had been remembered chiefly by the fact of his disappearance. The chapter was introduced by two editorial paragraphs and entitled "The Discovery of Bohemia." An abridged version under the present title was prepublished in The *Atlantic Monthly* (September, 1947).

Notoriously vague are the boundaries of Bohemia. "Is it a state, not of soul, but of the purse?," asked Huneker. As a way of life it is evidently both; it involves both social and psychological consequences; it offers both the vicissitudes of a precarious career and the adventures of an enlivened sensibility. Its earlier American devotee, in both respects, was Poe. But, though his work met affinities among the Pre-Raphaelites in England and even became the object of a cult among the Symbolists in France, he founded no esthetic school among his countrymen. His campaigns against didacticism and his experiments with technique were continued in the United States, not in organized movements, but by isolated figures. Whitman may seem, when we view the eighteen-fifties in retrospect, to have dominated the writers that forgathered at Pfaff's beer cellar under Broadway; but the official record of those forgatherings is Bayard Taylor's "Diversions of the Echo Club" (1872), a faint echo of mild diversions. A heartier atmosphere of literary conviviality was exhaled by San Francisco during the eighteen-sixties, but within another decade its Bohemians had become lions: Mark Twain, Bret Harte, and Joaquin Miller had drifted eastward. Oscar Wilde, carrying the gospel of Ruskin and Morris to the American lecture platform in 1882, merely created advance publicity for the Gilbert and Sullivan

Patience. For Howells, under the spell of Cambridge Brahminism, Bohemianism was "a sickly colony, transplanted from the mother asphalt of Paris, and never really striking root in the pavements of New York."

The *vie de Bohème* was deeply rooted in the interstices of European society, in the rift between artists and philistines, between a radical intelligentsia and a predominant bourgeoisie. In America where expansion left further room for individualism, the tensions were less explicit and the protests more superficial. When artistic flowering required intensive cultivation, however, Americans still sought training and encouragement on the other side of the Atlantic. What the Latin Quarter was to Parisians or Soho to Londoners, the whole of Europe was to them: a seacoast of Bohemia. Some of them, like Whistler, were destined for fabulous exploits within that international domain. Henry Harland, having tried unsuccessfully to catch the local color of Manhattan in his earlier stories, later emerged as editor of the *Yellow Book* and one of the arbiters of English estheticism. Francis Vielé-Griffin and Stuart Merrill were naturalized into the innermost circles of French poetry, and Merrill completed the cycle by translating a selection of Symbolist prose into his native language. But the contributions of the expatriates—unless, like Henry James, they were still preoccupied with American themes—belong to the foreign cultures they embraced. We are more concerned with repatriates, with the new ideas and attitudes they brought home from the Old World, with the enrichment—or, at any rate, the sophistication—they brought to the eighteen-nineties, which transcended the range of more genteel criticism by looking beyond England to the continent and beyond the art of literature to music and the plastic arts.

Thomas Beer has suggested that mauve, which Whistler defined as "pink trying to be purple," is the shade that characterizes this decade. It is an apt characterization of the popular blends that a domesticated Bohemianism produced. With the success of *Trilby* (1892), the Franco-English Du Maurier reinforced that picturesque and sentimental conception of the artist's life which the German-French Murger had popularized a generation before. The quizzical hedonism of Omar Khayyám, bound in crushed leather, made its appearance on many a parlor table. The Boston Irishman, John Boyle O'Reilly, tossed off a maudlin lyric, "In Bohemia" (1885), which was endlessly reprinted and parodied. Richard Hovey, after some translation from Mallarmé, collabo-

rated with the Canadian poet, Bliss Carman, in the breezy series of
Songs from Vagabondia (1894–1901). A vagabond pose, congenially
flouting the lesser conventions, was becoming respectable and even
profitable. Elbert Hubbard, reversing the process of William Morris,
converted art into industry; his personal literary organ, with conscious
and unconscious irony, was called *The Philistine*. Up-and-coming cities
now boasted of their Bohemian clubs; the oldest, established at San
Francisco in 1872, has outlasted the rest; its businessmen, to be sure,
have long outnumbered its more professionally Bohemian members. It
was in this club that the poet George Sterling committed suicide in
1926. Though he was a disciple of Ambrose Bierce, he was in his own
right the leader of Bohemia in California. Sterling lived into the age of
imagism and naturalism, still faithful to the kind of poetry that conveys
a "sense of the remote, the mysterious, the sadly beautiful." A year before he took his life he mourned the solemnity of the new era in which
there was no more "make-believe, no more masks and garlands." Of all
these symptoms the most significant was the eruption of "little magazines" throughout the country. Many of these were hardly more than
manifestos, but a few survived long enough to introduce lively talents
and open exciting horizons—notably the San Francisco *Lark,* the Chicago *Chap-Book,* and the cosmopolitan *M'lle New York.*

To distinguish a clear-cut direction or a guiding coterie behind these
fads and trends would be to oversimplify. Yet they point to the growth
of a class of self-educated intellectuals, whose characteristic form of
expression might be described as esthetic journalism. As a cultural influence it differed from its European counterpart, by striving rather to
educate than to shock the middle-class reader. As a means of education
it was not addressed to a privileged few or concentrated upon the past,
but eager to spread a wide awareness of contemporary developments in
taste and thought. Despite this world of difference between the academic and the journalistic, the lines were occasionally crossed. Charles
Warren Stoddard, whose South Sea vagabondage terminated in religious conversion, assumed the first professorship of English at the
Catholic University of America. Harry Thurston Peck, sometime professor of Latin at Columbia, subsequently edited the *Bookman* and
championed the moderns. Henry Adams, abandoning both a professorial and an editorial chair, could look down from the lonely eminence
of his leisure; whereas the esthetic journalists, enunciating views which
often paralleled his, had to write for a living. Though their American

market—to judge from George Gissing's account—was not quite so discouraging as Grub Street, they inevitably wasted a good deal of talent in boiling the pot. Freelances for better or worse, they accepted the conditions of their profession. Much of their writing was bound to prove ephemeral; some of it remains worthy of reconsideration.

2

The militant independence of the freelance is personified in Ambrose Bierce, the earliest American author after Poe to reflect the recognizable qualities of the movement. Resisting all other affiliations and categories, his restlessness finds its appropriate haven in Bohemia, which—according to his definition—was the "taproom of a wayside inn on the road from Bœotia to Philistia." A youthful veteran of the Civil War, a belated Argonaut to the west coast, he relived his affrays and disillusionments in the rough-and-tumble of the San Francisco press. Joining the American invasion of London during the eighteen-seventies, he mingled with the cockney wits, published some grimly facetious books under the pseudonym of Dod Grile, and even broke a lance in defense of the exiled Empress Eugénie. Failing to captivate the British public that lionized Clemens and Harte, he retreated to California where his later career linked the bygone frontier generation with younger writers like Jack London and George Sterling. His principal employer was the up-and-coming William Randolph Hearst, who was wise enough to give him free rein. His most effective journalistic coup was to prevent Collis P. Huntington from lobbying a railway-refunding bill through Congress. Bierce's separation from his wife, and the tragic deaths of their two sons, embittered his private life. After the turn of the century he made his home—insofar as he had one—in Washington, which afforded increasing scope to his misanthropy. At the age of seventy, after supervising the publication of his collected works and revisiting the battlefields of his youth, he disappeared across the Mexican border, leaving biography to trail off into legend.

No reader, thumbing through those twelve volumes of *Collected Works,* can avoid being struck by their monumental disproportion. As if in a last effort to compensate for the good books he might have written, Bierce padded the set with outdated editorials and stale hoaxes and forgotten polemics, disregarding his habitual distinction between journalism and literature. Frequently the degree of animus seems disproportionate to the issue, and usually the style is disproportionately superior to the subject. *Black Beetles in Amber* (1892) aims at the kind of elegant preservation that Pope accorded his enemies in *The Dunciad,* but Bierce's fluent verse seldom rises very high above its occasion. His prose, on the other hand, has a crisp precision which is almost unparalleled among his contemporaries; his puristic standards of usage, which he may have brought back from England, are set forth in his little handbook, *Write It Right* (1909). America needed, but did not want, a Swift. It needed the sharp reservations of the satirist, armed like Bierce with the weapon of wit. It wanted only the blunt affirmations of the humorist. "Nearly all Americans are humorous; if any are born witty, heaven help them to emigrate!," exclaimed Bierce. Though many of his satirical sketches suggest that Gulliver might have discovered another Brobdingnag in California, one of his serious essays laments "The Passing of Satire." His points were too fine, his targets too ubiquitous. His phobias included millionaires, labor leaders, women, and dogs. His values were ultimately the negative values of war.

Though *The Monk and the Hangman's Daughter* (1892) is still readable, though it skillfully handles the ironic situation of Anatole France's *Thaïs,* it is merely Bierce's revision of G. A. Danziger's translation of a German romance by Richard Voss. And, though *The Devil's Dictionary* (1906) is still quotable, it is no more than an alphabetical compendium of Bierce's deadliest witticisms and most philosophical epigrams. His securest achievement is concentrated in two volumes of short stories. "Denied existence by the chief publishing houses of the country," he informs us, *In the Midst of Life* was published privately in San Francisco under the original title of *Tales of Soldiers and Civilians* (1891). The second collection, *Can Such Things Be?,* attained a New York publisher two years later. There is no padding here. Defining the novel as "a short story padded," Bierce preferred the abbreviated form for its totality of effect. His technique of directing suspense toward a dramatic crisis is modeled on Poe, but Bierce's horrors are more realistically motivated: thus premature burial, in "One of the Missing," becomes a war casualty. Sometimes his settings encroach upon Bret Harte's territory, but Bierce's miners are far from sentimental, and even his "Baby Tramp" comes to a macabre end. Most of his denouements take place at graves. Editors, comprehensibly, were frightened away from these tales. Their violent obsession with sudden death cuts through the conventional twists of fiction to a mordant sense of reality. Dreams, flashbacks, hallucinations, as in "The Mocking Bird," provide irony but no escape.

Bierce's heroic theme, which Stephen Crane undertook a few years later, was not the Civil War in its strange grandeur, but its impact upon the individual consciousness. Every story is a single episode of conflict: son against father, lover against rival, a house—one's own—destroyed, a spy—one's brother—shot. Underlying them all, evoked in vivid imagery, is the contrast formulated in "An Affair of Outposts" between the civilian's preconceptions of military glory and the soldier's experience of ugliness and brutality. In "Chickamauga," an excruciating study in point of view, a child's idyl turns into a battle and the child turns out to be a deaf-mute. Further tales seek a moral equivalent for war in claim-jumping and psychic experiment, ghoulish practical jokes and pseudoscientific fantasies. Naturalism did not exclude the storyteller's concern with the supernatural, and Bierce's rationalism operates to lend credibility to his ghost stories. Peculiarly haunting is "The Death of Halpin Frayser," with its interpolation of Bierce's own recurrent dream, its Kafkaesque nightmare of the poet lost in the wood, its Freudian realization of "the dominance of the sexual element in all the relations of life." But his most nostalgic reminiscences are reserved for Chickamauga and Shiloh and Kennesaw Mountain. He himself is the lone survivor of "A Resumed Identity," a Rip Van Winkle of the Civil War to whom everything afterward is an anticlimax. Even when he describes the Sierras, in "The Night-Doings at Deadman's," it is with the eye of a former topographical officer in the Union Army:

Snow pursued by the wind is not wholly unlike a retreating army. In the open field it ranges itself in ranks and battalions; where it can get a foothold it makes a stand; where it can take cover it does so. You may see whole platoons of snow covering behind a bit of broken wall. The devious old road, hewn out of the mountain side, was full of it. Squadron upon squadron had struggled to escape by this line, when suddenly pursuit had ceased. A more desolate and dreary spot than Deadman's Gulch in a winter midnight it is impossible to imagine.

3

Lafcadio Hearn is not less completely the Bohemian for having remained a foreigner, a transient contributor to American literature. On his devious pilgrimage from the Old World toward the Orient, he spent more than twenty years in this country, and nearly all of his work encountered its audience here. Born in 1850 on an Ionian island to a Greek mother and an Anglo-Irish father, he had been educated sporadically in Ireland, England, and France. Emigrating in 1869, he was appalled by the grinding mechanisms of New York; he sought out connections in Cincinnati, and there obtained his earliest newspaper assignments. He was estranged from his friends, however, when they opposed his marriage to a mulatto. By 1877 he was glad to move on to the Latinized environment of New Orleans, where his journalistic and literary activities exfoliated. Always drawn toward the tropical and the primitive, he served for the better part of two years as correspondent in Martinique and the neighboring islands. Travel sketches in various periodicals and two or three miscellanies of exotic lore established his reputation, and he went to Japan in 1890 under the auspices of *Harper's Magazine.* When the customary misunderstandings arose, he was forced to seek other employment: he taught English in government schools, wrote editorials for the Kobe *Chronicle,* and lectured for a while in the Imperial University at Tokyo. Meanwhile he had fallen in love with the country, married a Japanese woman, and been adopted into her Samurai family under the name of Yakumo Koizumi.

The striking paradox of Hearn's career is that so deracinated a personality should ultimately sink his roots into so conventionalized a civilization. In one of his innumerable essays on "Ghosts" he refers to himself as

the civilized nomad whose wanderings are not prompted by hope of gain, not determined by pleasure, but simply compelled by certain necessities of his being,—the man whose inner secret nature is totally at variance with the stable conditions of a society to which he belongs only by accident.

Was it his hyphenated origin, his diminutive stature, or his disfigured eye that compelled him toward the Tennysonian vision of a summer isle, a savage woman, and a dusky race? Certainly, as his letters reveal, he was ill at ease among the professed improvements of the occident, and out of sympathy with "the Whitmanesque ideal of democracy." Murger's Bohemianism counterpoised the ideal of art for art's sake, and Wilde's derided lecture tour—which Hearn defended in the New Orleans *Item* —was an "acute provocative to the consideration of estheticism in the United States." From first to last he professed himself a romanticist; his boyish solace from the commonplace realism of city life had been the public library; afterward, when he gathered together a small collection of his own, he boasted that every volume was quaint or curious. Valuable by-products of this wayward bookishness were his graceful translations from Gautier, Flaubert, and Anatole France. Loti's *Madame Chrysanthême* was his prospectus for Japan.

> Knowing that I have nothing resembling genius, and that any ordinary talent must be supplemented with some sort of curious study in order to place it above the mediocre line, I am striving to woo the Muse of the Odd, and hope to succeed in thus attracting some little attention,

he had frankly resolved. Because he was never at home in America, he retained a traveler's perception of its strange corners and colorful survivals. As a reporter he specialized in the romance of reality; lurid murders and artists' models, madhouses and carnivals, voodoo rites and Creole cookery. His Louisiana friend, Père Rouquette, had lived among the Choctaws and written a *Nouvelle Atala;* the most charming memento of Hearn's sojourn in the West Indies was *Chita: A Memory of Last Island* (1889), which also embodies localized memories of *Paul et Virginie*. Local color, heightened by his imaginative strokes, blends into exoticism. The intense expressiveness of his own style is attributable to the quality he admired in Poe: "the color-power of words." American cities made him yearn for "a violet sky among green peaks and an eternally lilac and lukewarm sea." The Japanese tones of his later writing are more subdued. The suggestiveness of the word "ghostly" was for him an incantation; for him, as for many agnostics, fantasy replaced belief. Believing that ghosts represented ancestral experience, now banished by steam and electricity, he tried to recapture them in books like *Kwaidan* (1904).

"The dominant impression made by his personality," Huneker remarked of Hearn, ". . . is itself impressionistic." A posthumous title, *Diary of an Impressionist* (1911), subsumes his entire work, which—fragile and casual though it be—has extended since his death into a seemingly endless sequence of volumes. The books by which he is most likely to be remembered are the twelve that deal with his adopted country, from *Glimpses of Unfamiliar Japan* (1894) to *Japan: An Attempt at Interpretation* (1904). Their naïve charm has tended to fade in the light of more recent years. Hearn was anything but a shrewd observer of mores or politics, and his ignorance of the language disqualified him from interpreting the literature. His most memorable episodes are descriptions of shrines, gardens, fans, insects, and bric-a-brac. "A land where lotus is a common article of diet," where everything is marshaled in esthetic order, where egotistical individualism is conspicuous by its absence—as *Kokoro* (1896) reminds us—does not lack attraction. But Japan was already becoming aggressively and mechanically westernized, while Hearn, who continually warned his students against this unholy synthesis, was swept from his university post in a rising wave of hostility toward westerners. Tired of lotus-eating, he might have gone back to America if ill health had not finally overtaken him. He never escaped from what he had never found: himself. "Ironically," as Katherine Anne Porter points out, "he became the interpreter between two civilizations equally alien to him."

4

Since Hearn had departed from the United States at the very outset of the eighteen-nineties, he could only help from a distance to set the scene. And Bierce, though he heard "the note of desperation" sounded in the final decade of the century, had been shaped by a more rugged period. It was left for Edgar Saltus to play the sophisticate, to dramatize the cut-glass brilliance of the *fin du siècle*. Where the others were intellectually sequestered, he belonged to society in the exclusive sense of the term. Scion of a New York family, brother of a minor poet, he responded more fully to literary and philosophical studies in France and Germany than to the Columbia Law School from which he was graduated in 1880. His fellow student, Stuart Merrill, was enabled to function in an artistic milieu by remaining abroad; by returning home, where art was hardly more than an ornamental plaything, Saltus cast himself in the part of a dilettante and a dandy. His sobriquet, "the pocket Apollo," implies a varied endowment, and his legend is seasoned by three marriages and two divorces. His career on various newspapers was less sensational than his career in them. He traveled widely, gravitating in later years to southern California. Toward 1900, under the pressure of hack writing, his work begins to repeat itself; his earlier books best preserve the leisurely skepticism and nonchalant preciosity of his once fashionable manner. By the time of his death in 1921 it was thoroughly outmoded.

When Saltus is recollected, he is sometimes regarded as an American disciple of Oscar Wilde, to whom he devoted a succinct memoir.

Actually he parallels, rather than emulates, the English esthete, who was his junior by a year. In *Love and Lore* (1890), a year before the preface to *The Picture of Dorian Gray,* Saltus defended fiction against the prudishness of Anthony Comstock by recognizing only two kinds: "stories which are well written and stories which are not." Two years before *Salomé* he had touched upon the same subject, which was common property since Flaubert's *Hérodias.* Saltus, like Wilde, derived his critical outlook from France, as he duly acknowledged in one of his poems:

> I chat in paradox with Baudelaire,
> And talk with Gautier of the obsolete.

His first book, an anecdotal monograph, shows that he was also on speaking terms with Balzac. From these and other French writers, including Mérimée and Barbey d'Aurevilly, he translated extensively. German metaphysics, in its realistic and pessimistic phase, was a further influence. *The Philosophy of Disenchantment* (1885), a pocket exposition of the doctrines of Schopenhauer and von Hartmann, jauntily concluded that life was an affliction. *The Anatomy of Negation* (1886) followed logically as well as chronologically; it proceeded down the ages with the iconoclasts, pausing here and there to admire a shattered idol; Jesus, to cite the crucial instance, was "the most entrancing of nihilists but no innovator." Long afterward, reenchanted by theosophy, Saltus strolled through the museum of the world's religions in *The Lords of the Ghostland* (1907).

But philosophic doubt and religious denial were the starting point for epicurean pastimes. The next stage was history, and the ideal theme was Rome, not in its grandeur so much as its decadence. *Imperial Purple* (1892), a scandalous chronicle of the Caesars, luxuriated in passages that matched its title. Saltus, considering it his most sumptuous triumph, subjected the Tsars to a similar treatment in *The Imperial Orgy* (1920). Among his potboilers loomed a three-volume survey of great lovers, and *Historia Amoris* (1906) gave full indulgence to his rather prurient sense of the past. Under the guise of historical documentation it was possible to discuss matters still too delicate for fictional handling, and Saltus was well versed in those authorities that booksellers classify as erotica and curiosa. An unexpurgated library of such works, "everything, in fact, from Aristophanes to Zola," is catalogued in *Mr. Incoul's Misadventure* (1887). This piquant novel, the first of sixteen, observes an amoral code whereby murder and adultery are far less heinous than cheating at cards. A typical intermingling of pornography and hagiography, which reads like a collaboration between Flaubert and General Lew Wallace, is *Mary Magdalen* (1891). How it was received by Henry James, to whom it is dedicated, tempts speculation. Other novels, set against modern backgrounds, are spun out increasingly thin. Their mounting reliance on artifice and sensation, on perfumes and poisons, on bejeweled luxury and operatic vice, points directly to the detective story.

Not content, as a stylist, to contrive epigrammatic phrases, Saltus coined experimental words: grammatical audacities like "longly" or "parallely," imported novelties like "fatidic" or "lascive," along with other pedantries and Gallicisms. This brief specimen, from *Daughters of the Rich* (1909), is suggestive of the general effect:

An agony made of a thousand wounds, each distinct, each more lancinant than the other, caught and enveloped him. The torture of it thrust into being memories long ablated.

Diction like this can only be justified by an ironic tone. If some university had been endowed with a chair of irony, Huneker declared, Saltus might have found his niche. A latter-day Bohemian, Carl Van Vechten, has credited him with giving New York a mythology: "harpies and vampires take tea at Sherry's, succubi and incubi are observed buying opal rings at Tiffany's." But these fantastic shapes could not linger in that worldly climate without partaking of its corruptions. Saltus' preoccupation with the imperial theme was an oblique commentary on the private scandals of contemporary empire-builders; he compared the Vanderbilts to Caligula, sketched Delmonico's as if it were situated on the Via Sacra, and underlined the analogy between Newport and Nero's Golden House. The "Gold Book" compiled by Bradstreet's, the "Gilded Gang" frequenting the society columns, the alliterative collusion of "Manners, Money, and Morals" were the stuff of his essays and tales. These, if taken seriously, illustrate Pater's refined epicureanism; otherwise, we can take them as a comic supplement to Veblen's *Theory of the Leisure Class*.

5

In contradistinction to those that cut dashing figures or enact poignant roles against the esthetic backdrop, James Gibbons Huneker is less of an actor than a spectator. Whether before a stage or a table, whether at a piano or a desk, we think of him as comfortably seated. Owing perhaps to the advantages of this position, he was able to work out the implications of Bohemianism, both as a critical approach and as an attitude toward life, more explicitly than any other American writer. It was more than the warmth of a disciple that led H. L. Mencken to designate him "the chief man in the movement of the nineties on this side of the ocean." More precisely, Huneker protracted this momentum into the twentieth century; for his first book, *Mezzotints in Modern Music,* did not appear until 1899. But his long apprenticeship went back to the days when, as a Philadelphia schoolboy, he had escorted Whitman to concerts; when, as a musical student in Paris, Villiers de L'Isle-Adam had bought him a drink; when, as a pupil of Joseffy, he had taught piano for ten years at the National Conservatory in New York. His career as a critic, starting on the *Musical Courier* in 1887, continued through the *Sun,* the *Times,* the *World,* and other New York papers, interrupted only by occasional travels in Europe. Most of his twenty volumes were pasted together from magazine articles and newspaper reviews. He disliked being called a journalist, and styled himself with genial modesty "a newspaper man in a hell of a hurry writing journalese."

His rambling autobiography, *Steeplejack* (1920), introduces Huneker as jack of seven arts and master of none. Undoubtedly his interests ranged beyond his accomplishments, and he approached other fields with varying degrees of amateurishness; but he had qualified as a professional musician, and his criticism stays closest to the object when confronting the keyboard of his instrument. His most substantial book, *Chopin, the Man and His Music* (1900), for once subordinates biographical details to technical comments; while *Old Fogy: His Musical Opinions and Grotesques* (1913) playfully exposes romantic enthusiasms to classical prejudices. The Symbolist doctrine that conferred upon music the primacy of the arts was reinforced by Pater's dictum that all arts aspire to the condition of music. Thus encouraged to venture afield, Huneker recalls, he wrote of painting in terms of tone, of literature as form and color, and of life as a promenade of flavors. "I muddled the Seven Arts in a grand old stew. I saw music, heard color, tasted architecture, smelt sculpture, and fingered perfumes." In this pleasant state of synesthesia, the concert-goer became a gallery-visitor, working "in the key of impressionism." His hurried critiques became, if not adventures of a soul among masterpieces, then *Promenades of an Impressionist* (1910). Taste, to so practised an epicure, was no mere figure of speech; gusto was his canon, and degustation his critical function. His impressions of cities, in *The New Cosmopolis* (1915), were documented with menus. He would savor a painter, sip a composer, recommend an author, and announce, in *Variations* (1921): "There is no disputing tastes—with the tasteless."

To his axiom that the critic was primarily a human being, the corollary, expressed in *Unicorns* (1917), was: "All human beings are critics." And, when the critical medium was a part of the daily news, timeliness was as important as human interest. Paul Elmer More, in asking where Huneker dug up "all those eccentrics and maniacs," indicated the cultural lag between journalistic and academic criticism. *Iconoclasts: A Book of Dramatists* (1905) and *Egoists: A Book of Supermen* (1909) were pioneering enterprises which did much to direct the swirling currents of European modernism toward these shores. Huneker's pantheon was eclectic, if not eccentric; he exalted the individual above the type, the artist above the school; the dominating personalities were "Anarchs of Art" like Shaw and Nietzsche. If it seems incongruous that these image-breakers should themselves receive hero-worship, the incongruity is explained by a Nietzschean phrase which Huneker borrowed for one of his books, *The Pathos of Distance* (1913). Slyly he wondered whether the sordid circumstances of Gorky's *Night-Lodging* would be understood "in our own happy, sun-smitten land, where poverty and vice abound not, where the tramp is only a creation of the comic journals." But Europe had also a greater abundance of genius than his musical studies had trained him to expect from his compatriots. Poe, his father's acquaintance, was among his rare American admirations; but Poe, he thought, was no more American than English; and Poe, furthermore, would have been wiser if he had lived in Paris like Chopin.

The appropriate reward for Huneker's labors was that Remy de Gourmont and Georg Brandes respected him as a colleague. Though he could not vie with the acumen of the one or the erudition of the other, he acted as a well-informed and sympathetic American spokesman for the impressionism and the cosmopolitanism that they respectively exemplify. His style added a "personal note," an air of improvisation which now sustains the excitement of discovery and again diffuses into beery rhapsody and polyglot exclamation. Names invite epithets, which bristle with additional names: Huysmans, for example, is "the Jules Verne of esthetics." Allusions are multiplied into virtual litanies: a single page on Flaubert contains references to nineteen other artists. Titles reflect the paraphernalia of symbolism: *Ivory Apes and Peacocks* (1915). Two volumes of short stories about art and its problems, *Melomaniacs* (1902) and *Visionaries* (1905), fall somewhere between Henry James and O. Henry. Huneker's novel, *Painted Veils,* written at the age of sixty, ushered in the twenties. "In it," he confided, "the suppressed 'complexes' come to the surface." Sex, heavily orchestrated in the manner of Richard Strauss, comes to the surface of the old Bohemian fable; the seven arts are symbolized by seven veils, which ambiguously drape the seven sins. The prima donna heroine is an up-to-date incarnation of the goddess Istar, and the critic-hero—an Irish-American steeplejack of the arts—resembles Huneker. It is Remy de Gourmont who advises him to return to America, and it is Edgar Saltus who tells him he should have remained in Paris.

6

To return was no mistake; for the age of innocence abroad was expiring, and the time was ripe for sophistication at home. The Exhibition of 1893 made Chicago an international point of distribution for the latest artistic fashions. Concurrently, in many large cities, art museums and symphony orchestras were acquiring a public which needed guidance. Men like H. E. Krehbiel, Henry T. Finck, and W. J. Henderson did helpful work, but seldom strayed from the field of musical reviewing. The theater and the fine arts had exponents, but they lacked Huneker's breadth. His collaborator on *M'lle New York,* Vance Thompson, could report literary gossip and editorialize against philistinism; but Thompson's *French Portraits* (1900) owed its ideas, as well as its illustrations, to Gourmont's *Livre des Masques.* Percival Pollard would chat about central European literature in *Masks and Minstrels of the New Germany* (1911); earlier, with *Their Day in Court* (1909), he had driven home an invidious comparison. "The case of American letters," as Pollard had stated it, stood less in need of judicial inquiry than of medical diagnosis. The feminine bias, the commercial motive, the other symptoms were analyzed to show how quantity had superseded quality. Yet a neglected Boston critic, Walter Blackburn Harte, was Pollard's example and authority for the statement that the United States scarcely contained half a dozen writers who pursued literature as a serious profession. Bierce was his culminating instance of neglect, Huneker the exception that proved his rule: "A cosmopolitan, who happened to live in America. But who was not, primarily, interested in American art."

But if the trouble could be traced—as Pollard argued—to "our lack of proper criticism," the establishment of criteria depended upon a groundwork of importation and translation. The opinions Huneker imported, the books Hearn and Saltus translated, did much to eradicate the taint of provinciality that Henry James had detected in Poe. Though traditionalists had kept in touch with England, the current stimulus came largely from France. And, though the importers and translators were equally versatile as creative writers, their accomplishment was largely critical. Its results may be counted in educated audiences, rather than achieved masterpieces. Where literature had been traditionally connected with oratory and theology, it could now be envisaged through its relation to purely artistic disciplines; hence the old-fashioned didactic presuppositions gave way to estheticism. Art for art's sake was never a very positive credo, but it aided in releasing the artist from ulterior constraints—particularly the taboos of sexual reticence. Sometimes, it may seem to us, the prudery of the moralists was outmatched by the prurience of the esthetes; the struggle between them, at all events, would be prolonged and embittered before the subject could be faced in frank simplicity. To turn from subject matter to technique is to note the paradoxical devotion of a group of journalists to the cult of style. Affectation and mannerism did not obscure their genuine feeling for the cadence and the nuance. If they no longer excite us, it is because their successors reaped the benefits of their imitations and experiments.

What these isolated stylists had in common was the endeavor to reproduce experience at the level of consciousness, to relay sensations in unimpeded immediacy, which is connoted by the term *impressionism*. It is this method which Stephen Crane applied to naturalistic fiction in *The Red Badge of Courage* (1895), and which Lewis E. Gates reconciled with academic criticism in his essay on "Impressionism and Appreciation" (1900). Since impressionists are by nature individualists, they cannot be herded very closely together within a concerted movement; their lasting achievements, such as Bierce's tales, are likely to be the fruits of solitude. A negative program, however, may be discerned in their consistent antagonism toward middle-class standards, toward everything that the popular lady-novelists stood for, toward the distinguished—albeit inhibited—man of letters whom Bierce dubbed "Miss Nancy Howells." That the two men, born within a few years and a few miles of each other, should have ended so far apart emphasizes the divergence between the genteel tradition and the Bohemian protest. The latter developed, with the twentieth century, into a recognized opposition; it found a local habitation in Greenwich Village, and vociferous organs in *The Smart Set, Reedy's Mirror,* and *The Masses.* The Philistines were reduced by Gelett Burgess to Bromides, by Sinclair Lewis to Babbitts, and by Mencken to the *Booboisie.* The seacoast of Bohemia became the comic-opera kingdom of James Branch Cabell's novels, and romantic bookishness was pushed to its illogical conclusion in his *Beyond Life* (1919).

Whether we glance ahead to Cabell and Mencken, or backward to Poe and Whitman, it is clear that Bohemianism has continuously oscillated between the poles of escape and revolt; between an imaginative retreat from, and an iconoclastic attack upon, the restrictions of the commonplace. That our means of cultural expression have gradually broadened to comprehend both extremes is due, in large measure, to the work of the esthetic journalists. Edmund Wilson, paying his respects to Huneker and Mencken, has recently asserted that the heyday of the literary freelance is past; that such potentialities will hereafter be absorbed by staff-written periodicals, by educational institutions, or by Hollywood. If true, this terminates an epoch which goes back to the Civil War and reaches its height in the last years of the nineteenth century. The *fin du siècle* was confused by many contemporaries with the end of the world; Max Nordau's *Degeneration* (1895), which advanced pseudoscientific reasons for disliking modern literature, was widely circulated and approvingly underscored in America. But Americans could not wreathe themselves in the laurels of decadence, as self-conscious Europeans were doing; for, regarding the new century as peculiarly theirs, they welcomed its innovations. They did not always realize that their own eighteen-nineties harked back to the European sixties, to the ferment over impressionism, symbolism, naturalism, and nihilism. They chose instead to look forward to the American nineteen-twenties, to a generation which would win the struggles they had initiated. In short, they were not victims of the romantic agony, but the couriers of critical realism.

WILLIAM CARLOS WILLIAMS AND
THE OLD WORLD

On the continuous record of transatlantic encounters, Williams has presented a highly exceptional case, for reasons I have tried to explain in the following pages. They were written as the introduction to *A Voyage to Pagany,* when it was reprinted by New Directions in the fall of 1970; they had been printed under the present title shortly before in the *Yale Review* (Summer, 1970). Williams' novel as such—though it well deserved to be brought back into circulation—is hardly a work of art, as I freely admit. Yet its very artlessness is an artifice which, if it does not conceal art, at least reveals nature through its cultivated flatness of tone. Under the early Poundian assumption that art means Europe and that American means anti-art, the home-keeping artist tended to assume the protective coloration of the philistine.

The Atlantic Ocean has tended to act as a magnetic field for American writers, no two of whom have come to quite the same terms with those cultures on the other side. Critics like to polarize their problems into such dichotomies as Highbrow/Lowbrow, Paleface/Redskin, Virgin/Dynamo. But simplification is hazardous because the presence of Europe has so pervaded our background that the stance of every significant writer has been affected by it in some way or other. Whitman's reaction, to be sure, was at odds with Longfellow's response. Yet the strongest testimony has been lodged *a fortiori,* not by professed cosmopolites like Henry Adams or committed expatriates like Henry James but by local colorists like Irving, who celebrated Old Spain and Merry England as fervently as the Hudson River Valley and the western fur trade, or peripatetic regionalists like Cooper, who vainly sought to turn from Leatherstocking to European romances. It was through the grand tour chronicled in *The Innocents Abroad* that Mark Twain emerged as the humorous voice of America. Most of Hemingway's fiction, which the world accepts as the exemplification of a strenuous Americanism, takes place on foreign soil. This transatlantic impetus reached its fullest intensity with the artistic movement that surfaced after the First World War. Its impatient manifesto was a symposium of thirty intellectuals, edited by Harold Stearns and published in 1922 under the heavily ironic title, *Civilization in the United States.* Its inevitable break-up, under the economic and political pressure of the nineteen-thirties, was indicated twelve years afterward by Malcolm Cowley in his journalistic memoir, *Exile's Return*.

Meanwhile all sorts and conditions of Americans, doughboys and playboys, gold diggers and prophetesses, loners and joiners, businessmen and bums as well as Bohemian artists, had been making a continental sojourn, or at least a trip. Merely to list a small handful of titles and dates fould be to suggest at how many levels this had become a part of the national experience: *Three Soldiers* (1921), *The Enormous Room* (1922), *Mr. and Mrs. Haddock Abroad* (1924), *Gentlemen Prefer Blondes* (1925), *The Sun Also Rises* (1926), *Dodsworth* (1929), *Eimi* (1933), *The Autobiography of Alice B. Toklas* (1933), *Tender Is The Night* (1934), *Of Time and the River* (1935), *Nightwood* (1936). The point of convergence for these various pilgrimages would be what was then the world's capital of the arts. Someone has told the hero of the book that lies before us: "You know, dear, all good Americans go to Paris when they die, and we are dead, as far as they over there are concerned." To which his interior monologue frames a reply: "Yes, but are we good?" Having been there twice before, he clearly realizes that its touted frivolity is "America, not France." For the serious artist, if not for the *flaneur* of Montparnasse, Paris looks beyond the pleasure principle—here Freud is echoed in the original German. On the verge of his return, the pilgrim hails France as the "blessed home of all wanderers." But he is not at heart a wanderer, any more than William Carlos Williams himself, who managed to live within a half-mile of his birthplace for nearly all of his eighty years (1883–1963).

A Voyage to Pagany is the fictional reminiscence of a rare interlude during that firmly rooted existence, so much of it devoted to the practice of pediatrics and general medicine in the middle-class community of Rutherford, New Jersey, not far from the dreary industrial town whose epic he composed in *Paterson*. The paradox of his career was strengthened by the mixed strain of his parentage. From his mother, who seems to have exercised the greater influence on him, he inherited both Spanish and French blood. His English father, who had traveled widely in Latin America, never gave up British citizenship. Young Bill spent his fifteenth year in Switzerland, in the school at the Château de Lancy near Lake Geneva that he mentions here. During the following year in Paris he was privately tutored, since his French turned out to be inadequate for the Lycée Condorcet. As a medical student at the

University of Pennsylvania, he contracted his lifelong friendship with Ezra Pound, then pursuing his graduate studies in Romance languages. Theirs was a complementary relationship, sustained on both sides by personal affection and mutual respect, though they would be moving in opposite directions: Pound abroad on his quest for the spirit of romance, Williams homeward to push his own roots deeper into the soil along the Passaic River. It is not hard to read Williams' position between the lines of Pound's letters over the years; even the burlesque Americanese of the expatriate seems to mock the convictions of the nativist. "You'd better come across and broaden your mind [1909]" has its dialectical counterthrust in "I note your invitation to return to my fatherland [1917]."

If there is a touch of asperity in that last remark, it is because Pound, with "the virus . . . of nearly three bleating centuries" in his veins, was haughtily retorting to an American of the first generation. "And America! What the hell do you a bloomin' foreigner know about the place?" Williams has not even been west of the Maunchunk (N.J.) switchback. This letter was quoted in the polemical prologue to *Kora in Hell,* where the London expatriates are consigned to Williams' private inferno and Pound is singled out as "the best enemy United States verse has." In a subsequent letter Pound elaborated his clinical metaphor: Williams has avoided the endemic blood-poisoning because he had "the advantage of arriving in the milieu with a fresh flood of Europe in [his] veins." For his own part, from the first, he had criticized Pound's "unconstrained vagabondism." His correspondent, recoiling from the early constraints of Idaho and Indiana, was heading for the center, was putting himself in touch—indeed in command—of what he would later call "a live tradition." The real eccentric was the "dago immigrant" ("Finest possible specimen of course," Pound genially added), since he chose to stay behind and play the "old village cut-up." Williams, scientifically trained, approached his experimental objectives directly, and feared that those bookish courses which Pound pursued and prescribed would lead back to academic conventionality. In any case, the exile recognized that the hyphenated descent of his friend made him an authentic spokesman for the realities of *Patria Mia,* such as they were. From Paris, in 1922, he wrote to Rutherford:

. . . I don't really believe you want to leave the U.S. permanently. I think you are suffering from nerve; that you are really afraid to leave Rutherford. I think you ought to take a year off or a six months' vacation in Europe. I think you are afraid to take it, for fear of destroying some illusions which you think necessary to your illusions. I don't think you ought to leave permanently, your job gives you too real a contact, too valuable to give up.

Williams took up Pound's challenge, arranging a sabbatical leave from his practice. He was busy writing in New York during the last six months of 1923. Thence he and his wife embarked for Europe on January 9, 1924; they would disembark from their homecoming voyage on the twentieth of the following June. He sums it all up in his *Autobiography* as a "magnificent year," and its European itinerary would furnish the framework for *A Voyage to Pagany*. When the book appeared, it would be loyally dedicated to Pound, "the first of us all"—a vernacular counterpart for Eliot's dedication of *The Waste Land* to "il miglior fabbro." But, significantly, *A Voyage to Pagany* did not appear for four years; the immediate consequence of the journey was the renewed commitment of *In the American Grain*. D. H. Lawrence had recently brought out his seminal *Studies in Classic American Literature*, stimulating American writers and critics in their perennial search for a usable past. There was no flag-waving or eagle-screaming in Williams' rediscoveries among the explorers, the settlers, the founding fathers, and other predecessors. Mencken could not have been sharper in attacking "the inevitable Coolidge platform." Williams sometimes waxes apocalyptic, as he looks beyond the blandness of American life to "its— horrible temper," beyond its technological achievement to its "gross know-nothingism," beyond the puritanical inhibition to the lawless violence. From his six weeks in Paris he recalls a congenial dialogue with Valery Larbaud. Though the French had been much more humane than the English to the Indians, their colonies had failed because of their Latin sense of history. America's strength is its break with the past, Europe's weakness.

The Great American Novel—a parody of the genre, like the preliminary efforts of so many novelists—was written just before Williams' *Wanderjahr*, and is more intransigently nationalistic: "Europe's enemy is the past. Our enemy is Europe." *In the American Grain*, coming subsequently, illustrates with historical *collage* and critical commentary "the battle to establish a European life in the New World." Hence it may be read as a sequel to *A Voyage to Pagany*, wherein a copy of it retrospectively figures as "a keepsake." Its final emphasis, on grounds of immediacy rather than patriotism, is "Here not there." But the interaction would continue, prompting Williams to his brief sortie in the wake of Pound, his own exploration of "there," *là-bas,* Pagany. The collective name that he chose for Europe, though it had scarcely been repeated since the sixteenth century, was appropriate for his purposes. Pagans had originally been dwellers in rural villages; the early Christians used the term at Rome for those who still practised idolatry; more neutrally, a *paganus* was a person who did not share the prevailing beliefs. This relative concept could be reversed, as would be demonstrated in 1930–1932 by the publication in Boston of the little magazine, *Pagany: A Native Quarterly,* with Williams as a leading contributor and nativism as its literary program. The novel charts a return, via "old Pagany," to primal forces antedating both Europe and America. The central section, "At the Ancient Springs of Purity and Plenty," seeks to revive a sense of power and beauty through communion with "a resurgent paganism, still untouched." Long obscured by Christianity, and by the Renaissance, the pagan gods survive as stone images in the cathedrals.

In the *Autobiography* Williams speaks of *A Voyage to Pagany* as "my first (limping) novel." Since the junket of a husband and wife would hardly make much of a story, he decided to romanticize his material. In *I Wanted to Write a Poem,* based on a series of interviews with him by Ethel Head, he describes the genesis of the book more fully. It was composed at Rutherford as usual, albeit in the absence of Mrs. Williams and their two sons, who were then attending his old Swiss school. A laconic diary from 1924 served to nudge his memory and tap his imagination. "The protagonist was, of course, myself; his experiences, in a measure mine." Thus Dr. Evans, a forty-year-old physician from "the New Jersey town of P. where he was born," and born of immigrant stock, wants more than anything else to be a writer. "Loaded up with Americana—his love of America," he believes that Europe is "turning pagan." Since he is traveling alone, the actual Floss Williams—devoted companion, "the rock on which I have built," whose German-Norwegian parentage balanced her husband's admixture of bloods—has dropped out of the overt picture. Nonetheless, "the women figures in the story were frequently my conception of my wife," Williams confessed. And even more intimately: "There are other women, women the American might have desired to go to bed with, sometimes a woman whose face had registered in my mind, a woman out of the crowd." One of his uncomformable sonnets may epitomize Floss's role:

> With one woman
> I find all the rest . . .

On the other hand, few writers can have delivered so many babies, or have acquired so special a feeling for the moods and phases of womanhood. Elsewhere, again in the *Autobiography,* he tells us: "Men have given a direction to my life and women have always supplied the energy." In the novel his surrogate has already determined upon a direction, but the women help him to test the alternatives and confirm his resolution with their respective energies—and with resistance to them. A study of Williams' groping plays, *Many Loves* and *A Dream of Love,* might throw further light on the relation of his marriage to his fantasies.

If Eros does not personally intervene in the narration, which is so susceptible to her sway, it is because she has been deliberately exorcised. The publisher thought that the manuscript was too long, Williams frankly told his interviewer. Accordingly, the author decided to cut out "the best chapter in the book" and to publish it separately as a short story. It is entitled "The Venus," and would have come at the novel's midpoint. There the goddess is invoked through the painting of Botticelli and the statue from Cyrene; the invocation is heard as a verbal *Leitmotif;* but our Tannhäuser has definitely left this particular Venusberg behind. The tale, when we take it up, proves to be slight and poignant. It involves a beautiful blonde German girl who is staying at the same *pensione* with Evans in Rome, "the little *fräulein,*" "the Cyprian," with whom in the novel he has no chance to speak. In the story there is a conversation between them, little more, while they wander off from an excursion to the antiquities at Frascati. With Teutonic earnestness she raises the question: "What then is it like, America?" How can he explain what he himself, a kind of refugee, has been puzzling over? By contrast, the United States "seems less encumbered with its dead." He can show her a flint arrowhead, and she is momentarily attracted to the notion that Americans are almost savage, "not quite civilized." But the ultimate prospect seems "even more lonesome and frightening . . . than in Germany." Daughter of a Prussian general, resigned to taking her vows and becoming a nun, she too has considered and rejected the alternative world to her own.

Williams returned to the theme in one of his finest poems, "The Birth of Venus," which opens with a nostalgic glimpse of the Parade

Grounds at Villefranche—the well-remembered vista from his travels that reappears in both the *Autobiography* and *A Voyage to Pagany*. Now it is too late: "we / are not there." The sensory values of love, though reaffirmed, are harrowed by the negations and deprivations of war. Aphrodite, buried or in exile, has played an elusive part in latter-day fiction. Exhumed, she takes a stern revenge on a loveless bridal pair in Mérimée's *Vénus d'Ille*. In the guise of the Venus de Medici she fascinated Hawthorne, who evokes her image to symbolize the underground passions of *The Marble Faun*. One might have expected the antipuritan Williams, in a volume contemporaneous with *Lady Chatterley's Lover*, to have advanced the subject somewhat farther. But if Venus is the personification of that chthonic force which his traveler seeks in Pagany, then it must be said that either she eludes him or else he evades her. She has incarnated the artist's goal: "striving to cut between the show and the fact, . . . undeceiving, living—shedding fig leaves." Williams was once persuaded to hold forth publicly on the novel ("a form I have never respected"). Perhaps his disrespect colored his theories. His appeal to Carlyle's philosophy of clothes was more than metaphorical, since novels have so much to do with external appearances; and, of course, it has been their classic function to expose the actualities beneath. For Williams, however, the novel is little more than "a strip-tease"; only the poem can lay bare the nudity of things.

Figures of speech have their limits, and this one would never do to characterize the works of the major novelists. Yet it might help to distinguish between Williams' poetry, where he plays the realist (his word would be "objectivism" or "contact"), and the present novel, which—as he owned—"turned out to be much more romantic than I'd intended." The novels located on his own terrain, *White Mule* and *In the Money*, like most of his stories, would be unequivocally realistic. In *A Voyage to Pagany* little is made of the novelistic opportunities for characterization, observation of manners, or human relationships. Its burden is reflective and highly subjective, paying less heed to the impressions it gathers than to the impressionist who blends them in with his thoughts —thoughts on art, in the main, and its interconnection with the two hemispheres. "Florence, city of makers," of artists *par excellence*, inspires a meditation on the banks of the Arno, while the river itself, in continuous self-renewal, seems to be the prototype of art. "Reality, romance: it sums up, to make." All novels have combined the two components in varying proportions; the modicum of romance in *A Voyage to Pagany* stands out rather self-consciously because it has been super-imposed upon a spontaneous flow of autobiographical reality. Our identification with the problems and preoccupations of Dev (Dr. Evans-Williams) is all but complete. Evans recounts details which Williams remembered specifically from 1924: for instance, the three smiling Japanese tourists at Notre Dame or the joyous walk from Eze to Monaco. The get-together with the avant-garde really happened, and the character of Jack Murry was modeled on the Left Bank impresario, Robert McAlmon.

Williams did not aspire to be a Baedeker, and his topographical descriptions are often impressionistic to the point of distortion. When he calls the Santa Croce a cathedral, he is confusing it with the Duomo, and the confusion is triply confounded when he descries within it the tombs of Dante (buried at Ravenna) and of the Medici (adjoining San Lorenzo). Poet though he be, Dev is equally the compatriot of philistines like Sam Dodsworth, Mr. Haddock, and the excursionists of Mark Twain's *Quaker City*. The Forum leaves him cold; he is homesick in Venice; and when he tries to visit Ferney, "old home of the divine philosopher" (Voltaire), the house is closed and the gates are bolted. Nonetheless, like Gershwin's *American in Paris,* he responds with a peculiar zest to whatever comes within his wavelength. His appreciation of a particularly fastidious sequence of French wines is voiced by an indelibly American exclamation: "Wow!" The beer in Switzerland makes him worry about Prohibition at home. It is not surprising that, during his first night in Paris, he dreams of Walt Whitman. Leaves of grass, he discovers on a picnic by the Seine, can be symbols there as well as here. He is immeasurably more concerned with living humanity than with its historical monuments. At Carcassonne his attention wanders from the uninhabited fortress and its medieval legends to the modern settlement at its base, which is not so far removed from New Jersey after all. "People live here! Good God. And they are happy and they sent soldiers to the great war." People, with the consistent exception of Jews encountered on trains, draw out warm sympathies from him wherever he goes.

This cannot be regarded as a travel book, though it was apparently mistaken for such by its limited body of first readers. And no wonder; for its basic pattern is geographical, framed by arrival and departure and by a haunting sense of the oceanic depths beyond. The succession of settings might almost be Dantesque in their triplicity. The focus of the first section is on Dev's affair with Lou Martin, which seems to have motivated the whole adventure. Its principal locale is the Riviera, and the idyl seems to be more closely associated with the place than with the girl. Since he feels no deep chagrin, we need not, when she leaves him to marry her English tennis partner. Thereafter his motivation broadens and becomes more general: he is traveling to enlarge his view. The second section, proceeding from France to Italy, is the most scenic part of the book—although, in the absence of the blonde Venus, it sadly lacks a heroine. Instead we are faced with Dev's esthetic reflections; instead of dialogue, with his monologue, or rather with the interplay between his mind and the masterworks that interrogate it. Sightseeing can but excite "his lust to make," even as antiquity confirms his resolve "to make—new." The third section passes from art to science, insofar as it concerns Dev's professional interests. Now the scene is principally Vienna, to which Williams transposes some memories of a postgraduate year spent in pediatric studies at Leipzig University. In his admiration of his medical teachers, he can envisage a reconciliation of the sciences and the arts, of the disinterested pursuit of knowledge and the passionate cult of beauty.

Having rambled among the Italian monuments, the protagonist seats himself in the concert hall or the opera house—or, climactically, the Spanish Riding Academy—to continue his artistic education in Austria. Bach's Saint Matthew Passion presents him with the highest model, along with the realization that "Art kills time." Here the long-drawn-out message of Proust is condensed into three terse monosyllables, carrying a latent ambiguity: is art merely a pastime or does it confer immortality? A talk among medical colleagues, reflecting back the less permissive sexual attitudes in the States, recalls the exposure of Viennese puritanism that Shakespeare dramatized in *Measure for Measure*. Dev finds a musical mentor, as well as a mistress, in the American bluestocking, Grace Black. While they stroll along the Danube, it is she who voices the sharpest counterstatement against the homeland: its childish athleticism, its materialistic technology, the "political flimflam" of its democracy. Since the lovers are so divided by their cultural allegiances, they have no choice but to part. Heading for France again, Dev joins his sister Bess en route. We already know, from an earlier discussion, that she hates America even more than Grace does. Now, as they picnic by the Seine, she too pleads with him to stay in Europe, to quit his job and study it out. "Like Eliot?" he asks, and she answers: "Who is

Eliot? Like nobody." Rather than perform his "aesthetic duty to the Stars and Stripes," she would have him settle down with her and learn the secrets of life and art from the French. But he has seen the handwriting on the wall and read his own destiny in it. "Art," he has discovered, "is a country by itself."

Williams declared that the episode of the picnic had been suggested to him by the example of an expatriate brother and sister, the writer Lawrence Vail and the singer Clotilde. Into his fictitious account of the situation he has injected a hint of incest, orchestrated to a theme which reechoes from a performance of *Die Walküre,* where the Wagnerian siblings join together in the procreation of Siegfried. *"Brüder! Schwester!"* This association would seem to imply that it would be a decadent gesture for Dev to settle down with his "Seine Sister." But the implication is treated symbolically rather than psychologically; Williams' characteristic vein is innocence rather than decadence; Dev and Bess would simply be reverting to their childhood. It was for Thomas Mann to make the most of the same sinister *Leitmotif* in his "Blood of the Volsungs." Dev's three American women, then, remain in Europe. His most appealing heroine, the German Venus, has escaped from the novel, and the short story about her is a parable in which there can be no meeting between two minds or two worlds. The cycle is revivified by the ending, which is likewise a beginning as with Joyce and Eliot, when Dev catches sight of the Nantucket Lightship. Behind him lie the Seine, the Arno, and the Danube; ahead, once more and forever, the Passaic. It is easy to understand why the author should testify, while admitting freely its imperfections, that *"A Voyage to Pagany* was important to me in my education as a writer." He has told us something about its only previous publication in a modest edition by the Macauley Company of Passaic, N.J., with a jacket designed by his architect brother: " 'The Worm' encircling the world."

Williams regretted the neglect of his book, and hoped to see it reprinted some day. He felt it to be the most lyrical and descriptive of his prose writings, possibly because of its—for him—exotic subject-matter. Not that he had been conducting a travelogue or exploiting the picturesqueness of the scenery. The distance he keeps may be gauged by his uncertain handling of foreign names and phrases. This is far less important than the fact that he remains his unaffected self, that he so manifestly wrote to please himself. He was interested not in making an impression but in registering an impact. Though he said that Dr.

Evans represented him "as a person—not as a writer," the two are finally inseparable. When he tells us that Evans "was a man who enjoyed writing," he is obviously telling us about Williams. "He wrote because he loved it and he wrote eagerly, to be doing well something which he had a taste for, and for this only did he write." His boyish zest, his wide-eyed openness, and his spontaneous energy made him an especially responsive witness to the American-European encounter. Looking back upon *A Voyage to Pagany*, Williams wondered whether it might conceivably have been influenced by Henry James who was never one of his favorites. He need not have worried, for we cannot imagine Dev getting into one of those dark entanglements that seduced Roderick Hudson and menaced Christopher Newman. There may be some resemblance to Lambert Strether in the belated curiosity for finding out what one may have missed by having lived in Woollett rather than Paris. But no Jamesian personage would have made the westward crossing so happily, or found so much that was genuinely poetic in the American scene.

FOOTNOTES TO POETS, 1:
E. E. CUMMINGS

This brief appreciation was contributed to a special issue of *The Harvard Advocate* in honor of the poet (Spring, 1946). Perhaps I need not footnote the local allusions—except to recall that there was once a day when the name of a burlesque theater in Boston, the Old Howard, could hold appealingly wicked connotations for Harvard undergraduates. The stylistic effect that I was seeking to particularize in the case of Cummings involves what I have come to generalize as the quixotic principle. The principle has helped me to understand what had elsewhere struck me as a peculiar affinity between Cummings' poetry and Hemingway's prose (*Contexts of Criticism*). Cummings' more recent work, sustainingly fresh and increasingly resourceful, has strengthened the thematic metaphor in my original title, "Of Birds and Books." One might well think of the purple thrush in *73 Poems,* queried as to the meaning of death in life:

>   "if i
>   should tell you anything"
>   (that eagerly sweet carolling
>   self answers me)
>   "i could not sing"

When Cummings writes, "Birds sing sweeter than books tell how," he is singing his theme song. Poetry might be described, in his terms, as the vain attempt of books to emulate birds. An overwhelming consciousness of the abyss between them is perhaps responsible for his typographical gestures and stylistic outbreaks. Those who are not unnerved by such *frissons* will not find his poems difficult or cacophonous or even very formidably novel. Indeed none of our contemporaries has devoted himself, with a purer lyricism, to the perennial variation on the Wordsworthian note: on this linnet, that throstle, and those barren leaves. More bookish tastes, like the princess in the perverse fairy tale, may prefer the artificial nightingale to the real. The modern poet, like Yeats, may prefer "such a form as Grecian goldsmiths make," perched upon its golden bough at a drowsy emperor's court, to the birds that sing in the trees of more youthful countries.

But Cummings is not really a modernist; he is rather, like Joyce, a disaffected traditionalist, a bedeviled humanist, a banned singer, whose native strain of lyric affirmation—under pressure of congenial circumstances—has modulated into satirical negation. Circumstances, of course, go back to Cambridge, Massachusetts, to the traditional New England role of the minister's son, and to the need for living down the ghosts of Longfellow and Lowell. The original impetus seems to have recoiled from this academic background: from Professor Royce rolling down Divinity Avenue, Professor Shapley comparing the universe to a cookie, professorial anecdotes "out of Briggs by Kitty," and Radcliffe "uneyes safely ensconced in glass." Even the flowers were made of glass at Harvard, and the birds turned out to be "duckbilled platitudes"; it was one of those places where, as later succinctness would have it, "people became un." The daughters of Greenwich Village are caught, as it were, on the rebound from the dowagers of Brattle Street.

If Cummings escaped from the genteel tradition via Bohemianism, the First World War brought out his anarchistic tendencies. *The Enormous Room* is an unforgettable account of his unique experience, his accidental internment in a French prison camp. Whether it be classified as a war book or a prison book, it assuredly ranks among the finest American prose of the nineteen-twenties. By rediscovering the irreducible individuality of human beings, within the most squalid and narrowly regimented conditions, it confirms the discovery of Dostoevsky's *House of the Dead*—more recently reaffirmed in Jean Malaquais' *Les Javanais*. The Cummings hero wears nobody's uniform; he is distinguished like Olaf, "glad and big," by his ability to "take it"; he remains the picturesque underdog, the conscientious objector, the unregimented individualist. Travels in Russia complete the process of his disaffection; for the Soviets, as *Eimi* observes, carry standardization even farther than Cummings' compatriots. The "land of supernod" meets its match in the "kingdom of slogan."

The artist's problems are essentially what they have always been, but he now labors against greater odds, against "the noisy impotence of not and same." It is not he but "mostpeople" who lack positive values. In attacking their "unhearts" and "unminds," he is well aware that two negatives affirm, and that he is therefore defending sensibility and insight. But the rhetoric of the epoch, which Mencken designates Gamelielese, and which Cummings brilliantly demonstrates in his panegyric on Harding, is notoriously befogged by multiple negatives. "Everything is protected by cellophane against anything (because nothing really exists)." In a metaphor which is also an omen, he includes everything and nothing; he describes the stimulation and the exhaustion,

> absitively posolutely dead,
> like coney island in winter.

The sedge has withered from that landscape, and no birds sing. And no words, however feebly responding to artificial respiration, evoke the actualities that called them into being. Instead, the language reverberates back on itself, like

> songs containing the words country home and
> mother when sung at the old howard.

Younger poets, notably Kenneth Fearing, have developed a whole poetic diction out of Cummings' trick of reflating slogans and clichés. But the "busted harmonica" is not his best register, and his ventures into washroom epigraphy have tended to fade. His residual archaisms and habitual inversions have dated less, on the whole, than his attempts to talk out of the side of his mouth. His rearrangements of type and *calligrammes à l'Apollinaire* show, after all, quite as much preoccupation with form as his handling of the sonnet and the ballade. And his syntactic shifts, his substitution of nouns for verbs, his experimentation with adverbs as substantives, aim rather at a renewal of strained relationships than a reversion to anarchy. Ultimately the old and elemental relations prevail:

> Beauty makes terms
> with time and his worms,
> when loveliness
> says sweetly yes
> to wind and cold.

Time and his worms have kept busy, no doubt, while beauty has ebulliently renewed herself. But the burden of the lyricist has not greatly changed since Thomas Nashe wrote:

> Beauty is but a flower
> Which wrinkles will devour:
> Brightness falls from the air,
> Queens have died young and fair . . .

Behind Nashe, in the satirico-lyrical line, stands Villon, as the Middle Ages loom behind the Renaissance. *Ubi sunt?* Where are they now? What ever happened to Flora the beautiful Roman, or Bertha with the big feet? Or Alice or bestial Marj or Kitty, sixteen, 5 ft. 1 in.? Or, for that matter, laughing Allegra? Their presence yesterday and their absence today are equally conspicuous; the immediacy of here and now is accentuated by the mutability of then and there; and the recurrent counterpoint between love and death is poignantly restated. As the pattern extends from erotic themes to nature, in more recent lyrics, the apple orchards and New Hampshire mountains come into view. And, even though books can never "tell how," Cummings' books tell us what to look and listen for. Too often our heads are turned away from realities—not, like Don Quixote's, by reading too many romances—but by reading the advertisements in the slick magazines, by listening to the sweet singers on the radio, by drowsing over the mechanical contrivances of Hollywood.

> I'd rather learn from one bird how to sing
> than teach ten thousand stars how not to dance,

says Cummings in the final couplet of his *Collected Poems*. He leaves us confronting this characteristic alternative, which staunchly affirms while it doubly denies. Nor is his ultimate pun less characteristic; for it mechanically multiplies the star that danced at the birth of Shakespeare's Beatrice to the dimensions of some supercolossal Radio City Music Hall.

FOOTNOTES TO POETS, 2:
T. S. ELIOT

On the death of T. S. Eliot in 1965 a memorial service was held in the Harvard Church (January 20), at which Douglas Bush spoke succinctly and aptly about his career as a man of letters and I touched upon his local associations—"T. S. Eliot and Harvard." Both of these statements were published along with additional tributes in *The Harvard Advocate* (Fall, 1966), and Professor Bush's can also be found in his collection of essays, *Engaged and Disengaged*. My ceremonial epigraph and conclusion were, of course, supplied by the ode or hymn that Eliot had written for his class. That he had been elected a Class Odist rather than Class Poet is ironically anomalous; for, whereas the Poet is allowed free range, the Odist is expected to compose a new set of sentimental lyrics for the tune of "Fair Harvard" ("O, believe me if all those endearing young charms"). The classmate who was elected to write his own poem has not since been heard from in that line. And, though Eliot must have performed his more limited task as well as it could possibly be done, it is boggling to think of how many times the same conventional subject has been celebrated in the same anapestic tetrameters.

> For the hour that is left us, Fair Harvard, with thee
> Ere we face the importunate years,
> In thy shadow we wait, while thy presence dispels
> Our vain hesitations and fears.

And so the chain of anapests goes on, linking each successive class with Harvard by an ode to the same music. Let us pause for a moment to meditate, waiting in that shadow with the Odist of the Class of 1910. One of his classmates was destined to give the West its first eyewitness report on the Russian Revolution and, dying all too shortly thereafter, to be entombed in the Kremlin. Another, just emerging to prominence in the United States Senate, was killed in an airplane crash. Others survived to win the appropriate honors in business, public life, or the professions. How could it have been foreseen that this shy young scholar was embarking upon a long sequence of esthetic and spiritual adventures which would end by turning him into a legend for our time?

The danger, perhaps we can now see in retrospect, was lest he stay at Harvard and subside into a mere professor. He was headed in that direction via the usual detour, a traveling fellowship which enabled him to spend a year at the Sorbonne. After his return, he spent three years in the Harvard Graduate School, the third as an assistant in philosophy. It was to complete his dissertation on F. H. Bradley that he went abroad again to study at Oxford; and, had the war not broken out in 1914, he would probably have returned to take his doctorate. "Between the conception and the creation," to echo a later poem, "Falls the shadow"—the shadow of the University. The collection of manuscripts and memorabilia in the Houghton Library includes a letter from his cousin, President Eliot, telling him not to be foolish like Henry James, not to become an Englishman but to come home.

"Home is where one starts from," he has said: in his case, Saint Louis, on the great midcontinental river whose rhythms haunted him on the banks of the Thames. He has also said, "In my end is my beginning": his ashes will be buried in Saint Michael's church at East Coker, the Somersetshire village whence his ancestors migrated to New England. Thus he rounded out a cultural cycle, and Harvard was the halfway-station on his pilgrimage. The litany of his teachers held a generous place among his grateful acknowledgments: Lanman and Rand in Ancient Languages, Kittredge and Robinson in English, Woods and Santayana in Philosophy, Bertrand Russell as a visiting lecturer, above all Irving Babbitt. These were to him, like the sages in Yeats's Byzantine mosaic, the singing-masters of the poet's soul. And since this poet was notably learned, *doctus poeta,* something of the vast credit he earned from the world must accrue to the institution of learning that fostered his gifts.

Its presence, we might say in the language of his class ode, dispelled hesitations and fears. Summers at Cape Ann, poems and articles in the *Advocate,* visits to maiden aunts and to Mrs. Jack Gardner, *The Boston Evening Transcript*—such were the amenities of tradition for a youth from Missouri in the opening decade of the twentieth century. Soon enough he saw that, insofar as they prefigured a way of life, it was yielding—hesitantly, fearfully—to those importunities which he exemplified in the menacing person of "Apeneck Sweeney." Continuing his quest in the mother country, he would ground his future endeavors upon the rock of Anglican faith and British citizenship. He was welcomed, but as a newcomer, very much an American, a disturbingly original modernist whose horizons were etherized patients, whose human relations throbbed like taxis, who had syncopated "that Shakespeherian Rag."

Modern Europe, on the other side, offered no balm for intellectual snobbery or historical nostalgia. Rather, it inspired him to project what one of his many inspirers, Hermann Hesse, had called a glimpse into chaos, *Blick ins Chaos*. Only through an apocalyptic ordeal, through that refining fire whose prophet was Dante and whose day of wrath came with the Luftwaffe, could the individual discern any meaning in existence. As for culture, it would continue in the form of an ideal order, where time past flowed on into time present, restoring "with a new verse the ancient rhyme. / Redeem the time." The spirit, still "unappeased and peregrine," now moved "between two worlds become much like each other." This particular spirit, having remained a teacher in spite of himself, celebrated his homecoming to Harvard in 1932–33 as Charles Eliot Norton Professor of Poetry. Those of us who had the good fortune to meet him then were indeed his students already.

He was, he will always be, the literary mentor for my generation, even when we disagree with him. If I mention the fact that he published in his *Criterion* a senior essay of mine brashly taking issue with his views on certain Metaphysical Poets, it is because the very triviality of the example will illustrate how far he went out of his way in his personal kindness to younger and minor writers. In 1950 his gracious gesture, contributing his lecture on "Poetry and Drama," did more than anything else to establish a lectureship in memory of Theodore Spencer, our colleague and his friend. His visits to Cambridge during the last few years were charmingly sentimental occasions, designed to acquaint his sympathetic English bride with some of his older associations. To remember the austere sonority of his readings in Sanders Theatre, where he made a point of dwelling on his earlier poetry, is to be thankful that genius has been among us, casting its special brilliance on the loyalties we have shared. To conclude as his ode concludes:

> And only the years that efface and destroy
>   Give us also the vision to see
> What we owe for the future, the present, and past,
> Fair Harvard, to thine and to thee.

FOOTNOTES TO POETS, 3:
MARIANNE MOORE

Elliptically titled "A Note on Her French Aspect," these impressions appeared in *Festschrift for Marianne Moore's Seventy-Seventh Birthday,* edited by Tambimuttu in 1964. The format of that book was quite unworthy of the occasion, its distribution was negligible, and the duty of proofreading seems to have been disregarded. Therefore, if only to set the record straight, I welcome a reprinting. On the peculiarly Gallic and highly idiomatic subject of La Fontaine, I have never been fully confident of my own apprehension. But Miss Moore recreated something uniquely her own, and I shall always be grateful for the personal privilege of intensive correspondence and occasional discussion with her, while she was working upon it. In fairness to her, if in some embarrassment to myself, I should add that she discusses herself in her Harvard poem, "In Lieu of the Lyre," as

one whose "French aspect" was invented by
Professor Levin.

No one but a truly original poet would be so scrupulous with footnoted acknowledgments, and T. S. Eliot knows whereof he speaks when he says that Marianne Moore "has no immediate poetic derivations." Instead she has a richer attribute of the talented, which is more broadly significant: she has many affinities. These are hers by choice, as Henry James's were—by a series of choices no less fastidiously eclectic than his, albeit she has managed to cultivate her mandarinism without traveling far beyond Brooklyn. Some of her affinities are recognizable from the other side and from a distance, as I found when I taught a course in American literature to a class of Japanese students. Emily Dickinson was the only other one of our writers who elicited such complete appreciation from them. This kinship is as clearly manifested in dazzling insights as in reverberating off-rhymes. But Miss Moore can sustain the native note with a fuller orchestration, as in the Whitmanesque catalogue of a poem like "People's Surroundings." In deference to her quondam fellow townsman, Mr. Eliot, we may think of her as Anglo-American when remembering his allusion to the metaphysical qualities of her poetry. Nor should we forget the ancestral purport of "Spenser's Ireland."

Though she was not a member of the group that called themselves *Des Imagistes,* she has done more than they did to warrant their manifestos; and though she never underwent a period of expatriation in Paris, she too has derived inspiration from France—not so much from the *Symbolistes* as from the classical tradition. It is not for nothing that her given name is that of the national heroine, that she has proved herself capable of her own kind of *marivaudage,* or that she has set a personal style by wearing an elegant black *tricorne.* Her sympathy for French culture was eloquently expressed during the German Occupation in "Light Is Speech," which addressed itself to Bartholdi's famous statue in New York harbor and renewed the symbolic posture of Enlightenment. Her tribute to Molière, "To the Peacock of France," characteristically transposes his "je prends mon bien où je le trouve" into "taking charge of your possessions when you saw them." The principle she saliently put in practice, "that poetry should be as well written as prose," is credited by Mr. Eliot to Ezra Pound; but it had been enunciated by Victor Hugo nearly a century before. One of her rare exclamations or repetitions, "Neatness of finish! Neatness of finish!," seems to carry certain French overtones.

In practical terms, this direction has led to the most remarkable of her technical accomplishments, the use of syllabic versification in English. Its monument comprises the varied yet faithful stanzas of her exquisite translation of La Fontaine's *Fables,* where the human bestiary has been so thoroughly assimilated that the *esprit gaulois* is refined into a quintessence of Yankee wit. Equally close but less obvious, because it has more to do with viewpoints than with subjects, is her affinity with Montaigne. Miss Moore's first collective title for her poems was *Observations;* they may indeed be considered *Essays* in the original and exploratory sense. As the intellectual curiosity of the essayist weighs its object, the balance of thought is now tipped one way by an unexpectedly apt quotation, and again the other way by a startlingly specific example. "To a Steam Roller" might well be a latter-day counterpart of "Des Coches," wherein likewise

> The illustration
> is nothing to you without the application.

Some of the very topics, such as "Marriage," offer the same sort of occasion for digressing and coming round to the point, with much incidental pith:

> he loves himself so much,
> he can permit himself
> no rival in that love.

Such an observation would surprise us less, if it came from La Bruyère or La Rochefoucauld. Miss Moore, after she dangles her citations, usually succeeds in capping them with pointed remarks of her own:

> ... Caesar crossed the Alps 'on the top of a
> *diligence.*' We are not daft about the meaning, but
>   this familiarity
> with wrong meanings puzzles one.

And there are moments when her aphorisms touch the depths of tragic generalization:

> hope not being hope
> until all ground for hope has
> vanished.

The endless debate between nature and art is bound to be a sequence of shifting emphases; but, very generally speaking, the English poets have sided with nature and the French have taken the side of art. Here the dual allegiance reveals itself through a paradox: as a naturalist, Miss Moore is even more artful in her approach than Buffon. In its range and precision, her control over metaphor is almost Proustian. The markings of her lizard resemble piano keys; the habits of her pelican are linked to the career of Händel; the mussel opens and shuts its shell like

> an
> injured fan.

Yet, if her menagerie tends to become a museum, wherein the animal world is momentarily crystallized into semiprecious stones, she ultimately comes out on the side of life in "Critics and Connoisseurs." She tells us plainly that, better than the artifacts of the Ming Dynasty, she likes

> similar determination to make a pup
> eat his meat from a plate.

Prompted by a statement that New York is "the center of the wholesale fur trade," her imagery transforms the metropolis back into a predatory forest. On the other hand, the exotic and the intractable are domesticated, not to say civilized, in her practical vision:

> . . . here they've cats, not cobras, to
> keep down the rats.

It should also be noted that the analytical critic, who discourses so astringently on the understanding of art in "The Monkeys," turns out to be another cat—needless to add, a highly individualized specimen of its distinguished breed. Under so intense a gaze as this, imaginary gardens can turn into real ones, while mere toads can become as fabulous as hippogriffs.

REAPPRAISALS OF NOVELS, 1:
LES LIAISONS DANGEREUSES

The work discussed here seems unique in every way: the only work of fiction by its author, the outstanding novel of the French eighteenth century, the *reductio ad absurdum* of gallantry, the trenchant herald of Women's Liberation. Yet, as a model of style and structure, it likewise has its honored and early place in what I take to be the main line of realism. Hence, when the New American Library, Inc. reprinted the Aldington translation among the Signet Classics in 1962, I was pleased to fill in with this foreword.

The title of this novel is, and was meant to be, a warning: Danger! proceed at your own risk through a sequence of hazardous involvements. The actual phrase, *Les Liaisons dangereuses,* is expressly pronounced at the very end, where ironically it condemns the personage that has hypocritically invoked it during the course of an earlier discussion. The translation by Richard Aldington, a twentieth-century English man of letters who has shown a special affinity for the French eighteenth century, seems to be the best available (the only subsequent one that I have seen shows signs of dependence on his). He conveys a sense of the elegant verve and the paradoxical wit that combine to absorb the shocks of the story itself. But he calls it *Dangerous Acquaintances;* and his titular noun, "acquaintances," sounds too casual to be a match for that French word-of-all-work, *liaisons,* which takes on a slightly licentious undertone in non-Gallic ears. The innuendo seems quite warranted here; and though an author's footnote tells us that the term *roué* was falling out of fashion in his day, its meaning is still suggestive enough in English, where we still have some occasion to use it. We do not try to anglicize Victor Hugo's *Les Misérables* or even Françoise Sagan's *Bonjour tristesse.* Why, then, should we not retain the impact of this book's original name? The sinister connections that it exposes, moreover, ramify beyond the erotic sphere to encompass an entire social epoch in their network of intrigue.

Choderlos de Laclos (1741–1803) held a place in that society strategic enough to be involved in its intrigues and mediocre enough to survive its upheavals. First and last a military man, he ended his career as one of Napoleon's lesser generals. During his middle years, which were those of the Revolution, he was a pamphleteer and politician, slipping in and out of several contending factions, including the extremist Jacobins. He served as a kind of secretary and henchman to the opportunistic Duke of Orleans, who employed as governess Madame de Genlis, the authoress of edifying romances. Hence the historian Michelet could remark that the duke was flanked by vice on one side and virtue on the other. However, the identification of writers with what they write about is more conducive to censorship than to critical understanding. Laclos' private life seems to have been no more wildly irregular than that of other ex-aristocrats of his generation; after all, he married his former mistress. His notoriety was a direct response to his unlikely single work of fiction, which—from its publication in 1782— enjoyed the wide circulation that is usually the consequence of *succès de scandale*. He claimed to have utilized personal observations noted while he was garrisoned at Grenoble, the provincial capital where Stendhal was born the following year. Though the two would meet but once, appropriately in an opera box at Milan, *The Charterhouse of Parma* would be unthinkable without the *Liaisons dangereuses*.

The eighteenth century, in its leisure and literacy, was a great age for letter-writing. It is not surprising that the epistolary novel was one of its most characteristic literary forms. That convention, as opposed to fictitious memoirs or pseudo-biography, permitted a character to confide his most immediate thoughts and most recent impressions to the reader, without the interventions or delays of more formal narrative. It could be more intimate and more circumstantial; it could also be too monotonously repetitious and too arbitrarily contrived, unless the contrivance were handled with versatile skill. Credit for the widespread acceptance of the innovation is commonly accorded to Samuel Richardson. Taken up by Jean-Jacques Rousseau, it became a vehicle for his radical doctrines on human nature. Richardson's *Clarissa* fascinated and edified its readers by moralizing over a seduction, sentimentalizing its ill-fated heroine and making a melodramatic villain of her seducer, Lovelace. Rousseau, in his *New Eloise,* placed his Julie between a young lover and a middle-aged husband, resolving this triangle through mutual renunciation, an idealistic exercise in the new morality. Both of these fictional precedents are cited in the *Liaisons dangereuses,* which runs true to the realistic stance by casting a sardonic side-glance at its predecessors. The young lover is compared, by his mundane elders, to an unworldly hero of pastoral romance, Céladon. When the seduced heroine react naïvely, she is tartly admonished: "You would make an excellent figure in a novel."

It remained for Laclos to shift the focus back to the old immorality, as it were from chastity to the chase, from an outraged Clarissa to an outrageous Lovelace. Behind that vantage point looms a classic tradition of courtly gossip and worldly aphorism, cynical in mood and urbane in manner. Its seignorial attitudes come closer to the hard-boiled area of comedy, peopled with foolish virgins and predatory rakes, than to the committed domesticity of the ordinary novel. The spokesmen of the *Liaisons dangereuses* speak of themselves as actors on "the great stage" of gallantry; the chief gallant has a valet who plays his comic part by seducing his master's mistress' maid. Most novels, because they so wholly enlist our sympathies, seem to tend toward the subjective, the passive, the feminine. The subtitle of the Marquis de Sade's *Justine, The Misfortunes of Virtue,* might no less pertinently be attached to Henry James's *Portrait of a Lady* or *Wings of the Dove.* In each case, however divergently, we share a loss of innocence. Such a loss, from a more detached, more dynamic, more masculine point of view, may be envisaged as a gain of experience. It has been said of Laclos that he wrote about sex as cold-bloodedly and amorally as Machiavelli had written on politics—as Machiavelli indeed, we should add, had treated sex in his comedy, *Mandragora.* His handbook for power-hungry politicians, *The Prince,* had its amatory counterpart in Ovid's manual for would-be seducers, *The Art of Love.*

Such are the proudly vaunted principles of "the art of seduction," as practised by the immoralists of the *Liaisons dangereuses.* It is their innocent victim, the fifteen-year-old Cécile Volanges, who for them has "neither character nor principles," and whose depravation will feed their revenge against others. Her naïve response to the world outside the convent is relayed to a schoolmate through her opening letters, wherein she mistakes a kneeling shoemaker for an ardent suitor and wonders whether the ladies in the salons are blushing under their rouge at the gentlemen's stares. But we are not allowed to identify for long with endangered virtue; from the second letter our attention is alerted to the source of danger, the partnership between the widowed Marquise de Merteuil and her former lover, the Vicomte de Valmont. Theirs is the overview of intriguing gods, cavalierly sacrificing mere human beings to their own malicious quarrels and promiscuous amours.

Valmont, contemporary of Casanova, recounts his adventures like a sportsman at once fastidious and vainglorious, or like a general on the battlefield of sexual strategy, with many a mock-heroic bulletin. He is far too seasoned an amorist to regard Cécile as much of a conquest, although he takes a certain perverse satisfaction in corrupting a schoolgirl. She is incidental to the quarry he has been more avidly pursuing, the Présidente de Tourvel—all the more avidly because that pretty prude has religious compunctions, which only spice his libertine efforts to overcome her resistance.

Huysmans remarked that the suspense of the psychological novel hinged upon the question: will she or won't she? With Laclos that is all a foregone conclusion. We are simply curious to learn the details of "the inevitable fate": when and where and by what resourceful device or bold tactic will his redoubtable couple manage to pin down the ever-changing objects of their unending pursuit? Madame de Merteuil, in Valmont's absence, keeps him well informed of her teasing dalliance with the Chevalier de Belleroche. Suddenly she takes a wanton fancy to the less experienced Chevalier Danceny, mainly because he has been artlessly courting Cécile, so that the older pair becomes jointly engaged in debauching the younger. Madame de Merteuil's hostility toward Cécile, hypocritically masked and sincerely accepted as a confiding friendship, stems from a prior attachment to the Comte de Gercourt, who had left her for a certain Intendante, who left Gercourt for Valmont, who left the Intendante for Madame de Merteuil. It's a small world—not unlike Schnitzler's Vienna—and Gercourt is now the choice of Madame de Volanges for her daughter's hand. From what might already seem a full calendar of assignations, Madame de Merteuil takes a night off in order to conquer a conqueror of her sex, who has been arousing Valmont's envy, the undefeated Prévan. Meanwhile Valmont enjoys a parallel episode—on the farcical plane of Balzac's *Droll Stories*—when he encounters his old flame, the Vicomtesse, and they deceive both her husband and her lover.

An operatic catalogue of the situation would, in addition, reckon the courtesan Emilie, whose complaisance provides an accessible haven whenever Valmont is repulsed by the prudishness of Madame de Tourvel. Such calculations may not seem out of place when the game is so coolly played, when reason single-mindedly concentrates on making a plaything of passion, when it is not love but opportunity which flings the silly little heroine into the arms of the professional profligate. It does not require a very meticulous audit to note that, for Valmont and Madame de Merteuil, the story involves a carnal relationship with at least six other characters respectively, including one another and not excluding the obligingly deceased Marquis de Merteuil. Furthermore, their grand alliance blocks or breaks up relations between the other dramatis personae. When Madame de Merteuil fails to keep her bargain, to crown the downfall of Madame de Tourvel with the renewal of her own favors to him, Valmont retaliates by procuring Cécile for Danceny. It is her gesture of reciprocal spite that precipitates Danceny's challenge, the duel, Valmont's death, and Danceny's withdrawal into celibacy as a Knight of Malta. Nor is Gercourt drawn back into the vicious circle through marriage, since Cécile ends by taking the veil. As for Madame de Tourvel, she likewise returns—not to her conspicuously absent husband, the judge, but to a nunnery where mortal illness resolves her dilemmas. If the choreography of these entanglements could be plotted, it might fill in the implications of this sketchy diagram:

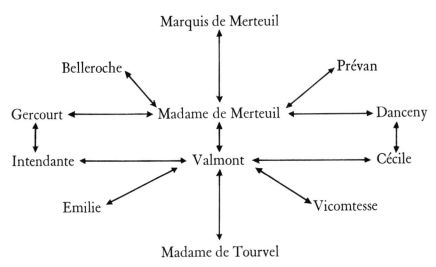

But the symmetry of this retrospective arrangement, with its total of thirteen *liaisons,* would be misleading, if it implied that the score was even between Madame de Merteuil and Valmont. Each is in a position to blackmail the other; they would be wiser if, as she suggests, like a pair of gamblers too well matched, they decided not to play each other. The real game is between these two accomplices, and their complicity turns into a mutually destructive campaign in the perennial battle of the sexes. He is much the simpler character: a dandy, a Don Juan, cold-blooded enough about women but head-over-heels in love with himself, chalking up each amorous success on the scoreboard of male vanity. She is less a coquette than a *femme fatale,* a self-professed Delilah, with a vengeance of hate to wreak on the opposite sex. Since, as she puts it, "hatred is always more clear-sighted and more ingenious than friend-ship," it is her clairvoyance and ingenuity that lend the book its unique perspective. It is she who lectures him like a schoolboy, and whose re-sentment flares up—along with her jealousy—when she suspects him of taking a conjugal tone with her. It is she who pens the "tender mis-sive" that, when he has copied and relayed it, brings about his rupture with her rival. And when she reveals herself most candidly, in letters LXXXI and CXIII, it is hard to imagine how a man could penetrate any farther into a woman's social experience and psychological animus.

Always the strict stylist, however loose in other aspects, Madame de Merteuil chides both her young correspondents upon the callowness of their epistolary styles. Yet Laclos himself is in full control of his char-acters' modes of expression, differentiating among them so nicely that we scarcely need the signatures of his dozen letter-writers. The dialecti-cal interplay of their minds, their choice of confidants, their shifts between town and country, the four-and-a-half-month continuity, the four-part structure, the rare but significant interventions of the author as editor—all of the technical components, in short, are as brilliantly managed as in the latest "midnight novel" of the current French school. And, of course, the nuances of polish applied to the dialogue and the narration could not begin to be equaled by latter-day novelists. Though the murky abysses are never far beneath the glittering surfaces, the language can refine specific misconduct into debonair generalization. Madame de Merteuil can epigrammatize with the deftness of a La Rochefoucauld:

"One should only permit excess with those one intends to leave soon."

"People rarely acquire the qualities they can dispense with."

"Love, which they tell us is the cause of our pleasures, is at most only the pretext for them."

At this kind of formulation, too, Valmont is her apt but less subtle disciple:

"As if it were very difficult to make a promise when you have decided not to keep it!"

Such maxims well deserve inscription among what William Blake called the proverbs of Hell. But they are not Laclos' considered advice to his readers, and it is wise old Madame de Rosemonde whose aphorism restores the ethical balance:

"Man enjoys the happiness he feels, woman the happiness she gives."

Madame de Merteuil has jauntily skirted this insight, when she confessed to Valmont about Belleroche:

"The perfect happiness he enjoys in being loved by me really attaches me to him."

However, her basic code is more purely selfish:

"Pleasure, which is indeed the sole motive for the union of the two sexes, is not sufficient to form a bond between them."

Noting that Kant's *Critique of Pure Reason* appeared just the year before, we might consider the *Liaisons dangereuses* as a critique of pure pleasure, a devastating attack on hedonism as a way of life. The farewell letter may be a manifesto of moral irresponsibility ("it is not my fault"); but Laclos visits heavy retributions upon his philanderers; and the double ruin of face and fortune may, for Madame de Merteuil, prove a fate worse than death. She and her ambivalent partner end by becoming cautionary examples, villains foiled at last by stern poetic justice. The viewpoint from which they are judged is hinted at the beginning, where—with the effect of juxtaposed mirrors—an Editor's Preface affirms the authenticity and the morality of this "collection," while a Publisher's Note insists that it is "only a novel," and could not actually have taken place in so enlightened an age. That irony does not mask the ulterior purport. Laclos had highly serious views about the upbringing of women, which are expressed in two posthumously published manuscripts. Something of a Rousseauist, he argues for a more natural treatment at every stage, and he is particularly concerned with the demoralizing consequences of the marriage of convenience. Thus his novel is an object lesson which puts flesh and blood on his feminist argument through the case of the sacrificed pawn, Cécile, and the figure of the avenging goddess, Madame de Merteuil, victim and exponent of lovelessness in the relation between the sexes.

This debauchery becomes, in turn, a flagrant symptom and a flamboyant symbol of the corruption of a whole society, the aristocracy of the Old Regime. When Valmont wishes that he had been trained as a pickpocket, his wish is a leveling comment upon his class. When lustful motives lead him to perform his one good deed, paying the taxes for a family that would otherwise be evicted and thereby "reduced to straw and despair," we are given a glimpse into the causes of the French Revolution. When his obliging servant, Azolan, draws the line at wearing livery, we are reminded of Beaumarchais' contemporaneous barber, Figaro, revolting against his arrogant master and heralding the proclamation of Liberty, Fraternity, and Equality in 1789. That, it would later be said, was a terminal date for *la douceur de vivre,* the sweetness of living, as it had been previously experienced through the rounds of fashion and flirtation at the court and in the châteaux. But wherever parasitical luxury flourishes, there will be idle frivolity, and —more often than not—the malign seductions of the sweet life, *la dolce vita.* This is a theme which, as the phrase may indicate, readily adapts itself to the usages of the film. Recently a cinematic version of the *Liaisons dangereuses* has renewed the controversies inherent in Laclos' original conception. It has been not only modernized but relocated at a skiing resort in the Maritime Alps. Their dazzling chill recalls the dictum of Baudelaire: "This book, if it burns, must burn like ice."

REAPPRAISALS OF NOVELS, 2:
THE CHARTERHOUSE OF PARMA

My study of Stendhal in *The Gates of Horn* made its tentative first appearance eighteen years earlier, under the rubric *Toward Stendhal,* as an issue of the intermittent periodical *Pharos* (Winter, 1945). To it was appended an open letter by George Mayberry, which had appeared in *The New Republic* not long before, on the occasion when the Scott-Moncrieff translation of the book was withdrawn from the Modern Library because it had attracted so little interest in this country. I should like to think that pamphlet contributed something to a change of attitude so far-reaching that we have lately been favored with an Anglo-American translation of Stendhal's *Life of Rossini*—one of the most trivial of his hack writings, riddled with errors and plagiaries, and limited by chronological circumstances to the first half of the subject's career. It was a pleasure to return to an author whose works I had studied as a whole, to attempt a more rounded appraisal of his masterwork, and to redress one warranted complaint that I had done less than justice to the ineffable Duchess of Sanseverina. This was the introduction to *The Charterhouse of Parma,* as translated by Lowell Bair and copyright by Bantam Books, Inc. (1960).

The happy few, to whom this book is dedicated on its final page, must have been multiplying in recent years. In 1943 the sole available English translation, that of C. K. Scott-Moncrieff, was dropped from a popular list of reprints because it had not proved popular enough to reward its publishers. Since then not only has it come back into print, but it has been accompanied by many of Stendhal's other and lesser works, some of them translated for the first time. Now Mr. Bair has given us at last an American *Charterhouse of Parma,* well designed for a wide circulation, which succeeds in catching the rapid pace and dynamic immediacy of its unique original. Scott-Moncrieff's version, like everything else he touched, had its literary qualities; yet it sometimes carried them to the point of mannerism or pedantry. Too often it rendered colloquial phrases by Anglicisms confusing to non-English readers. It also went out of its way to Italianize French words which might more pertinently have been Englished. The net impression is that of a British tourist determined to be our guide through Italy— whereas the author's personal rhythm and confidential tone should invite us directly, as they do here, to a complete absorption in his story. He would not himself have been surprised at this increasing measure of public acceptance. He had learned to accept his own career as a rather ineffectual man of the world, with a highly developed taste for travel, for the arts, and for the feminine sex, who had seen youthful service in the Napoleonic campaigns and was eking out his middle age at a minor consular post. The tangible fruit of his leisure, the outcome of so much scattered observation and accumulated experience, was his voluminous writing. Though it gained little recognition for him among his contemporaries, he does not seem to have minded. Addressing himself to posterity, he cultivated the special candor and the sharp penetration which it takes to reach that ultimate audience. Correctly he predicted that he would be rediscovered a generation after his death, and that he might not be fully appreciated until the middle years of the twentieth century. That he would ever find a following in the United States—a republic which he admired in principle and distrusted in practice—probably went beyond his expectations. Yet he would like us better today because we enjoy the opera; while we, in welcoming a new edition of his masterpiece, may congratulate ourselves upon our maturing appreciation.

It is not hard to understand why earlier editions lapsed, or why—with the exception of Balzac—the book attracted scant notice from contemporary critics. Balzac, in his enthusiastic review, declared that it ought to be read primarily by diplomats, statesmen, publicists, social leaders, the most distinguished artists, the twelve or fifteen hundred personalities dominating European life. Through this generous but somewhat intimidating overstatement, he evidently wanted to single out the particular charm it has for those who share its worldly wisdom; who recognize, from their own responsibilities and involvements, how subtly and shrewdly Stendhal has retraced the varying patterns of human interrelationship. Worldliness of this kind is more frequently conveyed by memoirs, aphorisms, or comedies than it is by the more subjective novel; and indeed there are elements of those other forms in *The Charterhouse of Parma*. When Balzac retitled it *The Modern Prince,* he implied that it might hold a further appeal for the less sophisticated, as a Machiavellian handbook introducing them to the ways of the world. But maturity is the password to Stendhal's domain; to the reader who lacks it, he will seem cold and cynical, as will Jane Austen, Congreve, Voltaire, and Montaigne.

In that respect Stendhal's previous major novel, *The Red and the Black,* has proved more appealing to younger sensibilities. It prepared the way for later fictional studies of the adolescent ego, of the ambition to become a superman, and of protest or revolt against an established system. Hence we could compare it with Dostoevsky's *Crime and Punishment,* Dreiser's *American Tragedy,* or Jean Genet's *Our Lady of the Flowers.* On the other hand, *The Charterhouse of Parma* is quite incomparable. No one but Stendhal could have written anything like it. Not that it is autobiographical, like so many of his other writings. Rather, it may be regarded as a testament of his last years, a consummation of all his strivings and strayings, the crystallization—to use a characteristic term—of his peculiar responses to a sequence of epoch-making circumstances. This may help to explain the remarkable feat of its composition, during the fifty-two days between November 4 and December 26, 1838. Dictation, though it may have led to a number of trivial inconsistencies, enabled Stendhal to sustain the note of improvisation, the conversational spontaneity of his style at its best. Its apparent effortlessness was grounded, as he might have claimed with Whistler, upon a lifetime's effort of artistic preparation.

Stendhal liked to base his fiction on actual documents, and he was particularly interested in first-hand anecdotes of the Italian Renaissance. In the present instance he was following an account of the grand courtesan, Vandozza Farnese: how her noble house had owed its rise to her notorious affair with Cardinal Borgia, who became Pope Alexander VI, and how her nephew Alessandro had survived intrigue and imprisonment to ascend the papal throne as Paul III. Here, with certain strategic differences, was an outline for Stendhal's narration. His focal point would still be the duchy of Parma; but he transposed the time from the sixteenth century to his own day, more than a hundred years after the long rule of the Farnese dynasty. The tale begins in 1796, about one year before the hero's birth, and ends shortly after his death, just before the pretended date of writing in 1830. The foreword misleadingly states that the place of writing was far away from Paris; actually Stendhal dictated the narrative while he was home on leave from his consulate at Civitavecchia, in his apartment on the Rue Caumartin. The plains of Lombardy, the banks of the River Po, and the waters of Lake Como seem all the sunnier for having been evoked through the mist and chill of a Parisian winter.

The allure of "delightful places" is made explicit in the quotation from Ariosto that heads the first volume. Stendhal's idyllic vision of Italy, as he makes clear by frequent cross-reference, is a critique of the

France he knew—which, in turn, was the beginning of the France we know, in its moods of calculation and restlessness. His autobiography, *The Life of Henri Brulard,* culminates with the mood of liberation he felt as a sublieutenant in Napoleon's Italian campaign of 1800. These emotions, transferred to Lieutenant Robert, charge the opening atmosphere of *The Charterhouse of Parma;* and Robert, destined to be a general at Waterloo, plays more than a walk-on part; for it is discreetly hinted that the hero, Fabrice, nominally the second son of the Marquis del Dongo, was really the offspring of the Frenchman's romantic *liaison* with the Marquise. Milan in the brief days of the French occupation, as capital of the Cisalpine Republic, represented a cultural fulfillment which meant so much to Stendhal that he had the word "Milanese" inscribed on his tombstone in the Montmartre Cemetery. It meant, along with more intimate recollections, a convergence of the new ideas set in motion by the French Revolution with those ardors and energies which for him were uniquely personified by the Italian character.

However, this euphoric possibility was cut off by the fall of Napoleon, and that is why the turning point of Waterloo forms the precipitating episode in the adventures of Fabrice. Under the wave of European reaction associated with the time-serving policies of Metternich, the Italian city-states were squeezed between the Austrian Empire and the temporal might of the Papacy. Their ill-starred regimes made repressive attempts to turn back the clock of history, which to Stendhal were as anachronistic as the powdered hair of his Metternichian politician, Count Mosca. Stendhal believed in enlightenment and continued to hope for progress; but, amid the revolutions and reactions of his epoch, he had lost his illusions about reforming human nature; and his Liberals, when they come to power, behave as ignobly as his Ultras. In effect, he possesses that rare insight which Lionel Trilling would call "the liberal imagination." Moreover, he has that even rarer talent, a liberal sense of humor. Instead of sketching his ideal state, he caricatures a utopia in reverse, a comic-opera principality depicted upon a scale which reduces its stateliest annals to absurdity. Well might he mockingly wish for an epic pen; for in Parma he created a realm which is ruled by the mock-epic spirit.

Such a setting presupposes a residue of disappointed heroism somewhere in the background. Its touchstone, for Stendhal, is the cult of Napoleon; and its most expressive reverberation is his treatment of Waterloo. This was the first time that the discomforting realities of modern warfare, as experienced by the befuddled participant, had been adequately presented in literature—so subsequent writers, from Tolstoy to Hemingway, have warmly acknowledged. The contrast between the heroic and the anticlimactic, between Fabrice's poetic anticipations and the newspapers after the battle, is Stendhal's refinement upon the technique originated by Cervantes and employed by all realists. That preliminary disillusionment serves as prologue to the grandiose anticlimax of Parma, its hypocritical court, and its reversal of values. Curbing his naïve idealism, Fabrice must strictly conform to outmoded standards of conduct and opinion. He must learn to play the game of careerism, which his mentors liken to the game of whist; and he learns so well that, before too long, he finds himself playing whist at the Prince's table. Still more appropriate is the recurrent metaphor of acting. Characters and situations are described as actors and performances; significant encounters take place at the theater; courtiers indulge in Commedia dell'Arte; hero and heroine communicate, at a crucial moment, by *recitative*.

The Charterhouse of Parma is not a historical novel, though it is framed by a hypothetical set of consequences to historic events. Despite its panoramic scope, it concentrates on the psychological sphere; it registers the impact and growth of awareness in the basic experiences of war, politics, love, and religion. Stendhal's novels characteristically follow the fortunes of some neophyte, who is initiated by his elders into the difficult problems of getting along in the world. Stendhal seems to identify emotionally with Julien Sorel, the self-made protagonist of *The Red and the Black,* in his quarrel against society. But toward the aristocratic conformist, Fabrice del Dongo, the author's attitude seems more detached, more closely to be identified with the young protégé's older sponsors. Like Homeric gods, they wangle his destinies; whereas Julien was both conspired against and conspiring, their conspiracies work on Fabrice's behalf. Count Mosca, the local Machiavelli, gives him the benefit of avuncular counsel because he himself is the lover of Fabrice's aunt, the incomparable Duchess of Sanseverina. She is approaching her forties, alas, while Mosca has entered his fifties, during a period when Fabrice—who was in his seventeenth year at Waterloo—is hardly more than twenty-three.

The shift of vantage point seems to accord with a growing consciousness of the difference between generations as the nineteenth century matured. Slight of stature, prone to tears, Fabrice is taken in hand by a series of motherly women, such as the jailor's wife and the *vivandière*. The dominant figure is, of course, the Sanseverina, a woman whose glamor seems to transcend the limits of merely literary creation. She is a Helen of Troy who, from the walls, directs the strategies of Trojans and Greeks alike; a Cleopatra who beguiles Pompey and Caesar and Antony, not in succession but simultaneously. Stendhal's reminiscence of his mother, who died in his infancy, was distinctly erotic; reciprocally, the Duchess is more than maternal in affectionate surveillance of her nephew. The irony is that, since her brother actually was not Fabrice's father, incest does not bar a romance between them. She is torn by jealousy when Fabrice, after many casual affairs, falls in love with his jailor's daughter, Clélia Conti; and Mosca, whose relation to his mistress is an adultery of convenience, repeats the pattern by becoming jealous of Fabrice. The single person who understands Gina Sanseverina is the doctor-poet Ferrante Palla, conscientious highwayman and self-nominated tribune of the people, whose entrance into the scene precipitates further reversals.

Overt theatricality masks an underlying sincerity on the part of such Stendhalian figures, which comes to the surface in desperate monologues or capricious gestures. They go through the polite motions, they keep up with courtly gossip: who's in, who's out. They are capable, in self-defense, of blackmail, double-crossing, most of the crimes that Stendhal takes pains to deplore. Sooner or later the moment is bound to come when their repressed passions erupt in public, like—as Stendhal repeatedly said of politics—a pistol-shot at a concert. Gina backs a revolution in Parma which Palla leads; and, though it fails, their fine Italian hands are to be detected in the Prince's assassination. Fabrice rather passively savors the fruits of nepotism, breaking out in an occasional duel or abduction; and yet his decisive acts are prompted by ardent and idealistic motives. Each of his successive initiations, military, political, and amatory, leads him—through a wayward sort of justice, preshadowed by numerous omens—to prison. He is incarcerated for his escapades in the brooding citadel of Parma, an imaginary landmark which resembles the Castle of Sant' Angelo at Rome. It casts its shadow over the book as the Spielberg, the fortress that symbolized Austrian repression, menacingly brooded over Stendhal's Italy.

Ideologically, then, the citadel is a monument to the constraining forces of despotism, a house of correction for Parma's invisible cohort of freethinkers. Yet, psychologically, it is not so repellent a symbol as that view of it might suggest. Its paradoxical fascination lures us, as we are lured by the prisons of Piranesi, not so much downward into the dark underground as upward to an emanation of light. Fabrice's clearest omen was manifested when Father Blanès hid him in the belfry, from which he could gaze down upon his native landscape. His feeling of ecstatic detachment prefigured the felicity he would experience in looking out from his tower at the Parmesan sky. True enough, his happiness is dependent upon the proximity of the charming Clélia, and their telegraphic courtship seems to have been predestined from their chance meeting several years before. Small wonder if, like the prisoner of Chillon, he regains his freedom with a sigh. And it is not without significance that his incarceration has lasted nine months, as if it were a regression to the womb. He makes a dashing escape, again prearranged through the intervention of Gina, who has her own mixed reasons for seeing him rescued from the confinement of Clélia's orbit. Inevitably, voluntarily, soon he returns to his blissful durance.

No compunction is wasted over his crime. Morally it is treated as the merest peccadillo, though it is politically exploited to embarrass the government with crises. Nor does anyone seem to be shocked at the fact that this callow rake is technically one of the religious. His novitiate, contrasted with his baptism of fire on the battlefield, seems to be no more than a matter of form, plus the proper clericalist opinions. Though he sincerely prays whenever his mundane affairs need divine assistance, it never occurs to him that his way of life taints him daily with the sin of simony. With the collusion of the snobbish Archbishop, he is hastily promoted to the top of the ecclesiastical hierarchy. He uses his position, along with certain histrionic gifts, in order to become a famous preacher. His sermons are theatrical attractions which draw the crowds from the rival *matinée,* and ultimately accomplish their amorous purpose: Clélia, now married to another, is persuaded to break her vow that she never will see Fabrice. She reverts to it, with practised equivocation, by arranging for trysts with him in the darkness. The child of their illicit union becomes, through an apt fatality, the secret object of competing affections and deceptions; less fortunate than his father, he does not survive them.

Thus love, when finally attained by Fabrice, is alloyed with unhappiness; while the Sanseverina, passionate creature that she has been, has been successively thwarted by three loveless marriages. War, as Stendhal's impulsive novice had dabbled in it, had turned out to be wholly bereft of heroics. Religion, which he has yet to take seriously, he has professed as if it were a branch of politics. Each of his initiations has left him in a deeper stage of disillusion. What next? What retreat but the somber institution that has lent the novel its name, and that does not appear in it until the concluding page? The Charterhouse is far less central than the citadel; its function is to stand apart from the story. Stendhal seems to have conceived his work in three volumes, to have completed two of them in detail, and then—at the last-minute behest of his publisher—to have rounded things off with a few abrupt and crowded paragraphs. Yet the shock of a tragic ending after the comedy, the prospect of solitude after so much society, is the logical solution. The gesture of withdrawal operates to restore the values that have been reversed; Stendhal's lovers, after all, have souls to think about; and though they may comply with the courtly hypocrisies, their determining choices are unworldly.

The Charterhouse means incarceration, for Fabrice, with a vengeance. Deliberately he has chosen the most austere and isolated of monastic disciplines—a decision stimulated, perhaps, by Stendhal's memories of the Grande Chartreuse near his birthplace, Grenoble. No Clélia will brighten the view from Fabrice's cell; no Sanseverina will preside over his fate; no Mosca will plot for his well-being. He will die young, within a year after taking his Carthusian vows, preceded by Clélia and followed by the Duchess. But he will doubtless have had the opportunity to review, in monkish contemplation, what he has lived through in passionate action. Stendhal has drawn a curtain across his penance, and he is remembered for his debonaire moments. Yet his world would be incomplete if he did not end by renouncing it, by rushing from the extreme of gay abandonment to the extreme of melancholy rigor. Between those extremes a vast distance is traversed and put into perspective, so that—from the Stendhalian heights—the scenery is magnificent and the overview exhilarating. As for the aftertaste, Stendhal himself summed it up in his favorite critical label, *sec*. That dryness is not of the dryasdust academy, nor is it the drouth of an esoteric wasteland. It is the bittersweet ebullition of sparkling wine.

REAPPRAISALS OF NOVELS, 3:
THE SCARLET LETTER

Another introduction—to another old favorite, which I have had some opportunity to discuss before, but less for its own sake than within the special focus of *The Power of Blackness*. When it was proposed that I reedit *The Scarlet Letter* for the Riverside Editions, I confess that I hesitated. Naïvely, it seemed to me that enough editions of the book were already available. The publishers, Houghton Mifflin, pointed out gently but cogently that, as heirs to the original publishers, Ticknor and Fields, they had good right to continue with an edition of their own. Then, as we investigated the state of the text, it soon became apparent that many inaccuracies had crept into it since Hawthorne's one proofreading, that it drastically needed a thorough reediting, that—except for the small first edition, now a highly valued collector's item—there were simply no reliable texts. This one (1960) may have given some impetus to the authoritative edition of Hawthorne's collected works, now being published by the Ohio State University Press under the sponsorship of the Modern Language Association.

We speak of a book as a classic when it has gained a place for itself in our culture, and has consequently become a part of our educational experience. But the term conveys further meanings implying precision of style, formality of structure, and, above all, concern for the basic principles that animate and regulate human behavior. Evaluated by these criteria, the list of unquestioned American classics is not a lengthy one. Often, with oblique regard for the alphabet, it is headed by *The Scarlet Letter*. This, among Hawthorne's larger works, has been generally rated as his characteristic best. It was also his first book-length narration—if we follow his own judgment in ignoring *Fanshawe,* an unsuccessful effort which went back to his college days. For some dozen years after graduation, he had retired to his mother's house in Salem, where he experimented with essayistic sketches and didactic tales, most of them evoking the regional past. A series of penny-a-lining assignments for Boston publishers, a brief job as measurer at the port of Boston, a season as a member of the utopian settlement at Brook Farm had not tempered that sense of isolation which underlay his need to communicate. Then his happy marriage and his paradisiac sojourn at Concord had released those flights of fantasy which reached their haven in *Mosses from an Old Manse.* But, since such writing was too delicate to support a growing family, his influential friends secured him part-time employment as Surveyor of the Revenue in the United States Custom-House at Salem.

Wedlock had made him belatedly sympathetic toward women and the relation between the sexes. Office-holding made him somewhat ironic about himself and his fellow office-holders and even the society they served. Given the austerity of his background plus the reticence of his temperament, both of these responsibilities had been steps to a hard-won maturity in his midforties, for Hawthorne as a man and as a writer. He admired the intellectuals of Concord and Cambridge, but he had seen enough of them to realize that his own mind would never march with any school of thought. After association with Bronson Alcott and Transcendentalism at its most impractical, he had welcomed "a change of diet." Yet he felt he must account to readers for his three-and-a-half years in an ineffectual bureaucracy, as well as for the circumstances that led to the termination of his appointment. His "autobiographical impulse," which came to the surface whenever he introduced a new work, joined forces with his homing instinct, which tended to focus his imagination on houses of varying kinds. Hence he gave his *Scarlet Letter* a local habitation by way of his introduction, "The Custom-House." Now that the Whigs had come back into office and Hawthorne—a staunch, if not an ardent, Democrat—was out of it, he could resume his true calling, the life of letters. But first he settled his score with politics, said farewell to his native town, and reverted to the colonial period, by gathering his latest impressions into a "sketch of official life."

That introductory sketch, which is one-fifth as long as the actual story, seems to have caused more immediate discussion than what it heralded. It may well have helped to create the unexpected demand for second and third editions within a few months. To the second edition Hawthorne added a preface, disclaiming partisan or personal malice, and refusing to delete or alter a single touch. It would not have become him to wax indignant over the Spoils System, from which he would benefit in his turn; instead, with cool amusement and obvious relief, he had set down a few reminiscences of his erstwhile colleagues. More serious is the objection some critics have leveled at "The Custom-House": that it offers an unsuitable preamble to *The Scarlet Letter* itself. There is indeed a contrast; but it has clearly been calculated; for Hawthorne's art is based on antithesis. It is as if, before conducting us into a realm of shadows, he wished to exhibit worldly substance at its most substantial. Yet the commercial routine of customs inspection harbors internal contrasts of its own. The names of Salem merchants, as entered in ledgers along with their respective imports and tariffs, are balanced against the shades of ancestral Hawthornes, witch-hanging Puritans who would frown upon their scion's weakness for writing story-books. The declining seaport is presented as the ghost of its bustling former self. A passing glance at the Gold Rush reminds us that, by 1849, the pursuit of material wealth had worked its way from New England to California.

But Hawthorne cannot give us more than "a faint representation of a mode of life not heretofore described." Contemplating the page that reality has spread out directly before him, he regrets his inability to probe its commonplaces for deeper significance. "A better book than I shall ever write," he sighs, "was there"—there, in that sphere of concrete observation which others were developing into the modern novel. He never thought of himself as a novelist; he was habitually "a romance-writer." The romance, as he defined it repeatedly, takes place in a twilit half-world "where the Actual and the Imaginary may meet." Hawthorne contrasts his busy days at the custom-house with his dreamy evenings at home in the parlor, where his imaginative faculties re-awaken amid the flicker of moonlight and firelight. The evolving shapes, though they seem strange and remote, are the familiar spirits that haunt his fiction: snow-images, soap-bubbles, mirror-reflections. But though he proceeds—through his domestic transition—from the contemporary and realistic to the legendary and symbolic, the shift of direction is not a means of escape. Rather, the quasi-historical setting allows him to question certain moralistic assumptions with a freedom and a candor which he could not have applied to a nineteenth-century subject. It is not the least of the book's achievements that, in the very epoch of genteel femininity, when America outdid Victorian England in the strictness of its taboos, Hawthorne's treatment of a triangle was hardly less of a challenge than D. H. Lawrence's.

As a customs officer, Hawthorne could cite such poetic forerunners as Chaucer and Burns, and could set an American precedent for the later Melville and Edwin Arlington Robinson. Moreover, as a keeper of records, he could shift to the storyteller's ground by employing a conventional device of romantic fiction; he could imagine that he had chanced upon his material in an ancient manuscript, which he described in meticulous detail, together with its faded and tattered yet gorgeous relic, the letter. This lent an air of authenticity to the tale, while enabling the narrator to assume a tone of editorial aloofness. It had the more potent effect of fixing attention upon the searing initial, promising mystery and inviting speculation from the very outset. Hawthorne's plan for the volume had been to include a number of shorter pieces; he mentions two of his neighborhood rambles, "Main Street" and "A Rill from the Town Pump." Many of his earlier stories had touched upon themes that *The Scarlet Letter* would spell out: notably "The Maypole of Merry Mount," where bright color and its studied avoidance emphasized the antagonism between Cavalier and Puritan views of sex. Frequently he used costume for characterization, as in "Lady Eleanore's Mantle," where a sumptuous garment symbolizes the pride of its owner and carries within it the germs of catastrophe. He was interested in characters who were not only isolated but marked by all too literal stigmata, such as the heroine of "The Birthmark," whose imperfection cannot be eradicated because it betokens Eve's original sin.

In "Endicott and the Red Cross," as the title specifies, the central object was a different sort of scarlet emblem. But, among the Salem crowd that has gathered to see the Popish sign renounced, we are given a memorable glimpse of an anonymous bystander:

There was likewise a young woman, with no mean share of beauty, whose doom it was to wear the letter A on the breast of her gown, in the eyes of all the world and her own children. And even her own children knew what that initial signified. Sporting with her infamy, the lost and desperate creature had embroidered the fatal token in scarlet cloth, with golden thread and the nicest art of needle-work; so that the capital A might have been thought to mean Admirable, or any thing rather than Adulteress.

Hawthorne was fascinated by that stern practice of branding convicted sinners, which he had encountered in his antiquarian reading. He refined upon it with a paradox, when he permitted the unnamed hussy to make a decoration out of her insignia of dishonor. Yet there was no real ambiguity; she was simply brazening out her shame; even her children knew what A stood for, embellished or otherwise. A jotted hint from a notebook of 1844, seven years after that fable, records Hawthorne's determination to study more deeply the character of such a protagonist. Persistently, he realized his intention three years later, when he undertook *The Scarlet Letter*. He was aware that the abbreviated epithet could not do justice to the full-scale portrait he was drawing, that moral judgments are not satisfactorily arrived at by the external application of labels. The perennial conflict of letter and spirit had been sharpened for him by the tension between the repressive legalism of Calvinistic tradition, on the one hand, and the Transcendental urge toward self-expression, on the other. If his starting point is condemnation, his objective is to reopen the case. His heroine's illegitimate child, precocious though she may be, does not accept or understand the stigma. And, along with her, we are kept wondering: "What does the letter mean, mother?—and why dost thou wear it?—and why does the minister keep his hand over his heart?"

The girl has a special affinity with the letter; for, if it is the mark of her mother's sin, she herself is the outcome and retribution. She, as her observers recognize, is "the scarlet letter endowed with life." As such she stands a little outside of the code that governs the others; like the infant Quaker in Hawthorne's "Gentle Boy," she is cruelly mistreated by the other children. Not being gentle, she retaliates fiercely, and acquires a reputation as an imp of evil, perhaps the devil's offspring. She is more appropriately depicted in the guise of an elfin sprite, a natural child in the fullest sense of the phrase, happiest when gracefully playing in her element, nature. Innocent enough to have been named Pearl, which signifies purity as well as great price, nonetheless she is wilder than an Indian, as wild as a bird or a breeze. She has learned her capitals in a hornbook; but, though Hawthorne alludes to the *New England Primer,* she has not mastered its most elementary lesson, where A stands for the archetypal sinner:

> By *Adam's* fall
> We sinned all.

Her innocence does not exempt her from the inherited evils of the flesh; but it does suggest that, as at the Garden of Eden, fatal temptations sometimes produce fertile consequences. Hawthorne was not attempting to subvert the Seventh Commandment or to demonstrate that adulteresses are admirable. He was concerned to show that fundamental morality is not so much a series of rigorous laws to be enforced by a meddling community as it is an insight to be attained through continuous exertion on the part of the individual conscience. Viewed in that light, it becomes conceivable for the adulteress to outgrow her discredited role and to grow into so admirable a person as Hester Prynne.

This kind of growth would be inconceivable if Hawthorne really were what he has so frequently been taken for, a mere allegorist. Hester could then do no more than live up to her label, like Bunyan's personified vices. But that is precisely where Hawthorne broke through the preconceptions of allegory to living situations. Though he was fond of pointing out object lessons or utilizing symbolic counterparts to embody his ideas, those ideas—when charged with feeling—transcend or transfigure their embodiments. The letter, which seems naïvely and narrowly explicit at first, gradually takes on its unique aura of intellectual suggestions and emotional associations. It is "a forcible type of moral solitude," for worse or for better: a curse which ostracizes its wearer, and yet—as the outcast develops morally—a blessing in disguise. Whereas Lady Eleanore wrapped herself in the mantle of pride, Hester wears the badge of humility. Like "the cross on a nun's bosom," it has a quality of sacredness; and Indian weapons seem powerless to transpierce it. More and more, it proves to be a talisman, though some of the hearsay about it seems open to doubt—its capacity to burn and glow and to project itself against the sky. At that level, we cannot solve the enigma, which slips away into the void like Melville's whale. However, we can reconsider the ethical standards whereby Hester has been judged and condemned. Her ambiguous A comes to mean, among other things, angel. Her shameful token is finally visualized, in heraldic terms, as a noble escutcheon upon her tombstone.

The book ends, as it begins, in retrospect, so that the characters are framed by the symbolism. In the interim, Hawthorne brings them to life by reinforcing their very resistance to the categories imposed upon them or to the types with which they are compared. Hester may represent, to the grim elders and their self-righteous goodwives, "the general symbol at which the preacher and moralist might point, and in which they might vivify and embody their images of woman's frailty and sinful passion." But, from her entrance, she transforms her disgrace into dignity. Her beauty, at odds with her spiritual condition, "made a halo of the misfortune and ignominy in which she was enveloped." Her taste for the beautiful, which has prompted her to embroider the letter, is one of the attributes that set her apart. The dash of red against her gray attire is a constant reminder of the differences between herself and the other colonists, whose somber dress proclaims their cheerless outlook. Moving from the prison to the pillory, she is forced to stand there in the statuesque pose of the Woman Taken in Adultery. Yet a Catholic witness, Hawthorne suggests, might—with esthetic justification—have likened her to a more profoundly appealing prototype: a painting of the Madonna. The child in her arms is thus, from one point of view, the confounding evidence of her guilt. From another, it is the innocent hope of future redemption. Like the letter by which it is prefigured, it concretely links profane with sacred love; it is the unbreakable bond between the sin and its expiation.

In his European romance, *The Marble Faun,* Hawthorne was to elaborate his conception of education by sin, of remorse as the teacher that broadens the sympathies and of suffering as the discipline that deepens the emotions. Similarly, Hester finds that her trespass endows her with "a sympathetic knowledge of the hidden sin in other hearts." Her ostracism gives her a vocation. Outlawed by the law-abiding, she is welcome only where misery prevails. Her good deeds and selfless interventions make her a byword among her fellow sufferers, and she rehabilitates herself as a Sister of Charity. Meanwhile, the letter has served as "her passport into regions where other women dared not tread." Liberating her from the conventions she has violated, it has encouraged her to think more freely and to form independent notions of right and wrong. Cut off from the Puritans, she approaches more closely than they to the speculative and skeptical spirit of the age, as expressed by more enlightened thinkers on the other side of the Atlantic. Had she been less of a woman and a mother, Hawthorne surmises, she might have become a prophetess like Anne Hutchinson; but her godly neighbors were even harder on their heretics than on their profligates. The alternative was the illicit path to the forest and to a witches' sabbath. Mistress Hibbins, who beckons Hester thither, is predestined to be hanged for witchcraft; yet she insinuates—what Hawthorne illustrates in "Young Goodman Brown"—that many of the town's respectable citizens, with impunity, devote their nights to the clandestine worship of the devil.

Hawthorne would have us remember that his settlers were not far from their English origins. They were the near descendants of the Elizabethans; and, though they could not have inherited the rich fancies of their forbears, something of the older lore and custom had weathered their harsher climate. Hawthorne's nomenclature catches, at least, the seventeenth-century atmosphere. Hester is an Anglicized variant of Esther, the name of the queen who redeemed her people in the Old Testament. William Prynne was one of the most fanatical of the

English Puritan controversialists. His surname has more pertinently belonged to Hester's husband, who—after making his appearance incognito—adopts the pseudonym of Roger Chillingworth. Here cross-reference is less pertinent; for William Chillingworth was a pioneering exponent of religious toleration; but Hawthorne seems to be playing upon the reverberations of "chilling." Two years afterward, in *The Blithedale Romance,* he would christen his cold-blooded villain Hollingsworth—an echo paralleled by the chiming names of the two hesitant heroes, Dimmesdale and Coverdale. As for Chillingworth, he is the most complete incarnation of a figure which Hawthorne was continually reexamining. This was the man of intellect whose obsession had deadened his sensibilities, the scholar-scientist whose experiments dealt ruthlessly with human lives. Shortly before *The Scarlet Letter,* he had been adumbrated in "Ethan Brand," but without convincing motivation for his fiendish curiosity. In 1847 Hawthorne had noted: "A story of the effects of revenge, diabolizing him who indulges in it."

Our first impression of Chillingworth is a dim one, a face in a sequence of pictures out of her past which flash through Hester's mind at the pillory. Within a page or two, she identitfies him as the stranger at the edge of the crowd; and he indicates, by a silent gesture, that the recognition is mutual. For him it is coupled with the shock of discovering how unfaithful she has been in his absence; and she, when he interviews her in prison, refuses to betray the identity of her lover. Up to this point, the moral superiority is on the side of the injured party, Chillingworth. He is bookish, elderly, slightly deformed, and entirely incompatible with a young wife, as he now is ready to admit. Leaving her fate to the auspices of the letter, he resolves to take the vengeance against his rival into his own hands. Step by step, he spies out his victim, tortures an already agonized conscience, and goads it on toward confession; and, in the process, Chillingworth himself is transformed into a virtual fiend. He is fatalistic about the parts that all three must enact: "It has all been a dark necessity." Chance or necessity operates to make Arthur Dimmesdale his fellow lodger and patient, since the young minister is in waning health, and since the scholar's scientific interests qualify him as a physician. His equivocal standing, in juxtaposition with the minister's pious repute, inspires the congregation to believe that their saintly champion is struggling against a diabolical agent. The ironic fact, of course, is that Chillingworth has been mortally wronged by Dimmesdale.

If Chillingworth plays Mephistopheles, he is not trying to beguile Faust into a seduction but to bring out his remorseful afterthoughts. As a doctor, Chillingworth perceives that the source of his patient's malady is not physical. There is "a strange sympathy betwixt soul and body" in Dimmesdale. Ultimately his body reveals the secret his soul has kept. Today we would call his illness psychosomatic, and look upon his colloquies with the leech as sessions with a psychoanalyst. Hawthorne's vocabulary may sound old-fashioned; yet we have scarcely penetrated beyond some of his psychological perceptions, such as his argument for the essential sameness of love and hate—which we might characterize, less elegantly, as the ambivalence of Chillingworth's motives. With Dimmesdale, the problem is Hawthorne's obsessive theme of secret sin—guilt-consciousness, suppressed and seeking catharsis. He first appears as a model of virtue, praying and exhorting the adulteress to disclose the adulterer, lest her unknown partner "add hypocrisy to sin." That the parson refers to himself is an irony which may pass unnoted, until the scalpel of Chillingworth's suspicion has laid bare "the interior of a heart." Then, in a "vain show of expiation," Dimmesdale goes through the motions of Hester's exposure. Alone, in the darkness, he ascends the scaffold. His night-watch is a Hawthornesque meditation, not unlike the critical chapter on "Governor Pyncheon" in *The House of the Seven Gables*. The vision in which it culminates, the letter A etched in red against the heavens, is either supernatural or subjective—Hawthorne deliberately equivocates.

Dimmesdale has undergone penance, but he has not achieved penitence; he has suffered, he has not been absolved. While "the outcast woman" is becoming a lay saint, he—"poor, fallen man"—is being overwhelmed by his unacknowledged sinfulness. Brilliant, sensitive, esteemed for his learning at Oxford and for his eloquence in the colonies, he is weak where she is strong. While she has emancipated herself, he is still entrammeled between his vows and his desires. An encounter in the woods between "the pastor and his parishioner," as Hawthorne dryly designates them, threatens to rekindle their latent passion. "What we did," Hester tells Dimmesdale, "had a consecration of its own." Nature, being heathen, sympathizes with this renewal; but Pearl remains, significantly, an antipathetic force; and the letter figures as a portent, momentarily flung into the brook and inexorably cast up again. The adulterous couple, like Dante's Paolo and Francesca, seem bound together by the very ties they have broken. They plan an elopement, a return to the Old World, unaware that the omniscient Chillingworth will be making his own plans to accompany them. In the meantime, on the day before they are scheduled to sail, the Reverend Mr. Dimmesdale has been accorded the duty and the honor of preaching an Election Sermon. It is that moment of triumphant pride which precedes a tragic fall. Hawthorne leads up to it by tracing Dimmesdale's inner vacillations and conflicting emotions, and by setting the outer stage for a closing scene which releases the pent-up dramatic suspense.

Hawthorne's art is related to the drama less immediately than to the pulpit. It is the product of a cultural environment dominated by the ministry, where a work of fiction—if tolerated at all—had to be an *exemplum,* an anecdotal example illustrating an ethical precept. Typical was Hawthorne's parable of the black veil put on by a blameless minister in order to remind his congregation of their undisclosed sins. This is the opposite of Dimmesdale's concealment, which is exemplified when he compulsively puts his hand over his heart. The scarlet letter is even more overt than the black veil, and Hester's sentence is intended to convert her into "a living sermon against sin." But living, as it is practiced by the preacher, does not square with his sermonizing. His preliminary exhortation rings hollow; his solitary vigil on the scaffold is an evasion. Though the Election Sermon, his valediction, stirs its hearers to enthusiastic acclaim, Hester hears only its sorrow-laden undertone. The key modulates from theology to psychology, as it usually does with Hawthorne. At the close of the story, as at the beginning, the chorus of townspeople is seen and heard, placing the situation in social perspective. The holiday, the festive procession, the modest relaxations from "Puritanic gloom" highlight the desperate seriousness of the spokesman for the occasion. His speech is not so much precept as example: he reascends the scaffold, bares his breast, and exposes the brand. To be at peace with himself, like Raskolnikov in *Crime and Punishment,* he must publicly confess.

Unlike Dostoevsky's hero-villain, Dimmesdale has already suffered his punishment, and he willingly yields up his life with his guilty burden. Characteristically, his final action is surrounded with metaphysical uncertainties, leaving readers a choice of interpretations. Thus, if they do not believe in heavenly miracles or in Chillingworth's devilish magic, the emergence of the letter may be rationalized as the result of Dimmesdale's self-laceration. We are even informed of "highly respectable witnesses" who have denied the phenomenon, together with any carnal relationship between the clergyman and the fallen woman, and have interpreted his death in her arms as an exemplary act of Christian humility. But Hawthorne pointedly discounts that version. Among the numerous morals that might be drawn, he stresses chastity or virtuous conduct less than sincerity and willingness to acknowledge one's faults: "Be true! Show freely to the world, if not your worst, yet some trait whereby the worst may be inferred!" Truth is the extenuating virtue to which Hester Prynne has held fast, despite her transgression. Unfaithful as a wife, she has not been "false to the symbol on her bosom." Whereas the priest has not only polluted his cloth, but—by playing the hypocrite—has degraded his virtues into vices, and must pay heavily for his atonement. Each of the pair is appropriately punished for having broken the sacrament of marriage. Yet neither is as much to blame as Chillingworth, their victim who has become their accomplice and persecutor. "That old man's revenge," says Dimmesdale to Hester, "has been blacker than my sin."

It has been destructive and self-destroying, whereas their union— though unhallowed—has been unselfish and has become creative. This transposition of values is underscored when Pearl, their visible tie, confuses Chillingworth with the devil, alias the Black Man. Pearl herself is a "living hieroglyphic," especially meaningful when bedecked with wild flowers. She claims to have come into existence by being plucked from the rosebush that so symbolically flowers among the weeds at the prison door. Once she fills in her mother's ornament with prickly burrs; again she outlines a green A upon her own dress in eelgrass. Hawthorne's belief in correspondences between the natural and the spiritual worlds is manifest in all his descriptions of foliage. The doctor picks his mysterious herbs in the graveyard, where they hint unspoken crimes to Dimmesdale. Whatever the idea, it is rendered concrete by the image. Conversely, the imagery is emblematic and always pictures forth —as Hawthorne would say—some concept or other. His descriptive mode is what he elsewhere calls "the moral picturesque." Many of his short stories read like essays, where the moralist discourses about a pictorial illustration. His method of building up a longer narrative is to articulate a chain of such episodes, under captions which are indications of dramatis personae, scenic effects, or stage directions. Each episode dramatically centers on what we might regard as a *tableau vivant,* a group of figures posed in revealing attitudes, summed up in an aphoristic remark by one of them or the implicit comment of some telling detail.

Hawthorne's flair for symmetry controls his neat arrangement of chapters, as well as the balanced prose of his sentences. Apart from its prologue, *The Scarlet Letter* consists of twenty-four numbered sections, which can be coherently grouped in twos, threes, fours, and sixes, as readers may notice. The conclusion rounds out a pattern established by the opening scene, with Hester, then Dimmesdale, in the pillory. Both of those scenes are public occasions; the latter has had its private rehearsal at the midpoint, Chapter XII, "The Minister's Vigil." All three —plus Chapter VII, "The Governor's Hall"—may be considered as ceremonials, bringing the major characters into the choric presence of the community. These alternate with more intimate revelations, monologues where consciences are examined in Hawthornesque solitude, or dialogues where they confront one another with searching interviews: Hester-Chillingworth, Chillingworth-Dimmesdale, Dimmesdale-Hester. This trio of principal actors, the parties to the conjugal involvement, augmented by its elusive consequence, Pearl, forms a cast succinctly completed by a few minor characters modeled on historic originals: Richard Bellingham, governor of the colony; John Wilson, senior pastor at Boston; and Mistress Hibbins, alleged to be a witch. The story moves along with the rhythm of a detective thriller, quickening as its network of suspicion tightens and is confirmed. Hester and Chillingworth recognize each other at the commencement; Chillingworth recognizes Dimmesdale by the middle of the book; and Dimmesdale, Chillingworth midway through the second half.

The culmination is the recognition scene where Dimmesdale lays his soul bare to the multitude. As he dies, the purport of the letter becomes a matter of common knowledge. Yet it is more significant for the self-knowledge it has been imparting to those involved with it during the seven probationary years since the beginning, when Pearl was some three months old. Hester, unable to set it aside or to stay away for long, will return to live and die in its service, as we learn from a glancing epilogue. Chillingworth, wilting "like an uprooted weed," will die within a year, bequeathing his considerable fortune to Pearl. Her future, as a young American heiress abroad, may provoke our curiosity; but that is another story, it has been suggested, which might be better left to Henry James. The time-span of *The Scarlet Letter* can be dated by Pearl's infancy:

roughly, she is a child in arms for the first four chapters, three years old in Chapters V–VIII, and seven by Chapter XII. These dates can be grounded historically through the allusion to John Winthrop's death—actually March 26, 1649—on the night of the minister's vigil. Twelve more chapters, constituting the second half, culminate about two months afterward on Election Day. This does not make the tale a historical novel; in spite of Hawthorne's documentary touches, he is preoccupied with morals, not manners; and his title page announces "a romance." A romance about Puritanism is bound to be somewhat contradictory; but here the contradiction is logically resolved through the interplay between puritanical constraints and romantic impulses, between the rigid observances of the market place and the tangled passions of the forest.

More broadly speaking, these alternatives dramatize such typically American dilemmas as those of introspection against extroversion, nonconformity against standardization, and skeptical detachment against material progress. What is distinctive with Hawthorne is his emphasis on the more difficult choice. Ordinarily it seems easier for our authors to depict characters—for example, John Steinbeck's—rough in outward aspect but pure in heart. Hawthorne's portraiture is more refined; yet it catches traits of anguish and terror which, though they may never be completely eliminated, are blandly masked by the smiling surfaces that a later breed of Americans seems to prefer. We are told that the Election Sermon projected a glorious vision of our national destiny; yet the repercussions we feel are neither hopes nor promises; they are the agonies of Arthur Dimmesdale. Sin and death are not absent from Utopia, Hawthorne asserts upon his very first page. He did not enjoy his pessimism; he would have preferred to write sunnier books. The few rays of sunlight that shine in *The Scarlet Letter* are associated, through the image of Pearl, with his affection for his own daughter. But his gloomy ancestors maintain the upper hand; and when he speaks of combining recreation with solemnity, his metaphor is an honorific version of the letter itself: "a grotesque and brilliant embroidery to the great robe of state." To have spun an imaginary bit of old cloth into a subtly colored evocation of the Massachusetts Bay Colony, darkly shading toward the wilderness beyond it—the storyteller's skill at making much out of little has seldom been more effectively exercised.

REAPPRAISALS OF NOVELS, 4:
THE HOUSE OF THE SEVEN GABLES

Since my chapter on Hawthorne as a novelist in *The Power of Blackness* was devoted to tracing certain themes, there has been satisfaction in coming back to each of his three major novels for an independent reconsideration: to *The Scarlet Letter* in the foregoing piece, to *The Marble Faun* in an essay contributed to a centenary volume in 1964 and reprinted in *Refractions,* and to *The House of the Seven Gables* in the following introduction to a reprint of the standard Ohio State text (Cleveland: Charles E. Merrill Co., 1969).

"A romance on the plan of Gil Blas," Hawthorne will tell us, "adapted to American society and manners, would cease to be a romance." It would be a picaresque novel, by definition; and Hawthorne's point is that the worldly ups and downs of such fiction would soon be surpassed by the actualities of daily experience in the United States. All of his longer narratives are therefore presented to us as romances rather than as novels, through prefaces which claim the latitude of a more imaginative approach to a more transcendent reality. He is especially anxious to distinguish between the nebulous fabric of his *House of the Seven Gables* and the literal terrain where we are bound to locate it. He had taken his official leave of his native Salem in the custom-house sketch that introduced *The Scarlet Letter* a year before. Writing now in some detachment at Lenox amid the Berkshires, he did not specifically mention that old seaport which anchored his locale to Essex County. Nor do his descriptions match, in all aspects, the seven-gabled landmark to which sightseers flock in Salem today. But his prefatory disclaimer may need a grain or two of salt. Certain resemblances to local traditions or to family associations strike us as something more than coincidental. He was surprised to hear of surviving Pynchons, who were not happy about his use of their surname. Closer to home were his own Hathorne ancestors, guilty of hanging witches in their day, and cherishing claims to a lost estate in Maine.

The House of the Seven Gables, among all of Hawthorne's romances, seems to be the one that best accords with our expectations for a novel. That is to say, it informs us much more fully than the others with regard to manners, practical arrangements, and the tenor of everyday life. It also seems to be the author's sunniest book—a relative distinction, in view of the shadows that tended to darken his vision. Yet here his other distinctive traits, his humor and his fancy, are given freer play and more balanced expression. Above all, his lifelong preoccupation with the past, sometimes nostalgic, sometimes ambivalent, here takes the sharply negative form of a critique and a shift toward the present. From first to last, from *Mosses from an Old Manse* to *Our Old Home,* Hawthorne made an ancient dwelling-place the matrix for his observations and fantasies. He could perhaps be accused, like his spokesman Holgrave, of talking "as if this old house were a theatre," the perfect setting for an ancestral melodrama. The haunted castles of Gothic romance were atmospheric contrivances for the unfoldment of mysteries and, ultimately, for the exorcism of ghosts. Hence the ghost story pointed the way to the detective story, with Hawthorne's half-credulous skepticism occupying a middle ground. Poe, his fellow American Gothicist, had similarly discerned the features of "a human countenance" in the façade of a "venerable mansion." The ruins of his House of Usher were a physical counterpart to the psychological decay of its doomed occupant.

The residence of the Pyncheons is more substantially built, though not untainted by dry-rot and damp-rot. Though we scarcely expect to encounter a feudal castle abutting upon a side street of a Yankee mercantile town, the aristocratic pretensions of this particular domicile set it apart from its democratic neighbors. As an incarnation of its owners' lives, its implications are both historic and social, suggesting a degeneration of their original Puritan strain. Since their title is legally valid and yet not morally clear, it raises larger questions regarding the basis of the society that has sustained it. Where there has been such obvious success, there must likewise have been some obscure failures in the background. If the house of Pyncheon represents the exploiting class, then the exploited have had their representatives in the Maule family, who once owned the land and were dispossessed but retained as builders and artisans. Nor has the heritage itself proved an unmixed blessing for its heirs. Among the various jottings and adumbrations that lead from Hawthorne's *American Notebooks* to *The Seven Gables,* a paradoxical entry suggests the dynastic plight: "To inherit a great fortune. To inherit a great misfortune." The preface even speaks, though with reservations, of a moral: "the folly of tumbling down an avalanche of ill-gotten gold, or real estate, on the heads of an unfortunate posterity."

And the opening chapter proceeds to ask whether each generation, merely by accepting its inheritance, has not compounded the sin of its forefathers.

The middle of the nineteenth century, more than any other period, was the heyday of revolutionary ideologies. It is not surprising that *The Seven Gables* questions the basic institution of property itself just as intensively as the recent *Communist Manifesto,* though from the Hawthornesque angle of the individual conscience. Nothing short of class struggle has spelled the difference between the capitalism of the landholding Pyncheons and the houseless poverty of the proletarian Maules. When the elderly hired man, Uncle Venner, discusses what he likes to call his "farm," he manages to make an old people's home sound like an outpost of Utopia. His scorn for heaping "property upon property" allies him, comments Holgrave, to "the principles of Fourier." Holgrave, the outsider, has endeavored to become a practising socialist, has lived among the Fourierists in their phalansteries, and has consorted with "all manner of cross-looking philanthropists"—such as the reformers at Brook Farm, whom Hawthorne would go on to satirize in *The Blithedale Romance.* Only the other day it has been reported that Holgrave had delivered a wild speech. Yet his nervous landlady, Hepzibah Pyncheon, feels no fears about him; lawless as he may seem, "he has a law of his own!" It is her brother Clifford, the aberrant member of the clan, who voices the strongest misgivings over the status quo. In the climactic moments of their attempted escape, his eloquence mounts to a searing denunciation of what they have left behind them and all that it stands for.

What we call real estate—the solid ground to build a house on—is the broad foundation on which nearly all the guilt of this world rests. A man will commit almost any wrong—he will heap up an immense pile of wickedness, as hard as granite, and which will weigh as heavily upon his soul, to eternal ages—only to build a great, gloomy, dark-chambered mansion, for himself to die in, and for his posterity to be miserable in. He lays his own dead corpse beneath the underpinning, as one may say, and hangs his frowning picture on the wall, and, after thus converting himself into an Evil Destiny, expects his remotest great-grandchildren to be happy there!

Given a theme of such panoramic possibilities, we are impressed by the self-imposed limitations of Hawthorne's artistic economy. The deliberate effect is to emphasize the suffocating atmosphere of the little world inside, as contrasted with the unknown forces at large outside. The chronological scope of the story, when it occasionally flashes back across two centuries, compensates to some extent for the narrowness of the contemporary circles to which it is mainly confined. There are four living Pyncheons and, though the crucial fact is not revealed until the end, there is one survivor of the Maules. Four of these are dwellers in the house for most of the interim; the fifth of them, "The Pyncheon of To-day," stays conspicuously in abeyance until the occasion of his fateful visit. This is Judge Jaffrey Pyncheon, the forceful head of the disintegrating dynasty, and the sole extant descendant who has lived up to the purse-proud values of their colonial ancestry. Hawthorne's portrayal of him is frankly external; it has no depth beyond a bland hypocrisy which masks an unregenerate villainy; and the benevolent smile does not always succeed in concealing the inherent frown. In this respect, the Judge has a polar opposite in his cousin, the old maid Hepzibah; for, though she is gentle and timid by nature, nearsightedness has given her the semblance of a perpetual scowl and a consequent reputation for bad temper. An appropriate *châtelaine* for an antiquated household, she stands closest to the center of the narrative.

It is set in motion by a crisis—one of the few, we surmise, in her uneventful career. In anticipation of her brother's homecoming, she has resolved to eke out their sorry pittance with a commercial venture. Hawthorne dwells upon the incongruity of the small shop beneath the gable along the street, upon the sixty-year-old spinster's qualms of despairing gentility, and upon the pathetic ineptitude with which she brings herself to mind the counter. Her long day's ordeal finds relief that night, with the sudden arrival of her country cousin Phoebe, who will henceforth add the charms and energies of youth to a situation grimly needing them. The building already harbors another young tenant in the enigmatic person of Holgrave. He is very much a man of his epoch, independent, autodidactic, humanitarian, a jack of numerous trades. If he is now "the artist," in Hawthorne's epithet, his art is significantly based on a new mechanical invention. A daguerreotypist, he makes "pictures out of sunlight," as he cheerfully puts it, and he will have further light to throw upon the central mystery. The fourth inhabitant, the latest comer, is as deeply introverted as he himself is turned outward. To Clifford Pyncheon, released after thirty years of imprisonment on a questionable charge, his sister's mouldering home presents a prospect of liberation. His spirit has long been broken, but it had never been stern enough to bear his cousin's tribal rivalry. What remains of him is an emaciated and frustrated esthete, as the lodger again perceives: "this abortive lover of the Beautiful."

These five characters, to all intents and purposes, constitute the dramatis personae: the worn-out brother and the pallid sister, the youthful couple thrown together by happier circumstances, and the looming figure that menaces the happiness of them all. In addition, when needed, Uncle Venner plays the philosophical servant, while little Ned Higgins is the most regular customer of the cent-shop and almost the only one we get to know by name. Two passers-by, a man named Dixey and a nameless companion whose wife has lost five dollars on a similar enterprise, form a sort of chorus for Hepzibah's luckless endeavor. The continuous animation of the street scenes without offers a running contrast to the claustral sense of stagnation within. It is a modest spectacle that Clifford sits watching, a series of genre-pictures framed by his arched window, with an Italian organ-grinder and his monkey lending an unwonted touch of exotic color. Clifford in his turn makes a characteristic gesture when he indulges in a childish caprice for blowing soap-bubbles. When a political procession unexpectedly marches down Pyncheon-street, he has to be restrained from plunging over the balcony into the throng. Like so many of Hawthorne's personages, he is torn by the conflicting impulsions toward society and solitude. He is moved, along with Hepzibah, to attend church one Sunday; but they hardly venture to cross their threshold into the open air. "It is too late," he sadly tells her, as they shrink back into the dark passageway. "We are ghosts!"

Yet the moment comes when they are forced to leave their imprisoning shelter, when briefly and bewilderingly they find themselves "in the midst of life!—in the throng of our fellow-beings!" Their means of flight provides an exciting alternative to their housebound manner of existence heretofore. This is nothing less than the latest and most advanced vehicle of material progress, the railroad. The impact of steam locomotion upon the last century could be traced through the great novelists; it supplants the Dickensian stagecoach; it figures as a leading motive in the life and work of Tolstoy; and Henry James arrives at his most poignant metaphor when, in the garden scene of *The Ambassadors,* his middle-aged hero confesses that he has missed the train. Clifford and Hepzibah have all too belatedly caught it; and, since they have no destination in mind, their journey turns out to be futile. But, while she cannot escape from the mental images of the past, he can momentarily free himself to delight in the technological novelty, to hail the future portended by electricity and telegraphy. His harangue, more eloquent than coherent, is the dramatic climax. Gradually his hopeful vistas are overtaken by his obsessive memories; aimlessly the two dismount and the train glides away, leaving them at an isolated junction; and once more he tries to follow her faltering steps, which can only lead them homeward. For her it has been a dream, for him a short-lived awakening to reality. "Everything was unfixed from its age-long rest, and moving at whirlwind speed in a direction opposite to their own."

The rapid movement of this chapter, "The Flight of Two Owls," establishes a calculated disparity with the leisurely pace of the book as a whole, and particularly with the static fixity of the next chapter, "Governor Pyncheon." This is the grand anticlimax, an ironic set-piece, a kind of inquest over the dominant character, stricken dead at the height of his pride and guile and ambition. The nemesis that had humbled the founding progenitor, Colonel Pyncheon, has stalked the Judge down in the Colonel's chair and stigmatized him with the congenital bloodstain of apoplexy. That stroke of poetic justice, which incidentally fulfills the wizard's curse of the eldest Maule, inspires a mocking and macabre revery. The Judge's watch ticks through the scheduled hours of the afternoon, the evening, and the night. His unfulfilled agenda becomes an exposure of his *modus vivendi*: the round of his engagements, the profit of his investments, the prize of politics within his grasp—for, as irony will have it, he misses the dinner where he is to be nominated for the governorship of the state. The visitation of death, so reluctantly acknowledged, reduces these mundane concerns to the plane of nothingness. "Time, all at once, appears to have become [/] a matter of no moment with the Judge!" The commentary rises to blank verse and sinks into a quasi-Shakespearean pun. Two years later, in *Bleak House,* Dickens would pronounce the same sort of funeral oration over the corpse of his officious attorney: "For, Mr. Tulkinghorn's time is over for evermore ..."

Hawthorne was self-consciously playing with his theme, and presenting his fantasies as hypotheses, when he summoned up the shades of the departed Pyncheons. "Ghost-stories are hardly to be treated seriously, any longer," he apologizes. We are conscious throughout of the narrator's presence; once he expressly tells us that he will enlighten us further "in another paragraph"; and the habitation itself is visualized through "the writer's recollection . . . from boyhood." In his attitude toward his subject matter, he often seems to be more of a casual essayist than a conventional storyteller. Thus he will introduce a scene with an aphorism or generalization: "Life, within doors, has few pleasanter prospects than a neatly arranged and well-provisioned breakfast-table . . ." When the sister thinks of entertaining her brother by singing and accompanying herself on the long-silent harpsichord, Hawthorne's reaction is sympathetically whimsical: "Poor Clifford! Poor Hepzibah! Poor harpsichord! All three would have been miserable together." The narrator, though he is virtually omniscient, withholds certain secrets from his readers; though he is ordinarily benign, he maintains some distance from his characters. Their defining characteristics are repeatedly stressed, not so much by epithets as by elegant variations: the old maid becomes an "elderly maiden." Hawthorne's style has a cultivated elegance which was already somewhat faded in its time, which is rich in reminiscence from earlier English writers, and which often touches off mock-heroic reverberations. Narration and description are interspersed with editorial comment, psychological analysis, and frequent moral judgment.

We are often reminded that the story follows the basic outlines of a morality. For Clifford and Hepzibah, the Judge is like Giant Despair, pursuing Christian and Hopeful in *The Pilgrim's Progress*. A money-minded New Englander passes the supplicant monkey "without imagining how nearly his own moral condition was here exemplified." But Hawthorne, the habitual spectator, is there to bring home the observation. Fiction, for him, must be a mode of exemplification, as is evident from his chapter headings—or from his notes on "Remarkables," many of which he has utilized in this volume. He cannot refer to "rank weeds" without parenthetically stating that they are "symbolic of the transmitted vices of society." The urchin who devours Hepzibah's stock of gingerbread cookies becomes, for duly specified reasons, "the very emblem of old Father Time." Trivial matters take on an emblematic significance, and incidental details are viewed as symbols of cosmic forces at work. The smile on the Judge's face has its metaphorical reduction in the labored shine upon his shoes. The beast-fable of Chanticleer and his two hens serves as a diminutive underplot, even as the scenes in the garden counterpoint those in the house. Hawthorne, in both, draws on the full resources of his pictorial talent. Here, as in so many of his shorter stories, actual pictures are used to enhance the characterization: the lowering portrait of the Puritan Colonel, the daguerreotype of the Judge which so strongly resembles it, and the delicate miniature of Clifford by Malbone. Holgrave will take another photograph at a conclusive moment.

> The author needs great faith in his reader's sympathy; else he must hesitate to give details so minute, and incidents apparently so trifling, as are essential to make up the idea of this garden-life. It was the Eden of a thunder-smitten Adam, who had fled for refuge thither out of the same dreary and perilous wilderness, into which the original Adam was expelled.

Hawthorne is peculiarly himself, both when he is communing informally with his reader and when he is relating his habitat to the landscape of the Fall. Some of his tales, like "The Birthmark" and "Rappaccini's Daughter," come to mind when we read the episode of "Alice Pyncheon," the eighteenth-century heroine who is mesmerized by the vengeful glance of a contemporaneous Maule. This tale is ascribed to the versatile Holgrave, and it comprises a tragic pendant to the narrative in its seriocomic fullness. Structurally, the romance shows the careful arrangement, the articulation of episodes, and the penchant for symmetry that are the hallmarks of Hawthorne's craftsmanship. His habit of antithesis comes out strongly in such juxtapositions as "May and November" or "The Scowl and the Smile." The book, consisting of twenty-one chapters, is divisible into three equal sections of seven chapters apiece. The first section, starting from a retrospective sketch of the house and its legend, brings together its four inhabitants, culminating with the chapter about Clifford's advent, "The Guest." That long-drawn-out day when Hepzibah opens her shop is covered by three chapters (II, III, IV). The continuity thence through the second section (VIII–XIV) takes about a month, whereupon the newly established routine is temporarily interrupted by "Phoebe's Good-Bye." Action quickens as we meet the crisis in the third section. Moving through another eventful day—the fifth of a storm—we spend the night with "Governor Pyncheon" (XV–XVIII), welcoming back the survivors on the morrow and reaching the solutions to their problems.

Hawthorne is at his best in rounding the transition from his eerie nocturnal watch to the light of a normal morning: the bustle of the tradesmen and children along the street, the emergence of Uncle Venner to do his chores, the unanswered tinkle of the shop-bell, the organ-grinder performing vainly before the deserted abode. An aura of suspense has been conjured up by the obscure linkage between the Judge's death and the cousins' departure, with suspicion pointing to them because of their panic. But reunion furnishes explanation, and all the remaining ambiguities are soon resolved in the terminal chapter. The secret the Judge was seeking, which might have been dimly apprehended by Clifford, has been well known to Holgrave, it mysteriously transpires. When he touches a hidden spring in the wall, the Colonel's portrait falls symbolically to the floor, and within the recess behind it lies an ancient deed from the Indians which validates the Pyncheons' claim to a vast eastern territory. Yet, since it has been obsolete for several generations, it can only help to exorcise Maule's curse. Moreover, Holgrave now explains his special knowledge by putting aside his incognito and revealing himself as a latterday descendant of the Maules. Since he and Phoebe have fallen in love, of course, the feud between the families will be forever pacified by their marriage. And since it likewise appears—by a final twist of coincidence—that the Judge's son has died abroad, she is the last of the line and will inherit the ultimate fortune.

With the lovers Hawthorne harks back, as he frequently did, as he would do at length in *The Marble Faun,* to the imagery of the primordial garden. "They were conscious of nothing sad nor old. They transformed the earth, and made it Eden again, and themselves the two first dwellers in it." One portent of this transfiguration is that the straggling plants associated with Alice Pyncheon have suddenly burst into crimson bloom. Another is that the overspreading elm has weathered the gale with but a single change: one of its branches has turned to autumnal gold, and gleams like the mystical bough that gained Aeneas his admittance to the world of shades. It could not be expected that Phoebe would wish to settle down under the seven gables, or that Holgrave would give up his resolve "to build a house for another generation." For the time being, they will live together with Hepzibah and Clifford—not to mention Uncle Venner and Chanticleer—at the country estate of the unlamented Judge. But though the elder pair seems entitled, at this stage, to accept the windfall and enjoy its amenities without much self-questioning, it is hard to imagine the bride and groom living there happily ever after. If they are still sensitive to houses, surely they will recoil again from the evil destiny personified by the builder and late owner. Holgrave is entrammeled in an implicit contradiction, more or less glossed over by hints that his radical zeal will mellow into conservatism when he becomes a responsible householder.

Hawthorne acutely sensed the weaker sides of both positions: the naïve inexperience of the modernist, wanting everything to be changed overnight, and the vested interest of the traditionalist, clinging and conforming to outmoded institutions. Yet, despite the compromise of its happy ending, *The Seven Gables* is essentially modern and iconoclastic in its emphasis. The cumulative burden of accusation falls squarely upon the past and upon its material legacy, property. The principal object lesson is the house itself, both as a monument of obsolescence and as a socioeconomic issue. Its owners themselves are victimized by its morbid influences; its transient guests are lucky to escape from its cobwebs, dust, and encrustations. The deliverance of the individual from some reclusive state to a viable relationship with "the whole sympathetic chain of human nature"—this is the simple pattern of an allegory which Hawthorne never tired of elaborating in one guise or another. In *The Seven Gables* we have his amplest, most concrete and vivid treatment of that problem, shadowing forth its relevance to our day. When Holgrave inveighs against "the influence which Dead Men have among living affairs," he is voicing an argument which Hawthorne had set down for himself in his notebooks. His attack on the dead hand of the past is actually a plea for facing the present, an affirmation more directly developed by his erstwhile Concord neighbor, Emerson: "Our age is retrospective. It builds the sepulchres of the fathers . . . Why should not we also enjoy an original relation to the universe?"

DICKENS AFTER A CENTURY

The centennial of the death of Dickens in 1970 was signalized by a resounding fanfare of literary tributes, an enormous accretion to a critical and scholarly bibliography which has been much expanded in recent years. Even Dr. Leavis seems to have relented for the occasion. This article was my small offering, published by the *American Scholar* in its sequence of "Reappraisals" (Autumn, 1970). My own renewal of interest has been taking further shapes in connection with the Victorian humorists.

I

"I never saw such a baby," exclaims the doctor in *Nicholas Nickleby*. There never was such a plum pudding, or whatever other object may have been served up, as there is when Dickens dishes it out. Nothing was ever so fine a specimen of its kind as those nonpareils which populate his fiction. The formula is slightly ambiguous; it could mean, of course, that they never had really existed. But rather it seems to affirm that their existence has been unique, that they have a certain quiddity or essence which reveals them as peculiarly themselves. Many of them likewise have attained a typicality, so that their odd names stand out as labels for attitudes: Pickwickian, Pecksniffian, Podsnappian. That there never was such a novelist as Dickens became evident at the outset of his career, when he accepted and gloried in the title of "the Inimitable Boz." It is not less evident a hundred years after his death. He has been widely imitated nonetheless, and by—along with lesser talents—Dostoevsky, Kafka, Shaw, and Brecht.

It might be said that the critical standing of Dickens has undergone two major changes, and that the first occurred when he died on June 9, 1870, midway through the composition of his fifteenth novel, *The Mystery of Edwin Drood*. There never was a writer who, during his lifetime, maintained so vital a contact with his readers. Since the novels came out serially, month by month and sometimes week by week, and since he wrote against monthly or weekly deadlines, an enormous and continuous feedback set the rhythms of his life. Like contributors to the *New Yorker,* he adapted the climate of the story to the appropriate season of the year. Each installment was in effect a one-man magazine, and its three or four chapters catered to the assorted interests of all the family with romance and satire, pathos and caricature, not to mention editorializing on current issues. Let us not forget that he was first of all a reporter, whose ear for the varieties of speech had been stenographically trained in court and Parliament.

But journalistic enterprise, which could probe the consequences of the New Poor Law in *Oliver Twist* or expose the scandal of the Yorkshire schools in *Nicholas Nickleby,* was merely the starting point. Sloppy, the mangle-boy in *Our Mutual Friend,* has a small share of his creator's gifts: "He do the police in several voices." (We have recently learned that this pithy sentence served as working title for another evocation of London street-cries, T. S. Eliot's *Waste Land.*) True mimetic genius, never content with bald reproduction, puts its own stamp on the objects of its mimicry. Dickens' "sharp perception of character and oddity" was self-proclaimed in a letter written at twenty, asking the manager of Covent Garden for a part in a play. That histrionic flair found implicit compensation throughout his writing. More explicitly, like Mr. Wopsle in *Hamlet,* he constantly involved his friends in amateur theatricals. Ultimately he consummated his love for the theater by his twelve-year affair with Ellen Ternan, an actress half his age. Through public readings, which ended by exhausting him, he played directly to his audience.

Thus the first change came when, ceasing to be a contemporary, he became a classic. A set of Dickens, despite the un-Victorian irony of his long-concealed private life, was accorded a special sort of domestic status, like a family Bible illustrated by Gustave Doré. His lifelong affinity with children was corroborated by the place he held amid their earliest serious reading. Just as Greek adolescents learned from Homer, so Dickens furnished generations of Anglo-Americans with their first articulated models of the world. Never mind if those models were heavily charged with more pity and terror than experience was likely to bring. The exaggerations were necessary, in order to make a full impact, and salutary, in arousing patterns of response. The historical point that we must note, which marks the second major change in Dickens' position, is that his works can less and less be reckoned—by one of his favorite phrases—as "household words." Indeed it has been a generation since a professor could take for granted that his students had read half of them before coming to college.

This is a simple corollary to the obvious fact that the television generation has meanwhile come of age; indeed its senior members now are crossing that precarious dividing line at thirty. It is not my purpose to discuss rival media, or to broach the problems of popular culture—though it may be pertinent to recall how masterfully Dickens controlled them through the literary instruments of his day. If his books have lost the consecration of the nursery and the schoolroom, then secularization brings certain advantages. They can be freshly rediscovered as books. To the intellectuals of the nineteen-twenties—in Bloomsbury, for example—he seemed much too middlebrow to be taken seriously. Consequently most critics benignly neglected him. Significantly, it was in the year of stress 1940 that the staunch and far-sighted George Orwell published his pioneering essay in revaluation. Shifting the interpretation from social toward psychological ground, Edmund Wilson contributed his penetrating biographical essay, "The Two Scrooges," during the following year. (Some sort of cycle in taste is rounded when we remember that 1941 was also the year that saw the demise of James Joyce.)

At the same time an Oxford don, Humphry House, in publishing his compact monograph, *The Dickens World,* welcomed our subject into the field of academic scholarship. Theretofore, with the predictable exception of one massive study in German, it had been studied chiefly by the hobbyists, collectors, and antiquarians who have kept their chatty periodical, *The Dickensian,* going for seventy years. Professional attention is now bearing such belated fruits as the compendious Pilgrim Edition of Dickens' letters and the reediting of his maltreated texts. Doctoral dissertations are multiplying; scholarly and critical publications are making as much of Dickens as of Melville or Faulkner; and Geiger counters are finding every rift of Noddy Boffin's dustheap richly loaded with symbolic ore. At all events, we have come a long way since Henry James was allowed to dismiss the book in question, *Our Mutual Friend,* as superficial. When he cavalierly asserted that it would be "an offense against humanity to place Mr. Dickens among the greatest novelists," James made clear why he himself—for all his charm and sensibility—does not belong in that class.

2

The Dickens who goes on casting his spell today is manifestly different from the author who so engrossed his contemporaries, or from that other author of the same name who exerted so wistful an appeal over the last generation of the nineteenth century and the first generation of the twentieth. To take the later first, because he barely existed, this was the pseudo-Dickens who virtually parodied himself in *The Old Curiosity Shop*. One of his weakest novels, it has at least the strength to move out of those premises after a chapter or two (reversing Stendhal's *Charterhouse of Parma,* which does not arrive at the announced location until the final page). Little Nell and her grandfather, dispossessed from the antiques, face some harsh realities in the Midlands, and conclude their pilgrimage among the Gothic antiquities of a rustic church and graveyard. Mr. House informs us that the original London antique-shop was torn down long ago; yet a tourist trap continues to operate in its name, associating Dickens with the quaint and picturesque past. In his time he hated the feudal past and addressed himself to the radical present.

His *Child's History of England* is peppered with value judgments bearing out such views. Both of his historical novels, *Barnaby Rudge* and *A Tale of Two Cities,* are headlong confrontations with the ambivalent nightmares of riot and revolution. The Dickensians gave their warmest allegiance to his first novel, *Pickwick Papers*—if we may call it a novel, when it calls itself a miscellany like *The Spectator Papers*. This providential work, which brought him fame and fortune at twenty-five, opportunely appeared in the pivotal year when Queen Victoria ascended the throne, 1837. But it is set a decade earlier, and it habitually harks back via the Regency toward the eighteenth century. Furthermore, it typically expresses the nostalgia of the cockney for the countryside. Dickens was well aware that the highroad ran in two directions. The "Yoho" of the stagecoach would soon be supplanted by the less melodious noise of the railway, whose herald he would become. He would become the laureate of chimney pots and areaways. And Mr. Pickwick's rural rides and sentimental excursions would lead back to much grimmer places, the law court and the prison.

Dickens is himself responsible for his association with the cult of Christmas, which he shamelessly exploited. Yet most of his *Christmas Stories* have their ghostly aspect. If they have a common moral, it is that Christmas comes but once a year; the tinsel is evanescent, and the plum pudding doled out sparingly. He may well have felt some temperamental kinship when he edited the memoirs of the sad clown, Grimaldi. Riotous as Dickens' humor can be, it is seldom far from heartache. There was much in him of Mark Tapley, that puritanical jester, who is so jolly by constitution that there can be "no credit in it" unless he sustains the jollity under the most trying conditions. Accordingly, he accompanies Martin Chuzzlewit through the severest of trials, actually the source of Dickens' greatest undeception, a visit to the United States—where he found public opinion so oppressive that he declared he could never have written his novels here. If we associate good cheer with Dickens, then we must recognize that he was whistling in the dark. Equally insistent was the impulse of *Pickwick*'s Fat Boy: "I wants to make your flesh creep."

We may be reminded of Bunyan's allegory, if not of Hogarth's plates, when we recall that *Oliver Twist* was subtitled *The Parish Boy's Progress*. Oliver's protesting gesture against the workhouse appeals as strongly to the sense of hunger as Dickens' holiday dinners appeal to the appetite. The visceral reaction he sought and gained has been accurately registered by William Saroyan: "I read *Oliver Twist* and said, 'What the hell kind of place is that?'" Where such earlier books called for the reform of particular social abuses, the later books are more general—and increasingly subversive—in their indictment of society as a whole. Government bureaucracy, as satirized in the Circumlocution Office of *Little Dorrit,* is perhaps an inevitable target. But the critique goes much deeper in *Bleak House,* when it assails the most fundamental of British institutions, the law. "Money cannot buy everything" may be the naïve lesson of the book whose full title brings it out: *Dealings with the Firm of Dombey and Son.* But *Hard Times* vies with Marx and Engels in its frontal attack upon business, laissez-faire economics, the industrial system itself.

The uncharacteristic austerity *of Hard Times* may help to explain why it is the only work of Dickens that F. R. Leavis admits to his private canon of great English novels. Even Dr. Leavis perceives that the grimness of Coketown is counterbalanced, to some extent, by Mr. Sleary's circus. Yet, although "people mutht be amuthed," this amusement is more pathetic than comic. Dickens' tractlike reportage on the striking workers can hardly withstand comparison with the close observation of Elizabeth Gaskell's contemporaneous novels of Manchester. Nor is his individualistic proletarian, Stephen Blackpool, any more convincing than his last holdout against parochial welfare, Betty Higden in *Our Mutual Friend.* There, in his last completed novel, his institutional imagination has outdone itself, with the sharpness of Swift's reversal in the Fourth Book of *Gulliver's Travels.* For now, in place of the organizing conception that usually related his dramatis personae to one another, the landmark is a monument to human disorganization, the detritus of civilization itself, the dustheap: refuse, garbage and debris. The song and film of *Alice's Restaurant* have been updating that metaphor of organized society as a dump.

Though Dickens worked for various philanthropic causes, he had no political program for solving the issues that he so graphically presented. If Cuffy and Duffy were voted into office, they would probably do no better than Coodle and Doodle—or, for that matter, the M.P. from Eatanswill. Dickens' courtroom recollections combined with his innate theatricality to produce scenes of comedy and suspense. Yet, always more of an advocate than a judge, when he tries his central case we never get to court. The fog that winds its way down Chancery Lane is the aura of legal obfuscation, the "Wiglomeration" of *Bleak House*. Its fictional entanglements are artfully contrived to underline the judicial ones. Sooner or later all of the characters stand interlinked by the bonds of interest—as several of them are by coincidental kinship—in a chain which extends from the proud estate at Chesney Wold to the fetid slum, Tom-All-Alone's, from the stately Sir Leicester Dedlock to the street-sweeping urchin Jo. A ray of sunshine, glinting down unexpectedly from the cross on the dome of Saint Paul's, conveys a cinematic suggestion that men might somehow live by other values.

3

Critical discussion of late has more than made up for the secrecy of Dickens in veiling the double trauma that did so much to shape his psychological outlook. His Micawberish father's imprisonment for debt had humiliated the twelve-year-old son still further by sending him to work in a miserable shoe-blacking factory. The episode has been fictionalized in *David Cooperfield,* where the youth is compelled to paste labels on wine bottles in Murdstone and Grinby's warehouse. Blacking-bottles turn up thematically, almost like King Charles's head in Mr. Dick's memorandum. We first encounter Sam Weller when he is performing his menial duties by blacking boots at the inn. As for the theme of paternal durance, shades of the prison house fall somewhere in nearly every volume. Even Mr. Pickwick is condemned to the Fleet. The two historical novels reach their respective climaxes with the storming of Newgate and the Bastille. Through the person of William Dorrit,

Dickens restaged his prodigal parent's sojourn in the Marshalsea. Often his fictional children reverse their family roles like Jenny Wren, treating her drunken father as a child.

Hence to the mooted question of child labor Dickens brought an unconfessed but experienced awareness which few Victorian reformers could match. Moreover his imagination, at its most impressionable stage, had been moulded by sudden exposure to poverty and by firsthand acquaintance with so many of London's saddest streets. Well might Master Humphrey shake his head over "the initiation of children into the ways of life, when they are scarcely more than infants." If they then appear to be precocious, they have earned the right. No other major writer has focused so intently on childhood, let alone unhappy childhood. There are more than thirty schools in Dickens' books, each of them a different kind of social microcosm. The deaths of children are his moral touchstones, as with poor Jo, and that of Little Nell may seem bathetic to our taste; yet Dickens, with his penchant for happy endings, was commendably firm in holding out against grief-stricken readers who sought a reprieve for her. It had to end that way because he had lived through it, with the death of his beloved young sister-in-law, Mary Hogarth.

" 'Tis the eye of childhood," we learn from *Macbeth,* "That fears a painted devil." This formulation is apt in suggesting on the one hand the narrative viewpoint of Dickens, the childlike nature of his sensibilities, and on the other the bugbears and grotesques, the nightmares that turn out to be all too real—such as the faces of Fagin and Monks, sneering at Oliver through the window of his not-quite-safe haven with Mr. Brownlow. There was never such a golden lad as Steerforth because he is glimpsed through the hero-worshipping glances of his junior schoolmate, David Copperfield. David also visualizes the Murdstones larger than life, more terrible than they would have appeared to adults, and many of Dickens' villains are no more than intimidating elders as viewed from the wide eyes of terrified adolescence—Mr. Gradgrind, for instance, as introduced while expounding his utilitarian pilosophy to the cowed pupils of Mr. M'Choakumchild's school. Orphans, waifs, street urchins, wards in chancery come closest to the center of consciousness. This is demonstrated by the narratives that Dickens wrote in the first person: David's, Pip's in *Great Expectations,* and Esther's half of *Bleak House.*

The utilitarian demand for "Facts, facts, facts"—Mr. Gradgrind's

Manchester refrain—has thus been transmuted by fantasy. Dickens never, for all his underlying concern with reality, professed himself a realist. Rather he might have promised, as Jemmy Trotter did to Mr. Pickwick, "a romance of real life." *Bleak House* was to reveal "the romantic side of familiar things." His chief Edwardian devotee, G. K. Chesterton, recognized in Dickens a "mythologist." Dickens tells us how he was fascinated, in his London boyhood, by the words "MOOR EEFFOC" on a swinging glass door. Before he thought of turning the letters around, they seemed an invitation to some adventure out of *The Arabian Nights*. Like Balzac or Baudelaire in Paris, like Gogol or Dostoevsky in Saint Petersburg, he poetized the modern metropolis. Every shop could be as interesting as the Old Curiosity Shop, not least the marine supply store of Sol Gills. That is why Dickens' stories have the quality of modernized fairy tales. They reenact the Christmas pantomime of the babes in the wood, with capitalism playing the part of the wicked witch. The age-old morality play of Everychild is brought up to date.

In the preface to *Oliver Twist* Dickens frankly confessed his moralistic intention: "to show . . . the principle of Good winning through every adverse circumstance, and triumphing at last." No wonder Oliver comes through so very abstractly, so little touched by adversity that he speaks a language he could never have picked up under the circumstances. Little Nell, too, is a principle of Good; and, since she fares so much less happily, it follows that the principle of Evil triumphs in *The Old Curiosity Shop*. This is incarnate in the exuberant monster Quilp, whose dwarfish figure seems modeled on Shakespeare's Richard III, and whose malevolence carries him far beyond mere self-interest or any sort of plausible motivation. Sometimes the forces of darkness seem so powerful, and the virtuous figures so frail, the malefactors so resourceful, and the balance of power so uncertain, that we must agree with Graham Greene and consider Dickens a Manichaean. However, there are countervailing forces of benevolence, avuncular philanthropists and professional benefactors like the Cheeryble brothers who befriend Nicholas Nickleby. Normally their pity allays the terror; flight leads to rescue, exile to return; and the orphan finds a surrogate for his lost parentage.

The allegorical conflicts are fought out against ever-changing odds. As the perspective broadens and deepens, it tends to overshadow the individuals caught up in it. Mr. Dombey may be punished for his pride,

Martin Chuzzlewit chastened for his selfishness. But the network of human relations becomes so complex, the alternatives so difficult to choose, that it is the condition of England which seems to be—as they say in Lancashire—"aw a muddle." The initial faith in philanthropy is displaced by the mordant radicalism that came to the surface with *Hard Times*. Regularly Dickens' last installments are grand finales, where lovers are united, old scores settled, and prizes handed out. But lost illusions—to echo Balzac's title—set the basic pattern for realistic fiction. Dickens planned to close *Great Expectations* with an unhappy ending; expectations had given way to disappointments; only the itervention of Bulwer-Lytton blurred the equivocal conclusion. *Our Mutual Friend*, though it crosses class barriers to unite its lovers, finally hears them condemned by "the voice of society." It may not be accidental that *Edwin Drood*, where the ghoulish strain is pushed farthest, never saw completion.

4

We cannot talk about Dickens without acknowledging his proneness to melodrama and sentimentality. Melodrama is drama in which we do not believe; sentimentality is emotion that we do not share. Hence, instead of identifying with a situation, we tend to be alienated from it. But alienation suggests a Brechtian clue to some of Dickens' most characteristic effects. One of his unsympathetic critics, the usually sympathetic Virginia Woolf, charged that "whenever plot burns low he throws on another character." Plot is distinctly minimal in Mrs. Woolf's own fiction, whereas Dickens constructed his plots with mounting elaboration, beginning from the periodical essay and ending with a murder mystery. Now, insofar as Inspector Bucket is the forerunner of Sherlock Holmes and Sam Spade, it can be observed that the modern novel has been relegating that vein of interest to the detective story or spy thriller. Serious novelists have concentrated mainly on characterization. Dickens was downgraded by E. M. Forster's well-known distinction between round and flat characters. But those simplistic metaphors were already superseded by the fourth-dimensional fiction of Tolstoy or Proust, which comes closer to the plane of Dickens than to that of Mrs. Woolf and Mr. Forster.

Admittedly, Dickens has something to answer for, which his ready imitators could reduce to clichés, such as the rough diamonds of Bret

Harte or the good-natured goons of John Steinbeck. His characters pursue, or rather overtake, that mellow tradition of English eccentrics which stems from my Uncle Toby and Parsons Adams and Primrose. What makes them most extraordinary—for we cannot expect them, all or any, to be plumbed by the introspection that Proust reserved for his ego—is their variety and plenitude. No less than 360 identifiable personages have been counted in *Pickwick Papers* alone. Taxidermists or bassoon players constitute a respectable, but rather specialized and limited, segment of the population. Who but Dickens would have thought of portraying Mr. Venus in his shop or Matthew Bagnet at home? Dickens' casts swarm with character-roles and bit-parts, even when they have little to do with advancing the situation. Purposes of the story momentarily call for a surgeon in *Bleak House,* Mr. Bayham Badger. Dickens enthusiastically throws in portrayals not only of Mrs. Badger but, through portraits pointed out on the wall, of her two lamented former husbands, Captain Swosser of the Royal Navy and Professor Dingo of European reputation.

Working on so vast a scale, Dickens frequently had to project a character through a few telling impressions. But such *tics* were keys to personality, like the clammy handshake of Uriah Heep. Playing by ear, he provided many of his spokesmen with verbal leitmotifs, such as Sam's Wellerisms or the *mots de caractère* of the Micawbers. Some of them speak an idiolect, a dialect spoken by a single person, notably Sairey Gamp in *Martin Chuzzlewit,* who speaks not only for herself but for her imaginary devotee, Mrs. Harris. All of them derive their special vividness from the fact that Dickens conceived them as dramatic roles, and some of them seem to be conscious of this fact: Dick Swiveller in *The Old Curiosity Shop,* whose speeches are medleys of tavern songs, romantic doggerel, and smart-aleck slang. Consciously the Boffins act out a play for the moral benefit of Bella Wilfer in *Our Mutual Friend*. Inevitably, in moving so quickly from book to book, Dickens indulged in a considerable amount of type-casting: such little mothers as Agnes Wickfield and Esther Summerson, such redeemable wastrels as Sidney Carton and Eugene Wrayburn. Yet here the variations are meaningful, and the successive versions bring out refinements.

Little Dorrit marks some improvement over Little Nell, while Little Emily belongs to a wholly different breed. "Little." Dickens' fondness for the diminutive is most revelatory when he is depicting those human growths which have been stunted by the big city, the Smallweeds and their ilk, Lilliputian types remembered from his apprenticeship as a lawyer's office-boy. Those who would consign his creatures to Mrs. Jarley's exhibit of waxworks should reconsider the psychological insight embodied in the scarred malice of Rosa Dartle (*David Copperfield*), the tormented lesbianism of Miss Wade (*Little Dorrit*), the smoldering tension of Bradley Headstone (*Our Mutual Friend*), the drug-induced schizophrenia of John Jasper (*Edwin Drood*). Although Dickens' method does not give us their thoughts, it makes us understand their behavior. Nor, in his maturity, is he so facile in linking external features to virtue and vice. Fagin, the evil Jew of *Oliver Twist,* is offset by the good Jew, Riah of *Our Mutual Friend*. The straight protagonist shows a marked development, starting from absolute scratch with Oliver, than whom nobody could be more straight. *Nicholas Nickleby,* even to its alliterative title, follows the easy-going picaresque pattern inherited from *Roderick Random* and *Peregrine Pickle.* So does Martin Chuzzlewit, though he has graver faults to be cured by his more hazardous journey.

With *David Copperfield* the picaresque form has grown into a *Bildungsroman,* an apprenticeship to life which is especially memorable because so much of it is deeply rooted in autobiographical reminiscence. Returning to this mode in *Great Expectations,* Dickens all but perfected it, though his terminal revisions and retractions somewhat marred that perfection. Though David's sentimental education has its up and downs, the direction is generally upward: the standard bourgeois ascent from rags to riches. Pip's social climb is both more tragic and more ironic. Behind his narration we seem to hear other voices, which hint that he has been pursuing false values and that his rise in the world is headed not unjustly for a fall. The recognition that he owes his fortune to the convict Magwitch, that his benefactor has been a malefactor, cuts through all the ethical lines that have previously been drawn and confirms the socialistic suspicion that property is theft. Similarly, the heritage in *Our Mutual Friend* is the insidious dustheap. The incognito role of the mutual friend John Harmon, not unlike that of Arthur Clennam in *Little Dorrit,* and not unlike that of the Caliph Haroun al Raschid in *The Arabian Nights,* is to explore the mysteries and palliate the inequities of Bagdad on the Thames.

Such was the role that Dickens had assigned to himself. Those novels in which he confronted the theme of revolution directly if retrospectively, though not altogether successful, must have taught him how to spread out the panoramic vistas of *Bleak House, Hard Times, Little Dorrit,* and *Our Mutual Friend.* The consciousness of suffering and folly imparted by these testamentary works would be intolerable, were it not for the wild flow of high spirits, the boundless energy and matchless gusto. Was Dickens, in the long run, an optimist or a pessimist? The answer must be that, like most of us, he was more or less manic-depressive. His abnormally acute gaze oscillated, with nervous volatility, from the Christmas tree to the Tyburn gallows. It is understandable and enviable that our comfortable parents and grandparents should have loved him for reflecting all their eupeptic images of quaintness, cheerfulness, and reassurance. We may be more struck by his visions of crime and violence, trials and prisons, pollution and protest, smug officialdom and desperate deprivation, urban blight and political divisiveness, mob scenes and picket lines, as we enter the second century of his posthumous fame.

PROUST, GIDE, AND THE SEXES

This demurrer is the only thing I ever wrote for the *Publications of the Modern Language Association,* wherein it appeared in June, 1950, together with a short and gracious rejoinder from Justin O'Brien. The line of argument against which I was demurring is indicated below, and I fear I did no more than scotch it; for it continues to wind its sinuous way through George Painter's massive but uncritical biography of Proust. Some twenty years ago it was really a breakthrough when such a problem could be seriously discussed in a scholarly journal; and Professor O'Brien's boldness in broaching it was matched by his fairness in meeting my objections, so that our controversy ended happily in a friendly debate at a subsequent meeting of the MLA. Since then, by his premature death, we have lost one of our most active and effective mediators between French and American culture.

The publication of "Albertine the Ambiguous: Notes on Proust's Transposition of Sexes" in the issue of December 1949 (XLIV, 933–952), reflects much credit on the courage of *PMLA* and on the candor of the author, Justin O'Brien. By isolating the most delicate of the many problems raised by Proust's great novel and reviewing it in the light of external and internal testimony, by pursuing and subsuming the trend of investigation that Robert Vigneron signalized thirteen years ago, this article makes it henceforth possible to discuss on the plane of scholarly inquiry what has heretofore subsisted at the level of literary gossip. Professor O'Brien is knowledgeably aware of the complexities and inconsistencies that hedge his subject, and he shows a courteous regard for interpretations which differ from his own. If I venture briefly to formulate my difference with him here, it is because he has cited me as a supporter of what ought now perhaps to be deemed a naïve and obsolescent view: the assumption that Proust, since he himself described Albertine as female, did not really envisage her as male. Somewhat more brusquely, in a later footnote, Professor O'Brien relegates this assumption to the realm of "serious error." I respectfully submit that, when mere acquiescence in a novelist's own designation of the sex of his heroine is held to be erroneous, we have reached a confusing epoch in the history of criticism. A heavy burden of proof falls upon any critic who sets his word against the word of the writer he is discussing. Until that burden is sustained by more rigorous arguments than Professor O'Brien has yet advanced, I shall go on believing that Proust means what he says.

The quotation that Professor O'Brien is kind enough to cite from an essay of mine should indicate that I am not unready to follow his line of interpretation, insofar as it leads us toward an understanding of Proust's character. Precise knowledge of the sex lives of our fellow men, for better or for worse, is hard to come by; at best, we eke out a meager amount of biographical detail with a good deal of psychological surmise; while statistics, such as Dr. Kinsey has attempted to gather, warn us against drawing categorical distinctions between normality and sexual inversion. Yet, by and large, what we know about Proust's sensibilities and predilections accords with those patterns of temperament and conduct which we loosely designate by the hybrid term *homosexual*. This fact, which no informed student of his life and work could seriously question, not only throws its obvious light on his explicit preoccupation with homosexuality; it lends authority to his exposition of that theme. We may go still farther, guided by the documentation that Professor O'Brien so helpfully provides, and note how the suspected limitations of Proust's experience help to explain certain equivocations, confusions, and improbabilities in his treatment of heterosexual relationships. To press such points very far, however, is to assume that Proust is never improbable or confused or equivocal when he addresses himself to other themes; and that relationships between the sexes, as described by heterosexual writers, are invariably convincing. More often than not, to be sure, Proust's *jeunes filles* have a boyish appearance; but so, for completely irrelevant reasons, have Shakespeare's. It may well be, as Professor O'Brien suggests, that Proust's conception of love was too subjective and pessimistic because of the abnormal circumstances under which he had known it. But literature would tell us, if life did not, that other men have reached similar conclusions by way of normal channels.

Let us freely grant that an emphasis on Proust's private life illuminates the motivation of *À la recherche du temps perdu* and accounts for many of the book's peculiarities. The question is whether it may not also seduce us into ignoring the author's considered aims and missing his more important artistic effects. Since he disclaimed the suggested keys to his characters, even where actual resemblances were close, we may at most regard Alfred Agostinelli as a source of inspiration rather than a model. If we imagine a masculine Albertine, we can well understand why she fails to provoke embarrassment when she (or he) goes about conspicuously unchaperoned. We are then faced with the ungrateful task of explaining why a young man should drape himself, not merely in Fortuny silks, but in less ambiguous attributes of femininity. Call him Albert for sake of hypothesis, and for "Gilberte" read "Gilbert"; there is something to be said for both of these readings. Should we not then, in all consistency, read "François" for "Françoise"—even though the latter remains as indubitably feminine as, in her altogether different way, the Duchesse de Guermantes? Once we commit ourselves to this process of *travestissement,* the work reduces itself to a travesty. What of Andrée, the chief object of the narrator's jealous suspicions? Is she to be transposed into André? In that case, the situation is turned into an unrelieved homosexual triangle. But if, as Professor O'Brien seems to think, Albert remains bisexual (to which I would agree, with the qualification that Albertine remains herself), it follows that Andrée must then be regarded as a normal young woman in love with Albert— despite the pains that Proust takes to establish her reputation as a lesbian. Further questions might be multiplied, but these may suffice to back my original contention that a change in the sex of Albertine introduces more difficulties than it settles.

Professor O'Brien's point of critical departure is a work which he has admirably translated, the *Journal* of André Gide. Now Gide, though one of the great witnesses of our time, is a hostile witness with respect to Proust: the colloquies between them, as recorded by Gide and cited by Professor O'Brien, can hardly be said to move toward a meeting of minds. It may be unfair to suspect Gide of resentment toward Proust for having—in a journalistic sense—scooped his big story. It is more significant that, toward their common theme, the attitudes of the two writers are diametrically opposed. Taking them at their word, we could document this contrast by juxtaposing the classical apologetics of *Corydon* and the biblical denunciations of *Sodome et Gomorrhe I.* Whatever the shape that Eros had taken for Proust, it must have left him in a deeply penitent frame of mind. If we are better acquainted with the facts of Gide's homoeroticism, it is because he went on to divulge them in *Si le grain ne meurt,* with an honesty which must be respected and an impenitence which need not be condemned. But neither should Proust's revulsion from pederasty be condemned as less honest than Gide's justification of it. It is true that the latter, by making an intimate confession, more bravely challenged public disapproval. Conceivably he may have felt that a homosexual writer who took a less personal stand on the issue of homosexuality was being unduly conventional and even hypocritical. But Proust had no special plea to put forward; after all, he was composing a work of fiction—a work whose success would be measured by his endeavor to transcend the limits of personality and to attain an objective perception of matters which are never very clear to the uninitiated and which the initiate too often romanticizes.

The variance between this approach and Gide's emerges strikingly from their conversation, where Gide is understandably repelled by the ugliness and bitterness of *Sodome et Gomorrhe;* and Proust, while frankly admitting the homosexual nature of his own recollections, defends their transposition into *A l'ombre des jeunes filles en fleurs* on the grounds that he intended to present a more attractive picture of heterosexual love. His intention was not to conceal what no one could have expected him to reveal, but rather to appeal—as writers, regardless of their peculiar traits, must always do—to the norms of human experience. Rightly or wrongly, unlike Gide, he cherished a conception of youthful innocence; its failure to burgeon and fulfill itself, its later perversion and ultimate corruption, mark the successive stages of his chronicle. The lyrical freshness of the earlier volumes is retrospectively sullied by hints that the girls on the beach, the not unnatural objetcs of a young man's fancy, were denizens of Gomorrah. Professor O'Brien's consistent misspelling of that biblical name is possibly symptomatic of his reluctance to accord it the weight that Proust seems to place upon it, for example in his essay on Baudelaire. Proust's epigraph from Vigny outlines his plot, the bisexual triangle, wherein the loved one hesitates between her heterosexual lover and his Lesbian rival. The sequence that begins with *Sodome et Gomorrhe* incarnates the apocalyptic vision of man and woman forsaking their natural relationship, deviating increasingly from the norm, each sex cohabitating finally with itself. Yet Proust, unlike his romantic predecessors, does not counterweight Sodom and Gomorrah with any vital and positive realization of man's love for woman or woman's for man. His treatment of the affair between Albertine and Marcel—and here my impression agrees with Professor O'Brien's—seems negative and somewhat unconvincing.

Nonetheless, though we may criticize it, I believe we must accept it at face value—and not, in Professor O'Brien's terms, metaphorically. Elstir's concept of art as metaphor is so general that it does not apply here with any particular force; the effect of narrative art, on the other hand, depends upon a literal acceptance of characters and situations as stated. Albertine may be perfunctorily realized, but she performs an irreplaceable function in a positively elaborated scheme of values, where the real heroine is not the mistress but the mother and the ethical touchstone is not sex but the family. Without presuming to judge between the Proustian and the Gidean codes, we can hardly fail to observe that traditional ethics are on the side of the former. Both men made the same kind of experiment in living, and Proust's confirmed standards that Gide's continued to question. This does not necessarily mean that one is correct and the other mistaken, but merely that Gide is intransigently individualistic while Proust was more and more conscious of social responsibilities. The contrast becomes a paradox when we remember that Proust began with hedonism and ended in asceticism, while Gide had been moving in the opposite direction. To speak of "immoral implications," as Professor O'Brien does, is to court invidious comparison, as well as to confound Proust's life with his work. Perhaps the two categories should be inseparable; certainly they come closer in Gide's morality, where fewer concessions are granted to the claims of esthetics. But the premise on which Proust's achievement rests is the poignant hope that work can make up for *le temps perdu,* that art can do penance for life, and that Proust the artist could outdistance Proust the man in his search for the true, the good, the beautiful. To read back the raw material of his experiences into his books is, therefore, to obtrude certain elements which he repudiated as false and bad and ugly.

Would Gide have preferred the sort of unabashed revelation that Jean Genet has more recently been giving the world? Readers of Genet's *Notre Dame des Fleurs* may well look back toward *A l'ombre des jeunes filles en fleurs* with renewed nostalgia for a moral order and a literary tradition which survive in Proust, if not beyond him. And Proust may well belong, as his earliest writings do, to the nineteenth century rather than the twentieth: to that class of novelists—eminently personified in Balzac—who still aspire toward wholeness, boldly resorting to imagination when observation breaks down, rather than falling back on the fragments at hand and exhibiting little more than their own entrails. Imaginative power, according to Coleridge, is tested by the writer's ability to deal with other conditions than those which immediately surround him. Few of our contemporaries dare to take such risks; and who can blame them for being unimaginative, if criticism forbids them to range beyond the limited series of episodes they happen to have lived through? Even Goethe, the most experienced of the moderns, would have been gravely restricted by the application of this canon. Goethe's insight into the complex relations between *Wahrheit* and *Dichtung* led him, in his own case, to perceive that *Werther* was a substitute for suicide. There, at all events, was a phase of human activity which could only be written about if it had not been experienced. It is a shorter step from Proust to Dickens, and from Proust's neurosis to Dickens' notorious marriage. Is it now to be urged that Dickens lived a lie, and that his many celebrations of domestic happiness have no validity? Because Gogol's biographers suspect him of having been an onanist, should we sneer at his stories and plays when they touch on romance?

It may be answered, of course, that these are extreme examples of how writers create what reality fails to supply. Precisely; and insofar as such vicarious creation is uncontrolled and unverified, it may prove to be fantastic, fictitious, false. The means of determining truth or falsity lie in the responses of its readers, each of whom in turn is circumscribed by the incompleteness of his scope yet anxious to enlarge it by the very act of reading. Thus the literary process involves a pooling of diverse experiences, a reciprocal arrangement which—in the crucial instance of Proust—makes the average reader conscious of much that is novel to him, but also draws upon ranges of association more familiar to him than to the writer. Universality is not to be identified with uniformity; and if the subjectivism of Albertine be approached as a metaphysical problem, there is no escape from the plight she symbolizes: the self-imprisonment of the narrator's ego, the fact that she is preordained *ex hypothesi* to elude him. Dorothy Richardson has sought to demonstrate that, in the last analysis, no man can write convincingly about women. Baudelaire sensed the dilemma when, in discussing what is commonly considered one of the master portraits of a woman in literature, he declared Emma Bovary to be a man. When Flaubert said, "Madame

Bovary, c'est moi," he explicitly acknowledged the transposition. But I do not suppose that Professor O'Brien, because of that acknowledgment, would urge us to make a hero of Flaubert's heroine. I hope he would rather agree that Flaubert was formulating the talent of all great novelists for imaginatively projecting themselves into other lives than their own, and thereby calling upon us to meet them halfway.

JOYCE AS CRITIC

When I revised *James Joyce: A Critical Introduction* in 1960, I vowed that I would add nothing more to that flood of commentary which—I may say, more penitently than boastfully—the first edition of my little book might have done something to release. I have found no difficulty in keeping that vow, except for two publications involving new material from the hand of the master, which I felt obligated to salute—if only to round out my own interpretation, such as it may have been. Accordingly, I would review the Trieste notebook published by Richard Ellmann as *Giacomo Joyce;* and when Mr. Ellmann and Ellsworth Mason edited their collection of Joyce's critical writing, I was happy to set down this account of it, which was published in the monthly organ of the Reader's Subscription, *The Griffin* (May 1959), under the title "The Rest Is Literature."

Recently, through the publication of *Contre Sainte-Beuve* and its English translation, *On Literature and Art,* we have been permitted to follow the steps by which Proust came to fiction via criticism. It was a longer and easier transition than that which turned Joyce the reader into a writer. Joyce's work seems to presuppose his own artistic vocation; with Proust the moment of self-realization comes as a belated surprise. And, whereas the sociable Proust—when asthma did not impede him—breathed the atmosphere of literary discussion, Joyce—in order to perfect his genius—cut himself off from a philistine society. Stringently he observed the working conditions laid down by his Stephen Dedalus: "silence, exile, and cunning." The consequence has spoken for itself above the hubbub of his early detractors and later enthusiasts. The compact but monumental corpus of his published writings has been increased since his death, notably by *Stephen Hero* and the *Epiphanies*. His manuscripts, highly cherished but widely scattered through Irish, English, and American libraries and private collections, stand in no danger of being neglected by scholars. A volume of his letters has appeared, and others are now being prepared. Truly we may say, as we pick up *The Critical Writings of James Joyce,* the regimen of silence has been broken.

"Critical"—as we worry that term today—may be too narrow and too intensive a label for this comprehensive and miscellaneous gathering. In the broadest sense of the world, Joyce may be said to have created nothing that was not critical. In a more professional sense, criticism was a sideline which he practised only to keep the pot boiling for two or three brief and hard-pressed intervals; and these critiques are interlarded with lively articles on various matters of nonesthetic interest, mainly political, not to mention an interview with a racing-car driver or an editorial on diseases of cattle. With the greatest artists, such as Ibsen, Joyce announced in his first published article: "Appreciation, hearkening is the only true criticism." Whether the author of *Ulysses* and *Finnegans Wake* could have counted upon so direct a hearing is an ironic question which might well be referred to his critics. If art was a distillation, as he believed with the Symbolists, then talking or writing about it was a dilution. When the quintessence had been attained and isolated, the residue was what Verlaine had dismissed from his *Art poétique:* "Et tout le reste est littérature." Accordingly, as Joyce defines it, "Literature is the wide domain which lies between ephemeral writing and poetry (with which is philosophy)."

Herein we encounter Joyce on the level of mere literature; the artist, relaxing from his formal self-portrait, casually sketches his contemporaries. Fifty-seven pieces, spanning a period of more than forty years, have been brought together within this book. The shapes they take are remarkably diverse: essays, lectures, pamphlets, broadsides, book reviews, program notes, jottings from notebooks, letters, schoolboy themes, satirical verse, reportage. A dozen pieces are translated from the Italian; two are reprinted in the original French. Ten have never been printed before, and most of the others under such obscure or remote circumstances that they have become collectors' items. The twenty-three book reviews are reedited from the all-too-limited edition that Mr. Mason brought out a few years ago, in collaboration with the late Stanislaus Joyce. His present collaborator, Mr. Ellmann, edited the posthumous memoir of Stanislaus, *My Brother's Keeper,* and is now completing what—we have reason to hope—should be the definitive biography of James Joyce. The editors have done their demanding job with unobtrusive authority; they have selected and assembled material which could only be tracked down and transcribed by devoted effort. Their introduction, though terse, is broadly suggestive; their notes are lucid, informative, and necessary, establishing a network of cross-reference between Joyce's major works and these residual productions.

The latter, in spite of their protean form and changing substance, are unified by the singleness of purpose with which Joyce wrote from life and lived his art. They begin with an exercise in composition, submitted to his Jesuit teachers at the age of fourteen and duly headed by the abbreviated Latin moto, "AMDG" ("For the Greater Glory of God"). They taper off in his fifty-sixth year with a protest against the pirating of *Ulysses,* communicated in rather clumsy French to the International P.E.N. Club and received—as we are informed by a final parenthesis—with loud applause. Both that invocation and that colophon are in character. Most of the pages between them derive from the preparatory stages of Joyce's career and document the achievements of his maturity. The paper on "The Study of Languages" adumbrates the concern that would earn him his living and spur him on to linguistic experimentation. An adolescent fragment entitled "Force" by the editors—though surely its key word is "subjugation"—posits a Joycean ideal of self-discipline, "the subjugation of a great gift." More concretely, it poses a metaphor:

When Aeolus has pronounced his fiat, there is no direct countermanding his order. That way the sailor cannot overcome him; but by veering and patient trial, sometimes using the strength of the Wind, sometimes avoiding it, now advancing and now retreating, at last the shifting sails are set for a straight course, and amid the succeeding calm the vessel steers for port.

This is already *Ulysses* in two sentences, one firm and forbidding, the other groping and pliable; for Aeolus, the god of the winds, is the opposing force embodied in the newspaper office; while the modern Odysseus, Mr. Bloom, is the patient sailor who veers in his homeward course. The same episode is foreshadowed again in an article, "The Shade of Parnell," where the fall of the Irish leader is compared with the failure of Moses to reach the Promised Land. The youthful Joyce, when he attacks a patriotic poet for using "those big words which make us so unhappy," or differentiates the "coherent absurdity" of Catholicism from the "incoherent absurdity" of Protestantism, is sharpening phrases to be flung at state and church by his fictional spokesman. When—at the behest of an Ulster acquaintance—he editorializes upon the foot-and-mouth disease, he himself plays a serious part which Stephen Dedalus will burlesque: "the bullockbefriending bard." Such adumbrations of motives later developed are certain to interest devotees of *Ulysses* and the *Portrait of the Artist as a Young Man.* Moreover, while we browse through the artist's studio, we should pause to note the approximations by which he gained his unique mastery. Here, for example, is a typical sentence from the earliest theme:

Fortune that glittering bauble, whose brilliant glimmer has allured and trifled with both proud and poor, is as wavering as the wind.

The sentiment, with its blurred metaphors, smells of the platitudinous classroom; the schoolboy has strained every verbal device in his naïve bag of tricks—personification, parallelism, antithesis, alliteration—to catch what he elsewhere calls "an innate symmetry" of language. This assimilation of clichés is the starting point for Joyce's virtuosity as a stylist. As he developed, he learned how to manipulate, mimic, and mock them; to show up hollow rhetoric by parody; to open up fresh insights by cutting across traditional patterns. Here, from his college magazine, is a parenthetical flight, which echoes a sophisticating influence:

... even she upon whose face many lives have cast that shadowy delicacy, as of one who broods upon distant terrors and riotous dreams, and that strange stillness before which love is silent, Mona Lisa....

The elusive cadence, appealing more to the ear than to the eye, would be recognizable as Pater's even without the pictorial trademark. Further experiments of the sort will lead on to the dazzling conclusion of "The Dead" or the unpunctuated epilogue to *Ulysses*. After such displays of virtuosity, the words themselves become the chief performers in *Finnegans Wake* and also in "From a Banned Writer to a Banned Singer," which is happily included and helpfully annotated in this recension. Here Joyce can combine his defense of an unappreciated artist, the tenor Sullivan, with a potpourri from the operatic repertory and—when the opera is Meyerbeer's *Huguenots*—with still another obsession, religious controversy. To the rhythm of the nursery rhyme, "Oranges and Lemons," the church bells of Paris ring in the Massacre of Saint Bartholomew:

Have you got your knife handy? asks the bellman Saint Andy. Here he is and brandnew, answers Bartholomew. Get ready, get ready, scream the bells of Our Lady. And make sure they're quite killed, adds the gentle Clotilde. Your attention, sirs, please, bawls big Brother Supplice. *Pour la foi! Pour la foi!* booms the great Auxerrois.

Joyce's criticism, not surprisingly, reflects his own preoccupations more fully than it does the authors he criticizes. High-handed as only a young reviewer can be, he misquoted more often than not—as the editors reveal—when he condescended to quote at all. He may not have had much choice in the books he reviewed; but he had no difficulty in pointing out what was wrong with the novels that came his way; and he managed to pay his respects to his favorite philosophers, Aristotle and Bruno. His greatest opportunity was a volume of folktales collected by Lady Gregory, which enabled him to deplore the childishness of the current literary revival. This was a personal gesture as well as a public stand, since it was through Lady Gregory's intervention that he was writing for the pro-English *Daily Express*. Hence Mulligan rebukes Stephen in *Ulysses:* "She gets you a job on the paper and then you go and slate her drivel to Jaysus." Joyce manifestly declared his independence from the movement by taking a patronizing tone with its patroness. He was similarly cavalier in his dismissal of the Victorian prophets ("a pompous professor named Ruskin," "Matthew Arnold has his own little opinion"). On the other hand, he was unbounded in his enthusiasm for the *fin-de-siècle* Messiah, Ibsen, whom he exalts by invidious comparisons at the expense of Rousseau, Emerson, Carlyle, Hardy, Turgenev, and Meredith.

Unfortunately, Joyce's lecture on the Irish Renaissance has been lost, though we are supplied with English versions of several other lectures delivered at the People's University of Trieste, along with contributions to the local newspaper, *Il Piccolo della Sera*. As a lecturer and journalist, Joyce specialized—with feelings habitually mixed—in "Ireland, Island of Saints and Sages," its literature and its politics. What else, where else was there, after all? If Ireland was "a country destined by God to be the caricature of the serious world," then Joyce was its predestined caricaturist. In the bitter ironies he directed against his compatriots, he maintained the position of a wildgoose, a cosmopolitan Irishman, keeping aloof from nationalism and seeking to Europeanize Irish culture. This is evident from his pamphlet, *The Day of the Rabblement,* which castigates the Irish Literary Theatre for failing to produce more plays by European dramatists. It was brash for a youth of nineteen to predict that the Renaissance would bog down into smug provinciality; however, time has borne out that prediction. It has outmoded George Moore, who was then a leading figure, but whom Joyce shrewdly described as an affected imitator of the continental naturalists.

Nor does it seem so presumptuous, in retrospect, that the adolescent pamphleteer should enroll himself among the iconoclasts as the successor to Ibsen.

The manifesto has its affirmative side. Its ringing peroration ("Even now that hour may be standing at the door") is paraphrased from Ibsen's famous welcome to the younger generation in *The Master Builder*. "Drama and Life," the discourse read by Joyce to his university classmates on an occasion which is dramatically set forth in *Stephen Hero,* ends with a similar tag-line from *The Pillars of Society:* "I will let in fresh air. . . ." In the same year, the promising year 1900, Joyce made his first appearance in print with an account of the dying master's last play, *When We Dead Awaken*. That allegory of art and its model, life, with its emphasis on reawakening, was to haunt Joyce again and again; but it must have seemed peculiarly inviting to him as he stood at the threshold of the new century. Clearly a "New School" was indicated; what it stood for was somewhat less clear than what it repudiated. Literature, as Joyce defined it pejoratively, was dead, and consequently to be distinguished from drama, which was alive. The term "dramatic" is Joyce's highest esthetic criterion, and with it he works his way toward the impersonal theory that will be expounded by Stephen in the *Portrait*. His essay on the poet Mangan, which is really a Shelleyesque apology for his own conception of poetry, strikes the concluding note of "continual affirmation" that will reverberate in the repeated "yes" of Molly Bloom.

Passages from notebooks, kept in the earliest years of expatriation and preserved through Herbert Gorman's biography, speculate on questions of pure esthetics, with the aid of Aristotle and Saint Thomas Aquinas. Yet Joyce's abstractions tend to take concrete forms—a tendency which, in scholastic jargon, he would have called "whatness" or "quiddity." Thus the Aristotelian principle of catharsis not only becomes a literal purgative but a symbol for censorship and the confessional in his scurrilous poem, "The Holy Office." That brilliant piece of Swiftian doggerel, with its contrasting image of Ibsen's stag pursuing his lofty course alone, has its sequel in another poetic broadsheet, "Gas from a Burner," written upon the suppression of *Dubliners* and distributed to friends and enemies as a kind of farewell to Ireland. Both of those lampoons achieve their cathartic effect upon the plane of low comedy. Everything Irish is bumptiously satirized, including the author who takes himself so seriously in those books where the artist is the protagonist. Joyce's rare testimonials to other writers, such as Hardy or Pound, are solemn and self-preoccupied. His actual correspondence in later years, unlike these *juvenilia* and *marginalia,* is disappointingly querulous and constrained. He was never comfortable in the role of a man of letters; but he was fond of projecting his personality into a rich variety of comic impersonations. There, as in *Finnegans Wake,* his gift for self-parody found its dramatic fulfilment.

> Who is the meek philosopher who doesn't care a damn
> About the yellow peril or the problem of Siam
> And disbelieves that British Tar is water from life's fount
> And will not gulp the gospel of the German on the Mount?
> It's Mr. Dooley,
> Mr. Dooley,
> The broadest brain our country ever knew
> 'The curse of Moses
> On both your houses'
> Cries Mr. Dooley-ooley-ooley-oo.

This Mr. Dooley is obviously an American cousin of Shem the Penman; he is likewise a music-hall mouthpiece for Joyce's neutralism in World War I. It is fitting that his latest verses should mark a return to Ibsen, and that his epilogue to *Ghosts* should be an exorcism of gloom. It may well be, as the editors suggest, that Joyce himself—through the voice of Captain Alving—is telling us we must take him for better or worse:

> Nay more, were I not all I was,
> Weak, wanton, waster out and out,
> There would have been no world's applause
> And damn all to write home about.

TRAGEDY, REVOLUTION, AND ANDRÉ MALRAUX

This was the very first review I wrote for publication—though not the first published, since it was written for a quarterly, the *Sewanee Review* (July, 1937), wherein it was entitled "Tragedy and Revolution," while soon afterward I started writing for the weekly *Nation*. Having been dazzled by the impact of *La Condition humaine,* which had been awarded the Prix Goncourt when I was a student in Paris, and having been one of a sponsoring group which raised questions at Harvard by inviting André Malraux to speak on behalf of the Spanish Loyalists, I was anxious to express my admiration. Though the book at hand was not a major effort, anything he touched was likely to excite a certain tension. "Bliss was it in that dawn to be alive," as Wordsworth said of the French Revolution. The weary road that has been traveled since can be measured, to a striking degree, by the tergiversations of M. Malraux's later career. Yet I think he has shown an inner consistency in questing for the heroic, even though it has proved so elusive, and that he has been true to his own adventurous nature, if not to any ideology.

To the novelist no man is a hero; he is a subject for observation—psychological or sociological as the case may be. The novel is the product of a free, self-critical, middle-class society, and its prevailing convention for the last hundred years has been to approximate the ordinary level of experience in that society. A novelist does not stray beyond that level without being suspected of artificiality and bad taste. The earlier novels of André Malraux, and certainly his present one, have aroused this suspicion; critics have discerned in them an attempted revival of romanticism, a downright employment of melodrama. Now it is true that the faded trappings of the romanticists corresponded to no reality in the lives of the comfortable generations that followed, but a century ago, when the Spielberg cast its shadow over Europe, there was a very real menace of reaction to give point to the rhetoric of Byron and edge to the irony of Stendhal. Today no less, when shades of the concentration camp fall across the world, writers—with Malraux in their vanguard—are beginning to make us aware that violence and cruelty are not atavistic survivals or figments of the far-fetched literary imagination, that we live once more in stirring times, that we shall witness clashes which involve beliefs as well as interests. That is why it is no paradox to find the Communists sponsoring the return to a heroic literature or to discover a novelist who actively supports their collective program making the staunchest assertion of the dignity of the individual.

Malraux began his quest for a hero by following the wake of Conrad to the East, where emotions could seem less encumbered with the triviality of more familiar circumstances. There, particularly in *Man's Fate,* he set characters as involved and irresponsible as André Gide's against the backdrop of the Chinese Revolution, mingled their personal concerns with the welfare of a whole mass movement, and frustrated both in a defeat so crushing that it ennobled those who felt it. Thus, although he has been writing in the subjective tradition, the comprehensive nature of his theme lends a certain objectivity to his novels and differentiates his heroes from the introverted line of Renés and Adolphes and Dominiques. Yet there is always an indeterminate gap between the underlying forces and the mind or minds through which they are fragmentarily perceived; it is the isolation sensed by Garine— hero of Malraux's untranslated first novel, *Les Conquérants*—in the midst of coolies' syndicates, students' clubs, and the drums and banners of the Red Army.

Before a group of writers recently Malraux testified to his admiration of Dostoevsky, Cervantes, and Defoe, each of whom had been imprisoned or pilloried and had returned to write the book of solitude. *Days of Wrath,* too, is a book of solitude. Compared with Malraux's other books, there is a difference of scale; it is much slighter in length and scope, its workmanship invites more detailed examination, it achieves concentration and immediacy by confining its protagonist to prison for the first five chapters. In the last three, after the German authorities have blundered on to another suspect and released Kassner, the panorama begins revolving through a hailstorm into Czechoslovakia, which becomes the setting for a brief reunion with his wife and child before resuming his underground task. Only in outline is this a chronicle of adventure. There are two roles, according to the author, "the hero and his sense of life," and the components of classical tragedy are engendered between them—"man, the crowd, the elements, woman, destiny." The scene is the mind of Kassner, chained to his lonely rock by Might and Force, prey to the vulture of introspection.

The canons of tragedy are partially satisfied, in a number of books, by imitating actions which are serious and even complete, and which inspire pity, if not fear. The conditions usually lacking are that the action be of a certain magnitude and that the style be suitably embellished. Of these, the second condition is fulfilled more frequently than the first, for portentous subjects are rarer than gifted writers. Both qualities characterize Malraux; he attains magnitude by his relation to the revolutionary movement and embellishment by a technique that gives *Days of Wrath* its literary interest. Here, since the situations are conventional, it is the texture that matters. Kassner wastes no resentment on his Nazi inquisitors, no remorse over the sacrifice of his nameless comrade, no suspense about the inescapable certainty of his return. He is preoccupied with dreams, arguments, hallucinations, thoughts of death, reminiscences of the German village of his childhood, fantasies on his campaigns in Siberia. There is even a moment, at the crucial point of the book, when he breaks out into monologue.

Malraux's style is as lyrical as the music that Kassner imagines to console himself for the numbness of his bruises and the darkness of his cell. Throughout it is intense and supple, capable now of bare directness and again of sudden ranges of suggestion. Haakon Chevalier's English is always faithful and often distinguished. A sentence describing the approach to the hall in Prague where Kassner seeks his wife may be quoted as an example, not of the translation, but of the difficulties that confronted the translator:

> Dans une atmosphère de championnat du monde, de kermesse et de menace, quinze à vingt mille hommes étaient massés, entourés de forces de police au coin des rues dans des reflets d'armes.

What is lost is the arresting effect of syllepsis and the rhythm of the single sentence, while perforce allusions are amplified and closely woven images unraveled, so that the three English sentences almost double the wordage of the single French one.

> The atmosphere of the meeting reminded Kassner both of a world-championship match and a village fair. At the same time it was full of menace. Fifteen to twenty thousand men were massed together, surrounded by police-forces with gleaming weapons who stood in clusters on the street corners.

Malraux has not, in the self-denial of conversion, cast aside the analytical equipment that the bourgeois novel has accumulated. Rather, he is anxious to extend its use, to reduce to sensation the loss or gain of liberty, a precarious journey by plane, the novelty of a foreign capital, the primary emotions of sex and fatherhood. Kassner's search for Anna is counterpointed by the banalities of a radical meeting. A final glance at his hands evokes, by association, the hours he spent in his cell thinking of suicide and waiting for his nails to grow back. The hands, indeed, may be the hands of Lenin, but the voice is the voice of Proust. Malraux is well aware that, whatever the size of the subject, the novelist's only unit of measurement is the impact of events on the individual consciousness. An explorer of new phases of experience as well as undiscovered cities, he shares the activity of his heroes as they share his curiosity. Together they have become revolutionists for the same reason that Ernest Hemingway's heroes become matadors. The difference lies in the minds of those who believe that a revolution is a nobler spectacle than a bullfight.

For ideologically the revolution may be only the means to an end, but psychologically it is an end in itself. Malraux has the intelligence to see that there is no necessary connection between revolution and Utopia, and the courage to dispense with the usual revolutionary eschatology. In this respect, as in so many others, he is more definitely the disciple of Proudhon and Sorel than of Marx and Engels. Revolution, if it is to be justified at all, must be justified here and now, in the lives of its adherents. To them Malraux can hold out few immediate hopes, not even to see the consequences of their acts, but only "to escape from the common lot of man" in action, "to convert destiny into consciousness" in art. Whatever action does not achieve, art may; for it is comprehending the events in which one participates that is important, and Malraux is certain of the issues, if not of the outcome. Meanwhile, it is an inestimable advantage for a literary man to live in a heroic age. The revolution has been fought and won again and again on paper by more zealous novelists. They fail because they try to impose upon the reader a new set of values, and Malraux succeeds because he is willing to appeal to the old ones.

THE HARVEST OF THOMAS MANN

When *Joseph the Provider* first was published—the English version concurrently with the German—I reviewed it for the *New Republic* (July 10, 1944) under the somewhat topical heading "Mann: from Ur to OPA." The context was not inappropriate for a novel which indirectly reflects Mann's American sojourn and even echoes some of the liberal ardors of the day. My review was revised and enlarged into its present form for a collection edited by Charles Neider, *The Stature of Thomas Mann* (New York, 1947). I am glad to see reprinted here my appreciative reference to the English translation by H. T. Lowe-Porter, inasmuch as she reacted with such distress when I later reviewed *Doctor Faustus* and criticized her handling of that more difficult task for both false archaisms and unacknowledged cuts. (A thoroughly misleading account of this tangential episode has been given by John C. Thirlwall in a book on the Mann-Lowe-Porter relationship, *In Another Language.*) With the completion of the *Joseph* cycle, Mann reached the apogee he had set for himself at the very moment when the world's hopes for peace seemed to be on the point of realization. But the optimism of that moment would not prevail for long; the harvest preceded a winter of discontent. Mann became increasingly disillusioned with his adopted country and spent his final years in Switzerland. In his last works he returned to his earlier themes: sickness, decline, artistic alienation. If this was anticlimactic, in the terms of his career, it honestly mirrored the larger anticlimax of history.

"Except a grain of wheat fall into the earth and die, it abideth by itself alone." To this text the earlier works of Thomas Mann provided a comment, with their dying fall, their concern for the pathological, and their consciousness of isolation. The title of his first story was *Fallen;* the subject of his first novel, written at twenty-five, was the decadence of the German burgher; in a remarkable sequence of sketches he went on to expound the riddle of the artist, whose gifts were a blessing to mankind and a curse to himself. In 1918 Mann contributed to the German war effort his *Reflections of a Non-Political Man,* an earnest and unhappy defense of *Kultur* against such exponents of *Zivilisation* as his pacifist brother Heinrich. His own arguments for the old order were later ascribed to the authoritarian Naphta, and answered by the humanist Settembrini: "Everything is politics." Thus *The Magic Mountain,* written at fifty from the alpine summits of postwar internationalism, broadened the dialectic between art and society. The large-hearted Peeperkorn set an example of brotherhood and sacrifice; the convalescent Hans Castorp, singing a *Lied* of Schubert, marched down again into the battles of the flatland. The Naphta-Settembrini debate could only be settled by force; taking a leaf from Turgenev's *Fathers and Sons,* Mann staged a duel between them; his liberal fired in the air and his fascist committed suicide. Germany would have to choose, his Russian heroine warned his ambivalent hero. Germany chose soon afterward—and Mann, after what must have been an agony of hesitation, chose the other side. Already *Mario and the Magician,* as early as 1929, had dramatized the fall of Italian fascism with the portentous detonation of a pistol-shot.

"But if it die," and in 1933, when the first volume of *Joseph and his Brothers* was published, Europe was nearing the crisis, "it beareth much fruit." With the publication of *Joseph the Provider,* the last volume of his tetralogy, Thomas Mann, looking toward his seventieth year and the completion of the Second World War—might be said to have reaped his harvest. His literary self-consciousness, the conviction of his high-calling, accentuates the parallel between himself and his latest hero, and allows him to look—with Joseph's detached attitude of irony and complacency—upon the vicissitudes that have turned his exile into a triumph. The storyteller's wandering star, which he so poignantly invoked at the outset of his story and of his wanderings, has brought him a long way. It has ended by bringing him the kind of public reception that Joseph received at the foreign court of Egypt: even the ceremony of "gilding" is not without its analogies in the sphere of publishing and reviewing. Just as Joseph considers the Egyptians a "quaint and comic" people, so Mann, in the environs of Hollywood, must know what it feels like to live in a "monkey-land." He must also know the significance of the gesture he made when he came to America a few years ago: the isolated artist taking out his citizenship papers. And American fiction, with its symbolist traditions, offers an appropriate haven for his writing. We cannot read of the declining Buddenbrook family or of Hans Castorp lost in the snow without recalling the ponderous fancy that plays around Judge Pyncheon in *The House of the Seven Gables* or the allegorical zeal that glosses the whiteness of the whale in *Moby-Dick.*

We are less likely to remember that Mann is still working in the Goethean tradition of the pedagogical novel. That genre, to our way of thinking, is scarcely a novel at all; but the forms of fiction, always protean, are changing faster than ever today. Once more we seem to be accustoming ourselves to didacticism in the arts; indeed hagiography has become a best-seller with Franz Werfel's *Song of Bernadette*. Hence it is not impertinent to suggest, of a writer who has just completed a prose narrative of more than two thousand pages, that he is scarcely a novelist. (Neither was Sterne, and Mann has recently testified to the stimulation his work derived from *Tristram Shandy*.) Mann is more interested in projecting ideas than in telling stories. Both *Buddenbrooks* and *The Magic Mountain* were conceived as short stories, and then amplified with Teutonic thoroughness to their encyclopedic scale. As for the Joseph story, it would be hard to improve upon the succinct narration of Genesis xxv.1, and Mann has not tried. He is rather a commentator than a narrator; he comments so fully on the circumstances and implications of his theme that little is left for the critic except to admire. Repeating—or perhaps we should say anticipating—Schiller's distinction between naïve and sentimental poetry, Mann is acutely aware of the distance that separates primitive myth from modern knowledge. He bridges it by playing the scholiast, enveloping his text in wordplay and numerology, notes and queries, exegetics and homiletics. A full page of Talmudic explication follows the three words, "I am he." Often the very simplest assumption requires the most complicated explanation. Sometimes the reader nods, and sometimes the author, as when he calls photography to his aid. Such imagery helps us to visualize not Joseph, but a German tourist in pith helmet and sunglasses.

To hold their audience, while discarding the habitual devices and advantage of the *raconteur,* is a technical feat which few writers could accomplish. Mann does this by sustaining a rich texture, by embroidering what he has called—referring to the imaginary masterpiece of Gustav von Aschenbach—a "tapestry-novel." With a virtuosity which we may recognize, if not appreciate, he echoes the sonorities of Luther's German; we may well be grateful for Mrs. Lowe-Porter's skill in translating them into the comparable English of King James. If the book is not a novel, it is a fruitful collaboration of poetry and scholarship, a brilliant exercise of the historical imagination, a striking exhibit in the museum of latter-day culture. Mann's development out of naturalism toward symbolism—"from the bourgeois and individual to the typical and mythical," in his own significant phrase—is thoroughly consistent; for he is continually seeking the symbolic in the temporal, continually finding "the eternal present." Writing of the twentieth century A.D., he indicates the typical in a welter of particulars. Writing of the fourteenth century B.C., he particularizes his archetypes, as Joseph candidly admits. Into the deep well of the past Mann has taken his naturalistic equipment; he has conveyed life out of the tombs that the Egyptologists have excavated; he has created some memorable vistas of the ancient world, not quite so vivid as Flaubert's perhaps, but impressively solid. As if it were yesterday, or indeed today, he has recreated the New Kingdom at the end of the Eighteenth Dynasty. He even permits us an archeologically accurate glimpse of the perennially fascinating Nefertiti. He plausibly identifies the biblical Pharaoh with the youthful mystic Ikhnaton, whose cult of the sun-god does not seem far removed from prehistoric Jewish monotheism. Mann thereby strengthens the identification between his mythical theme and our contemporary diaspora.

Our reviving preoccupation with myth, he has elsewhere stated, represents "an early and primitive stage in the life of humanity, but a late and mature one in the life of the individual." Taking as long a retrospect as the mind can reach, the saga of Joseph is a work of old age. Stately and studied, visionary and discursive, it has the minor key and the complex orchestration, the grand manner and the flagging intensity, that we expect from the later works of the masters. In its cyclic structure it closely parallels the contemporaneous productions of Joyce and Eliot: "In my end is my beginning." The tale has been told—and Mann's repetitions and anticipations stress the point—not once nor twice but many times. Everything has happened before and will happen again. "After all it was a sacred play," the moribund Jacob declares by way of epilogue. Characters enact their parts with the sense of fulfilling a pattern, breaking out into songs and rhymes at the happy ending. Ikhnaton is half-embarrassed in his role of *deus ex machina,* Joseph supremely confident as he reincarnates the mystery of Adonis. Since he is not merely the dying god but also the hermetic trickster, "not only a prophet but a rogue as well," his career is picaresque as well as prophetic. Something of a prig, something of a show-off, he has flaunted his marvelous dreams and his coat of many colors. His sin has been artistic self-absorption; the favorite son has held aloof from his brethren. He must learn to place his gifts at the disposal of society, to interpret the dreams of others. Literally he has gone down into the foul pit; figuratively he has gone down into the nether world of Egypt; still a third time he must go down into the house of bondage before he can emerge triumphant, bringing fruitfulness to the land. The downward movement of the first three volumes ripens into the success story of *Joseph the Provider*.

For provision is foresight; in telling, as Mann points out, there is an element of foretelling; and his eyes, as he approaches the climax of the epos, turn toward the future. The artist, never a mere custodian of tradition, is forever *rerum novarum cupidus*. Having been ushered in by a Dantesque introduction, a vertiginous "Descent into Hell," the cycle is now rounded out with a "Prelude in the Upper Circles," spoken by a Miltonic angel with a cosmic sense of humor. To suggest still further continuities, the disturbing episode of Tamar is interpolated, with its promise for the Messianic line of David and the subsequent cycle of Jesus. Mann's self-confessed "mania for treatment *ab ovo*" has taken him back to the cradles of civilization in Ur of the Chaldees and the valley of the Nile. His far-ranging prospect, not less timely than timeless, extends to the current outposts of the United Nations Relief and Rehabilitation Administration. To a world which is undergoing the widest realization of Pharaoh's nightmares, Mann offers the newest application of Joseph's prophecies. As we read between the hieroglyphics, they all add up to a planned economy in a welfare state: the stars, the sheaves, the dying grain, the bread and wine of communion, the lean and fat kine of scarcity and abundance. Joseph himself, no longer a scribe and a slave, must now be a minister of agriculture with a global conscience. It is hardly coincidental that, in Mann's lecture on *The Theme of the Joseph Novels,* he expressed such warm admiration for Henry Wallace. Joseph's agrarian reforms, his ever-normal granary, his rationing and taxation, his exploitation of the rich barons and generosity toward the little men, his tact with the priests of Amon, his regulation of business, his socialization of property, his Nile Valley Authority, his Office of Price Administration—his platform, in short, should win the liberal vote. Osiris comes forth by day and lo, a New Deal! "And ye shall eat the fat of the land," we read in the Bible and John Steinbeck.

It is strange how so familiar a tale can maintain its suspense. Each successive book involves the protagonist in a more entangled set of human relationships: ancestry in the first, brotherhood in the second, sex in the third. In the fourth book all of these conflicts attain their resolution. No recognition scene is more strongly charged with conflicting emotions than the meeting between Joseph and his father, and Mann is at his masterly best in treating "the painfully beautiful motif of re-union." The paternal quest of so many modern writers ends here in the patriarch's arms. The *Brüderkrieg* of recurrent folklore resolves in for-giveness and reconciliation. For resisting temptation Joseph has already paid the penalty; now he reaps the reward. As he fulfills his mission and emerges from Mann's commentary, he is no longer a portrait of the artist, nor the culture hero of a persecuted race; he is civilization itself. And Mann, by the unanswerable dialectic of events, has become our most enlightening *Zivilisationsliterat*—not less enlightening because he has brought along, to the heights of his final accomplishment, his darker vision of the depths. His final symbol is the Thummim, the synthesis of light and shade, blessing and curse. "What constitutes civil-ized life is that the binding and traditional depth shall fulfill itself in the freedom of God which belongs to the I," he has learned. The ego, in discovering the idea of God, has emancipated itself from collective un-consciousness. Having veered toward the opposite extreme of artistic individualism, it has gradually found its ultimate equilibrium in the recognition of social responsibilities. It has lived up to the original covenant. "And," to let the author supply the most important footnote, "the contrast between esthetic and civil tendencies, between isolation and community, between individual and collective is fabulously neu-tralized."

Between the thesis of the *Bürger* and the antithesis of the *Künstler,* the dialectical interchange is now complete. Mann has vastly changed, and so has the old Hanseatic town of Lübeck, since the days when he described himself to his fellow citizens as "a bourgeois storyteller." As a citizen of the world, a *Weltbürger,* in the years that have hurriedly fol-lowed the Weimar Republic, he has painfully adumbrated his own conception of the city of men. Humanistic as well as humanitarian, this would unite the best features of Athens and Moscow; it would realize the contrasting ideals of Hölderlin and Marx. And if it is somewhat rhetorically proclaimed in Mann's articles and speeches, it is imagina-tively approximated in his later fiction—particularly in *Joseph the Provider.* Consequently, the outcome of Mann's tetralogy is life and fertility, where the burden of Wagner's was death and destruction. Al-ways the exponent of German culture, Mann, beginning to write in its decadent period, premised his writing on Nietzsche's definition of a human being: "the sick animal." Inevitably, as Mann's position became more central, his biography has become what he once termed an *imitatio Goethe,* and his emphasis has shifted from sickness to health—in Goethe's terms, from romanticism to classicism. In an early sketch, *A Weary Hour,* Mann associated the artist's vocation with the sickly genius of Schiller. In *The Beloved Returns,* gravitating toward his healthier and more cosmopolitan model, Mann has latterly reenacted Goethe's quarrel with his short-sighted countrymen: "They think they are Germany—but I am." Now, beholding a liberated Germany once more, he approaches Faust's climactic moment:

> Solch ein Gewimmel möcht ich sehn,
> Auf freiem Grund mit freiem Volke stehen.

It is good to be reminded of that other Germany, whose voice now rises with some of its former authority above the Tohu-Bohu of muddled motives and opportunistic attitudes, whose recuperating wisdom will be profoundly needed in the epoch of privation and plenty that lies ahead. The immediate situation confronting Europe, which is rather a famine than a feast, hardly accords with the festival spirit of Mann's concluding volume. But his love-feast is the necessary sequel to the "feast of death" that was predicated by his military conclusion to *The Magic Mountain.* The naturalism of *Buddenbrooks* reached its last decaying stage in Mann's detailed prognosis of a typhoid case. The symbolism of *The Magic Mountain,* taking the sanatorium as its point of departure, was basically therapeutic. But the upward direction of Hans Castorp's pilgrimage terminated in a sudden descent, while Joseph's underground explorations—happily ending after many ups and downs —ascend toward an *O altitudo!* On that rarefied level it is not Joseph but his descendant, it is Moses who appears in a postscript as Mann's avatar. The Germans, by an ironic reversal of circumstance, are now identified with the children of Israel; while the expatriate writer, no longer a displaced person, is virtually recognized as the father of his people. In *The Tables of the Law* he does not lead them out of the wilderness; he righteously administers a shattering rebuke for the profanation of their heritage. Mann's recent decision to make this country his Pisgah will not make milk and honey flow in Germany. His continued presence, however, should enlarge our own perspective. It is his contribution as much as anyone's, if we can look back to the war and say, as Karl Jaspers said at the rededication of the Heidelberg Medical School: "We have won insights into the reality of the world and man and of ourselves."

INTRODUCING VLADIMIR NABOKOV

Today it would be simpler and more appropriate to say that this subject needed no introduction. But, having been introduced to him soon after he came to America in 1940, it was my pleasure to reintroduce him to a Cambridge audience on April 10, 1964, when he gave a reading from his own works under the auspices of *The Harvard Advocate* at Sanders Theatre, Harvard University. Though I had the privilege of being in close touch with him throughout his American period, I had somehow not ventured to write about him for publication, and had been prevented by the pressure of other responsibilites from contributing to the issue of *TriQuarterly* dedicated to his seventieth birthday. Now he stands in little need of commentators—quite the contrary. Yet, since he did not take amiss these introductory comments, I should like to read them into the record.

The speaker of the evening—like Socrates—has the gift of raising questions rather than dissipating them, but there is one question which his very presence on this platform should dispell. Perhaps because of all you have heard about him, perhaps because of all you have read attached to the butterfly signature, you may have gathered the impression that Vladimir Nabokov is a fictitious character. The answer to that question is that, if he were a character in a novel, it could only be a character in a novel by Vladimir Nabokov. Tonight we have an empirical, as well as an ontological, argument for his existence.

Matthew Arnold described the plight of the writer a hundred years ago as "wandering between two worlds." How simple! How uncomplicated! How comparatively comfortable and potentially monotonous that must have been—what with only two worlds, both of them conveniently located on the same planet and, as T. S. Eliot has added in recent years, "two worlds become much like one another!" Mr. Nabokov does not stand at the checkpoint between the Russia of his birth and the America of his naturalization, for he has many worlds. He controls his plurality of worlds with a firm but agile hand, like a bunch—*une grappe,* the French would say—of brilliantly colored balloons. Some he inflates to perilous magnitudes; others he punctures with explosive sharpness; and still others he allows to escape, and to soar higher and higher until they are out of sight.

One of them, the world of youthful memories, is so perfect because it was closed forever in 1917. Another is as wide open as the expressways of the Far West, bordered by cacti, irrigated by beer cans, illuminated by neon, orchestrated by jukeboxes, and populated by nymphets. One of those worlds takes the form of a chessboard, another of a thesaurus. Another is a limbo of émigrés and displaced persons, polyglot taxi-drivers and dictators down on their luck, in nostalgic cafés on anonymous boulevards. Still another is the fabulous and faraway kingdom of Zembla, whose exiled prince shambles incognito across an American campus, where he teaches basketball-players the aspects of the Russian verb.

The world of *The Gift*, Nabokov's evocation of Russian culture in exile—and I quote from the preface to the recently published English translation of the Russian novel—is "at present as much of a phantasm as most of my other worlds." Recalling the writers he knew and read in those days, Mr. Nabokov has written, in his volume of reminiscences published in this country as *Conclusive Evidence* and in England as *Speak, Memory:*

But the author that interested me most was naturally Sirin. He belonged to my generation. Among the young writers produced in exile he turned out to be the only major one. Beginning with the appearance of his first novel in 1925 and throughout the next fifteen years, until he vanished as strangely as he had come, his work kept provoking an acute and rather morbid interest on the part of critics. Just as Marxist publicists of the eighties in old Russia would have denounced his lack of concern with the economic structure of society, so the mystagogues of emigré letters deplored his lack of religious insight and of moral preoccupation. . . . Conversely, Sirin's admirers made much, perhaps too much, of his unusual style, brilliant precision, functional imagery and that sort of thing. Russian readers who had been raised on the sturdy straightforwardness of Russian realism and had called the bluff of decadent cheats, were impressed by the mirror-like angles of his clear but weirdly misleading sentences and by the fact that the real life of his books flowed in his figures of speech, which one critic has compared to "windows giving upon a contiguous world . . . a rolling corollary, the shadow of a train of thought." Across the dark sky of exile, Sirin passed, to use a simile of a more conservative nature, like a meteor, and disappeared, leaving nothing much else behind him than a vague sense of uneasiness.

Naturally, Sirin interested the author of that paragraph, since Sirin was the pen name under which he had written his Russian works. When

Sirin vanished in 1940, the twinkling new star of Nabokov appeared in the Anglo-American firmament.

Now you must not suppose that any foreign-born writer, however gifted with power over words, could attain Nabokov's mastery of English style by taking a few Berlitz lessons. His infancy, in an aristocratic and liberal family, was attended by English governesses; he himself attended university at another Cambridge; and his first prose publication, after his early emergence as a poet, was a translation of *Alice in Wonderland*—what else? He shares a birthday with Shakespeare, so that he too should be having a jubilee later this month. Born in the latest possible year to be a child of the nineteenth century, consequently he conveys its heritage of self-cultivation and free expression into our epoch of mechanization and uniformity.

When he came to the United States, he lived for a number of years in this Cambridge, while writing his first English books, teaching Russian at Wellesley College, and making his professional contributions to the corruscating science of lepidopterology at the Agassiz Museum. Later, during the period when he was professor of literature at Cornell University, he returned to Harvard one year to teach Slavic and General Education. Hence he has personal friends, as well as literary admirers, in this little world; and, since he held some of his lectures in this very hall, we hope that he will regard this evening as a kind of homecoming. Indeed it might not be out of place for me to reveal that his Alpinist son, while an undergraduate at Harvard, once climbed the spire of this building—in the days when Memorial Hall still had a spire.

The thirteen exemplary novels of Nabokov (eight in Russian, three of those translated into English, and five of them originally in English), his haunting stories and virtuoso poems, his memoir and critical study of Gogol, and his admirable translations, which will culminate in his version of and commentary upon Pushkin's *Evgeni Onegin*—all these cannot admittedly be classified within the boundaries of merely national literature or, for that matter, merely conventional genres. Yet it has always seemed to me that his temperamental affinities are luminously clear. They are with Turgenev and Flaubert and our Henry James, with Proust and Joyce—and it's hard to think of any others more recent. For he may well be the last of the Mandarins, that vanishing breed of writers characterized by their combination of ingenious originality, intransigent individuality, dedicated artistry, and the highest culture.

"My private tragedy," wrote Mr. Nabokov in his postscript to *Lolita*, "is that I had to abandon my natural idiom, my untrammeled, rich, and infinitely docile Russian tongue for a second-rate brand of English, devoid of any of those apparatuses—the baffling mirror, the black velvet backdrop, the implied associations and traditions which the native illusionist, frocktails flying, can magically use to transcend the heritage in his own way." Obviously, we are here to discount that modest disclaimer. All too few of our contemporaries, born to English wordplay, can prestidigitate with it as he can. Watch him closely, then. He has many tricks up his sleeve. Mr. Nabokov.

"A MATTER OF NATIONAL CONCERN": THE REPORT OF THE COMMISSION ON OBSCENITY AND PORNOGRAPHY

A concern with the case of Joyce and—to some extent—with that of Henry Miller got me involved in this particular problem, a problem for all of us which seems to be increasing both in breadth and in complexity, and which will undoubtedly be subjected to further juridical modification. I had already touched upon the current attrition of censorship, together with some of its implications and consequences, in an essay on "The Unbanning of the Books" (*Refractions*). The official endeavor to deal with the question objectively was therefore welcome, and the official endeavor to sweep it under the rug was therefore shocking. We shall be hearing more about it within the near future. This review-article was written for the fifth volume of *The Yearbook of Comparative Criticism* (Pennsylvania State University Press, 1972), edited by Professor Joseph Strelka and devoted to the theme of Literary Criticism and Sociology.

The argument was already an old one when Plato addressed himself to it, and he chose to take the traditional side. He excluded most poetry and some music from his ideal republic, on the premise that they would weaken men's characters by appealing to the baser passions. Aristotle responded by formulating his theory of catharsis, arguing that men would be purged of their dangerous impulses through the fictitious experiences they vicariously underwent. The dialectical conflict between those two positions has never been fully resolved; indeed it has broadened and sharpened during the past two centuries, as the reading habit has been democratized. Books were often banned or censored in earlier periods, but mainly for religious or political reasons. Sexual offenses were dealt with by the law, which has mirrored the moral code of given times and places. The attempt to reduce or prevent such offenses through the censorship of suggestive literature does not seem to have taken much hold before the nineteenth century. Sex was, after all, the most private of private matters, and the freedom to read and publish has been one of the West's most hard-won liberties. Moreover, no one has conclusively demonstrated the ill effects of any kind of reading upon its readers. The question has been raised on many occasions, yet the most influential of all critical handbooks—Aristotle's—testified to the contrary. Jimmy Walker, Mayor of New York in the nineteen-twenties, shrugged the problem off with the declaration that no nice girl was ever seduced by a book.

Well, Emma Bovary may not have been a very nice girl, although she certainly thought of herself as such. On the other hand, it could be said that Mayor Walker's skeptical generalization is lacking in due respect for the power of the printed word. Witness to this power was borne by Dante's Francesca, when she told of reading a romance with Paolo one day and of suddenly ceasing to read it by mutual agreement. The ambiguous name of that romance was *Galeotto,* which signifies not only Galahad but also "go-between." That books could act as panders is the assumption that leads to blanket legislative controls, and consequently to legal actions which can be instigated by any reader who smells some potential offense in what he reads. The prudery of the Victorians was officially legislated by Lord Campbell's Act in 1857—the year in which France watched the trial and acquittal of *Madame Bovary.* The criterion that was long to prevail in Anglo-American courts is generally referred to as the Hicklin rule—though this is an injustice to the memory of Benjamin Hicklin, who had reversed a charge of obscenity in his intermediate court of appeals. When the prosecution appealed the case in 1868, Hicklin was overruled by Lord Chief Justice Alexander Cockburn, who proceeded to promulgate the test for which he merits the commemoration: "whether the tendency of the matter charged as obscenity is to deprave and corrupt those whose minds are open to such immoral influences and into whose hands a publication of this sort may fall."

This test was so readily accepted and applied, by American judges as well as British, that its wording is echoed almost verbatim by the Supreme Court of the United States, ruling on the Rosen case in 1896. The federal statute that had made it a crime to send obscene matter through the mails would be forever associated with Anthony Comstock, the self-appointed guardian of public morality. In cooperation with the Y.M.C.A., he had lobbied so successfully that both houses of Congress passed his bill in 1873 after less than a total hour of debate. Here, as in Great Britain, the avowed intention was to protect the morals of the young from being depraved and corrupted—albeit at the cost of keeping mature adults from access to such classics as *The Arabian Nights* or *The Decameron* and of inhibiting the publication of such important contemporaries as Dreiser or Shaw. The logical consequence, as phrased by Judge Curtis Bok in a Pennsylvania decision of 1949 legalizing the local sale of novels by Faulkner and others, was to "put the entire reading public at the mercy of the adolescent mind." Not only post offices and customs houses but libraries and school boards, not to mention publishers and booksellers, felt and relayed those puritanical pressures which Mencken liked to call Comstockery. The middle generation of our century, however, brought about a marked reversal of that tendency. Its turning point was the verdict of Judge John M. Woolsey in 1933, upheld on appeal by the opinion of Judge Augustus Hand, which allowed *Ulysses* to be published in the United States.

"Whilst in many places the effect of *Ulysses* on the reader undoubtedly is somewhat emetic," Judge Woolsey held, "nowhere does it tend to be an aphrodisiac." In a similar vein, Judge Hand described the notorious final chapter as "pitiful and tragic, rather than lustful." Had the net impression been more erotic, a judgment on that basis might well have been adverse. Both of these judges were willing to consider the novel as a whole, rather than excerpts taken out of context, and to apply a more sophisticated test for obscenity than the Hicklin rule: the novel's impact not upon a child but upon the *homme moyen sensuel*. Both were at considerable pains to distinguish serious fiction from pornography, as Joyce himself had been, and as D. H. Lawrence was in his turn. It has become increasingly difficult to maintain such a distinction in recent years. Mr. Justice Stewart has remarked that, while perhaps he could not define hard-core pornography, he knows it when he sees it; but, significantly, this remark supported his finding that the film in the Jacobellis case was not pornographic. How can the hard core be recognized, then, or has it altogether melted away? Justices Black and Douglas have consistently based their often dissenting opinions on the grounds that an unabridgeable freedom of expression, as guaranteed by the First Amendment to the Constitution, should be absolute. The trend of Supreme Court cases has its landmark in the Roth decision of 1957, which found against the defendants. Mr. Justice Brennan, speaking for the majority, tried to draw a line which would indicate the limits of constitutional protection:

All ideas having even the slightest redeeming social importance—unorthodox ideas, controversial ideas, even ideas hateful to the prevailing climate of opinion—have the full protection of the guarantees, unless excludable because they encroach upon the limited area of more important interests. But implicit in the history of the First Amendment is the rejection of obscenity as utterly without redeeming social importance.

Sin may still be subject to condemnation here; but the loophole of redemption has been opened, since social value is determined by rapidly changing community standards. *Lady Chatterley's Lover* and *Tropic of Cancer,* though each is unquestionably obsessed with sex in its different way, could thus be redeemed during the early nineteen-sixties. *Lolita,* which a number of American firms had considered but not dared to publish, came out under a Parisian imprint in 1955; Putnam's was able to bring it out in New York by 1958; and it has never suffered from prosecution. In 1963 Putnam's resurrected from under the counter the *Memoirs of a Woman of Pleasure* better known as *Fanny Hill,* which had never heretofore been regarded as anything other than pornographic, and indeed had occasioned the first obscenity trial in American history. When its extensive record of suppressions was reversed by the Supreme Court in 1966, Justice Brennan declared that it fell within the protective area he had previously delimited: "a book cannot be proscribed unless it is found to be *utterly* without redeeming social value." How far short of utter its prurience falls is a nice speculation. At a time when monosyllabic taboos are so very casually violated, it may be that John Cleland's judicial readers were charmed by the euphemistic fastidiousness of his mock-heroic sexual metaphors. That literary qualities may be in themselves redemptive controverts the older notion that they enhance the seduction. Yet the very fact that a work of this sort has been handed down to us from the past lends it historical standing as a sociological document.

The term *pornography,* as literally derived from the Greek, means no more than writing about whores—a fair description of the shelf where Cleland may stand with Aretino and Restif de la Bretonne, all now redeemed by time and valued by society. (Recently Morse Peckham has devoted a rather pretentious monograph to the esthetic status of this genre.)[1] As for *obscenity,* its etymology is as obscure as its interpretation is subjective. The original meaning of its Latin adjective was, not inappropriately, "ill-omened." Later usage, making *obscene* synonymous with "foul" or "filthy," illustrates how moralistic arguments utilize the imagery of purity and pollution. *Dirt* and *smut* seem frequently to function for the dirtier words they have proscribed. "A thing is obscene if, considered as a whole, its predominant appeal is to prurient interest . . ." So runs the definition of the American Law

1. Morse Peckham, *Art and Pornography: An Experiment in Explanation* (New York, 1969).

Institute, as quoted by Justice Brennan in *Roth* v. *United States*. It is hard to see why this specification does not fit *Fanny Hill,* which must have been a harder book to defend than either *Lady Chatterley's Lover* or *Tropic of Cancer.* Since the same lawyer, Charles Rembar, was chiefly responsible for the successful defense of all three, it is valuable to have his personal account of that sequence of trials in a volume provocatively titled *The End of Obscenity.*[2] Mr. Rembar claims and deserves a large share of the credit, assuming that credit will be accorded, for having widened Justice Brennan's loophole to the point where no publication whatsoever would seem altogether devoid of redeeming social value. The present situation is characterized, by Mr. Rembar himself, as a *seductio ad absurdum.*

The legislative point of view diverges from the judicial. The Comstock Act may be obsolete today, yet the Congress still votes unquestioningly for virtue as defined by those who profess it loudly. It was evidently a mood of reaction against the increasingly permissive drift of legal opinion which in October 1967 prompted the passage of Public Law 90–100, designating the problem as "a matter of national concern." The legislation, introduced by Senator John McClellan of Arkansas, called upon the President to appoint an advisory commission which would make appropriate recommendations, after a thorough investigation of the traffic in obscenity and pornography, including—and among the conventional verbiage, this would turn out to be an innovative proviso—"a study of the causal relationship of such materials to antisocial behavior." Four specific tasks were assigned to the commissioners: (1) to survey the state of the laws controlling and defining pornography, (2) to inquire into its operation and scope as a business, (3) to evaluate its effect on the public, "and particularly minors," and (4) to recommend proposals for its regulation, "without in any way interfering with constitutional rights." In January 1968 President Johnson appointed a panel of eighteen members, whose elected chairman would be William B. Lockhart, Dean of the Law School at the University of Minnesota and a leading authority on obscenity law. With one striking omission, the commission represented a fair sampling of the various other interests involved: public officials, professional women, the clergy, social scientists, educators (but not from the humanities). Literature and the arts had no direct representation, unless we count the presence

2. Charles Rembar, *The End of Obscenity: The Trials of Lady Chatterley, Tropic of Cancer, and Fanny Hill* (New York, 1968).

of a librarian. This might be ascribed to philistinism, rather than illiberal intentions, on the part of the President and his advisers.

The controversy surrounding the commission, during and after its two-year deliberations, has been much better publicized than its 646-page report. Two of the commissioners—the Rev. Morton A. Hill, S.J., president of an organization entitled Morality in Media, and the Rev. Winfrey C. Link, administrator of the McKendree Manor Methodist Retirement Home—broke away from the procedures and policies of their colleagues at an early stage, and held public hearings all over the country to dramatize their belief in more rigorous controls. When one of the commissioners—Senator Kenneth B. Keating of New York—was compelled to resign on becoming Ambassador to India, the incoming President Nixon was given his single chance to affect the results. He appointed a namesake of the former incumbent, the Cincinnati lawyer Charles M. Keating, Jr., who had qualified himself by his energetic activities on behalf of censorship and had founded a pressure group known as Citizens for Decent Literature, Inc. Mr. Keating was consistent in his campaign to obstruct and discredit the majority, boycotting their executive sessions, abstaining from their final vote, and filing suit to enjoin against publication until he had prepared his own dissenting report. Meanwhile overwrought accounts of the majority report had been leaked to the press and to a congressional committee. Even before it was published, a White House spokesman announced that the President was at variance with it. Just seventeen days after the Government Printing Office had issued its small official edition, it was rejected by the Senate. Shepherded again by Senator McClellan, a condemnatory resolution was passed without debate by a vote of sixty to five.

The irony of the circumstance is twofold. On the one hand, obviously the Congress got something quite different from what it thought it had bargained for; it had wanted dogma and was offered dubiety. On the other, a new administration, whose watchwords were law and order, had been embarrassed from the very first by this holdover from a muddled if well-meaning liberalism, and was all too happy to join in the general effort to sabotage it. Shortly before the elections of 1970, President Nixon released a statement seething with indignation, declaring that he had "evaluated" the report—he does not say he has read it—and that he both "categorically" and "totally" rejects "its morally bankrupt conclusions."[3] As a defender of decency, which one might almost

3. See the *New York Times*, October 25, 1970, p. 71.

be led to think that the commission had attacked, he repeatedly de-
nounces "smut" and "poison" and—using a less old-fashioned word—
"pollution." Thus he begs the initial question that the commission was
established to study, the definition of obscenity: when is it smut and by
what canon? In the name of "an open society" he reverts to the ideology
of the Hicklin rule: "If the level of filth rises in the adult community,
the young people in our society cannot help but be inundated by the
flood." Heatedly, in language strongly influenced by the rhetoric of
Commissioner Keating's dissent, he calls for more antismut laws and
prosecutions in every state and at every level. "American morality is not
to be trifled with." The services of Dean Lockhart and his hard-working
fellow commissioners are finally rewarded with the most thankless of
discharges: "The Commission on Pornography and Obscenity has performed a disservice."

This "shabby political treatment" did not go unreproved by such
monitors as the *New York Times,* which pleaded with legislators to
"give the commission's report the belated benefit of a fair and rational
hearing," since they had been too busy campaigning at the time they
had voted for its repudiation.[4] Speaking more broadly, on behalf of
twenty-five civic, educational, and literary organizations, the National
Book Committee has appealed for a thoughtful reconsideration and a
fuller public dialogue on the issues raised by the report—an appeal to
which I, for one, am hereby venturing to set down a tentative response.
Though the government did as little as possible to distribute the report,
it is now available in commercial editions.[5] A spurious version of it,
closely resembling the dissident reports, had come out in advance; an
edition of the report itself, richly illustrated by pornographic exhibits,
also kept curiosity stirred up. There has even been a documentary film,
Red, White, and Blue, which inclines toward the latter shading. The
actual text, while it is somewhat clogged by the competing jargons of
law and the behavioral sciences, endeavors to come to grips with its
peculiarly elusive and sometimes distasteful subject matter. But, in contrast to those question-begging adjectives which so often figure as
accusations ("lewd," "lascivious," "lustful," and "licentious," to stay
within the bounds of alliteration), the report consistently attempts to
neutralize its material by such antiseptic phrases as "sexually oriented."
The degree of consensus is roughly a little more than two-thirds.

4. *New York Times,* February 10, 1971, p. 42.
5. *The Report of the Commission on Obscenity and Pornography* (New York, 1970).

Twelve of the eighteen commissioners voted for it in its entirety, two dissented in part, three dissented completely, and Mr. Keating abstained.

Despite the absence of letters among the professional fields reflected in the membership of the commission, the report abounds in implications bearing on the complex interaction between society and literature. Hence there is particular need for these to be scrutinized and discussed from the vantage point of literary criticism. In 1920 Mencken had complained that the courts would not admit critical opinion in evidence for prosecuted books. Latterly the defense has had more and more opportunity to call upon critics as expert witnesses, and Mr. Rembar attests the strategic role that they have played in a number of his cases. If the issue depends on whether a book has any literary merit, actually that is the very quality of which the critic is supposed to be the best judge. The book would not be on trial unless it stood at the borderline between literature and pornography, in the estimation of some, and he is presumably consulted to help the court draw that line. But how can literature and pornography be conceived as mutually exclusive categories? Objectively, the latter is merely a specialized branch of the former. If a work of pornography is legally identifiable as involving obscenity, then it may now be redeemed by the nonobscene elements it contains—if indeed it contains them—and Mr. Rembar, as I understand him, would find some ground for every book to meet this countertest. Has he not rescued Cleland, as well as Lawrence and Miller, for American readers? Yet even his open-minded ingenuity might be hard put to discover the strain of mitigation in those works of Cleland's pseudonymous heirs which line the lurid counters of Forty-second Street.

At all events, the pornographer's trade has come out from underground, and the commission's first panel has obtained a good deal of information about it to share with us. The mere fact that it operates in the open makes it look less sinister, though undeniably sordid, an agent of esthetic if not ethical degradation. The businesses that purvey it seem to be fly-by-night affairs, gathering tenuous profits from a limited volume of sales, even when individual prices are high. Sales for "adult only" magazines are estimated at between $25,000,000 and $35,000,000 in 1969, whereas during that same year the income of *Playboy* alone—which is considered mildly erotic but not pornographic—reached the total of $66,000,000. Cinema is the only medium that comes close to big business in this line, counting box-office receipts of somewhat less than half a billion dollars. But here the spectrum runs from downright "sexploitation" (skin-flicks or stag movies) through so-called art films (usually foreign imports) to standard Hollywood products rated *X* (no patron under seventeen admitted) or *R* (patrons under seventeen must be accompanied by a parent or guardian). The *X* rating is hesitantly attached, though flamboyantly advertised; it covers less than 6 percent of the motion pictures subject to the Production Code Administration. Pictorial representation differs considerably from verbal in some of the problems it presents; the source of its excitations is nearer the surface. Often the two media are combined, as in photographically illustrated marriage manuals or medical handbooks. These, like the classical texts once hidden away as *erotica* or *curiosa* and today universally procurable, assert a claim to legitimacy which cannot be vaunted by pornographic potboilers.

Facts and figures regarding the production and distribution of pornography are more accessible than an understanding in any depth about what goes on in the crucial process, consumption. There is still enough peep-show furtiveness in the atmosphere of pornographic bookshops for their customers to be wary of interviews. Field observations report that the average consumer of this product tends to be a solitary white male, aged between twenty-one and fifty-five, married more often than not, dressed pretty much like any other man in the street—and not too much unlike him in sexual habits, insofar as these can be discerned. If women are seldom to be seen in such purlieus, it is because pornography, written for an exclusively masculine readership and focusing upon woman as a sex object, has been sexist with a vengeance. But that inequity may be grounded in nature, for the researches of Dr. Kinsey and others indicate that women are less sexually responsive than men to visual and literary stimuli. This does not mean that women are less capable of arousal (*pace* Dr. Masters and Mrs. Johnson), but the evidence suggests that they feel more aroused by romantic subjects than by explicitly sexual ones. Since—as I began by noting—the moral and legal arguments for censoring books and pictures have always hinged on their presumptive influence over human character and conduct, and since so little has been understood as to precisely how this influence is effected and with what consequences, it is the report of the commission's second panel on "The Impact of Erotica" which should be its most interesting contribution, as it has already been its most controversial.

Many of this panel's findings are as predictable, or else as inconclusive, as the usual tabulation of a sociological questionnaire. The inverse correlation between church attendance and pornographic indulgence will be no surprise to either moralists or libertarians. Nor can we dismiss the possible hazards of obscenity because, in a canvass of current opinion, only 2 percent of those interviewed believe it is one of "the two or three major issues facing the country today." This simply proves that we are not so steeped in vice as the citizens of Sodom and Gomorrah. Given the national problems that have been ranked ahead of obscenity by the respondents (war, race, the economy, youth, law and order, drugs, pollution, poverty, moral breakdown, government, foreign policy, education, overpopulation, as preferentially listed), it would take another Anthony Comstock to assign a higher priority to his peculiar obsession. The determination of community standards by door-to-door sampling makes for simplistic questions and inconsistent answers. For example, 56 percent of the people may believe that "sexual materials lead to a breakdown of morals"; yet only 1 percent of them admit this in their own case; and few can think specifically of any instance. Exposure to pornography was linked with juvenile crime by 58 percent of the police chiefs questioned. Large majorities in other groups—psychiatrists, social workers, and others versed in conditioning rather than crime—made little connection. Their negative conclusion is supported by further studies in the incidence of sex crimes by both juveniles and adults, which did not vary greatly during the nineteen-sixties, in spite of the manifold increase in sex-oriented materials.

Much of the commission's two-million-dollar appropriation has been employed to foster programs of research, which will be detailed in ten supplementary volumes of technical reports and summarized with graphs and tables in the body of the report. (Among the numerous teams of sociologists and psychologists working upon these projects, a sense of ironic propriety might single out the name of D. M. Amoroso.) This collective endeavor, unwittingly commissioned by the Senate's interest in causation, breaks new ground by bringing empirical data to bear upon the effects of pornography. Admittedly, it is hampered by limitations and obstacles. The time was rather short for a full-range study of after-effects. Children, the principal objects of concern, were decidedly *hors du combat* for such encounters as could be devised under such conditions. University students who volunteered would have their motives suspected, and would become a subject for congressional reprehension. One might add that experiment with human guinea pigs, while never failing to outrage the obscurantists, likewise offers a standing invitation to Aristophanic burlesque or Swiftian satire. (Aristophanes would have been delighted to hear about the phalloplethysmograph.) The essence of Bergsonian absurdity is achieved when the superimposition of the mechanical on the living takes place within the sphere of sex itself. But, though some may be amused—while others are outraged—by the techniques so ingeniously developed for registering physical response to psychological stimulus, discovery can take no other course. That sexual arousal can be measured has with males been a comic byword, which may now be scientifically implemented for both sexes through the therapy of Masters and Johnson and the experimentation sponsored by the commission.

"Such direct measurements entail problems pertinent to the invasion of privacy," to quote the understatement of the commissioners. They are not unaware that "the instrumentation involved" may unduly excite or inhibit "the object which is measured." Objectivity so attained is all too narrowly limited, to say the very least, but it carries the will for exactitude and concreteness as far as it has yet ventured into this problematic zone. A central series of controlled experiments typically exposes groups of subjects to barrages of erotic photographs, slides, films, and reading matter, and—as the exposures are repeated or discontinued—charts the curve of reactions, both physiological and behavioral. The immediate reaction is the sort of intensification that might have been expected from so concentrated an incitement. But that priapic reflex soon gives way to an interval of satiation and a gradual falling-off in responsiveness. Shakespeare may have anticipated the pattern, when his Duke commands in *Twelfth Night:*

> Give me excess of it, that, surfeiting,
> The appetite may sicken, and so die.

Some of those subjects who were confined for electronic observation, as we learn from the report, had been provided with a surfeit of periodicals, most of them excitably pornographic, and were encouraged to browse as freely as they desired. Many of the browsers ended by turning to the *Reader's Digest*—an extreme gesture of practical criticism. We who have not submitted ourselves to so complete an immersion, but have sampled the stimulants when they have drifted our way, could reaffirm the sense of boredom induced by their repetitions and limitations. The report is disarming in its conclusion, based on its many avenues of inquiry, that it cannot demonstrate any causal relationship between pornography and delinquency. But this may be no more than a default in the face of uncertainty, a failure to develop methods for coming up with any conclusion at all.

"If a case is to be made against 'pornography' in 1970," so the panel's negative induction is summed up, "it will have to be made on grounds other than demonstrated effects of a damaging personal or social nature." This is not to deny that erotic themes are sexually stimulating, even as tragic or comic themes may elicit tears or laughter. Readers may not cry or laugh aloud when confronted with tragic or comic scenes, nor may they necessarily "achieve orgasm through nonintercourse means"—as the report, with heavy-handed delicacy, puts it—by responding to pornographic excitation. We shall never know to what extent consumers of pornography make deliberate use of it for such purposes, and accordingly the report does not pursue that opaque probability. Nevertheless the common assumption behind it offers a significant testimonial to the undeniable fact that erotic material provokes a sexual response. However, since masturbation is the least social of acts, and since hygienic counsel no longer preaches that it is personally damaging, it affords no grounds for any ban. The case against "pornography"—and note how the cited sentence neutralizes the word with quotation marks—must be made on the ever-debatable grounds of morality. In the last analysis, the question is whether moral arguments should be fortified by legal sanctions, or whether a broader conception of legality should prevail. The commission's third panel concerned itself with positive approaches short of repression, such as codes for self-regulation in pertinent industries. Surveying ways and means for the improvement of sex education, it found an incidental usefulness in some of the controverted materials.

When district attorneys were queried as to the obscenity trade within their local jurisdictions, less than a third of them replied that it was a matter for serious concern. This reflects particularly the innocence of the less heavily populated counties, where pornographic enterprise would not be financially rewarding. The replies from the urban districts, where diversity works against conformity to an old-fashioned set of values, registered much greater apprehension. It is here that the Citizens' Action Groups have been organized, whose resolve to police the mores of the community implies an ultimate recourse to the law. Thence we are brought to the legal considerations of the fourth and last panel, which has struggled to clarify the confusion it has faced, reporting an "almost universal dissatisfaction with the present law." The historical background is sketched; the existing statutes and the federal agencies are canvassed; but the focus is on the sequence of judicial modifications that has unfolded with such bewildering rapidity during the thirteen years since the Roth decision. At the moment there are three accepted criteria, all of which must be met if a book is to be ruled obscene: (1) appeal to a prurient interest, (2) patent offensiveness by contemporary community standards, and (3) utter lack of redeeming social value. None of these definitions has any precision whatever, and each of them entails some degree of subjective judgment. The difficulty of deciding in their light on matters so inherently ambiguous has been pushing judges, juries, law enforcement officials, and the public—along with booksellers, publishers, and authors—toward an impasse of ambiguity. Furthermore:

A series of decisions of the Supreme Court, generally rendered without opinion, has given an exceedingly narrow scope of actual application to the constitutionally required three-part standard for adult legislation. These decisions leave it questionable whether any verbal or textual materials whatever may presently be deemed "obscene" for adults under the constitutional standard and suggest that only the most graphic pictorial depictions of actual sexual activity may fall within it. Present law for adults is therefore largely ineffective.

The development of constitutional doctrine has been oriented, by Dean Lockhart and his colleagues, against the larger perspectives of changing public opinion. Cross-reference to the obscenity laws of fifteen other countries discloses inconsistencies and trends which are comparable to those of our own. The pace has been set by Denmark, the pornographers' Land of Cockaigne, where an increasingly permissive attitude during the nineteen-sixties culminated in the abolition of all legal restraints on commerce in pornography for adults. Statistics based on the records of the Copenhagen police for that period show a dramatic decline in the incidence of sexual offenses. This civilized model should be reassuring to those who fear the turbid inundation prophesied in President Nixon's jeremiad. Four factors, then, have pointed the report in a parallel direction: (1) the comparative insignificance of the pornographic market, (2) the dearth of psychosexual evidence demonstrating antisocial effect, (3) affirmative measures through sex education and more open discussion, which require no special legislation, and (4) cutting the Gordian knot of entangled laws and obfuscating precedents. Finding "no warrant for continued governmental interference with the full freedom of adults to read . . . ," the commission recommends that "federal, state, and local legislation prohibiting the sale, exhibition, and distribution of sexual materials to consenting adults should be repealed." There are qualifying recommendations which would prohibit the sale or display of sexual materials to minors, and would impose restrictions on public exhibits and on the use of the mails for offensive advertising. (Bills designed to meet this last complaint have currently been introduced into Congress.)

After such knowledge, what forgiveness? Differences of viewpoint among the members of the commission, which must at times have rendered their sessions volcanic, come out in an appendix more than half as long as the report itself. Two behavioral scientists concur, but want to move farther toward total repeal. Two concurring physicians view the subject as "a nuisance rather than an evil." For a Methodist minister, the report is "a milestone in the history of human communications." A Jewish rabbi, not unsympathetic to its findings thus far, feels that more thorough investigation is needed. Commissioners Hill and Link have drawn up a lengthy counterstatement, whose strident pitch is struck in the opening sentence: "The Commission's report is a Magna Carta for the pornographer." Unshaken in their faith that pornography is the cause of vice and crime, they circularly proceed to roll back history since Roth. Obscenity should be redefined so that nothing could ever redeem it. Some of the experimental research is vulnerable, it must be conceded, to the methodological objections that they press. Tighter censorship, stricter legislation, and more frequent prosecutions are proposed *inter alia,* under the somewhat ominous byword of "vigilance." Not only films but rock lyrics and underground newspapers ought to be subjected to licensing boards and preliminary clearances. As for what Mr. Keating would call "the Danish solution," Messrs. Hill and Link explain that "we are a different culture with a greater commitment to the Judeo-Christian tradition." If this is not Pharisaism, it is crass ignorance, which should not put down the compatriots of Kierkegaard and Grundtvig.

Commissioner Keating, who concurred in the Hill-Link report, has gone on to write a minority report of his own at equal length. It is a fitting anticlimax to the volume—and to his own nonperformance on the commission, which he assails in volleys of mixed metaphor, calling for an investigation of the investigators (their "ivory-tower views" go "unhoned by the checks and balances of a competitive, active, real world"). The precision of his fuming prose can be gauged when he attacks the Supreme Court for "the flaunting of morality." What he apparently meant to say was "flouting," which has almost the opposite meaning; but those two words are frequently confused by mixed-up persons, especially in thermodynamic moments. Like his clerical co-adjutors, he is manifestly embarked upon a religious crusade: "For those who believe in God . . . no argument against pornography should be necessary." Nonetheless he is nothing if not argumentative, arming himself with quotations from such authorities as Marcel Proust, Arnold Toynbee, Whittaker Chambers, Spiro T. Agnew, John N. Mitchell, and J. Edgar Hoover. The documentation includes a list of addresses where pornography can be obtained, as well as a gloating series of sexual case histories, most of them hearsay. Mr. Keating has his own legislative pro-gram; he has prolific suggestions for running the country, the states, the cities, and above all private lives; he has a detailed plan for turning California into a kind of police state. And, of course, he has his Citizens for Decent Literature, which can boast the honorary membership of 124 congressmen plus eleven senators, notably the Hon. Barry Goldwater and the Hon. Strom Thurmond.

If this counterreport reads like a travesty, self-refuted by its overkill, we should note that it is wielding more influence in "the competitive, active, real world" than the Lockhart Report. Mr. Keating, as a minor-ity of one, is the only commissioner to whom the White House has been willing to listen. His diatribe sets a tone which reverberates through the President's discharge (a tone which might correctly be de-scribed as "the flaunting of morality"). In view of the Congress's treat-ment of the report, and of the hopes expressed for a narrower line from a reconstituted Supreme Court, it is more than conceivable that we may witness a widespread tightening of codes and bans. That should bring us one step nearer to Plato's republic—and to the official prudery and legislated morality that enter hand in hand with totalitarian regimes. Both of the dissenting reports look upon Dean Lockhart with a sus-picious eye because of his association with the American Civil Liberties Union, as if he should be disqualified from his present assignment be-cause of a prior commitment to free speech. A dialectic of permissive-ness versus repressiveness emerges from the confrontation between a libertarian majority and a regulative minority. The commission's *donnée* was the ultraliberal turn that the courts had been taking. Surprisingly this seemed to be justified, rather than discredited, by the empirical studies of sexual materials. Finding no positive evidence of their harmful effects, the report had no warrant for recommending the abridgment of basic rights. "Surely," said Justice Frankfurter in a similar situation, "this [would be] to burn down the house to roast the pig."

The recommendation of the disregarded majority, as Clive Barnes points out in his preface to the reprint, turns the "matter of national concern" into a private matter. To leave it there, if possible, would be a happy ending. Critics of the report, though they mostly incline toward laissez-faire economics, are less inclined toward individualism in the field of morals. Messrs. Hill and Link, refusing to accept the negative conclusion with regard to harmfulness, insist that the burden of proof lies on the other side. If it has the slightest potential for harm, let the book show cause why it should not be banned. For the majority, it had seemed more dangerous to curtail freedom than to risk contamination. Though that choice seems clear to liberals, it must still be made with some embarrassment. Above and beyond our lingering uncertainties, pornography is without doubt a nuisance. The dissolution of the hardcore concept has brought some strange bedfellows together; cheap shockers jostle once-forbidden classics on the polychrome list of the Grove Press. It is true, as the report submits, that "dirty words" as such have lost their obscene force. This may be a loss both for colloquial speech and for literary style. It was their proscription from polite discourse that lent them their expletive vigor. When we think of what those dashes or initials used to portend, of the elegant circumlocutions of Cleland, of Hemingway's wry habit of substituting the word *obscenity* itself, or of Joyce's sparing, shocking, and self-conscious introduction of the familiar monosyllables into print, then Norman Mailer's casual scurrility seems much too easy, childish, and self-indulgent.

If everything is permissible at the level of publication, then at the level of criticism we must bear a new responsibility. If we shift our value judgments from ethics to esthetics, it is still our duty to discriminate art from trash. This is the critical consequence of the report; the other, perhaps the major, consequence is scientific. Rightly the commission claims, as one of its contributions, to have placed "the dimension of human sexual behavior on the agenda for further inquiry." It has shown how art, in its problematic relation to sex, can be a control for that inquiry. The deliberations of the Commission on Obscenity and Pornography were slightly overlapped by those of another national Commission on the Causes and Prevention of Violence, an overlapping which resulted in a curious contradiction. Though this other group did not undertake any research projects of its own, it did find certain television programs demoralizing for children, and concluded by proposing some curbs. It is worth noting that one commissioner—Otto N. Larsen—was a member of both groups, voting for causation and regulation in the one case and for nonregulation in the other. Are we to infer that violence is more contagious than sex, or merely that it is more dangerous and less desirable? As debate continues and enlarges, it appears that the censorship of pornography has its advocates in law and social science, as well as in the Presidency and the Congress.[6] Whether we can turn back at so advanced a stage, without jeopardizing that individual freedom which the report puts highest among its mixed concerns, will all too soon be seen.

6. See Walter Berns, "Pornography vs. Democracy: The Case for Censorship," and the ensuing discussion, *Public Interest,* XXII (Winter, 1971), 3ff.; Irving Kristol, "Pornography, Obscenity and the Case for Censorship," *New York Times Sunday Magazine,* March 28, 1971, pp. 24ff.; also Herbert L. Packer, "The Pornography Caper," *Commentary,* LI, 2 (February, 1971), 72–77.

BIBLIOGRAPHY

INDEX

BIBLIOGRAPHY

CC: reprinted in *Contexts of Criticism* (1957).
GH: revised and assimilated into *The Gates of Horn* (1963).
R: reprinted in *Refractions* (1966).
GC: reprinted in *Grounds for Comparison* (1972).

The Broken Column: A Study in Romantic Hellenism (Cambridge: Harvard University Press, 1931), 76 pp.

"John Cleveland and the Conceit," *Criterion,* XIV, 54 (October, 1934), 40–53.

"Literature and the Lively Sciences," *Atlantic Monthly,* CLV, 3 (March, 1935), 303–311.

"Skelton and Oxford" (correspondence), *Times Literary Supplement,* XXXV, 1788 (May 9, 1936), 400.

"Selden's Spectacles," *Sewanee Review,* XLV, 1 (January, 1937), 24–39.
"Portrait of a Homeric Scholar," *Classical Journal,* XXXII, 5 (February, 1937), 259–266; *GC.*
"Small Trade Wind," review of *Great Trade Route* and *Portraits from Life* by Ford Madox Ford, *Nation,* CXLIV, 13 (March 27, 1937), 358–359.
"In Times of Realism," review of *Three Comrades* by Erich Maria Remarque, *Nation,* CXLIV, 17 (April 24, 1937), 485–486.
"The Novel, No," review of *The Novel and the People* by Ralph Fox, *Nation,* CXLIV, 23 (June 5, 1937), 651.
"A Parthian Glance," review of *The Pretender* by Lion Feuchtwanger, *Nation,* CXLIV, 24 (June 12, 1937), 684.
"The Professor's Novelist," review of *Anatole France, 1884–1896* by Edwin Preston Dargan, *Nation,* CXLV, 2 (July 10, 1937), 51–52.
"Tragedy and Revolution," review of *Days of Wrath* by André Malraux, *Sewanee Review,* XLV, 3 (July, 1937), 171–174; *GC.*
"Anne to Victoria to Wallis," review of *Anne to Victoria,* ed. Bonamy Dobrée, *Nation,* CXLV, 6 (August 7, 1937), 154–156.
"Mann and Superman," review of *Freud, Goethe, Wagner* by Thomas Mann, *Nation,* CXLV, 11 (September 11, 1937), 270.
"Divided Front in Minnesota," *Nation,* CXLV, 14 (October 2, 1937), 346–348.
"Newtonian Cosmology," review of *War with the Newts* by Karel Čapek, *Nation,* CXLV, 18 (October 30, 1937), 482–483.
"Shakespeare the Surrealist," review of *Shakespeare's Young Lovers* by E. E. Stoll, *Nation,* CXLV, 26 (December 25, 1937), 720.

"The Brown Book of Heinrich Heine," review of *Heinrich Heine: Paradox and Poet* by Louis Untermeyer, *Partisan Review,* IV, 2 (January, 1938), 50–53.
"Innovation and Collective Talent," review of *New Writing, Spring 1937,* ed. John

Lehmann; *New Writing, Fall 1937*, ed. John Lehmann; *New Letters in America*, ed. Horace Gregory; *New Directions in Prose and Poetry, 1937*, ed. James Laughlin IV; *The Writer in a Changing World*, ed. Henry Hart; in *Nation*, CXLVI, 7 (February 12, 1938), 185–187.

"Snakes in Iceland," review of *Literarry Opinion in America*, ed. Morton Dauwen Zabel, *Nation*, CXLVI, 8 (February 19, 1938), 216–219.

"DeVoto and His Epoch," review of *Bernard DeVoto: A Preliminary Appraisal* by Garrett Mattingly, *Nation*, CXLVI, 12 (March 19, 1938), 167–169.

"Seven Satires: Penance for Cocktails, Macaronic, The Fall of Manchester, Rolling Stock, In the Empire Style, Aetiological Fable, Concordat" (verse), *Sewanee Review*, XLVI, 2 (April, 1938), 206–211.

"Pompes Funèbres de Troisième Classe," review of *Four French Novelists* by Georges Lemaître, *Partisan Review*, IV, 6 (May, 1938), 54–57.

"La Citadelle de Parme: Stendhal et Benvenuto Cellini," *Revue de Littérature Comparée*, LXX, 2 (April–June, 1938), 346–350.

"Prospectus for an Unpublishable Treatise," *Sewanee Review*, XLVI, 4 (October, 1938), 432–437.

Ben Jonson: *Selected Works*, ed. with an introduction by Harry Levin (New York: Random House, 1938), 1010 pp.; London: Nonesuch Press, 1940; introduction reprinted in *Ben Jonson: A Collection of Critical Essays*, ed. J. A. Barish (Englewood Cliffs, N.J., 1963); and in *GC*.

"Minnesota," review of *Minnesota, a State Guide*, Federal Writers' Project, *Boston Evening Transcript*, February 4, 1939, sec. iv. p. 1.

"Tragedy and Comedy: A Statement," *University Review*, V, 3 (Spring, 1939), 217–219.

"New Irish Stew," review of *Finnegans Wake* by James Joyce, *Kenyon Review*, I, 4 (Autumn, 1939), 460–465.

"On First Looking into *Finnegans Wake*," *New Directions, 1939*, pp. 253–287; forms the basis of ch. III, sec. 1 and 2 of *James Joyce: A Critical Introduction* (see 1941); abridged version in *James Joyce: The Critical Heritage*, ed. R. H. Deming (London, 1970).

Review: *Studies in Beaumont, Fletcher, and Massinger* by Baldwin Maxwell, *Boston Evening Transcript*, February 10, 1940, sec. v, p. 2.

"Last Essays of Babbitt," review of *Spanish Character and Other Essays* by Irving Babbitt, *New Republic*, CIII, 1354 (November 11, 1940), 670.

"If We Had Some Eggs," review of *Hamlet* by Henry Miller and Michael Fraenkel and *The Expense of Greatness* by R. P. Blackmur, *New Republic*, CIII, 27 (December 30, 1940), 905–906.

"Wallace Stevens" (statement), *Harvard Advocate*, CXXVII, 3 (December, 1940), 30.

"Pseudodoxia Academica," *Southern Review*, VI, 2 (Autumn, 1940), 263–269; extract reprinted in *The Critic's Notebook*, ed. R. W. Stallman (Minneapolis, 1950).

James Joyce: A Critical Introduction (Norfolk, Connecticut: New Directions, 1941), xii + 240 pp.; revised paperback edition (1961); London: Faber and Faber, 1944, xiv + 256 pp.; revised paperback edition (1968); ch. II, sec. 2 reprinted in *Critiques and Essays on Modern Fiction*, ed. J. W. Aldridge (New York, 1951); II, 1 in *Essays in Modern Literary Criticism*, ed. R. B. West (New York, 1952); I, 3 in *Modern British Fiction*, ed. Mark Schorer (New York, 1962); in *Joyce's Portrait: Criticism and Critiques*, ed. T. E. Connolly (New York, 1962); in *Portraits of an Artist*, ed. William

Morris and Clifford Nault (New York, 1962); and in *The Portrait of the Artist,* ed. C. G. Anderson (New York, 1968); extract in *Twentieth Century Interpretations of A Portrait of the Artist,* ed. W. M. Schutte (Englewood Cliffs, N. J., 1968); in *A New Directions Reader,* ed. Hayden Carruth and James Laughlin (New York, 1964); French translation by Claude Tarnaud (Paris: Robert Marin, 1959); Spanish translation by Antonio Castro Leal (Mexico City: Fondacion de la Cultura Economica, 1959); Italian translation by Ariodante Marianni (Milan: Mondadori, 1966); Spanish translation of final chapter by José Rodríguez Feo in *Orígines,* III, 10 (Spring, 1946).

"Poet on Omnibus," review of *Victor Hugo: A Realistic Biography of the Great Romantic* by Matthew Josephson, *New Republic,* CVII, 1456 (October 26, 1942), 552–553.
"Regrets" (correspondence), *Partisan Review,* IX, 5 (September–October, 1942), 446.
John Wilmot, Earl of Rochester: *A Satire against Mankind, and Other Poems,* ed. with an introduction by Harry Levin (Norfolk, Connecticut: New Directions, 1942), 31 pp.; introduction reprinted in *GC.*

"The Poetry of Geopolitics," review of *The Tragicall History of Christopher Marlowe* by John Bakeless, *New Republic,* CVIII, 8 (February 22, 1943), 260–261. See also correspondence, ibid., CVIII, 13 (March 29, 1943), 415–416.
"Jonson's Metempsychosis," *Philological Quarterly,* XXII, 3 (July, 1943), 231–239.
"Poets of Poetry," review of *The Heritage of Symbolism* by C. M. Bowra, *New Republic,* CIX, 8 (August 23, 1943), 260–261.
"Invitation to Romanticism," review of *Romanticism and the Modern Ego* by Jacques Barzun, *New Republic,* CIX, 17 (October 25, 1943), 584–586.
"The Novel," in *Dictionary of World Literature: Criticism, Forms, Techniques,* ed. J. T. Shipley (New York: Philosophical Library, 1943), 405–407; new edition entitled *Dictionary of World Literary Terms* (Boston: The Writer Inc., 1970), 215–217.

"Nations of Niobes" (verse), *Quarterly Review of Literature,* I, 2 (Winter, 1944), 73.
"Balancing Falstaff," review of *The Fortunes of Falstaff* by J. Dover Wilson, *New Republic,* CX, 19 (May 8, 1944), 632–634.
Jules Laforgue: "Two Pigeons" (translation), *Accent,* IV, 3 (Spring, 1944), 131–139; reprinted in *Accent Anthology,* ed. Kerker Quinn and Charles Shattuck (New York, 1946), 129–140.
"Verdade e Ficçâo," *Pensamento da America,* III, 7 (July 4, 1944), 96, 104 (Portuguese translation of *GH,* III, 1).
"Mann: from Ur to OPA," review of *Joseph the Provider* by Thomas Mann, *New Republic,* CXI, 2 (July 10, 1944), 49–50; enlarged version in *The Stature of Thomas Mann,* ed. Charles Neider (New York, 1947), 211–217; *GC.*
"Everybody's Earwicker," review of *A Skeleton Key to Finnegans Wake* by Joseph Campbell and Henry Morton Robinson, *New Republic,* CXI, 4 (July 24, 1944), 106–107.
"Through the Looking Glass," review of *For the Time Being* by W. H. Auden, *New Republic,* CXI, 12 (September 18, 1944), 347–348.
"Reading between the Lines," review of *Imaginary Interviews* by André Gide, *New Republic,* CXI, 18 (October 30, 1944), 570–572.
"Flowers of Good," review of *Baudelaire: A Criticism* by Joseph Bennett, *New Republic,* CXI, 25 (December 18, 1944), 841.
"Introduction," *Three Tales* by Gustave Flaubert, trans. Arthur McDowall (Norfolk, Connecticut: New Directions, 1944), pp. 1–12.

"Toward Stendhal," *Pharos*, 3 (Winter, 1945), 5–70; *GH*, ch. III.

"Meditation on a Battlement," review of *Hamlet: Traduction nouvelle d'André Gide*, *New Republic*, CXII, 17 (April 23, 1945), 559–560.

"Taine y su influencia en la critica literaria," *Orígenes*, II, 5 (April, 1945), 3–8 (Spanish translation by José Rodríguez Feo of "Literature as an Institution"; see 1946).

"Album Leaf" (verse), *Harvard Wake*, I, 4 (June, 1945), 11–12.

"Tell It Not in Gath," review of *The League of Frightened Philistines* by James T. Farrell, *New Republic*, CXIII, 4 (July 23, 1945), 105–106.

"A Serious Frenchman," review of *Basic Verities* and *Men and Saints* by Charles Péguy, *Sewanee Review*, LIII, 3 (Summer, 1945), 486–489.

"Playwright as Pedagogue," review of *The Use of the Drama* by Harley Granville-Barker, *New Republic*, CXIII, 10 (September 3, 1945), 292–293.

"The Real Thing," review of *Three Short Novels of Dostoevsky* with an introduction by Thomas Mann, *New Republic*, CXIV, 2 (January 14, 1946), 56–57.

"Civilized Nomad," review of *Lafcadio Hearn* by Vera McWilliams, *New Republic*, CXIV, 16 (April 22, 1946), 588–589.

"Lower Criticism," review of *Dickens, Dalí and Others* by George Orwell, *New Republic*, CXIV, 18 (May 6, 1946), 665–667.

"Falstaff Uncolted," *Modern Language Notes*, LXI, 5 (May, 1946), 305–310.

"The Quintessence of Hawthorne," review of *Hawthorne's Short Stories*, ed. Newton Arvin, *New York Times Book Review*, June 16, 1946, pp. 1, 37.

"Literature as an Institution," *Accent*, VI, 3 (Spring, 1946), 159–168; reprinted in *The Novelist as Thinker*, ed. B. Rajan (London, 1947); in *Criticism: The Foundations of Modern Literary Judgment*, ed. Mark Schorer, Josephine Miles, and Gordon McKenzie (New York, 1948); in *A Little Treasury of American Prose*, ed. George Mayberry (New York, 1949); in *Literary Opinion in America*, ed. M. D. Zabel (New York, 1951; Italian edition, 1964); in *Introduction to Literary Criticism*, ed. Lionel Trilling (New York, 1970); and in *Criticism: The Major Texts*, ed. W. J. Bate (New York: Harcourt, Brace, Jovanovich, 1970); excerpt in *A Grammar of Literary Criticism*, ed. L. S. Hall (New York, 1964); Spanish translation by José Rodríguez Feo in *Orígenes*, II, 5 (April, 1945); Italian translation by Oreste Frattoni in *Inventario*, I, 2 (Summer, 1946); Polish translation by Boguslaw Grodzicki in *Tematy*, V, 18 (Summer, 1966); *GH*, ch. I, sec. 2 and 3.

"Lives of the Novelists," review of *The Life of the Heart: George Sand and Her Times* by Frances Winwar, *The Letters and Private Papers of William Makepeace Thackeray*, ed. Gordon Ray, *The Trollopes* by Lucy Poate and Richard Poate Stebbins, *Charlotte and Emily: The Brontës* by Laura L. Hinkley, *Tolstoy and His Wife* by Tikhon Polner, *The Crack-Up* by F. Scott Fitzgerald, and *Freudianism and the Literary Mind* by Frederick J. Hoffman, in *American Scholar*, XV, 2 (Spring, 1946), 245–251.

"Of Birds and Books," *Harvard Wake*, 5 (Spring, 1946), 61–63; *GC*.

"Poet on a Pedestal," review of *Aragon: Poet of the French Resistance*, ed. Hannah Josephson and Malcolm Cowley, in *Kenyon Review*, VIII, 2 (Spring, 1946), 318–322.

"Self-Condemned Playboy," review of *The Condemned Playground* by Cyril Connolly, *New Republic*, CXV, 2 (July 15, 1946), 49–50.

"The Humanities in General Education," *Harvard Alumni Bulletin*, XLIX, 2 (October 12, 1946), 76, 77.

"Report on Round Table Conference on General Education" (mimeographed report of symposium), Haverford College (November 16, 1946), 10 pp.

"Stendhal in Technicolor," review of *Stendhal* by Matthew Josephson, *New Republic*, CXV, 18 (November 4, 1946), 595–597.

"Grandeur and Decadence," review of *Balzac* by Stefan Zweig, *New Republic*, CXV, 22 (December 2, 1946), 730–733. See also "A Reviewer Protests" (correspondence), ibid., CXV, 24 (December 16, 1946), 834.

"Opening a Window on the Outdoors," review of *The Masterpiece* by Emile Zola, *New York Times Book Review*, December 8, 1946, pp. 3, 61.

"James Joyce," *Atlantic Monthly*, CLXXVIII, 6 (December, 1946), 125–129 (abridgment of introduction to Viking Portable Library edition; see 1947).

"Life Without Father," *Atlantic Monthly*, CLXXIX, 1 (January, 1947), 97–101; *R.*

"Writers from Aakjaer to Zweig," review of *Columbia Dictionary of Modern European Literature*, ed. Horatio Smith, *New York Times Book Review*, February 23, 1947, pp. 4, 30.

"Metacriticism," review of *The Kafka Problem*, ed. Angel Flores, *Yale Review*, XXXVI, 2 (Winter, 1947), 354–356.

"America Discovers Bohemia," *Atlantic Monthly*, CLXXX, 3 (September, 1947), 68–75; fuller version printed as "The Discovery of Bohemia" in *Literary History of the United States*, ed. R. F. Spiller, Willard Thorp, T. H. Johnson, and H. S. Canby (New York, 1948), II, 1065–1079; *GC.*

"Toward Balzac," *Direction*, 3 (Fall, 1947), 5–74; *GH*, ch. IV.

"*Don Quixote* and *Moby Dick*," in *Cervantes across the Centuries*, ed. Angel Flores and M. J. Benardete (New York: Dryden Press, 1947), pp. 217–226; Spanish translation in *Realidad*, II, 5 (September–October, 1947), 254–267; *CC.*

The Portable James Joyce with an introduction and notes by Harry Levin (New York: Viking Press, 1947), 760 pp.; revised paperback edition (1965); published in England as *The Essential James Joyce* (London: Jonathan Cape, 1948); Penguin paperback edition (1963); French translation of introduction by Magali Patchett-Morsy, Marie-Claude Peugeot, and Paul Rozenberg in *Configuration Critique de James Joyce*, vol. I-1, ed. M. J. Minard (Paris, 1959).

"Flaubert: Portrait of the Artist as a Saint," *Kenyon Review*, X, 1 (Winter, 1948), 28–43; *GH*, ch. V, sec. 2.

"A Letter in English by Stendhal," *Harvard Library Bulletin*, II, 1 (Winter, 1948), 123–125.

" 'Modern' Art—and 'Modern' Novels," review of *The Dehumanization of Art* and *Notes on the Novel* by José Ortega y Gasset, *New York Times Book Review*, June 6, 1948, p. 4.

"Proust's First Published Writings," review of *Pleasures and Regrets* by Marcel Proust, *New York Times Book Review*, August 1, 1948, p. 3.

"Dr. Mann versus a Teutonic Mephisto," review of *Doctor Faustus* by Thomas Mann, *New York Times Book Review*, October 31, 1948, p. 5.

"Marcel Proust," *Atlantic Monthly*, CLXXXII, 4 (October, 1948), 85–89; fuller version printed as introduction to *Letters of Marcel Proust*, ed. and trans. Mina Curtiss (New York: Random House, 1949), xv–xxiv; slightly revised for paperback edition (1966).

"Flaubert and the Spirit of '48," *Yale Review*, XXXVIII, 1 (Autumn, 1948), 96–108; *GH*, ch. V, sec. 1.

"A Harvard Education: What Is It? II. The Humanities" (symposium), *The 1947–1948 Harvard Album*, pp. 28–33.

"Clinical Demonstration on Four Poets," review of *Sex, Symbolism, and Psychology in Literature* by Roy P. Basler, *Saturday Review of Literature*, XXXII, 1 (January 1, 1949), 14. See also correspondence, ibid., XXXII, 7 (February 12, 1949), 22.

"Theodore Spencer" (with David McCord), *Harvard Alumni Bulletin*, LI, 8 (January 29, 1949), 343.

"K. as Commentator," review of *The Penal Colony, Diaries, 1910–13, Diaries, 1914–23* by Franz Kafka, *New Republic*, CXX, 6 (February 7, 1949), 25–26.

Review: *Essays in the History of Ideas* by Arthur O. Lovejoy, *Isis*, XL, 119 (February, 1949), 85–87; *GC*.

"An Echo from *The Spanish Tragedy*," *Modern Language Notes*, LXIV, 5 (May, 1949), 297–302.

"An Unpublished Dialogue by Marcel Proust," *Harvard Library Bulletin*, III, 2 (Spring, 1949), 257–267.

"Carteggio inedito Svevo-James Joyce," *Inventario*, II, 1 (Spring, 1949), 106–138.

"Facets of Shakespeare," review of *Shakespeare Survey*, ed. Allardyce Nicoll, *Shakespearean Comedy* by T. M. Parrott, *The Populace in Shakespeare* by Brents Stirling, *Playwriting for Elizabethans* by M. C. Hyde, in *New York Times Book Review*, August 7, 1949, pp. 5, 24.

"Joyce's Sentimental Journey through France and Italy," *Yale Review*, XXXVIII, 4 (Summer, 1949), 664–672; French translation by Magali Patchett-Morsy and Paul Rozenberg in *Configuration Critique de James Joyce*, vol. I–2, ed. M. J. Minard (Paris, 1960); *CC*.

"The Timeless Old Soldier," review of *Don Quixote* by Miguel de Cervantes, trans. Samuel Putnam, *New York Times Book Review*, September 25, 1949, pp. 3, 33.

"What Shakespeare Had to Say," review of *Shakespeare's World of Images* by Donald A. Stauffer, *New York Times Book Review*, October 30, 1949, p. 5.

"The Jewish Writer and the English Literary Tradition" (symposium), *Commentary*, VIII, 4 (October, 1949), 363–364.

Review: *Theory of Literature* by René Wellek and Austin Warren, *Germanic Review*, XXIV, 4 (December, 1949), 303–306.

"Some European Views of Contemporary American Literature," *American Quarterly*, I, 3 (Fall, 1949), 264–279; reprinted in *The American Writer and the European Tradition*, ed. Margaret Denny and W. H. Gilman (Minneapolis, 1950); paperback edition (1963); included in *CC* under the title "A Gallery of Mirrors."

"Definizione del realismo," *Inventario*, II, 3 (Autumn, 1949), 8–14 (translation by Anna Lambertini of "What Is Realism?"; see 1951).

"Courses in the Humanities at Harvard University" (with I. A. Richards, J. H. Finley, Jr., and Andrews Wanning), *The Humanities in General Education*, ed. Earl J. McGrath (Dubuque, Iowa: William Brown Co., 1949), pp. 244–260.

"The Essential James Joyce" (correspondence), *Times Literary Supplement*, XLIX, 2508 (February 24, 1950), 128.

Review: *Der Pessimismus bei Thomas Hardy, George Crabbe und Jonathan Swift* by G. van den Bergh, *Erasmus*, III, 3–4 (March 10, 1950), 159–160.

"Everybody's Shakespeare," review of *Shakespeare of London* by Marchette Chute, *Sergeant Shakespeare* by Duff Cooper, *The Real Shakespeare* by William Bliss, *The Time Is Free* by Roy Walker, *The Twelfth Night of Shakespeare's Audience* by John W. Draper, *The Appreciation of Shakespeare*, ed. Bernard M. Wagner, in *New York Times Book Review*, March 26, 1950, pp. 7, 30.

"F. O. Matthiessen as a Scholar" (correspondence), *New York Times*, April 14, 1950, p. 22.

"Fragment of a Great Confession," review of *The Green Huntsman* by Stendhal, trans. Louise Varese, *New York Times Book Review,* May 28, 1950, p. 5.

"Proust, Gide and the Sexes" (controversy with Justin O'Brien), *Publications of the Modern Language Association,* LXV, 4 (June, 1950), 648–652; *GC.*

"An Explication of the Player's Speech (*Hamlet,* II, ii, 472–541)," *Kenyon Review,* XII, 2 (Spring, 1950), 273–296; reprinted in *Hamlet,* ed. Cyrus Hoy (New York, 1963); and in *The Question of Hamlet* (see 1959).

The Defense of Poetry: Harvard Summer School (mimeographed record of conference; Cambridge, August 14–17, 1950), 165 pp., *passim.*

"Cervantes' Other Masterpiece," review of *Three Exemplary Novels* by Miguel de Cervantes, trans. Samuel Putnam, *New York Times Book Review,* October 22, 1950, p. 5.

Statement in *F. O. Matthiessen: A Collective Portrait,* ed. Paul M. Sweezy and Leo Huberman (New York: Henry Schuman, 1950); reprinted from *Monthly Review,* II, 6 (October, 1950), 293.

"With 'Sunny Coldness,' Stendhal Viewed His Age," review of *The Telegraph* by Stendhal, trans. Louise Varese, *New York Times Book Review,* December 10, 1950, p. 5.

"From Priam to Birotteau," *Yale French Studies,* 6 (Autumn, 1950), 75–82; *GH,* ch. II, sec. 5.

"Balzac et Proust," *Hommage à Balzac* (Paris: Mercure de France, 1950), 281–308; Italian translation by Luigi Berti in *Inventario,* III, 4 (Spring, 1951); original English version in *CC.*

"Notes on Convention," *Perspectives of Criticism* (Cambridge: Harvard University Press, 1950), pp. 55–83; Italian translation by Luigi Berti in *Inventario,* III, 3 (Autumn, 1950); *R.*

Perspectives of Criticism, Harvard Studies in Comparative Literature, XX, ed. Harry Levin (Cambridge: Harvard University Press, 1950), xiv + 248 pp.; London: Oxford University Press, 1950; New York: Russel and Russel, 1970.

"An Author and His Limits," review of *Henry James* by F. W. Dupee, *New York Herald Tribune Book Review,* May 27, 1951, p. 14.

"The Tradition of Tradition," *Hopkins Review,* IV, 3 (Spring, 1951), 5–14; Italian translation by Luigi Berti in *Inventario,* IV, 2 (March–April, 1952); Dutch translation by Halbo C. Kool in *Amerikaans Cultureel Perspectief* (1954); Serbian translation by Mario Suško in *Putevi,* XI, 6 (November–December, 1965); *CC.*

"Chekhov: From Hack to Master Craftsman," review of *Chekhov* by Ronald Hingley, *New York Times Book Review,* June 3, 1951, p. 5.

Review: *Scourge and Minister: A Study of Hamlet as Tragedy of Revengefulness and Justice* by G. R. Elliott, *Shakespeare Quarterly,* II, 3 (July, 1951), 259–260.

"What Is Realism?," in *A Symposium on Realism* arranged by Harry Levin, *Comparative Literature,* III, 3 (Summer, 1951), 193–199; reprinted in *Aspects of Fiction,* ed. H. E. Hugo (Boston, 1962); excerpt in *A Grammar of Literary Criticism,* ed. L. S. Hall (New York, 1964); Italian translation by Anna Lambertini in *Inventario,* II, 3 (Autumn, 1949); unauthorized Chinese translation in *Wên I Yüeh Pao* (Taipei); Serbian translation by Zvonimir Radeljković in *Putevi,* XIII, 6 (November–December, 1967); *CC.*

Review: *The French Education of Henry Adams* by Max I. Baym, *New England Quarterly,* XXIV, 4 (December, 1951), 542–546.

"Observations on the Style of Ernest Hemingway," *Kenyon Review,* XIII, 4 (Autumn, 1951), 581–609; reprinted in *American Critical Essays,* ed. Harold Beaver (Oxford,

1959); in *Hemingway and His Critics*, ed. Carlos Baker (New York, 1961; Italian edition by Mondadori, 1962); in *Hemingway: A Collection of Critical Essays*, by R. P. Weeks (New York, 1962); in *The Personal Voice*, ed. Albert Guérard, John Hawkes, and Claire Rosenfield (New York, 1964); in *The World of Words: A Language Reader*, ed. Burnet Kottler and Martin Light (Boston, 1966); in *Moderne englische und amerikanische Literaturkritik*, ed. Willi Erzgräber (Darmstadt, 1969); and in *Essays in Stylistic Analysis*, ed. H. S. Babb (New York, 1972); Polish translation by Leszek Elektorowicz in *Tematy*, VI, 22 (Summer, 1967); *CC*.

"*Madame Bovary:* The Cathedral and the Hospital," *Essays in Criticism*, II, 1 (January, 1952), 1–23; reprinted in *Madame Bovary*, ed. Paul De Man (New York, 1965); Spanish translation by José Rodríguez Feo in *Orígines*, IX, 32 (Winter, 1952); Italian translation by Luisa Franchini in *Inventario*, IV, 5–6 (September–December, 1952); *GH*, ch. V, sec. 3.

"Retrospect," *Comparative Literature Newsletter*, 1 (Spring, 1952), 1–2.

"Essays on Several Occasions," review of *The Necessary Angel* by Wallace Stevens, *The Lost Childhood and Other Essays* by Graham Greene, *Two Cheers for Democracy* by E. M. Forster, in *Yale Review*, XLI, 4 (Summer, 1952), 615–618.

Review: *Character and Society in Shakespeare* by Arthur Sewell, *Shakespeare Quarterly*, III, 4 (October, 1952), 370–371.

"The Department of Comparative Literature," *Yearbook of Comparative and General Literature*, ed. W. P. Friedrich, I (Chapel Hill, 1952), 42–45.

The Overreacher: A Study of Christopher Marlowe (Cambridge: Harvard University Press, 1952), xiii + 204 pp.; photographic reprint (Gloucester, Mass.: Peter Smith, 1966); London: Faber and Faber, 1954, 231 pp.; paperback edition (Boston: Beacon Press, 1964); reprinted in paperback under the title *Christopher Marlowe: The Overreacher* (London: Faber and Faber, 1965); abridged version of ch. IV in *Shakespeare's Contemporaries*, ed. Max Bluestone and Norman Rabkin (New York, 1961); part of ch. VI in *Marlowe: A Collection of Critical Essays*, ed. Clifford Leech (New York, 1964); abridged version of ch. III in *Critics on Marlowe*, ed. Judith O'Neill (London, 1969); ch. V in *Macmillan Casebook for* Dr. Faustus, ed. J. D. Jump (London, 1969); and in *Twentieth Century Interpretations of Dr. Faustus*, ed. Willard Farnham (Englewood Cliffs, N.J., 1969).

"La Littérature comparée: Point de vue d'outre-atlantique," French translation by Jean Bruneau in *Revue de littérature comparée*, XXVII, 1 (January–March, 1953), 17–26.

"Portrait of the Artist as a New Zealander," review of *Katherine Mansfield* by Anthony Alpers, *Yale Review*, XLIII, 2 (Winter, 1954), 310–311.

"When Flaubert Revealed His Deepest Feelings," review of *The Selected Letters of Gustave Flaubert*, trans. Francis Steegmuller, *New York Times Book Review*, January 24, 1954, p. 3. See letter of correction, February 21, p. 25.

"The Ivory Gate," *Yale French Studies*, 13 (Spring, 1954), 17–29; reprinted in *Academic Discourse*, ed. John Enck (New York, 1964); Italian translation by Mimma Desmaele in *Inventario*, IV, 3–6 (May–December, 1954); Spanish translation by José Rodríguez Feo in *Ciclón*, I, 4 (July, 1955); *R*.

"Unfrocked Professor," review of *The Literary Essays of Ezra Pound*, ed. T. S. Eliot, *Yale Review*, XLIII, 4 (Summer, 1954), 602–604.

"Castles and Culture: America and the Gothic Tradition," *Times Literary Supplement*, LIII, 2746 (September 17, 1954), xliv; reprinted in *American Literature Today*, ed. Alan Angoff (New York, 1957); and in *The Power of Blackness* (see 1958).

Review: *Stendhal et la voie oblique* by Victor Brombert, *Romanic Review,* XLV, 3 (October, 1954), 216–219.
"The Gulfs of Academe," *Atlantic Monthly,* CXCIV, 4 (October, 1954), 77–79.

"An Urgent Awareness," review of *The Opposing Self: Nine Essays in Criticism* by Lionel Trilling, *New York Times Book Review,* February 13, 1955, pp. 3, 30.
Review: *The Structure of Literature* by Paul Goodman, *Modern Language Notes,* LXX, 2 (February, 1955), 124–126.
"Back to Shakespeare: Modern Research and Elizabethan Staging," *Center,* II, 1 (February, 1955), 14–18.
"Criticism in Crisis," *Comparative Literature,* VII, 2 (Spring, 1955), 144–155; German translation by Heinz Politzer in *Die Neue Rundschau,* LXVIII, 1 (January, 1957); Italian translation by Lina Angioletti in *Inventario,* XIV, 1–6 (January–December, 1959); another German translation by Liselotte Skudrzyk in *Moderne amerikanische Literaturtheorien,* ed. Joseph Strelka and Walter Hinderer (Frankfurt, 1970); *CC.*
"The Poetics of French Symbolism: Introductory Note," *Romanic Review,* XLVI, 3 (October, 1955), 161–163.
"American Theater Today," Japanese translation by Fumi Takano in *American Ways of Thinking,* ed. Takeyasu Kimura (Tokyo: Tokyo University Press, 1955), pp. 39–56.
"Art as Knowledge," in *The Unity of Knowledge,* Columbia University Bicentennial Series, ed. Lewis Leary (New York: Doubleday & Co., 1955), pp. 189–207; *CC.*
Autobiographical statement in *Twentieth Century Authors: A Biographical Dictionary of Modern Literature,* ed. S. J. Kunitz (New York: H. W. Wilson Co., 1955).

Review: *Hamlet: Father and Son* by Peter Alexander, *Shakespeare Quarterly,* VII, 1 (Winter, 1956), 104–107; reprinted in *The Question of Hamlet* (see 1959).
"New Frontiers of Knowledge in the Humanities," *Harvard Library Bulletin,* X, 2 (Spring, 1956), 155–165; reprinted in *Frontiers of Knowledge* (Waltham: Brandeis University, 1958); *CC.*
Review: *The Literary Symbol* by William York Tyndall, *Modern Philology,* LIV, 1 (August, 1956), 53–55.
Review: *James Joyce and the Cultic Use of Fiction* by Kristian Smidt, *Anglia,* LXXIII, 4 (Summer, 1956), 533–535.
"James Joyce, un individu dans le monde," *Révue de Métaphysique et de Morale,* LXI, 3–4 (July–December, 1956), 346–359; reprinted as "James Joyce et l'idée de littérature mondiale" in *CC.*
"The Landscape Gardener's Grave" (verse), *Quarterly Review of Literature,* VIII, 4 (Fall, 1956), 282.
"The Example of Cervantes," *Society and Self in the Novel,* ed. Mark Schorer (New York: Columbia University Press, 1956), pp. 3–25; reprinted in *Perspectives USA,* 16 (Summer, 1956); translated in its German and Italian editions, *Perspektiven* and *Prospetti;* also reprinted in *Cervantes: A Collection of Essays,* ed. Lowry Nelson (New York, 1969); *CC.*
William Shakespeare: *Coriolanus,* ed. Harry Levin (Baltimore: Penguin Books, 1956), 164 pp.; included in *The Complete Pelican Shakespeare,* ed. Alfred Harbage (Baltimore, 1969); introduction reprinted in *Shakespeare: The Tragedies,* ed. Alfred Harbage (New York, 1964).
Symbolism and Fiction (Charlottesville: University of Virginia Press, 1956), 43 pp.; reprinted in *Learners and Discerners,* ed. Robert Scholes (Charlottesville, 1964); and in *Perspectives in Contemporary Criticism,* ed. S. N. Grebstein (New York, 1968);

excerpt in *Strategies in Rhetoric: From Thought to Symbol,* ed. T. E. Kakonis (New York, 1971); *CC.*

"But Unhappy Emma Still Exists," review of *Madame Bovary* by Gustave Flaubert, trans. Francis Steegmuller, *New York Times Book Review,* April 14, 1957, pp. 1, 4; reprinted in *Opinions and Perspectives from the* New York Times Book Review, ed. Francis Brown (Boston, 1964).

Review: *L'Influence de Ruskin sur la vie, les idées, et l'oeuvre de Marcel Proust* by Jean Autret, *French Review,* XXX, 5 (April, 1957), 417.

Review: *Letters from Goethe,* trans. Marianne von Herzfeld and C. A. M. Sym, *New York Times Book Review,* September 3, 1957, p. 3.

Contexts of Criticism, Harvard Studies in Comparative Literature, XXII (Cambridge: Harvard University Press, 1957), xiii + 294 pp.; paperback edition (New York: Atheneum Press, 1963); London: Oxford University Press, 1957; Spanish translation by Edgar Rodríguez Leal published as *Interpretaciones Criticas* (Caracas: Universidad Central de Venezuela, 1968). Includes the following articles not previously published: "Contexts of the Classical," "Society as Its Own Historian," and "The War of Words in English Poetry."

Review: *Hawthorne's Tragic Vision* by Roy R. Male, *American Literature,* XXIX, 4 (January, 1958), 491–492.

Review: *Literary Criticism: A Short History* by W. K. Wimsatt, Jr., and Cleanth Brooks, *Modern Language Notes,* LXXIII, 2 (February, 1958), 155–160. See also exchange with Professors Wimsatt and Brooks, ibid., LXXIII, 7 (November, 1958), 557–560.

Review: *Shakespeare and the Allegory of Evil: The History of a Metaphor in Relation to His Major Villains* by Bernard Spivak, *Renaissance News,* XI, 4 (Winter, 1958), 279–281.

Review: *Realismo e Simbolismo* by Agostino Lombroso, *American Literature,* XXX, 2 (May, 1958), 262–263.

Review: *Joyce and Aquinas* by William T. Noon, *Speculum,* XXXIII, 3 (July, 1958), 426–427.

"The Antic Disposition," *Shakespeare Jahrbuch,* XCIV (1958), 175–190; reprinted in *Macmillan Casebook for Hamlet,* ed. J. D. Jump (London, 1969); and in *The Question of Hamlet* (see 1959).

Autobiographical statement in *Harvard Class of 1933: Twenty-fifth Anniversary Report,* ed. Donal M. Sullivan (Cambridge, 1958), 644–646.

The Power of Blackness: Hawthorne, Poe, Melville (New York: Alfred A. Knopf, 1958), xii + 263 + ix pp.; paperback edition (New York: Vintage Books, 1960); London: Faber and Faber, 1958; parts of chs. I and III reprinted in *The Scarlet Letter,* ed. Sculley Bradley, R. C. Beatty, and E. H. Long (New York, 1962); excerpts from ch. V reprinted in *Twentieth Century Interpretations of "The Fall of the House of Usher,"* ed. Thomas Woodson (Englewood Cliffs, N.J., 1969); also in *Twentieth Century Interpretations of Poe's Tales,* ed. W. L. Howarth (Englewood Cliffs, N.J., 1969).

"Philippe-Jules-Fernand Baldensperger" (minute), with J. H. Finley, Jr., Marcel Françon, and F. M. Rogers, *Harvard University Gazette,* LIV, 23 (February 21, 1959), 114–115; *GC.*

Review: *Kommentar zu Shakespeares Richard III: Interpretation eines Dramas* by Wolfgang Clemen, *Modern Language Notes,* LXXIV, 2 (February, 1959), 164–166.

"Art versus Life," review of *Claybook for James Joyce* by Louis Gillet, *Joyce among the*

Jesuits by Kevin Sullivan, *Our Friend James Joyce* by Padraic and Mary Colum, in *Yale Review*, XLVIII, 2 (Winter, 1959), 269–272.

"The Rest Is Literature," *Griffin*, VIII, 4 (May, 1959), 5–11; *GC*.

Review: *On Literature and Art* by Marcel Proust, *French Review*, XXXII, 6 (May, 1959), 594–595.

"Some Meanings of Myth," *Daedalus*, LXXXVIII, 2 (Spring, 1959), 223–231; reprinted in *Myth and Mythmaking*, ed. H. A. Murray (New York, 1960); *R*.

"The Heights and the Depths: A Scene from *King Lear*," *More Talking about Shakespeare*, ed. John Garrett (London and New York: Longman's, 1959), pp. 87–103; reprinted in *King Lear*, ed. Russell Fraser (New York, 1963).

Curriculum vitae and statement in *The Society of Fellows*, ed. Crane Brinton (Cambridge: Harvard University Press, 1959), pp. 185–186.

The Question of Hamlet (New York and London: Oxford University Press, 1959), xi + 178 pp.; paperback edition (Viking Press, 1961); new paperback edition (Oxford University Press, 1970); excerpt in *The Reader's Encyclopedia of Shakespeare* ed. O. J. Campbell and E. G. Quinn (New York, 1966), p. 300; extracts reprinted in *Twentieth Century Interpretations of* Hamlet, ed. David Bevington (Englewood Cliffs, N.J., 1968).

"Form and Formality in *Romeo and Juliet*," *Shakespeare Quarterly*, IX, 1 (Winter, 1960), 3–11; reprinted in *Four Centuries of Shakespearean Criticism*, ed. J. F. Kermode (New York, 1965); in *Modern Shakespearean Criticism*, ed. A. B. Kernan (New York, 1970); and in *Twentieth Century Interpretations of* Romeo and Juliet, ed. Douglas Cole (Englewood Cliffs, N.J., 1970).

Review: *Critical Writings* by James Joyce, *A Second James Joyce Miscellany*, ed. Marvin Magalaner, *The Sympathetic Alien* by J. Mitchell Morse, in *Criticism*, II, 1 (Winter, 1960), 103–106.

Review: *Paul Elmer More* by A. H. Dakin, *New York Times Book Review*, April 17, 1960, p. 16.

Review: *Dark Conceit: The Making of Allegory* by Edwin Honig, *Comparative Literature*, XII, 2 (Spring, 1960), 177–178.

"What Was Modernism?," *Massachusetts Review*, I, 4 (Summer, 1960), 609–630; reprinted in *Varieties of Literary Experience*, ed. Stanley Burnshaw (New York, 1962); Italian translation in *Inventario*, XVIII (January–December, 1963); *R*.

Review: *The Power of Satire: Magic, Ritual, Art* by Robert C. Elliott, *Comparative Literature*, XII, 3 (Summer, 1960), 265–267.

"Notes on *Troilus and Cressida*," *Harvard Crimson*, October 14, 1960, p. R-7.

Review: *E. E. Cummings: The Art of His Poetry* by Norman Friedman, *American Literature*, XXXII, 3 (November, 1960), 342–343.

"Literature and Exile," *Essays in Comparative Literature*, Washington University Studies (Saint Louis, 1960), pp. 1–20; abridged version in *Listener*, LXII, 1594 (October 15, 1959); *R*.

"Introduction," *The Charterhouse of Parma* by Stendhal, trans. Lowell Bair (New York: Bantam Books, 1960), pp. v–xii; *GC*.

"Preface," *The Singer of Tales* by Alfred B. Lord, Harvard Studies in Comparative Literature, XXIV (Cambridge: Harvard University Press, 1960), pp. xiii–xv; German translation by Helmut Martin, *Der Sänger Erzählt* (Munich, 1965).

Irving Babbitt and the Teaching of Literature, Inaugural Lecture (Cambridge: Harvard University, 1960), 28 pp.; sec. 4 reprinted as "Irving Babbitt and the New Humanism," *Harvard Alumni Bulletin*, LXIII, 5 (November 26, 1960), 209–211; *R*.

Nathaniel Hawthorne: *The Scarlet Letter,* ed. with an introduction by Harry Levin (Boston: Houghton Mifflin Co., Riverside Editions, 1960), xxvi + 262 pp.; enlarged edition published under the title *The Scarlet Letter and Other Tales of the Puritans* (1961), xxvi + 404 pp.; introduction reprinted in *Freedom and Discipline in English,* Commission on English of the College Entrance Examination Board (New York, 1965); and in *GC.*

"Not Enough Politics" (interview), *Comment,* I, 4 (May, 1961), pp. 7, 16.
"Outstanding Books, 1931–1961" (symposium), *American Scholar,* XXX, 4 (Fall, 1961), 614.
"English Literature of the Renaissance," *The Renaissance: A Reconsideration of Theories and Interpretations,* ed. Tinsley Helton (Madison: University of Wisconsin Press, 1961), 125–152; paperback edition, 1964; *R.*
"The American Voice in English Poetry," *Actes du VIIIᵉ Congrès de la Fédération Internationale des Langues et Littératures Modèrnes* (Liège, 1961), 83–103; reprinted in *Emory University Quarterly,* XXII, 3 (Fall, 1966); *R.*

"Shakespeare Today," *Proceedings of the American Philosophical Society,* CVI, 5 (October 11, 1962), 422–426; Italian translation in *Inventario,* XVIII (Spring, 1964).
Review: *The Word Irony and Its Context* by Norman Knox, *English Studies,* XLIII, 5 (October, 1962), 449–451.
"Foreword," *Les Liaisons Dangereuses* by Choderlos de Laclos, trans. Richard Aldington (New York: Signet Classics, 1962), pp. xii–xiv; *GC.*

"Apogee and Aftermath of the Novel," *Daedalus,* XCII, 2 (Spring, 1963), 206–219; Polish translation in *Tematy,* II, 8 (Autumn, 1963); *GH,* ch. VIII, sec. 2 and 3.
Review: *Chekhov, Stendhal and Other Essays* by Ilya Ehrenburg, *New York Times Book Review,* July 7, 1963, p. 5.
"Leech-Gathering," *Times Literary Supplement,* LXII, 3204 (July 26, 1963), 567; reprinted in *The Critical Moment: Literary Criticism in the Nineteen-Sixties* (New York: McGraw Hill, 1964); German translation in *Kritiker unserer Zeit,* ed. Hans Mayer (Stuttgart, 1964); *GC.*
"Commonwealth of Massachusetts versus *Tropic of Cancer*" (testimony), *Henry Miller and the Critics,* ed. George Wickes (Carbondale: Southern Illinois University Press, 1963), pp. 168–174.
"Presentation to I. A. Richards of the Loines Award for Poetry," *Proceedings of the American Academy–National Institute of Arts and Letters,* second series, XIII (1963), 250–251.
The Gates of Horn: A Study of Five French Realists (New York: and London: Oxford University Press, 1963), x + 554 pp.; paperback edition (1966); ch. II, sec. 6 and 7 reprinted in *Approaches to the Novel,* ed. Robert Scholes (San Francisco, 1966); V, 5 in *Flaubert: A Collection of Critical Essays,* ed. Raymond Giraud (New York, 1964); V, 3 in *Madame Bovary and the Critics,* ed. B. F. Bart (New York, 1966).

"*Othello* and the Motive-Hunters," *Centennial Review,* VIII, 1 (Winter, 1964), 1–16.
"*France-Amérique:* The Transatlantic Refraction," *Comparative Literature Studies,* I, 2 (Spring, 1964), 87–92; reprinted in *Comparative Literature: Matter and Method,* ed. A. O. Aldridge (Urban, 1969); *R.*
"Marlowe Today," *Tulane Drama Review,* VIII, 4 (Summer, 1964), 22–31.
"Renato Poggioli, 1907–1963" (minute), with Herbert Dieckmann, J. H. Finley, Jr., A. B. Lord, and Wiktor Weintraub, *Harvard University Gazette,* LX, 8 (November 7,

1964), 55–56; reprinted in *Lives of Harvard Scholars: A Selection, 1957–1967* (Cambridge: Harvard University Information Center, 1968); *GC.*

Review: *Marlowe: A Critical Study* by J. B. Steane, *Renaissance News,* XVII, 3 (Autumn, 1964), 232–234.

American Comparative Literature Association: Report on Professional Standards, with A. O. Aldridge, C. B. Beall, Haskell Block, Ralph Freedman, Horst Frenz, J. C. La Drière, Alain Renoir, and René Wellek (mimeographed, 1964), 8 pp.

"*Macbeth:* The Play, the Playwright and His Theater," in *Macbeth* by William Shakespeare (Boston: Houghton Mifflin Co., 1964), pp. vii–xviii.

"A Note on Her French Aspect," *Festschrift for Marianne Moore's Seventy-Seventh Birthday,* ed. Tambimuttu (New York: Tambimuttu and Mass, 1964), pp. 40–44; *GC.*

"Perry (Gilbert Eddy) Miller," *Year Book 1964* (Philadelphia: American Philosophical Society, 1965), pp. 136–140; *GC.*

"Renato Poggioli," *Yearbook of Comparative Literature,* XIII (1964), 124–125.

"Statues from Italy: *The Marble Faun,*" *Hawthorne Centenary Essays,* ed. R. H. Pearce (Columbus: Ohio State University Press, 1964), pp. 119–140; paperback edition, 1968; *R.*

"The Golden Age and the Renaissance," *Literary Views, Critical and Historical Essays,* ed. Carroll Camden (Chicago: University of Chicago Press, 1964), pp. 1–14; extract reprinted in *Twentieth Century Interpretations of* The Tempest, ed. Hallett Smith (Englewood Cliffs, N.J., 1969).

"Two Comedies of Errors," *Stratford Papers on Shakespeare, 1963,* ed. B. W. Jackson (Toronto: W. J. Gage, 1964), pp. 35–57; *R.*

"Reflections on the Final Volume of *The Oxford History of English Literature,*" *Forum for Modern Language Studies,* I, 1 (January, 1965), 4–16; *R.*

"Toward a Sociology of the Novel," *Journal of the History of Ideas,* XXVI, 1 (January–March, 1965), 148–154; *R.*

"Reducing Shakespeare," review of *Shakespeare Our Contemporary* by Jan Kott, *A Window to Criticism* by Murray Krieger, *The Poetry of Shakespeare's Plays* by F. E. Halliday, *Shakespeare's Poems,* ed. J. M. Osborn, L. L. Martz, and E. M. Waith, in *Yale Review,* LIV, 2 (Winter, 1965), 261–264.

"Semantics of Culture," *Daedalus,* XCIV, 1 (Winter, 1965)), 1–13; reprinted in *Science and Culture,* ed. Gerald Holton (Boston, 1965); paperback edition, 1968; *R.*

Review: *A Natural Perspective: The Development of Shakespearean Comedy and Romance* by Northrop Frye, *Comparative Literature,* XVII, 3 (Summer, 1965), 278–279.

"Janes and Emilies, or the Novelist as Heroine," *Southern Review,* new series, I, 4 (October, 1965), 735–753; *R.*

"Wonderland Revisited," *Kenyon Review,* XXVII, 4 (Autumn, 1965), 591–616; reprinted in *Aspects of Alice,* ed. Robert Phillips (New York, 1971).

"Preface," *The Spirit of the Letter* by Renato Poggioli (Cambridge: Harvard University Press, 1965), pp. vii–xi.

"Shakespearean Nomenclature," *Essays on Shakespeare,* ed. Gerald W. Chapman (Princeton: Princeton University Press, 1965), pp. 59–90.

"The Shakespearean Overplot," *Renaissance Drama,* VIII, ed. Samuel Schoenbaum (Evanston: Northwestern University Press, 1965), 63–71.

William Shakespeare: The Comedy of Errors, ed. Harry Levin (New York: New American Library, 1965), xxxviii + 176 pp.; reprinted in *The Complete Signet Classic Shakespeare,* ed. Sylvan Barnet (New York: Harcourt, Brace, Jovanovich, 1972).

"The Unbanning of the Books," *Atlantic Monthly*, CCXVII, 2 (February, 1966), 77–81; reprinted in *Harbrace College Reader*, ed. Mark Schorer, Philip Durham, and Everett L. Jones (New York, 1968); and in *Perspectives on Pornography*, ed. D. A. Hughes (New York, 1970); Japanese translation in *Japan–America Forum* (April, 1967); R.

"Paradises, Heavenly and Earthly," *Huntington Library Quarterly*, XXIX, 4 (August, 1966), 305–324; revised and augmented version in *Encounter*, XXXII, 6 (June, 1969); reprinted in *The Myth of the Golden Age in the Renaissance* (see 1969).

Review: *Un Problème de littérature comparée: Les études de thèmes, essai de méthodologie* by Raymond Trousson, *Comparative Literature*, XVIII, 3 (Summer, 1966), 273–274.

"Comparative Literature" (correspondence), *New York Review of Books*, VIII, 5 (October 6, 1966), 35.

"Eliot and Harvard" (memorial address), *Harvard Advocate*, C, 3–4 (Fall, 1966), 34–35; GC.

"Shakespeare in the Light of Comparative Literature," *Friendship's Garland: Essays Presented to Mario Praz*, ed. Vittorio Gabrieli (Milan, 1966), II, 381–400; reprinted in *Comparatists at Work*, ed. S. G. Nichols and R. B. Vowles (Waltham, Mass., 1968); R.

Countercurrents in the Study of English, Sedgewick Memorial Lecture (Vancouver: University of British Columbia, 1966), 34 pp.; GC.

Refractions: Essays in Comparative Literature (New York and London: Oxford University Press, 1966), xi + 359 pp.; paperback edition (1968).

"From Terence to Tabarin: A Note on *Les Fourberies de Scapin*," *Yale French Studies*, 38 (May, 1967), 128–137; GC.

Review: *Correspondance de Georg Brandes*, ed. Paul Krieger, *Scandinavica*, I, 2 (November, 1967), 126–127.

Why Literary Criticism Is Not an Exact Science (Cambridge: Heffers, 1967), 27 pp.; Cambridge, Mass.: Harvard University Press, 1967; GC.

Review: *James Joyce: Giacomo Joyce*, ed. Richard Ellmann, *New York Times Book Review*, January 21, 1968, p. 22.

"The Dissemination of Realism," *TriQuarterly*, 11 (Winter, 1968), 163–178; included without postscript in *Actes du Ve Congrès de l'Association Internationale de Littérature Comparée: Belgrade, 1967* (Amsterdam: University of Belgrade, 1969); Hungarian translation by Szabó Akosné in *Helikon*, XIV, 2 (Winter, 1968); GC.

"Comparing the Literature," *Yearbook of Comparative and General Literature*, XVII (1968), 5–16; GC.

"Some Paradoxes of Utopia," *Edward Bellamy: Novelist and Reformer*, Union Worthies, 23, ed. H. C. Martin (Schenectady: Union College, 1968), 16–22; reprinted in *The Myth of the Golden Age in the Renaissance* (see 1969).

"Thematics and Criticism," *The Disciplines of Criticism: Essays in Literary Theory, Interpretation, and History*, ed. Peter Demetz, Thomas Greene, and Lowry Nelson, Jr. (New Haven and London: Yale University Press, 1968), pp. 125–145; Italian translation by Dante Della Terza in *Strumenti Critici*, 9 (June, 1969); GC.

"Two *Romanisten* in America: Spitzer and Auerbach," *Perspectives in American History*, II, ed. Donald Fleming and Bernard Bailyn (Cambridge: Harvard University Press, 1968), 463–484; volume reprinted as *The Intellectual Migration* (Cambridge: Harvard University Press, 1969); GC.

"The End of Elizabethan Drama," *Comparative Drama*, III, 4 (Winter, 1969–1970), 275–281.

"Quoting and Telling," review of *The Poetics of Quotation in the Novel* by Herman Meyer, *Novel*, II, 3 (Spring, 1969), 278–279.

"Hail to the Hero" (correspondence) *Time*, XCIII, 23 (June 6, 1969), 14.

"A Question for the Faculty" (symposium), *Harvard Bulletin*, LII, 1 (September 15, 1969), 44–45.

"From *Gusle* to Tape-recorder," *Comparative Literature Studies*, VI, 3 (September, 1969), 262–273; *GC*.

"Witnesses on Harvard" (correspondence), *Harper's Magazine*, CCXXXIX, 1434 (November, 1969), 11.

"Introduction," *The House of the Seven Gables* by Nathaniel Hawthorne (Cleveland: Charles E. Merrill, Co., 1969), pp. v–xv; *GC*.

"Two Magian Comedies: *The Tempest* and *The Alchemist*," *Shakespeare Survey*, XXII (1969), 47–58.

"The Modern Humanities in Historical Perspective," *The Future of the Modern Humanities*, I (Cambridge: Modern Humanities Research Association, 1969), 1–27; *GC*.

The Myth of the Golden Age in the Renaissance (Bloomington: Indiana University Press, 1969), xxiv + 231; London, Faber and Faber, 1970.

"Neglected Books" (symposium), *American Scholar*, XXXIX, 2 (Spring, 1970), 332.

"William Carlos Williams and the Old World," *Yale Review*, LIX, 4 (Summer, 1970), 520–531; reprinted as introduction to *A Voyage to Pagany* by William Carlos Williams (New York: New Directions, 1970); *GC*.

Review: *The Theory of Comedy* by Elder Olson, *Comparative Literature*, XXII, 3 (Summer, 1970), 286–288.

"Nepotism Rules" (correspondence), *Modern Language Association Newsletter*, II, 4 (October, 1970), 4.

"Charles Dickens, 1812–1870," *American Scholar*, XXXIX, 4 (Autumn, 1970), 670–676; Spanish translation by Aída Fajardo in *Sin Nombre*, II, 1 (1971); *GC*.

"The Quixotic Principle; Cervantes and Other Novelists," *Harvard English Studies*, I (1970), 45–66; *GC*.

"Evangelizing Shakespeare," review of *Shakespearean Tragedy: Its Art and Christian Premises* by Roy W. Battenhouse, *Journal of the History of Ideas*, XXXII, 2 (April–June, 1971), 306–310.

"Program Note," *Othello* by William Shakespeare (Loeb Drama Center, Cambridge, Mass., November 11–14, 17–20, 1971).

"William Shakespeare," in *Atlantic Brief Lives: A Biographical Companion to the Arts*, ed. Louis Kronenberger (Boston: Atlantic Monthly Press, 1971), pp. 699–701.

INDEX

Harvard Studies in Comparative Literature

* Out of print